I0109987

Praise for *Another War Is Possible*

"*Another War Is Possible* is a compelling invitation to revolutionaries of the past, present, and future to think critically and historically about their years of struggle. Rothaus's captivating memoir of global justice militancy beyond puppets and platitudes is painfully honest, admirably humble, and at times simply hilarious."
—Mark Bray, author of *Antifa: The Anti-Fascist Handbook*

"My activist generation (born in the 1970s—anyone remember Generation X?) knew exactly one window where it wasn't all gloom: the high tide of the so-called antiglobalization movement from 1999 to 2001. For once, it seemed fundamental social, political, and economic change was possible—worldwide! With 9/11, at the latest, that window was shut. If you want to read an account of those exceptional years from the radical fringes of the movement, here it is. With all respect to academic treatises, NGO evaluations, and Democratic Socialists of America type musings, this is where the revolution becomes palpable. Destined to turn into an instant movement classic, *Another War Is Possible* tells the frontline story of attacking a system that we all know is heading toward Armageddon. It is insightful, it is smart, it is funny. Hardly ever has it been easier to endorse a book. Read!"
—Gabriel Kuhn, author of *Sober Living for the Revolution*, *Soccer vs. the State*, and *Antifascism, Sports, Sobriety*

"In an age where anarchist ideas are being both embraced by a new generation of activists and demonized by the rich and powerful, Rothaus shines a light onto those who were punching Nazis and fighting the police before the rise of Trumpism. Part riot diary and part personal reflection, *Another War Is Possible* is a must-read for anyone looking for both an exciting page-turner and an inside look at militant anticapitalist and antifascist resistance."
—*It's Going Down*

ANOTHER WAR IS POSSIBLE

MILITANT ANARCHIST EXPERIENCES IN THE ANTIGLOBALIZATION ERA

Tomas Rothaus

PM

Another War Is Possible: Militant Anarchist Experiences in the Antiglobalization Era
© 2025 Tomas Rothaus
This edition © 2025 PM Press

ISBN: 979-8-88744-105-4 (paperback)
ISBN: 979-8-88744-115-3 (ebook)
Library of Congress Control Number: 2024942919
Interior design by briandesign

10 9 8 7 6 5 4 3 2 1

PM Press
PO Box 23912
Oakland, CA 94623
www.pmpress.org

Printed in the USA.

To all those whose conscience shone so
bright that it set the streets on fire

La barricada cierra la calle, pero abre el camino

CONTENTS

ANOTHER WAR WAS POSSIBLE

CrimethInc.

It was the end of the twentieth century, and capitalism had triumphed.

"Really existing socialism" had collapsed. Elections were taking place everywhere, bringing new politicians to power to sign neoliberal trade agreements. In place of dictatorships, the free market reigned victorious.

Francis Fukuyama declared it "the end of history," proclaiming "the end-point of mankind's ideological evolution and the universalization of Western liberal democracy as the final form of human government."[1]

For politicians, advertising agents, and corporate executives, it was a time of jubilation.

The social ferment of the 1960s had ebbed. In the United States, radical politics largely subsisted in subcultural milieux—environmental movements, radical bookstores, the hip-hop and punk scenes. Europe also had the rave scene, the squatting movement with its network of social centers, and the vestiges of the powerful movements of the mid-twentieth century. On the opposing side, there were fascists, but they, too, were largely confined to subcultures. Outside those enclaves, social peace prevailed, as everyone scrambled to get their piece of the pie or waited for their ship to come in.

It was a fools' paradise. Globalized capitalism was moving wealth around faster and further than ever before, but in the process, it was concentrating it into fewer and fewer hands, slowly immiserating the vast majority. Anarchists knew that the apparent unanimity around the new world order would not last forever. Eventually, there would be another round of conflicts and history would continue moving forward. The real question was how the lines would be drawn.

> *We met at hardcore punk shows. We were reading about the Panthers, the Yippies, the Ranters, the Diggers, Up Against the Wall Motherfucker. When we heard that someone had spray-painted NEVER WORK on the wall of the Boulevard de Port-Royal during the May 1968 uprising, we took it literally, embarking on a life of crime.*
>
> *Others, like the author of this book, took a different approach, drawing on a different toolset. We quit our jobs; they unionized their workplaces. We squatted buildings; they did tenant organizing. We rejected formal organization; they created federations. We hitchhiked to events; they showed up with vans full of gear.*
>
> *Eventually, we began to run into each other at conferences and demonstrations.*
>
> *Everything that rises must converge.*

Fortunately, anarchists were not the only ones who had a bone to pick with the reigning order. On the first day of 1994, just as the North American Free Trade Agreement took effect, the Zapatista Army of National Liberation (EZLN) rose up against the Mexican government in Chiapas, setting a powerful example of grassroots struggle against neoliberalism. Inspired by the EZLN and other anticolonial and anticapitalist movements, people around the world began to organize protests, networks, occupations, global days of action.

To most people in the United States, taking on the authorities seemed absurd, if not downright quaint. Corporate media journalists refused to even say the word "capitalism" aloud, substituting "antiglobalization" as if we were part of a worldwide movement for parochialism. The bitterest conflicts were over "violence"—to be precise, over whether it was acceptable to respond in kind to the perpetual top-down violence of the state. But the most difficult challenge was to enable people to imagine that the capitalist world order was not inevitable, that another world was possible.

Nonetheless, for a few years—let's say, from 1999 to 2001—the chief conflict playing out on the global stage was between neoliberal capitalism and the grassroots movements that opposed it. On June 18,

1999, thousands of people converged on London for a day of action heralded as the Carnival Against Capitalism, during which some of them almost succeeded in destroying the London Stock Exchange. The following November, demonstrators successfully blockaded and shut down the summit of the World Trade Organization in Seattle. Over the next two years, almost every major international trade summit occasioned fierce street conflict.

> *"Should we try to get across?" I shouted, but we were already running, it was a split-second decision, we were already on the bridge by the time she answered, "Let's do it, we're doing it," and we were sprinting for the other side. Behind us, I could hear the pop-pop as the cops fired tear gas and rubber bullets; around us, I could hear the impact of the bullets, the clatter as the canisters landed, the hiss as their noxious contents filled the air; ahead, I couldn't see anything, the gas blotted out the sky, there was only the unknown—and beyond that, if we were lucky enough to reach it, a city to destroy, a world to create.*

The stakes were higher than we knew. If all of the people who were on the losing end of cutthroat capitalism failed to grasp that it was the source of their misfortunes, they would be susceptible to nationalism, racism, xenophobia, and demagoguery when they realized that the market was not fulfilling their hopes. But if we could make our case that capitalism was the chief cause of their misery, they might join us in our efforts to build a new society. There was a short window of time in which it seemed possible that we might succeed.

This was the war in which the author of this book participated—a war fought to forestall all the senseless wars that came afterward. We were fighting for a world in which all human beings could encounter each other as equals, in which the profit imperative would not trump the needs of human beings or the threat of climate change.

> *We set out from the campus at noon. Hundreds of people were there, ready, suited up—hoods, helmets, shoulder pads, the works. One group was pushing a full-size catapult. I was walking behind some people who were pulling a giant puppet representing the World Bank. Sledgehammers kept falling out onto the asphalt from inside the papier mâché.*

Among the crowd, I recognized his crew from the inaugura-
tion the previous January. You develop an instinct for such things,
even when everyone is masked. In idle social conversations and
online forums, we were rivals. But in a situation like that, you want
everyone there.

At some point, the police drove a water cannon right at the
crowd. A certain masked anarchist ran right up to it and smashed
out the window before it could get a clear shot at us. The driver
pulled away in a hurry.

Well, that's fucking crazy, *I thought.* Wow.

Perhaps if everyone had been able to see what was coming, more
people would have fought as hard as the author of this book. Few understood how dire things could get.

★

Unfortunately, we were not the only force contending to determine
how the lines of conflict would be drawn in the twenty-first century.
Provoked by centuries of colonial violence, Salafi jihadists attacked
the Pentagon and the World Trade Center on September 11, 2001.
Neoconservatives in the Bush administration snatched the opportunity to invade Afghanistan and then Iraq, precipitating the so-called
clash of civilizations they had been fantasizing about. The new century
opened with a series of bloodbaths.

This declaration of war served to obscure the possibility of any
other war, any other stakes for which people might fight. The authorities in the United States and their symmetrical adversaries in al-Qaeda
aimed to assert their rivalry as the central conflict in history, sidelining
the rebels in Chiapas and the demonstrators who had shut down the
Seattle WTO summit.

In the United States, authoritarian socialist parties took advantage of the situation to seize the initiative from anarchists and other
horizontally organized projects, gaining control of the antiwar movement through front groups (Not in Our Name for the Revolutionary
Communist Party, ANSWER for the Workers World Party). The trans-
formative grassroots models of the visionary anticapitalist movement
gave way to reactive protests addressing uncaring politicians.

The US government passed the Patriot Act. The FBI stepped up operations targeting Muslims in particular, but also environmentalists and animal liberation activists. Politicians expanded and militarized the police. On November 30, 1999, the government of Seattle had fielded just four hundred police to defend the summit of the World Trade Organization; in 2017, twenty-eight thousand security personnel defended Donald Trump's inauguration.

Overseas, the brutal US occupations of Iraq and Afghanistan cost nearly a million lives, driving more people into the ranks of the jihadists. The rise of the Islamic State in Iraq and Syria a decade later showed that the invasions had only strengthened the forces that the neoconservatives purported to be attacking. In 2010, when a wave of revolutions began in Tunisia and spread across the Mideast, it hit a wall in Syria in part because of the Islamic State and its supporters. We'll never know what the uprisings of the Arab Spring and other social movements in the region could have accomplished if not for the harm wrought by the so-called War on Terror. When the Taliban recaptured Afghanistan in 2021, it only underscored how pointless as well as destructive the US invasions had been.

The violence and poverty that resulted from all of these wars, occupations, and insurgencies drove refugees toward Europe from Africa and the Mideast by the millions. Something similar was taking place south of the US border, as the havoc wreaked by the North American Free Trade Agreement and the militarization of police and paramilitaries plunged whole regions into bloodshed. Nativists on both sides of the Atlantic took advantage of the refugees' desperation to drum up racism and fear.

Meanwhile, in the former Eastern bloc, capitalist profiteering left many people worse off economically than they had been before the fall of the Berlin Wall. This generated waves of nationalism, enabling autocrats like Vladimir Putin and Viktor Orbán to consolidate control. Emulating their model, politicians like Donald Trump, Jair Bolsonaro, and Giorgia Meloni came to power in the Americas and Western Europe. They channeled the rage of the eroding middle class toward openly fascist politics, encouraging their supporters to blame refugees, queer and trans people, Jewish people, and "communists" for the ways the free market had failed them.

Driven by rampant industrialism, climate change hammered coast-lines and incinerated forests. The COVID-19 pandemic ... the spread of conspiracy theories and disinformation ... the concentration of wealth in the hands of a few billionaires ... the genocide in Gaza—all of this will be familiar to you unless it has been eclipsed by even worse by the time you read this. The Russian invasion of Ukraine is not the last of the wars to come if we continue down this road—wars made possible by the consolidation of autocratic power and inevitable by economic and ecological crises. Looking at the weaponization of refugees on the border between Belarus and Poland and the use of prisoners as cannon fodder in Ukraine, we can see that—unless we change course—life is going to be increasingly cheap in the twenty-first century.

On June 18, 2023, exactly twenty-four years after the Carnival Against Capitalism in London, the lead article in *The New York Times* acknowledged what we had been saying for a quarter of a century: capitalist globalization creates catastrophic wealth inequalities, wrecking the biosphere and generating extreme-right nationalism.[2] The article recited all the talking points of the average anticapitalist protester of 1999, right down to the criticisms of the International Monetary Fund. Even the capitalists themselves now wish that we had won.

All of these tragedies had yet to occur when the struggles described in this book took place. Who knows—if more of us had fought harder, we might have averted some of them.

But we can't fault the author of this book. He was always on the front lines.

We ran into each other at a book fair some years after the events described in these pages. I recognized him from the streets, but we had never had a proper conversation.

Unexpectedly, we hit it off immediately. In person, it didn't matter that I was an adventurist dropout and he was a boring platformist.

He wanted to know if we were going to release a sequel to a certain controversial memoir we had published about a delinquent living on the run. "Politically, it's trash," he said. "But as a story, it's so exciting."

I didn't share his high opinion of it. I thought the humor compensated for the lack of character development, but speaking as a career criminal, the subject matter was positively banal. We had printed it as a strategy to undermine the materialism and timidity of kids from the suburbs, not to appeal to seasoned anarchists like himself.

He persisted. "Come on, you have to do a sequel!"

I told him that he should write a memoir of his own, recounting his adventures in the streets. "That would be worth publishing," I said.

It only took him two decades.

★

World history is a vast stage. On the scale of all humanity, each of us is only one out of billions. But it is up to us how we approach our role in the drama. We can see ourselves as spectators and passively accept our fate—or we can understand ourselves as protagonists and set out to discover how much influence we can exert on the course of events.

The author of this book took the latter approach. As a result, he participated in a surprising number of the historic events of the turn of the century. The litany of his adventures attests to how much a single person can accomplish with a bit of determination, whether in a time of social peace or of pitched conflict. Fortunately, he survived and, with a little encouragement, managed to write down some of what he experienced.

The result is the valuable historical document that you are holding in your hands. Not everyone who lives through epoch-making street fighting on three continents has the opportunity to write such a memoir. Buenaventura Durruti didn't.

Like Peter Kropotkin's *Memoirs of a Revolutionist* or Emma Goldman's *Living My Life*, this book offers a firsthand record of a pivotal time period. You can learn more about what things were really like from such a text than from any secondhand summary.

But this is not simply historical reference material. None of the struggles described in this book have reached a conclusion. All of them continue on a much larger scale and with even higher stakes: the struggle against fascism, against the violence of borders, against the subordination of ecosystems and communities to the demands of capitalism, against the violence of the police and the military, against autocratic power.

Another war was possible—and it still is today. If the consequences of our failure to abolish capitalism at the turn of the century were two decades of butchery, economic crisis, ecological disaster, and fascist reaction, think what will ensue if we fail to rise to the challenge this time. History didn't have to turn out the way it did in 2001—and it doesn't have to continue down that road now. This book remains timely because it tells part of a story that *you* have to finish.

There are many ways to participate in these struggles. Physically fighting fascists and police officers is only one of a wide range of tactics, and it is hardly the most important. From the author of this book, you can learn what some of those who came before you tried and what you might be able to do yourself. We—the survivors of the previous round—will be fighting alongside you.

If we don't speed it on its way, capitalism will take another century or more to collapse. It will sweep us into wars like nothing we have seen before. The resulting catastrophe will bury all of us in the wreckage.

Let's fight together for a better future. Another war is possible.

INTRODUCTION

We are so often the untold story, the unwritten poem. The stories of our adventures, our struggles, our hopes, and our aspirations are told by our enemies, who portray us as wide-eyed, bomb-throwing maniacs and vandals; by mild-mannered moderate reformers who will grant us understandable motivations but deny us reasoned political agency; by academics who look at us like exotic animals.

There are many reasons for this. For starters, political conviction. The firm belief that what mattered and matters foremost is not the isolated individual and their personal experience, but our collective ideas and motivations. Our conviction in not only the desirability but also the achievability of a world built on foundations radically different from those of the world today. Where on the ashes of a society organized for the benefit of capital—where resources are hoarded by those who have seized them and are assigned and distributed not to further the collective good of society, its needs, and the maximum expression of the individual but to facilitate the further accumulation of wealth in the hands of an ever-more-powerful few—we could build a new one organized around the principles of mutual aid, solidarity, and voluntary association. Our conviction that we could replace this dictatorship of capital that masquerades as a democracy—a democracy in which most are reduced to wage slavery and the central aspect of their lives, the workplace, where they spend the bulk of their waking moments, is a space as dictatorial as any—with one in which work is organized to further the needs of both the individual and the collective. One in which humans are free to flourish to their full potential and no Einsteins are lost having "lived and died in cotton fields and sweatshops."[1] One in which access to goods, capital, and services is granted "from each according to his ability, to each according to his needs," allowing us all to live better while working less, until such a point as the workplace is no longer a central aspect of our lives.[2] A society in which nationalism, religion, borders, and the state have been definitively replaced with mutual aid, solidarity, freedom, and socialism.

What matters is not the who but the why above—and so we write our calls to action, our post-action analysis, but rarely our personal stories. And beyond political conviction there's yet another of the many compelling reasons for this: security culture.

"What the hell are you doing? What is this, a confession? Have you lost your mind? Loose lips sink ships!" And so forth. It's my younger self, who I have had to see and hear throughout this entire process, looking at me in outraged disbelief as I try patiently over and over to explain that it's been twenty years and I don't think the state cares anymore about who conspired to throw what rock where in 2001. That it's fine. And that just in case, it'll all be anonymous.

Once I've managed to silence that outraged voice, the younger and less understanding version of me comes roaring back with his next objection: "Maybe, fine. But who the hell do you think you are?" He is the voice of humility. Of the not unreasonable argument that if we believe firmly that the mask was not merely a defense against state repression, but also a metaphor of our belief that what mattered was the why and not the who, then who are *you* to be telling the story of a generation of revolutionaries? Of a sea of people numbering in the thousands upon thousands, of whom you were just one?

Conviction. Security culture. Humility. All reasonable arguments, but also precisely the reason historical accounts of radical struggles and social movements so often skew toward the written record of the moderates, the timid, the "now is neither the place nor the time" crowd, and the "violence has never achieved anything" herd.

So I push back against the objections of young anarcho-orthodox me one more time, trying to explain patiently that just as reading the stories of the participants in the waves of rebellion of the preceding generations inspired us—of Bill Ayers and his *Fugitive Days* and of Ann Hansen's *Direct Action*, to name just two among several—so too might reading about our experiences, adventures, and motivations inspire others. And that too is a contribution to preserving, maintaining, and advancing struggle.

So here we are. This is just the story of a life. Or, as it turns out, due to editorial and length concerns, a brief period of one life. One life, one perspective, one person. With all of my prejudices and subjectivities, particularly colored by the enthusiasm and confidence of youth. But it's the story of a life intertwined with the story of thousands upon thousands with whom I shared an idea, a utopia. And most importantly, we shared the desire, the need, to give our best toward making that utopia a reality. Failing that, we tried to taste it in the fleeting moments and experiences we created together. I've tried to represent others, those individuals with whom I shared this path and these experiences, as best as I can. If anything, I wish my creative writing and literary skills were better, so that I could much more fully develop their characters and portray more completely the incredible, kind, and unique individuals with whom I shared the path of anarchist struggle. I am fully aware that we are seldom as well represented as when we represent ourselves. Those comrades whom I could still find, and who were open to it, I spoke to and interviewed at length, letting them speak in their own words or at least ensuring that they felt properly represented by the dialogue attributed to them. As for those whom the passage of time seems to have swallowed forever, I hope desperately that if they were to someday read this, they will see at least an accurate reflection of their motivations and experiences in my recollections.

★

We are anarcho-syndicalists on the shop floor, green anarchists in the woods, social anarchists in our communities, individual-ists when you catch us alone, anarcho-communists when there's something to share, insurrectionists when we strike a blow.
—CrimethInc., "Fight Where You Stand"

It's perhaps fitting to lead here with a quote from CrimethInc. Those few unlucky ones who are familiar with the minutiae of early 2000s

North American inter-anarcho squabbles and camps will remember that we, the Barricada, NEFAC (Northeastern Federation of Anarcho-Communists), and assorted anarcho-communist camps (which was possibly the dominant anarchist tendency of the time, reaching, for example, a peak of four separate NEFAC-federated anarcho-communist collectives in the city of Boston alone in 2000) were publicly and vocally critical of CrimethInc. in our publications. We of course thought it important, and healthy, for our movement to have the debates necessary to flesh out its ideas, practices, and directions. But less well known is that while we were critical and "opposed to each other" in public and in the battle of ideas, we had a comradely bond forged in battle. A bond that—unlike Barricada, NEFAC, or most of our more formal organizations—still lasts to this day.

Personally, I was uncompromising in the field of ideas, probably to the point of sectarianism and not being a much-loved character among those who identified more with other tendencies in anarchism. But in practice, my sense of political belonging and ideological affinity was always pragmatic, oriented toward the general anarchist camp. My priority was always effective action and an anarchism that was as relevant as possible in the social struggles of the day, more so than ideological purity. And so unsurprisingly, while living in the Athens of the '90s I fell in with a more insurrectionary "anarchism means war" tendency. In the post-general-strike Paris of the late '90s, I quickly found myself in the anarcho-syndicalist CNT (Confédération Nationale du Travail) on the one side and in antifascist circles combating the rise of the far right on the other. In the US, it was platformism and finding our role in the antiglobalization movement. And finally, although it's outside the time period of this book, a decade in the politically deeply eclectic world of the German autonome antifa. Because you fight where you stand.

If you are looking for slavish devotion to anarchist orthodoxy, you won't find it here. I've always been and still am a true believer in the anarchist idea—of a society free from state and capital; a society free from all forms of discrimination, oppression, and institutional authority; one in which the collective knowledge, wealth, and efforts of society are put toward the common good, freeing us from the constraints of wage labor and the logic of productivity, so that individuals may be free to live life to the fullest extent of their desires. But I see anarchism as a vibrant and living school of thought. Of course, I draw inspiration and guidance from the ideas of those who came before us, but I also draw conclusions from the changing realities around me and the concrete struggles I participate in.

Maybe others have had or will have different experiences, but these are the lessons I draw from my own experience, born of practical realities from struggle in five different countries on three continents. Others may reach different conclusions, which are equally valid, but mine is that this is the reality of active political participation and engagement. Of refusing to observe the course of history as a mere witness. Of choosing to be a participant, and striving to be a protagonist. Struggle cures sectarianism, and praxis tempers dogmatism. Would I today join the Democratic Socialists of America in the US? Vote for Syriza in 2010s Greece? Vote yes on the constitutional reform in Chile? Of course not, on all counts. But I would hope that I would be understanding of those who do and would prioritize what we have in common rather than focusing on where we differ. Unlike in my youth, I would hope that I would be able to try to build bridges with those individuals, though not necessarily with their political organizations, and use those bridges to convey my anarchist vision and praxis, rather than attacking them or bludgeoning them with it.

There is a constant tension running through these stories. For one, because tension and contradiction are naturally human, but also because more often than not the writer is the me of today, while the protagonist is the me of two decades ago. They do not always see eye to eye. In many cases, the anarchist of twenty years ago reached similar conclusions, through measured political analysis, to the one of today, but back then raw desire and passion translated into actions not necessarily aligned with reasoned analysis. Often these contradictions were waved away by one of two go-to phrases: "If I wanted to care about opinions, I'd have been a politician" and "If I wanted to always find an excuse not to act, I'd be a Marxist-Leninist." And so there is constant contradiction.

The perceived contradiction of pitting mass-based organizing and education against the urge and desire for immediate and uncompromising action and revolt. The contradiction in desiring to bring about *le grand soir* (roughly "the great night") and the final victory of libertarian social revolution while still recognizing the benefits of partial victories and leftward shifts in society. The contradiction in advocating for social anarchism and mass movements while feeling a growing disdain for large swaths of society as they cheer the advances of capital, state surveillance, and fascism like trained seals whose minds have been irrevocably colonized. In being aware of the dangers of the authoritarian left and virulently defending anarchism and anarchists from them, with arguments as well as with weapons, while also recognizing that more often than not they have been the comrades sharing front lines with us. In advocating and living a total and frontal war against the state and capital while also engaging in concrete and limited struggles to obtain concessions from both of them. The contradiction between a life of activism, organizing, and militance that was probably 99 percent composed of endless meetings, mind-numbingly boring antifascist research and surveillance efforts, thankless hundreds if not thousands of hours manning info stands or giving out literature, late nights alone hunting for the right words for a text or call, followed by hours of collective discussion about every word and term, of hours upon hours and weekends upon weekends walking around with a flag, often in the gray and rainy cold of winter, surrounded by robocops and hostile civilians—and a book that makes it seem like this is somehow a particularly exciting way to live, highlighting the exceptions rather than the rule of a life of anarchist militancy.

There is a tension between the rejection of militarism and the concept of revolutionary vanguard formations, while speaking about cadre and differentiating between civilians and people who chose to live as I and many of those around me did—who, although it took me years to realize and accept it, have the life experiences, and often traumas, of combatants rather than civilians. The tensions of a deep aversion to violence on a personal level, while at the same time not only being constantly faced with it but often initiating it ourselves out of recognition that if we wish to put an end to the unimaginable violence and needless suffering caused by the logic of capital and the authority of the state, or of fascist mobs and movements, there is only one road—and to pretend it is a peaceful one only renders us weaker in our efforts at liberation, thus allowing for a greater and longer-lasting violence exerted on society as a whole.

There are tensions and contradictions everywhere, and many remain unresolved. I grappled with them for years, as one should, so much so that I saw them as yet another obstacle (beyond the above-mentioned) to writing such a text. The decades of writing political texts and demonstration calls clearly took a toll: In my mind, if you write it is to transmit a message. To educate. To agitate. To convince and spur to action. If you yourself are incapable of deciphering what message it is your text is trying to convey, then chances are you shouldn't be writing it. Or at least, you shouldn't be writing it as a political text.

So I instead began writing for a small but important audience: for my children. Because they were too young to remember most of these events, but the consequences of my actions have had, currently have, and will continue to have a significant impact on their lives. If nothing else, I felt I owed it to them to explain, as best as I could and as honestly as I could, why their father lived as he lived and what motivated the decisions he took. Why did they grow up in a house with ten other people? Why when we were sitting in our room playing board games were there suddenly hundreds of police officers outside? Why did we take a completely unexpected and unplanned vacation to a foreign country? But most of all, why did I one day disappear? Why did we split up? Why can I be visited but can never visit? Why did I never return to where we lived? (Note that the aforementioned children didn't yet exist during the time period that, due to length constraints, ends up being covered in this book. A lot of this subject matter, and answers to these questions, will show up in another book, covering the years after 2002.)

Most of all, I wrote to attempt to explain to them who I am, where I came from, what shaped me, and what motivated my actions. So that one day in the future when they judge me — and they will judge me, as all children eventually judge their parents — they might do so less harshly. Or at the very least with the benefit of the whole story to base their verdict on. Hopefully, they might understand that at least in my mind, if I chose struggle, I didn't choose it *over* them. I chose struggle *for* them. This, too, is a contradiction. A brutal one. One that I'll probably contend with for the rest of my life.

The inescapable arm of the consequences of my past is merciless. Reaching effortlessly, usually at seemingly randomly cruel moments, from decades ago to my life today. Threatening to endanger us all, throwing up invisible walls preventing us from being together, stopping me from being with my family at will. And every time it does so, it comes accompanied by a chorus of recriminations. How could you do this? How could you be so irresponsible? How could you risk so much for an idea so far-fetched? How could you expose others who depend on you to the consequences of your actions, without their consent? For what? Utopia? Have you not seen the world around you? It's a jungle of individualism, competition, violence, obscurantism, and greed. You fought for an impossible fantasy, with real-world consequences for you and those who love you, trust you, depend on you.

I have to remind myself that to the me of then, there was no alternative. No decision to be made. That in my eyes the best and most important example I could hope to provide for them as a human being was to not accept needless suffering and a criminally illogical social and economic system as an inescapable fatality. That while many things might be considered normal in the world around them, they are under no obligation to accept them as such. That being outraged by injustice and senseless death and violence, no matter how widespread or accepted they are, is to remain human in the face of the machinery of legalized oppression. That normal, legal, and accepted don't necessarily mean right. That no matter the cost, the price, or the legality, our conscience should always rebel against the world of authority, commodity, borders, and the exploitation of human by human. In short, that we should always strive to choose the side of dignity.

But more and more, when harassed by this particularly aggressive and painful contradiction, I am convinced that I had no choice in the matter. It was, after all, what my conscience demanded of me. Of course, maybe it would have been easier to adapt to capitalist society, to become a wage slave, to concern myself only with the task of providing food, shelter, and comfort. But what kind of life lesson would that be? Be concerned with the world, with society, with the understanding that your freedom is inextricably linked to the freedom of others ... but do so only safely, while you are young, and then once you have a family limit yourself to looking out for you and yours?

Even so, there came a point when I attempted just that. Not only because the repression became too intense and the isolation too great, but because in my mind from this point on—isolated and exiled—any further political action that exposed me to legal or physical danger was almost absurd from a cost-benefit analysis. There was nothing more to gain for the movement or my ideas with whatever I had left to lose. For me, political action and the life of an anarchist had to be always all day, every day. The front line or nothing. Anything less was cowardice and treason. While I paid lip service to the idea that anarchism should be an inclusive space—where the sympathizer, the curious newcomer, and everyone and anyone should feel welcomed and appreciated—this was by no means a concept I extended to myself.

So I put my best foot forward in the project of drowning my conscience and becoming a good citizen. A model participant in capitalist society. And to be fair, I had a very good run at it too. I benefit from the privilege of a lot of social capital, don't consider myself white but certainly benefit from white skin privilege, and speak several languages fluently. Also, in a shocking twist of fate, anarchism has provided me with a certain skill set that is both useful and well compensated in capitalist society. But despite my best efforts, reality kept getting in the way of my attempts to find my peace with rainbow capitalism. My conscience insisted on rebelling against the sight of kids in cages. Of a two-year-old toddler drowned on a beach at the altar of a border. Murdered because he and his parents lacked the correct piece of paper. Of human beings reduced to mere equations, sacrificed in a pandemic to guarantee the continued accumulation of capital. At comrades fighting and dying in the streets, desperately trying to push back the waves of fascists and white supremacists.

I had to accept that anarchism and the moral coordinates it provides me are inextricable from me as a human being. While it's very likely an easier way to live, I just don't have the luxury of extirpating them from my being. Accepting this fact, I realized that what was imperative was to redefine my relationship to it.

Eventually, and with the invaluable help of more than a few comrades, I began to see that I, too, owe myself the mercy of understanding that it is not only acceptable to struggle in forms that don't involve your body and the constant risk of injury, death, or prison, but also valuable. That, as in life, in political action there are also stages—chapters, so to speak. And that the key to both finding happiness as an individual as well as being effective in struggle is to know when it is time to close a chapter, walk away as gracefully as possible, and start a new one. That my mind can also be a weapon, not only to strategize for how to best wage material combat against the enemies of a liberated and egalitarian society, but to contribute with my thoughts and experiences. Experiences that—thanks to a few geographical twists of fate putting me repeatedly in the right places at the right time, and the fanaticism leading me to seek out, or create, those times and places when they didn't magically fall into my lap—I had accumulated more than a few of. It's not only acceptable, but important. It's okay to put down your weapons, if you at least try to help those who come after you to wield them better.

So the weapon at my disposal today is writing, and not just for the kids, but also to do what I can to preserve the collective memory of our movement. Not to give lessons, because the character of "old man veteran of movements past talks down to the next generations" is universally reviled, and rightfully so. If the sentence starts with, "When I was young ... ," you can probably feel free to tune out. Not to mention, what lessons would I, or the collective *we* of anarchists past, even have to give, and how relevant are our experiences? From the outside looking in, the movement in the US today seems larger than ours ever was. We had to mobilize for months and across the entire continent to put together a black bloc of maybe one thousand people. Now we see them spring up on a weekly basis, with hundreds of disciplined comrades showing up simultane- ously in Oakland, Portland, Seattle, Washington, Atlanta, Chicago, and everywhere in between. Where we carried the occasional shield, baton, radio, and helmet, today's militants display a level of preparation when they take to the streets that makes ours feel almost comically quaint.

It is also true, though, that current anarchist and radical genera- tions, particularly in North America, seem to find little to nothing from previous ones to draw on, expending time and energy reinventing the wheel and often wading unknowingly into mistakes already made. This is an attempt to at least provide my perspective on some of those expe- riences and mistakes, so that others can have it as a tool when making decisions today. But it's just one person's perspective, and the beautiful part about anarchism is that you are completely free to take it or leave it. And that said, few things could give me more joy than to feel that my experience or perspective is useless, or less relevant, not because it is outdated or irrelevant per se but because it has been largely surpassed.

But experience doesn't have to be tactically relevant. The sharing of experience, of stories, of anecdotes, can be motivationally relevant. Hopefully you'll laugh at our stupidity, shake your head at our sectar- ianism, smile condescendingly at our innocence—while being inspired by our adventures and misadventures.

Whatever our different contexts, however the world and our enemies might change, I believe the essence of how to nurture the anarchist idea and build its movement remains the same: Reach out to those who see how broken our world is and feel the urgency of change but lack the hope in an alternative to struggle for it. Expose and confront those cynical enough to see the devastation and needless suffering around us but rationalize and justify it because they benefit from this reality. Be an unflinching opponent of the apologists of nationalism, sexism, racism, and capitalism whom we do not seek to convince, but to oppose and defeat.

But most of all, look kindly on those who see this world as broken and strive to change it with us, even when we might disagree on how to best go about doing so. Those who refuse to sit idly by as society accelerates needlessly into ecological collapse, while never-before-seen-in-human-history advances in technology and productivity are put at the service of wealth accumulation, instead of toward human-kind living plentifully with ample time for leisure as we could. Those whose conscience drives them to reject the growing fascist threat and the capitalist normality of inequality that breeds it. Those who stand by us and share a barricade with us, no matter if that barricade is literal or metaphorical.

This book is the first part in a much longer adventure. It's a snapshot of our story, a glimpse into our state of mind, a moment in our experiences—as one individual lived and interpreted them. It's my little drop of water into the river of anarchy, and if it helps in even the smallest of ways in the task of that river one day becoming the raging rapids that will sweep away the world of state and capital, clearing the path for the one of anarchy and communism, then it's just as valuable a weapon as I've ever wielded.

Be boundless in your solidarity. Passionate in your love. Audacious in your adventures. Unforgiving in your rage.

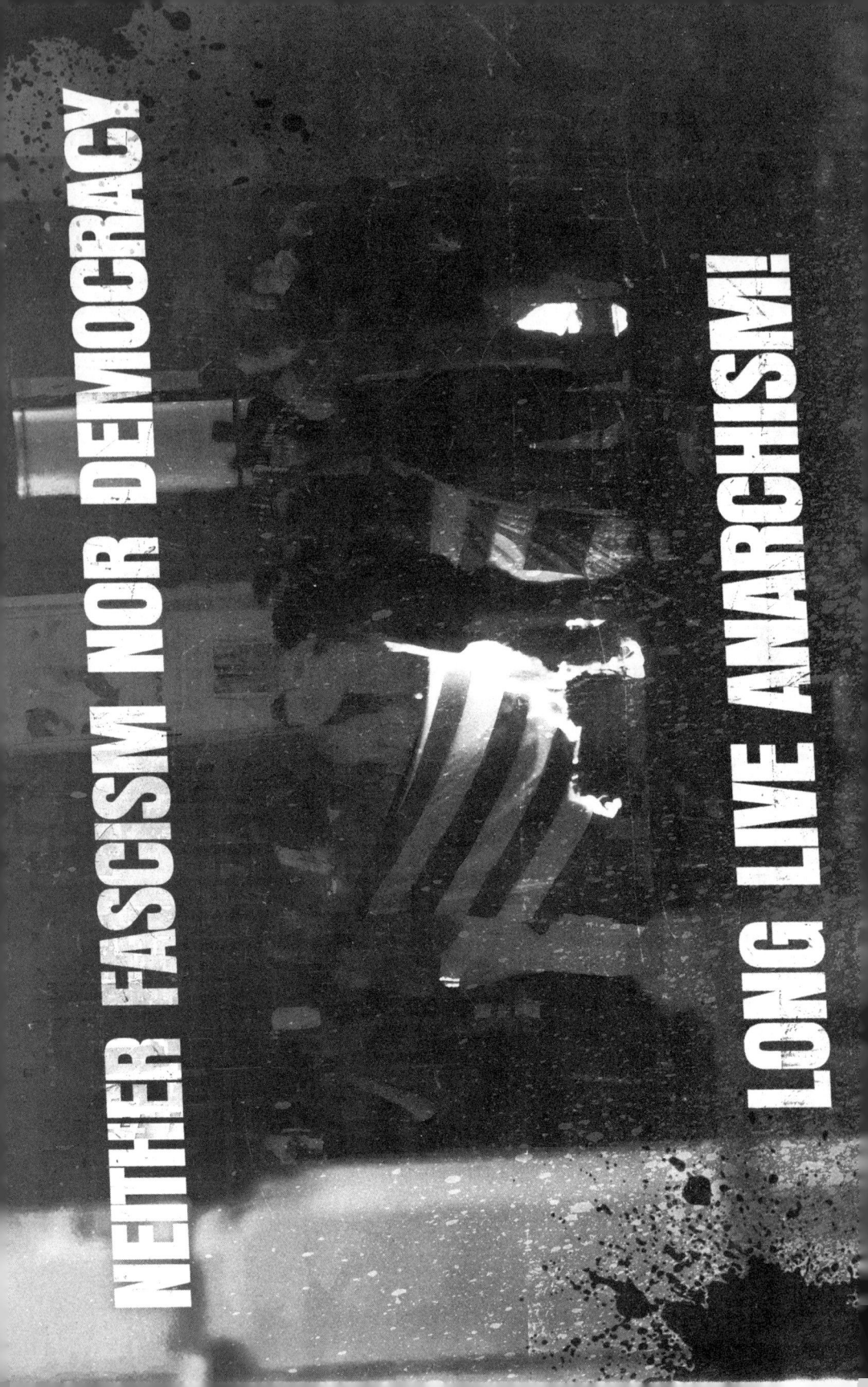

NEITHER FASCISM NOR DEMOCRACY

LONG LIVE ANARCHISM!

PROLOGUE

Outskirts of Athens,
November 17, 1995, 22:00

The Greek television channels of the 1990s had an entertaining tradition of providing live coverage of ongoing riots, and I have them to thank for discovering modern anarchism. Being barely a teenager who had only recently moved to Athens, I didn't yet have many friends, and my limited comprehension of the language meant that as far as TV programming went, my options weren't great. So I was greatly appreciative when whatever terrible Greek soap opera or water polo match I was watching (yes, they televise water polo in Greece, and I was sometimes bored enough to watch) was interrupted by the "incidents downtown."

The coverage and scenery were usually more or less the same. On one side, some middle-aged news anchor in a suit droning on about "hooligans, vandals, hoodlums, and other dregs of society" while the camera shot either from a helicopter or from comfortably behind the lines of police. Sometimes there would be an actual journalist with the cameraman, giving exasperated and outraged commentary from behind the police lines. On the other side stood groups of a few dozen to a few hundred people, masked and many of them with the typical rioter look of the time, which meant jeans and bomber jackets, which were often turned inside out to reveal the neon-orange inner lining. The setting was always pretty much one of two. It was either some place downtown on the margins of some demonstration called by mainstream unions and political parties, or it was the immediate surroundings of a university, more often than not the famed Athens Polytechnic University, and the latter was the case that day.

The scenes this particular night were impressive, and the confrontations were clearly significantly more intense than usual. There seemed to be an endless horde of masked youths at and around the gates of the university, and the images on TV were a constant stream of clouds of tear gas, barricades, and firebombs flying in every direction. It all made for exciting viewing for a young teenager, but as far as I understood, this was just the usual antics from "the hoodlums who infiltrate and hijack the legitimate demonstrations of the good citizens and protesters."

My understanding of Greek was still pretty basic, but I could clearly make out that what these people, these supposed "mindless vandals and hooligans with no political message who are just out for destruction," were chanting about clearly had to do with freedom, something about "against authority," and something or other "against nationalism." Just as I was grappling with this, several more masked figures emerged from the gates of the Athens Polytechnic with a gigantic Greek flag in their hands. They promptly proceeded to light it on fire. Through the noise of the indignant news anchor lecturing about how "they respect nothing, not even our beloved patriotic emblems," I heard them chant "*zito i anarchia*," which essentially translates to "long live anarchy!"

Shortly afterward, still with the backdrop of a constant back and forth of firebombs versus tear gas, I witnessed on live television as they proceeded to hang yet another enormous Greek flag on the main gate of the Polytechnic ... and promptly lit it on fire.

And this was the moment that changed my life, probably forever. I started trying to focus on the chants and graffiti around them. I caught something about "the passion for freedom" in a chant and saw "Neither Fascism nor Democracy" on a wall. Slowly it dawned on me. These were actual, existing, modern-day anarchists. Anarchism was not, as I had believed to that day, a late-nineteenth-century ideology that, while seemingly appealing, had died off almost a century ago.

I had become aware of the idea of anarchism as a pre-teen thanks to the mainstream "punk" trend of the mid-'90s, namely the Offspring and Green Day. (Please don't judge me ...) Somebody told me that if I liked "punk rock" I should listen to the Sex Pistols, and somehow I had gotten my hands on a *Never Mind the Bollocks* cassette. "Anarchy in the UK" seemed like a pretty good song, but I had no idea what this word "anarchy" meant. Curious as I was, and this being (at least in my universe) pre-internet times, I headed to the library and looked the word up in the encyclopedia. I could have encountered any of the terrible, shallow, and ignorant descriptions of the word that are par for the course in most publications. Instead, by a pure stroke of luck, the entry on "anarchism" in the *Encyclopedia Britannica* I held in my hands was written by none other than Peter Kropotkin. The first two paragraphs read:

> ANARCHISM (from the Gr. ἀν- and ἀρχή, contrary to authority), the name given to a principle or theory of life and conduct under which society is conceived without government—harmony in such a society being obtained, not by submission to law, or by obedience to any authority, but by free agreements concluded between the various groups, territorial and professional, freely constituted for the sake of production and consumption, as also for the satisfaction of the infinite variety of needs and aspirations of a civilized being. In a society developed on these lines, the voluntary associations which already now begin to cover all the fields of human activity would take a still greater extension so as to substitute themselves for the state in all its functions....
>
> If ... society were organized on these principles, man would not be limited in the free exercise of his powers in productive work by a capitalist monopoly, maintained by the state; nor would he be limited in the exercise of his will by a fear of punishment, or by obedience towards individuals or metaphysical entities, which both lead to depression of initiative and servility of mind. He would be guided in his actions by his own understanding, which necessarily would bear the impression of a free action and reaction between his own self and the ethical conceptions of his surroundings. Man would thus be enabled to obtain the full development of all his faculties, intellectual, artistic and moral, without being hampered by overwork for the monopolists, or by the servility and inertia of mind of the great number.[1]

It was difficult to believe what I was reading. This seemed incredible, and it articulated the instinctive dislike I felt for authority in a way I couldn't imagine existed. I quickly proceeded to see what, if any, actual books on "anarchism" might be available at the library. They had one. This library, in Athens, Greece, of all places in the world, had one single solitary book on anarchism, and it was nothing less than *The Haymarket Tragedy*, by the prolific and brilliant historian of anarchism Paul Avrich. Five hundred pages that painted a vivid and moving portrait not just of the actual Haymarket martyrs, but of the entire anarchist community, their ideas, their convictions, and their sacrifices. I devoured the book in a couple of days, the way most teenagers might go through a good video game.

And then I hit a dead end. Living on the outskirts of Athens, with no access to the internet, and speaking not much Greek, I couldn't find any references to anarchism or anarchists more recent than the turn of the nineteenth century. So I concluded that this must have been a great idea, but unfortunately one with no connection to the present day. But from the book and the encyclopedia, I had enough of an understanding of political theory to understand that anarchism was a type of communism, and that communists were also against both capital and the state. They only seemed to disagree on the road to get there. And communists of the Marxist variety not only existed, but you could find them just about anywhere in Greece (where the Stalinist Communist Party of Greece, KKE, was still garnering a solid 10 percent or so of the vote at that time). For better or worse, I encountered members of the Greek branch of the Maoist Revolutionary Internationalist Movement selling newspapers (what else?) while in the city one day. Apparently there was a "people's war" raging in Peru, and Chairman Gonzalo had recently been captured.[2] This was especially grave since he was the great mind behind the science of "Marxism-Leninism-Maoism-Gonzalo Thought," which would lead the masses to inevitable eventual victory in the protracted people's war. Not only did this seem fascinating, urgent, and momentous, but they told me if I came to their meetings, they could provide me with news and texts to read, in Spanish! So began my brief childhood flirtation with Maoism.

It ended abruptly on Friday, November 17, 1995. As the TV broadcast the image of Greek flags going up in smoke, so did my interest in Maoism. Now that I had deciphered the code, even through the lens of the mainstream media's coverage, I could see that the language of anarchism and antiauthoritarianism was all around those battles. In the banners, graffiti, chants, and even the forms of action and targets. I briefly considered trying to head over there, but I guess I was reasonable enough to decide that my barely teen self trying to somehow safely make it through the cops and to the side of the demonstrators—and then going up to a random masked anarchist in the middle of a riot and saying, "Hey! Speak English? Spanish? I too am interested in anarchism!"—was probably not a great plan.

I didn't sleep that night as I sat glued to the television watching the clashes unfold. I was still awake when, sometime after dawn, the police were given permission to violate the asylum. They entered the university and arrested 504 anarchist militants that morning. The anarchists exited the Polytechnic with arms locked and to the chant of, "The passion for freedom is stronger than any prison cell!"

PART 1

RISING TIDE: THE PARIS YEARS

ADRENALINE, VIOLENCE, AND A PROGRAM

1
YOU NEVER FORGET
YOUR FIRST TIME

Paris, 1996

One can never provide enough examples of what can never be said enough times. Yes, the state and capitalist order may be powerful. Yes, they are armed to the teeth. And yes, they do have all sorts of techniques, technologies, and assorted government agencies dedicated to the sole and singular purpose of shutting us up, terrifying the hell out of us, and, when that all fails, locking us the fuck up.

But their greatest weapon is far and away the paralysis their propaganda and culture of fear imposes on us. The flu-like contagion that gets to the bones of everyone who questions the world around them and tells them that the enemy is all-knowing, all-seeing, all-powerful. That resistance is futile, and that if you fail to grasp that concept, you will be going to jail and your life will end.

I know the lie well. I believed it. Even when I was already on the "dark side" (the good side!), it still gripped me with unshakable force. I'll never forget the day it went away. I was living in Paris, and it was sometime in 1996. It was early on a weekday, and I was supposed to be in school. So instead, of course, we were outside the Palace of Justice, putting pressure on the judges deciding whether they would deport an anarchist comrade of ours, whose name and alleged crimes I can no longer recall, back to his home country of Italy, where he would be sent straight to prison.

We milled about for a few hours, about a hundred of us chatting in the cold, hanging out on the sidewalk and mainly being bored and anxious. I had just recently begun going to demonstrations and other such happenings. In my youthful exuberance, I truly expected there to be some indescribable sense of joy and power and magic and other such exciting feelings at being surrounded by hundreds or thousands of like-minded crazed folk.

Unfortunately, I wasn't really feeling it. Mainly, it was just a mob walk from point A to point B. Rather boring, and in the Parisian wintertime, usually unpleasantly cold and often wet.

Suddenly, what we all knew would happen, happened. Deportation was the verdict. And before I knew it, everybody was pouring off the sidewalk and into the middle of the damned avenue. Cars were blocked, buses were stopped, and hundreds of important people in business suits were prevented from getting to important places in order to do important things.

Are these people insane? I thought. *Do they not know this is illegal?* I joined in. My thoughts raced furiously. I was breaking out of the box, stepping beyond the boundaries, disobeying the rules. Something vague about stepping out of the world of the spectacle and into another one scuttled across my mind.

We were the living dead! They would catch us, put us in jail forever. My life was over! My poor mother, I hadn't even said goodbye! Hell, she thought I was at school!

Wait, what is this?! There was a feeling in my gut. Fear, eating me alive? Nope, wasn't it. *What is this?* I felt queasy, and while I didn't know if that was a word, it was definitely the feeling. My veins were bigger, I could feel the blood flowing. I was trembling.

It feels good.

CRS robocops (as we called the riot cops in their full regalia) came running down the street. The strange feeling only got stronger. I still thought my life was over and I was headed to jail forever, but suddenly I didn't care. I felt strong, fearless. They could do what they wanted to me, but I was fighting for what was right, to hell with the consequences (so functions the mind of a young, self-righteous anarcho!). My ponderings about life as a prison martyr were interrupted when I was clobbered in the ribs by a baton. Strangely, I didn't feel pain. I realized what the feeling was. Adrenaline! The troublemaker's greatest and most precious drug. And I recognized what it gave me: power! *I'm invincible!*

I hit him back. Straight under the face mask, right at the chin. What could be more logical? An agent of the repressive forces of the state strikes me, I strike him the fuck back. How had it taken me fourteen years of my life to figure this out? After a few seconds, which seemed like minutes and which I'd savor for the rest of my life, we were retreating and dispersing. Succumbing to superior armament and numbers. During the retreat, I watched as comrades broke a window. I ducked into the metro, jumped the turnstiles—*I didn't pay for the subway, now I'm really going away for life!*—and escaped to safety.

I sat on the subway recapping the events of the day and waiting for the world to end. An avenue was blocked in one of Paris's finest areas, the economy was (however infinitely insignificantly) affected, officers of the law were injured, and property was damaged. I was afraid to move. Not being one for drugs, I imagined this might be what it felt like to be a paranoid stoner. *Oh my God, she's looking at me ... he knows, they all know ... I have "criminal" written on my face.* At any moment the SWAT team would come flying through the windows and "take me down." They would get me. They always caught the lawbreakers. This was the undeniable truth, anybody who has ever watched *COPS* or *World's Wildest Police Videos* knew this. I waited a bit longer for the world to end.

It never did.

I'm sure somewhere deep inside, I'm still waiting.

This was probably the singular most important and exciting realization of my life. That the state is not all-seeing and all-knowing. It is not all-powerful. A whole new world unfolded before my eyes with five minutes of troublemaking. Statues of powerful and invincible enemies crumbled before my very eyes. Corridors of possibility transformed themselves into raging wild jungles, where anything not only could be, but would be! The monopoly of violence was broken. The sandcastle of fear and paralysis lay in ruins, washed away by the tide of adventure, spontaneity, and rebellion. And atop these ruins, we stood. Just me and some other like-minded Crazies (capital *C*), armed with adrenaline, violence, and a program. I may be plagued by megalomaniac tendencies, but it really felt like this!

It's a feeling I highly suggest to everyone.

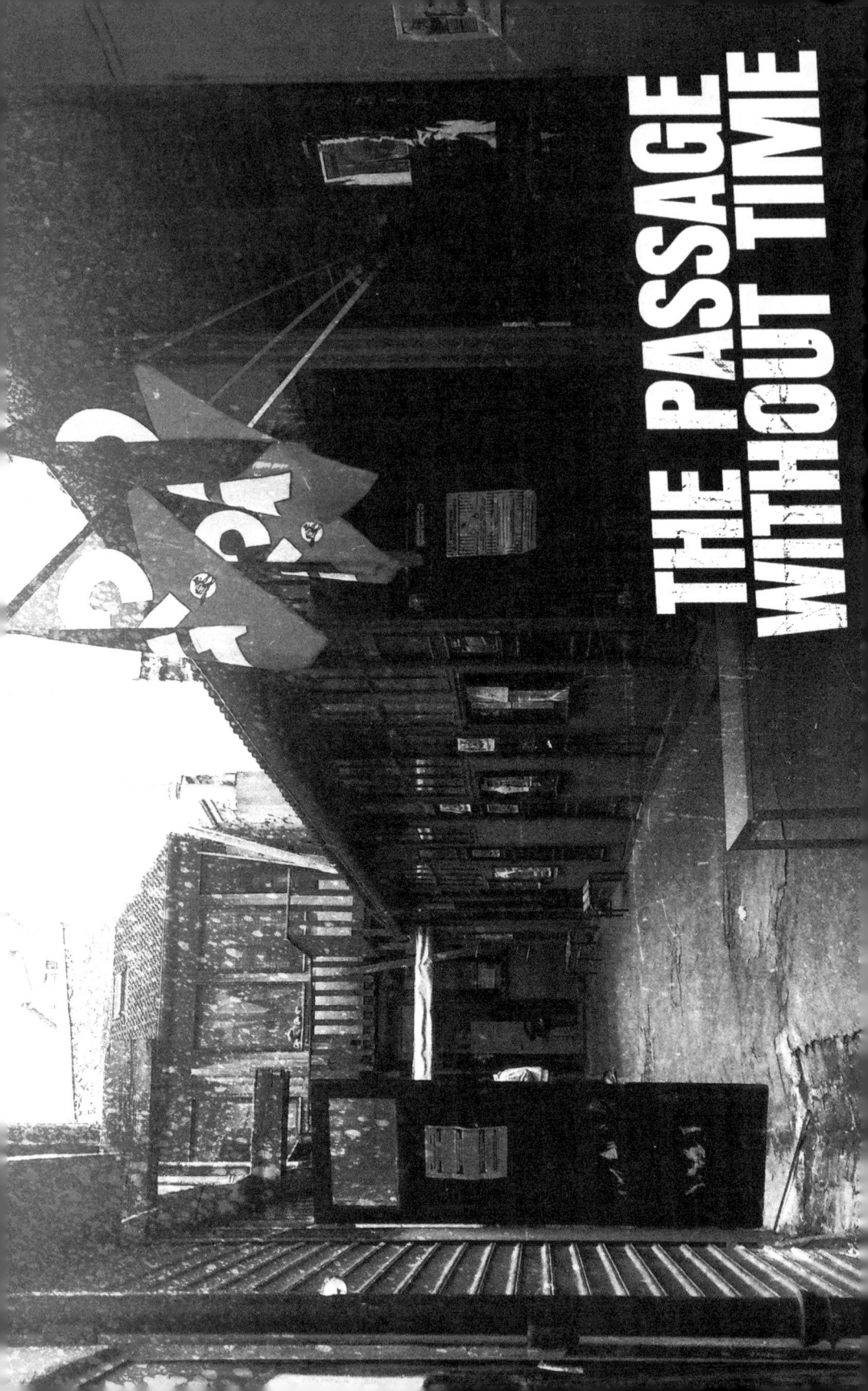

THE PASSAGE WITHOUT TIME

2
33 RUE DES VIGNOLES
Paris, 1997

They say that books are a door to another world, but what if I told you that until not too many years ago in Paris, there was one specific magical door that accomplished this exact thing in reality? A door that, when passed through, brought to life a world that was only supposed to exist in books.

To find this hidden door, you have to crisscross Paris on a bicycle like a rabid banshee, alternating between swerving wildly through traffic and yelling at tourists for standing stupidly in the bicycle lane. (At least, that's how I usually got myself there. I had just returned from a year or so in Argentina and everything was new and exciting, so I was always in a hurry.) But you could also just simply step off the metro at the Avron stop and into the 20th arrondissement of the city's east side. You'll be meters away from the Place de la Nation, iconic start or end point of many if not most Parisian demonstrations, and surrounded by the smell of *grec frites*, kebab and French fries, coming from one of the several immigrant-owned restaurants in the area. Gentrified as Paris is, the 20th arrondissement is still one of its most popular and diverse neighborhoods.

You begin your walk in the direction of the Père-Lachaise cemetery, less than a mile or so away. It's the world's most-visited cemetery and a place teeming with history. Most in popular culture know it as the final

resting place of the Doors' Jim Morrison, but for us radicals and revolutionaries it is the location of the infamous Communards' Wall, a stark
reminder of the potential price in blood of revolutionary struggle. The
spot where, on May 28, 1871, 147 of the final 200 of the Paris Commune's
combatants were shot following desperate and often hand-to-hand
combat among the gravestones, after having entrenched themselves for
a last stand against the advancing Versaillaise army of counterrevolution.

But that's not where you are headed today, and after only a few
short blocks on a typically wide tree-lined Parisian boulevard, you take
a right turn onto a narrow, winding side street, the Rue des Vignoles.
You'll walk for a few minutes among the quintessentially Parisian two-,
three-, and four-story residential buildings before you notice to your
left an alleyway. You have arrived at number 33 of the Rue des Vignoles.

Somehow even narrower than the Rue des Vignoles itself, let's call
it comically narrow, the approximately fifty-meter-deep alleyway is an
unexpected sight, akin to Gru's house in *Despicable Me*—by no means
because it is ugly, mind you, but because it is positively cartoonish in
how it differs from the rest of its immediate surroundings. While the
surrounding buildings are several stories tall, the structures on both
sides of the alley are only one story, and the wooden touches to the
cement structure give it all an almost rural look. It is, to say the least,
an unexpected sight in central Paris. As you turn past the iron gate at
the alley's entrance, you notice the quaint Parisian cobblestone ground
below you, as well as the rather unusual paint job on the buildings to
both sides: a powerful, vibrant tone of red, with doors and shutters
painted black.[1]

As you walk into the alley, you will pass a fair amount of doors on
both sides that open onto interesting sights and sounds. From the first
on your right, you will hear the distinctive sound of shoes rhythmically
stomping on wood as you pass by the home of the Flamenco in France
association. Farther in and to your left, past the red and black flags
emblazoned with the initials CNT in bold white letters to your right, you
will find a door that opens into a large hall. If you were to peer in through
that particular door, depending on the time and day, you would be liable
to encounter just about anything: from hundreds of kids going crazy at
a punk rock or rap show, to people of all ages having lively debates about
every topic under the sun, to political activists engaging in self-defense
and combat sport classes, as well as hours-long organizational meetings

of union branches and radical collectives. There are several more such fascinating doors, one even leading into a room filled with nothing but dozens of banners and hundreds of red and black flags. But none of these is the door that concerns us right now.

The door we are looking for is hidden, again fittingly for a magic portal, at the very end of this alleyway, giving the precise directions to reach it also an almost storybook quality: *Head down a winding side street, into the narrow cobblestone alleyway, inside of which, at the end and to the left, on a signless door that leads into a windowless room, you will find what you are looking for.* And although I did find it, I didn't really know that it existed until I stumbled upon it, much less was I actively looking for it.

★

It's late afternoon on a weekday, and, like a perfectly normal teenager, following school and football practice I head over here for some meeting or another. It's one of my first times at the 33 Rue des Vignoles, if not the first, so chances are I was there for a meeting of the autonomous and antiauthoritarian CAE, short for Collectif Anti-Expulsions (the Anti-Deportation Collective). Lost and not knowing which room our meeting is in, I hear voices coming from the behind the windowless door in the back. As I approach the door, I realize they are speaking in Spanish, which I'm always happy to hear. (My French is good, but I feel more comfortable in Spanish.)

I open the door with the intention of asking if the CAE meeting is here, or if they know where it is. Before I say anything, I'm put off balance by what I see inside. Two or three dusty old wooden desks, the room lined wall to wall and floor to ceiling with shelves full of books, all of which seem like they could have comfortably been published in the 1940s. Inside sit three or four bearded old men, the youngest of whom was probably comfortably into his seventies. What I want to say, in Spanish, is, "Excuse me, but do you happen to know where the CAE meeting is?" But, a little flustered and with typical teenage awkwardness, what I blurt out is the significantly less elegantly articulated, "Who are you?" They look at me with what I assume is amused silence, probably also a little surprised at being addressed in Spanish by a child inside their own offices and in a tone that implies that it is they rather than I who are intruding, while I rephrase my question.

Another one of the old men replies, always in Spanish, and by the time he finishes his sentence I have lost all interest in my meeting: "The meeting you are looking for is probably next door, in the large hall. We are the CNT in exile and the International Antifascist Solidarity"—known as SIA, the initials for Solidaridad Internacional Antifascista—"and this is our office."

From the iconic address and the mention of the initials CNT earlier, many will have already deciphered where I was: the Parisian headquarters of the Confédération Nationale du Travail, the French anarcho-syndicalist union.[2] And you might be aware, as I was, that the French CNT was formed in 1946, out of a union of exiled Spanish CNT members, anarchist CGT (Confédération Générale du Travail) members disgruntled with the Stalinist Communist Party's domination of France's then and still largest labor union, and some former participants in the French antifascist resistance. What I was blissfully unaware of, although it now seems like it might have been a little obvious, was that the French CNT headquarters at 33 Rue des Vignoles also contained the offices of the incredibly still-existing Spanish CNT in exile, as well as that of the SIA. The history of the Spanish CNT, and of the epic struggle against international fascism and for social revolution waged by its more than one million adherents in the course of the Spanish Civil War and revolution of the 1930s, is well known to this date, but that of the SIA significantly less so, as it pertains primarily to the much lesser known story of what became of those hundreds of thousands of men, women, and children who were displaced in 1939 in what came to be known as La Retirada (The Retreat), fleeing Spain after the dream of a stateless and classless libertarian society was militarily defeated by the combined forces of Stalinism, international fascism, and the inaction of the Western capitalist states.

Founded jointly by the CNT, FAI (Iberian Anarchist Federation), and FIJL (Iberian Federation of Libertarian Youth) in May 1937 during the immediate aftermath of the tragic May Days confrontations in Barcelona pitting anarchists and the Trotskyist POUM (Workers' Party of Marxist Unification) against Stalinists, the SIA was conceived to be simultaneously both a humanitarian organization and a political organization advocating for anarchist ideas. The original objectives were to provide material aid and support behind the front lines of war while addressing the urgent need to improve anarchist networks of international solidarity,

DIMANCHE 6 OCTOBRE 1946

SOLIDARITÉ INTERNATIONALE ANTI-FASCISTE

 **S. I. A.**

Section Départementale de la Loire - Saint-Étienne

GRAND MEETING

~~~ **OU ?** ~~~

En St-Etienne le DIMANCHE 6 OCTOBRE à 9 h. 30 du matin à la grande Salle des Fêtes de la Bourse du Travail on aura le plaisir d'entendre pour la première fois à St-Etienne la voix de S. I. A.

En cet acte prendront la parole sous la présidence de

BERNARDO PAU

Secrétaire du Comité Régional de Lyon de S. I. A.

Alexandre MIRANDE

Membre du Comité National de S. I. A.

SANS SICART

Membre du M. L. E. et C. N. T. en France

Ils vous feront connaître pourquoi a été créée la "' Solidarité Internationale Antifasciste" à travers les frontières.

Nota - Les mêmes orateurs prendront la parole le SAMEDI 5 OCTOBRE à 20 heures, salle des Concerts à RIVE-DE-GIER.

Imprimerie TERRIER-CONQUIS - St-Etienne

A 1946 poster announcing a public meeting of the SIA in Saint-Étienne, a suburb of Paris.

thus improving the supply of both medical supplies and weapons for the anarchist war effort, as other similar organizations such as the Socorro Rojo (Red Aid) were dominated by the Stalinist Communist Parties of their respective countries and thus funneled aid almost exclusively to the Stalinist-controlled People's Army.

An article in the 1978 edition of the SIA's annual calendar reads: "The culminating moment of the work of the S.I.A. in France was as the final defeat in the war in Spain was unfolding. During those tragic days, the delegates of the SIA Committee, together with comrades from the Spanish Committees for Antifascist Action, faced an avalanche of refugees who were being channeled into the concentration camps. . . . [SIA] comrades traveled tirelessly all the roads which became a veritable via crucis for those thousands of men, women, children and elderly, wounded and invalids, who entered France fleeing the Francoist bullet," with many even suffering legal repercussions in France for their solidarity.[3]

While organizing aid and solidarity to the thousands upon thousands who crossed the border into France in the course of La Retirada to escape the advance of fascism, meaning certain death for many of them, might have represented the peak of the SIA's activity and its most epic moment, the organization continued its work for decades to come, rendering aid and support to those joining the guerrilla and underground struggle against Francoism, and today it still engages in support of antifascist and immigrant struggles in France. It remains "independent of all political or religious entities" and engages wherever "there are new aggressions against humanity and in the face of the unacceptable treatment afforded to the most vulnerable.... SIA chooses to take action against injustice and resignation. True to the spirit of its original struggle for the total respect of the individual, SIA focuses on aid to victims of oppressions, be they state, religious, or partisan based."[4]

I was unaware of the existence, much less history, of the SIA when I opened the door and stumbled into their offices that afternoon. But I enthusiastically inquired, and the old men in that room (and they were, I have to sadly admit, almost always all men) were happy to oblige. I don't know if a young Spanish-speaking anarchist reminded them—some of the "younger" ones who only knew Spain and the revolution through the stories of the parents whom they had accompanied into exile, at least — of their youth and how they themselves were originally drawn to anarchism through the stories of their parents and the community of exiles in which they grew up. Or if I was a stand-in for the grandchildren most of them probably already had but who, speaking out of statistical probability, were unlikely to have a keen and burning interest in the history of struggle and sacrifice made by their grandparents for the dream of a free society. Or if it was quite simply in their nature, and they would have received anyone with the same openness and enthusiasm.

But the fact is, from that moment on, if there was a day I knew I was headed to "the 33," as we called it, for a meeting or event, I made it a habit to arrive several hours early and enjoy a *grec frites* while listening to the memories, lessons, and experiences of those who had lived in the flesh the anarchist attempt to storm the heavens. Their stories were at times powerful, moving, and inspiring, and at others heartbreaking and tragic. Yet, despite all that these men had been through, I never noticed even the slightest hint of bitterness or regret in them. (To be fair, obviously, if you were bitter or regretful about your or your parents' engagement in anarchist struggle some six decades earlier, you were pretty unlikely to be spending your weekday afternoons sitting in the offices of the CNT in exile.)

"Education. Agitation. Organization. Weapons."

I was a child then, barely a teenager, so I didn't fight. To be honest, I didn't even really understand everything that was happening. So maybe my memories are too innocent. It's possible that exile and the stories of my parents of a distant and lost world have colored my recollections to imagine a harmonious utopia that is far from reality. After all, though we didn't see violence in Barcelona until the May Days really, in the end it was still a society at war. But the violence still seemed to us like a distant, and glorious, thing. I didn't see the dead and wounded returning from the front, I didn't really understand that some of those leaving to the front would never again return to their homes and families. All I saw were the massive farewell parades, the enthusiastic militia fighters, the cheering crowds, and the cars and makeshift tanks flying red and black flags, emblazoned with the initials CNT-FAI. And those initials, especially CNT, were suddenly everywhere!

I remember movie theaters, grand halls traditionally reserved for the privileged and well-off of the city, suddenly draped in CNT banners and adorned with red and black flags. They were showing newsreels and movies depicting not only the war effort but the revolution, and proudly announcing that the workers had collectivized the operation, that it now belonged to all of society, and that they had federated with other similar operations that were now being operated by the revolutionary workers' unions. These kinds of announcements were everywhere around the city, and the phenomenon was not just in the smaller industries. The hallmarks of a modern, large, urban city, such as the taxis, the tram system, and even the eventually infamous telephone central, had all been collectivized and were in the hands of the workers (almost always CNT workers), the owners either having been forced out or, more often than not, having fled.

Those who came into the city from the countryside gave excited talks in halls and on the streets. Again, I recall the excitement on people's faces, the flags flying, the enthusiasm, and I remember hearing that "el comunismo libertario," libertarian communism, had been implemented in the countryside, and that the landowners, soldiers, and priests had fled. I distinctly recall somebody excitedly exclaiming that in some places, currency had been abolished and the people of the town were free to take what they needed from the storage deposits, which to my childish mind seemed incredible!

Again, I'm merging my own childhood memories, which are mainly of the sentiments and moods I felt in the city and in the people around me, with what I would later come to understand through reading as well as through talking with the older people who actively participated. I am now aware, obviously, that an incredible and historic social and economic process was taking place. Economically, a seizing of the means of production by society, not by the state, and its immediate reorganization to supply the needs of society rather than the profits of capitalists. The real-world implementation of libertarian communism, not just in smaller rural communities, but in a large, urban, modern city of millions like Barcelona. Like I said, all of that I came to really understand later, but what I immediately noticed, clear and obvious even to the eyes of a child, was the cultural revolution.

What I saw was the tip of the iceberg: Workers walking with pride, their heads held high. Entire swaths of society, used to constant oppression and exploitation, now walking the city with the broad smiles of free people on their faces. I suddenly heard much less of the formal usted *and much more of the comradely* compañero *on the street. Restaurants were suddenly for everyone, and we were welcomed on the trams by people wearing red and black bandannas announcing with a smile that we didn't have to pay. I saw women not only participating in public life but proudly holding weapons and headed toward the front lines.*

What I also didn't see, and only came to understand quite a few years later, was that this was the fruit of the momentous labor of decades carried out by the anarchist movement. The eyes of a young child only saw the tip of the iceberg, but below the water line was an enormous mountain of effort and sacrifice that had made that moment possible. Decades upon decades of libertarian propaganda, of education, of organization, of implanting the anarchist idea of economic and individual freedom from both oppression and exploitation, a constant agitation about the importance of women's rights and freedoms, of personal responsibility and discipline against vices used to keep us asleep and enslaved. And, of course, a vibrant and militant defense of anarchism of our organizations, and of the people. Educación, agitación, organización, y armas. *[Education. Agitation. Organization. Weapons.]*

Obviously I'm paraphrasing these recollections, but those four words, in that specific order, I remember distinctly. Aside from that, though, these conversations took place almost a quarter century ago, and obviously these people, actual guardians and historians of a lived utopia forced into exile, are no longer among us. Despite having spent an inordinate amount of hours with them, I remember no names and feel uncomfortable putting words into the mouths of those who can no longer express for themselves whether they feel they are being accurately represented or not, although I'm confident that I am representing the spirit of their ideas and our interactions accurately. What is also likely, though, and by likely I mean absolutely certain, is that I too am merging memories and condensing different talks with different people into one. Particularly since the setting was always the same: the same room and more or less the same time of day, the old men sitting in the windowless room, as far as I could tell eternally writing letters or arguing about obscure matters among themselves, while a rotating cast of one or two of them spoke with me.

The Camps, La Nueve, Patton's Anarchists, and the Liberation of Paris

Of all the fascinating but much less well known stories that those men in that room shared with me over the course of several years, the one I remember most distinctly was one of what came after the defeat in Spain. Of the camps, of the resistance against fascism in France, and of its eventual liberation from Nazi occupation. Of anarchists fighting under the command of General Patton and being among the first in the liberation of Paris. We were talking about the time after La Retirada, of women and children literally being housed in French prisons while fighting-age men were separated from them and taken to internment camps. "So, did they keep you in the camps until after France was liberated from the Nazis?" was my half question, half assertion. I asked it absentmindedly, assuming "yes" to be the obvious and only possible answer.

Great was my surprise when my question was met with a playful face of feigned outrage and the very Spanish exclamation of "¡Pero que dices chico!?" (roughly "What are you talking about, child?!").

According to an article in Spain's El País newspaper (the country's most read), "When the Germans occupied France, many of the prisoners fell into German hands and were transferred to the Mauthausen-Gusen concentration camp, and it's true that many died there." The exact numbers are actually that about 15,000 were transferred to German concentration camps, 5,122 of whom would eventually perish at Mauthausen.[5] Many others who survived were actually conscripted by the Germans to provide forced labor not at the camps but across Europe wherever the German war effort required it. Such was the case of the father of Manuel Rodriguez. Rodriguez, born in 1936 and having fled from Spain to France together with his parents toward the war's end, recalls that some of his first childhood memories are of "being housed in a French prison, locked in a cell at night, and not seeing my father for years."[6]

Fortunately, almost miraculously even, in the process of writing this text, I ran into a radio interview with him, from which the quote above comes. Manuel Rodriguez is eighty years old at the time of the interview, but he sounds young. There's youth in his voice and youth in his spirit. It's free of the cynicism and bitterness so common of age. Clearly a free spirit, a rebel heart, and an unflinching belief in utopia— precisely because of and despite having seen and experienced some of the absolute worst of humanity—apparently helps keeps you young at heart. In the interview, he describes not seeing his father from 1939 until 1944, when thanks to the help of SIA his father was able to locate him and his mother. Promptly thereafter his father was able to escape from the Germans, return to France and to his family, and join the resist-ance—only to be promptly arrested again after being betrayed by a local police officer. "He is loaded onto a wagon … headed to Germany, one of those wagons originally intended for beasts not humans, but manages to escape. He returns to his town and once again contacts the resist-ance and says, 'Listen, I've been in the camps, I've been on the German war effort, I escaped so as to not aid the Germans, I've been betrayed and arrested, and I don't want this to happen again.' The resistance commander and another person went to the local police station and announced, 'The Spaniard is back, but if anything happens to him there will be problems,' and he was never touched again."[7]

Others who had also escaped joined the antifascist resistance in the guerrilla fight against the Vichy government. But some of those who fled to North Africa, many thousands as well, would eventually become La Nueve, the 9th company in General Leclerc's 2nd Armored Division, and they were the first to enter Paris in 1944. I distinctly remember being told, "It's a shame Manuel isn't here to tell you about it himself."

The Manuel in question is Manuel Pinto Queiroz-Ruiz, more commonly known as Manuel Lozano. Manuel Lozano passed away in 2000, so my time in Paris coincided with the last years of his life. I don't know, or can't recall, if I didn't meet him because our paths didn't cross, or if he was physically present less often at the CNT due to his age, or if I did indeed meet him and just don't remember. But I do remember learning his story, and that of La Nueve, in the third person, so not from Manuel himself.

Manuel Lozano, born in 1916, was not just the last surviving member of La Nueve, he was also a lifelong anarchist militant and organizer with the CNT in exile. In Evelyn Mesquida's book *La Nueve: Los españoles que liberaron París* (La Nueve: The Spaniards who liberated Paris), he recalls the day when, still a young anarchist, he watched the military rebels who had risen up against the Republican government occupy his hometown of Jerez. "My father," who was also an anarchist, "told me I had to flee immediately and helped me to escape. He didn't want to come with me, and was executed shortly after." Manuel recalls that, according to an uncle of his, his father's last words were, "You might execute me, but you'll never get my son."[8]

"I was still very young, but in those times, living through so much tragedy, we grew up immediately."[9] After years of war and fighting on numerous fronts, in March 1939 the twenty-two-year-old Manuel, fleeing from the fascist advance, boarded the fishing boat *La Joven Maria*, headed for the North African port of Oran, at that time still a French territory. He was arrested the day after his arrival and placed in what he describes as "a camp, surrounded by barbed wire and guarded at all times.... The conditions were terrible. On the second day of my detention, I asked to speak to the camp director. He was of Arabic origin, small, well dressed, but very cynical. I told him I wanted some soap and a towel to wash myself. And the guy, hands in his pockets, starts turning around while laughing and saying, 'You think this is a hotel? This is a concentration camp!'"[10]

In 1942, "when the allies landed in Africa, we were all freed," says Manuel.[11] He immediately enlisted in the Corps Francs d'Afrique (African Volunteer Corps) to continue the fight against fascism on the African front. There, he was pitted against the troops of the feared German general and military theorist Erwin Rommel, also known as "the Desert Fox." "His troops were considered elite. We were able to defeat them, and I've always wondered how I managed to survive that hell, or how I survived what came after."[12]

Immediately following the victory on the North African front, he and thousands of other Spanish exiles and refugees enlisted to continue the fight against fascism, as part of what came to be the 2nd Armored Division of the Free French Forces. Since Spaniards were particularly numerous in its 9th Company, it came to be known as La Nueve, "the Ninth": "The majority were socialists, communists, anarchists or unaffiliated men hostile to Franco, while others were deserters of concentration camps for Spanish refugees in Algeria and Morocco. While still fully integrated soldiers in the French Army, they were permitted to wear the tricolor Republican flag on their uniforms. As it was composed almost entirely of Spanish soldiers, Spanish was used as the common language within the company and the officers also came from the Spanish ranks."[13]

In 1943, while still in Africa, the company received a significant amount of armament and armored vehicles from the US Army, christening their vehicles with names such as *Guernica*, *Madrid*, *Teruel*, and *Resistance*. One with the name *Les Pinguins* was so named only after the French superior officers rejected the original proposal of *Buenaventura Durruti*.[14]

On the night of July 31, 1944, La Nueve landed on Utah Beach in Normandy, where they were integrated into the Third United States Army, under the command of none other than General George S. Patton. For the next three weeks, La Nueve would engage in fierce clashes with German troops around France, including fending off attacks by the Waffen-SS, Adolf Hitler, and Das Reich divisions of the Nazi army. As Mesquida writes in *La Nueve*: "The company's anarchists revealed their courageous character during this battle, as one mortar unit carried out a coup de main attack [an attack relying on the elements of speed and surprise to swiftly defeat the opponent] 3 km behind German lines on 14 August, taking 130 German prisoners, capturing 13 vehicles, and liberating 8 Americans."[15]

It is a landmark moment that for decades was all but erased from history for its political inconvenience. Fascist Spain of course had no use for it, and it was damaging to the nationalist French discourse claiming that the liberation of France was exclusively achieved by the French themselves. But the reality is that not only were thousands of internationalists, many of them from Germany and North Africa, as well as approximately fifteen thousand Spaniards, integral to the anti-Nazi and anti-collaborationist effort, they were indeed the very first to enter the city of Paris. Just over three weeks after landing on mainland Europe, on the night of August 24, and following the lead of the resistance-led uprising against the German occupation of Paris, which had begun just four days earlier, the anarchists and Spanish republicans of La Nueve were the first troops to enter the city, proceeding almost immediately to occupy German high command. On the following day, as triumphant Allied troops poured into the city, the Spanish fighters of La Nueve participated in the victory parade under tricolor Spanish republican banners (red and black ones were apparently not quite

A comrade from La Nueve makes the anarchist salute during the liberation of Paris.

so welcome), four of their half-tracks even being assigned to escort General Charles De Gaulle.

"Who Knows If We Could Have Been Able to Change the Course of History?"

The war did not end in Paris for La Nueve, as they participated in battles across France pushing the Nazi forces back, even eventually penetrating into Germany and participating in the Allied capture of the "Eagle's Nest" on May 5, 1945. By this point, thirty-five La Nueve fighters lay dead, with another ninety-seven wounded. With many others having been transferred to other units in the French Army, very likely as a precautionary measure against preserving an organized and battle-tested group of foreign radicals now that the Nazi threat was no longer imminent, only sixteen Spaniards remained active in the company.

Naive as it may seem today, many if not most of those who joined the fight against the Nazis sincerely and deeply believed that, as a matter of course, the attention of the Allied forces would turn to the liberation of fascist Spain once the Nazis were defeated. While of course eager to defeat fascism on the international scene, the intentions of the Spanish antifascists could not have been more explicit, as Manuel Lozano himself states: "We entered into the Leclerc Division thinking that after France, we would continue on to liberate Spain."[16] While the memory and sacrifice of the antifascists of La Nueve would be minimized and almost erased from history in the decades to come, the first betrayal and disillusion would come almost immediately after the liberation of France. In 1985, Manuel says, "After Strasbourg, we understood that we would not be sent to liberate Spain. In my company, La Nueve, everybody was prepared to desert with all the armament. Campos, the head of our section, contacted the guerrilla fighters of the Unión Nacional who were fighting in the Pyrenees. But the Unión Nacional was controlled by the communists, and we had to abort that idea."[17]

Manuel is asked what would have happened if they had indeed been able to continue to Spain, join forces with other guerrilla fighters, and relaunch an offensive against Franco: "We would have taken the entire division, and not just the division but also all the other battalions in which there were Spaniards. We had studied everything. With the trucks loaded with armament and materials, with gasoline, we would have made it all the way to Barcelona. In that case, who knows if we could have been able to change the course of history?"[18]

Manuel and La Nueve indeed didn't continue into Spain, a place in which Manuel would never again set foot. But in 1970, they entered the space at 33 Rue des Vignoles, where a plaque at the entrance now reads:

> On this place
> the Spanish exiles
> of the Confederación Nacional del Trabajo,
> veterans of Mauthausen, of the resistance
> of the liberation of Paris
> combatants of liberty and of social justice
> will never cease in their labors for a different future.

There, for decade after decade, they kept not only the memory but also the dream of a classless and stateless utopia alive, albeit in exile. And it was there where almost thirty years later I stumbled onto them.

The Home of Utopia in Exile

Had it been just a historical society, as groups of exiled Spanish anarchists in some other places sometimes were, the impact on me might

CNT demonstration in Paris, sometime in 1998.

not have been the same. Sure, I had a keen and urgent sense of history, but more so I was concerned with action. But this wasn't just old men in a dark and dusty room reminiscing about glorious times gone by.

Some of those old men, and, in the cases of the older ones, their children, or the children they had inspired through their example, sacrifice, and perseverance, were the anarchist youths who raised the black flags during the uprising of May '68. The generation that followed them, in turn, brought the spirit of rebellion and direct action to the wave of general strikes that paralyzed France and terrified the bosses in 1995—and with it a growth and resurgence of the French CNT, which quickly ballooned to over five thousand adherents. And we, those who were a bit younger still, stood directly in that tradition—of an unbroken chain of anarchist education, agitation, and struggle spanning almost a century. As Manuel Rodriguez put it, "If this exists today, it's because the comrades have existed, because of their struggle, sacrifice, and labor."[19]

Inspiring as the world of the CNT in exile in that room was, it was still only one aspect of the rich and multigenerational anarchist ecosystem that existed in the CNT headquarters at that time.

The different generations and strands of anarchism weren't just connected metaphorically, they literally coexisted in this one space, and you could experience them all just by jumping from room to room at different times and days. At one moment in one room, it could be a meeting of the CNT-Nettoyage (cleaning workers' union), formed in 1988 and representing "hundreds of workers coming from the most precarious sectors of the proletariat, mainly immigrants, often *sans-papiers* [undocumented "illegals"]"[20]—while in the next room the very classically anarchist and very much autonome-dominated Collectif Anti-Expulsions could be found plotting the next occupation or mass action directed against the state machinery of deportation or the companies and corporations who collaborated with the state to make detention and deportation of human beings possible. From the construction workers' union, to university students, to a teachers' union, and even the sadly short-lived grouping of anarcho-syndicalist high school students we formed, the place was a living lesson in the practical application of multigenerational, diverse (at least, more diverse than elsewhere), and multifaceted anarchism.

A las Barricadas

Negras tormentas agitan los aires	*Black storms shake the air*
nubes oscuras nos impiden ver.	*Dark clouds blind us*
Aunque nos espere el dolor y la muerte	*Although pain and death [may] await us*
contra el enemigo nos llama el deber.	*Duty calls us against the enemy*
El bien más preciado es la libertad	*The most precious good is freedom*
hay que defenderla con fe y valor.	*It must be defended with faith and courage*
Alza la bandera revolucionaria	*Raise the revolutionary flag*
que del triunfo sin cesar nos lleva en pos.	*Which carries us ceaselessly toward triumph*
Alza la bandera revolucionaria	*Raise the revolutionary flag*
que del triunfo sin cesar nos lleva en pos.	*Which carries us ceaselessly toward triumph*

Negras tormentas agitan los aires	*Black storms shake the air*
nubes oscuras nos impiden ver.	*Dark clouds blind us*
Aunque nos espere el dolor y la	*Although pain and death [may]*
muerte	*await us*
contra el enemigo nos llama el	*Duty calls us against the enemy*
deber.	
	The most precious good is freedom
El bien más preciado es la libertad	*It must be defended with faith and*
hay que defenderla con fe y valor.	*courage*
	Raise the revolutionary flag
Alza la bandera revolucionaria	*Which carries us ceaselessly*
que del triunfo sin cesar nos lleva	*toward triumph*
en pos.	*Raise the revolutionary flag*
Alza la bandera revolucionaria	*Which carries us ceaselessly*
que del triunfo sin cesar nos lleva	*toward triumph*
en pos.	
	Get up, working people, to the
En pie el pueblo obrero, a la	*battle*
batalla	*[We] have to topple the reaction*
hay que derrocar a la reacción.	
	To the barricades! To the
¡A las barricadas! ¡A las	*barricades!*
barricadas!	*For the triumph of the*
por el triunfo de la Confederación.	*Confederation*
¡A las barricadas! ¡A las	*To the barricades! To the*
barricadas!	*barricades!*
por el triunfo de la Confederación.	*For the triumph of the*
	Confederation

These are the lyrics to the famous Spanish Revolution–era CNT and anarchist battle hymn "A las Barricadas." But I'm not reading them from a book or listening to them in some black-and-white documentary. Nor is it the old men in the windowless room singing it nostalgically. None of that. I'm in the large hall at 33 Rue des Vignoles on a random Saturday night in 1997. I've spent the day doing who knows what at the 33, and to be honest very possibly nothing productive. By then I had been given my own set of keys to the place, and there is a greater than zero chance that I was just there because having my own keys to the place made me feel very happy and important, and so I sometimes spent my day alternating between chatting with the old men from the CNT in exile and staring stupidly but happily at the room with all the red and black flags. Either way, I'm already here, and apparently at night there is a concert in the large hall with some punk or Oi! band that I've never heard of called Brigada Flores Magon—so obviously I've stayed for that.

And even though I didn't really need any more of a poetic hook to illustrate to me the connection between the CNT, its decades of anarchist struggle, and the proud tradition we were inheriting and tasked with continuing, I got one that night anyway. The first surprise of the night is that what I have been expecting will be a scraggly-looking group of punk kids—you know, as punk bands tend to be—is actually five guys with short, cropped hair and clean-cut looks.[21] They launch into a ska-laced tribute to the Zapatista uprising in Chiapas that isn't bad, followed by a song against militarism that is a little too hardcore for my taste, when suddenly I hear the distinctive first chords of "A las Barricadas," except that for the first time in my life, they aren't contained in an old recording but are blaring from a contemporary electric guitar and in a room full of energetic young people singing enthusiastically along. It is a painfully obvious metaphor for the bridge connecting our past and present.

After their set, I head over to buy a drink and a sandwich at the bar, where I notice that, in a very much anarchist and punk rock vein, the rock star who was just playing guitar onstage, to the extent that yelling from a three-foot-high stage at maybe one hundred kids can be considered rock star status, is now busily at work preparing sandwiches. I buy a ham and cheese sandwich as an excuse to start a chat with him and ask, "Do you speak Spanish?" since his singing on the chorus to "A las Barricadas" seemed suspiciously accent free. We start chatting, about life, anarchism, subculture, football, how we got here ... and as it turns out Victor is originally from Mexico and gravitated toward the CNT when he was eighteen, through his involvement in its Comité Chiapas (Chiapas Committee) and then its antifascist work, until eventually he landed in its university student wing. "When I started in 1994, the university students, especially at Nanterre, were really the motor of the CNT." For the record, the Nanterre university he is talking about is none other than the historic hotbed of university radicalism that was

A May Day luncheon at the 33 Rue des Vignoles, 1998.

the catalyst for the uprising of May '68. "Mathieu and I, Mathieu is the singer of the band by the way, lived really far out in the banlieue, so we didn't really make it out to Vignoles that often. But when we did, I had a little bit the same impression as you. It's a place that stands almost outside of the passage of time, and where you can find all kinds of people. First, there's these almost mythical characters, these old men at the end of the hallway, exiles of the revolution and civil war. And politics aside, there's a very strong emotional and affective side to it. These are actual humans who were ready to give their lives for what we believe in. It was fascinating for me, because in my case I had reached anarchism, obviously intellectually through books and pamphlets, but physically basically until I arrived at the CNT only through punk rock subculture. But here suddenly there's this place with all kinds of people—besides the CNT in exile there was CNT Construction, CNT Postal Workers, CNT Education with professors, and so on. Generally just people of all stripes. On a lot of them you could still find hints of their subcultural youth, but it no longer defined them. It didn't define their anarchist politics, and their aging out of or losing interest in youth subcultures didn't mean abandoning their anarchist politics." As a bearded old man, who clearly has maybe had a glass of wine or two too many, walks by cheerily humming "A las Barricadas," Victor laughs and points out, "That doesn't mean there isn't a ton of charismatic characters here, though, and it's definitely a plus."

He goes on to describe how "Mathieu and I were much younger than the rest, so we were basically like the mascots. But we always felt welcomed, respected, and included." While he says it, I can't help thinking that if they were the "young mascots" at age eighteen, I at several years younger still might end up in CNT childcare. But my self-conscious musings about my age are interrupted when he mentions something or other about the first real struggles they experienced being in and around the general strike of 1995, an event I am obsessed with for obvious reasons—like, for example, the working class barely flexing its collective muscle and grinding capitalist society to a halt in defense of its interests—but also missed personally experiencing by just over a year, as I was still living in Athens at that time.

"We had to sleep at comrades' apartments in the city if we wanted to participate in the actions, since the effectiveness of the strike made it impossible for us to travel back and forth to our suburbs." The effectiveness of the strike was indeed unquestionable, as it lasted two months and succeeded in forcing the right-wing government to call off its reform attempts, which primarily consisted of the cutting of thousands of jobs from the train and metro branches while raising the minimum retirement age. Victor describes "the incredible power and energy on the streets" and then goes into the interplay between the presence of the CNT as a public and visible force, an actual trade union, and the organizing work of its members, but how they also "wore different hats," at times taking off the CNT sticker to engage in more militant actions. "This dichotomy some present, between day-to-day organizing and more spectacular forms of confrontation, is false. We're the same people, doing the day-to-day organizing, and simply wearing a different hat when it comes time to occupy a university, fight the fascists, carry out an expropriation, or simply march as an anarchist bloc in the streets."

Inspiring as this all is, we quickly veer into the inevitable "But what happened?" The strike succeeded in pushing back the right-wing government, mobilized millions of people, and enjoyed widespread popular support in spite of the "inconveniences" it generated for many. But obviously, le grand soir has not come and capitalism and the state are nowhere near being abolished. Still working his shift preparing sandwiches, Victor explains, "Yeah, a lot of us got a very harsh but important lesson there. Everything was in place, it was a general strike, the stuff of our dreams, but sometimes we would arrive at a demonstration, and if we tried to talk to random people, usually unionized workers themselves, often decades older than us, about anarchism and revolution, we were often greeted with smirks, if not outright dismissal. And in the middle of this wave of resistance, we couldn't help feeling small and far from our goals when suddenly, for example, the CGT union bloc would arrive, with its security service ten times larger than ours, often composed primarily of actual cops, and brush us aside like flies. Clearly, our influence was minimal, and all the stones in the world wouldn't change that. So how do we create revolutionary consciousness? It has to be built. Everything has to be built. Those guerrillas in the fields back in South America or in Mexico who we often idealize, they didn't fall from the sky. The collectivizations in Spain, that wasn't just ten crazies in an affinity group, there's a whole context and organizing behind that."[22]

An old man standing in line chimes in, in Spanish: "*Asi es chavales*," which translates roughly to "That's the way, kids," before adding, "It's not easy being an anarchist." It was another one of the old men from the magic door to history in the room next to us, who for some reason has stuck around for the punk rock show.

Twenty years later, when talking about those times, Victor would recall precisely these situations, "standing there making sandwiches when suddenly these heroes from a bygone era, who we often rightly or wrongly—through probably rightly—placed on a pedestal would suddenly show up to chat with us. They were old men and we were almost children, but they interacted with us as equals and still projected so much enthusiasm despite all the accumulated defeats. Even the simple act of being at a DIY event, in the space of a self-managed and revolutionary union, standing there making sandwiches and chatting, I like to think we were putting our small grain of sand together toward *le grand soir*."[23]

Otros Vendran (Others Will Come)

It was a veritable multiverse of anarchism, with different generations, styles, forms of action, and political concepts coexisting. Of course not without tensions and controversies, since a healthy movement is like a family, and no family is healthy without its fair share of arguments.

Brigada Flores Magon members and parts of the "Brigada Red Army" crew at a CNT demonstration, May 1, 1998.

We bickered about the loud parties and concerts and what their effect on our relationship with the neighbors might be. We argued about our image on the streets, as sometimes we were criticized for the macho image we might be projecting, as us young ones generally made up the CNT security service at demonstrations, and a small horde of young men sporting cropped haircuts, boots, and bomber jackets maybe wasn't the most welcoming and diverse public-facing image of what was supposed to be a multigenerational and antipatriarchal workers' movement. Other times, half jokingly and half seriously, the old men of the CNT in exile would point disapprovingly at the hammer and sickle or Soviet imagery on our shirts, patches, or pins—which we sported not out of political conviction but rather because it was most effective at provoking and setting off our fascist or nationalist enemies—reminding us that in Spain the Stalinists "carried out a cleansing of Trotskyists and anarcho-syndicalists with the same energy as in the Soviet Union."[24] Other times our disagreements were more urgent and substantial, such as what struggles of the day to get involved with and in what capacity, as well as what forms of action and organization were compatible with the essence of anarchist ideas and objectives—a question that, as far as I understand, indeed ended up being primarily responsible for the latest split in the CNT in 2012.

But in the end, at least back then and despite whatever momentary bickering and disagreements we might have had, we agreed on the essence of the matter: The presence of all of us, of all these facets of our movement and our ideas, made us a broader space, a more open and welcoming movement, a stronger force on the streets, and generally contributed to the construction of an anarchist pole of dual power.

The magical door at the end of the hallway is now shut. They pushed against the hands of time for as hard and as long as they could, keeping the door open so that others could follow them through it. But apparently, even in a place "outside of time," time stops for no one. They have now left us, and even most of their children have left us. They gave decades of their lives, all of their lives, so that the ideals of a free society, of libertarian socialism, might not die in that room. The door may have shut, but I and many others who had the luck and privilege of peering inside, and who in a way were brought together by the influence of that generation, now have the responsibility of taking as much as we can from there. Of ensuring we do everything and more in our power to share what we learned from them and put it into practice, with the understanding, as I was once told in that room, that "if not us, then you. If not you, then others will come," and one day utopia will no longer be banished into exile.

3

"EUROPE, JEUNESSE, RÉVOLUTION"

Paris, May 1998

On the Run: Paris, Rue des Chartreux, May 9, 1998, Sometime Around Sunset

"Europe, jeunesse, révolution!" The chant echoed like thunder, bouncing off the walls of the grand buildings of Paris's elegant 6th arrondissement neighborhood. I stood just across the street, not twenty meters away, eating an ice cream while trying to look as casual as possible. "Europe! Jeunesse! Révolution!" Even louder now, from hundreds of mostly young mouths in a sea of Celtic crosses, bomber jackets, and hunting jackets. I, alone, looked away. I was terrified. "EUROPE! JEUNESSE! RÉVOLUTION!" Louder than ever. "Europe, youth, revolution," a classic of the French radical right. I decided it was unwise to be looking away. Hundreds of militant fascists on the streets of Paris was not exactly a normal occurrence; an innocent bystander would probably be looking at them.

So I looked in their direction again. Still protected by my cunning disguise, the ice cream. I had purchased it in the hopes that it would make me look innocent and uninvolved. As I looked over, I unintentionally locked eyes with one of their security service members. Black leather jacket, long hair, scraggly college-intellectual beard, white security armband, walkie-talkie in one hand and Palestinian kaffiyeh in the style of the modern fascists of the day around his neck. Because, you

FACING THE FASCISTS

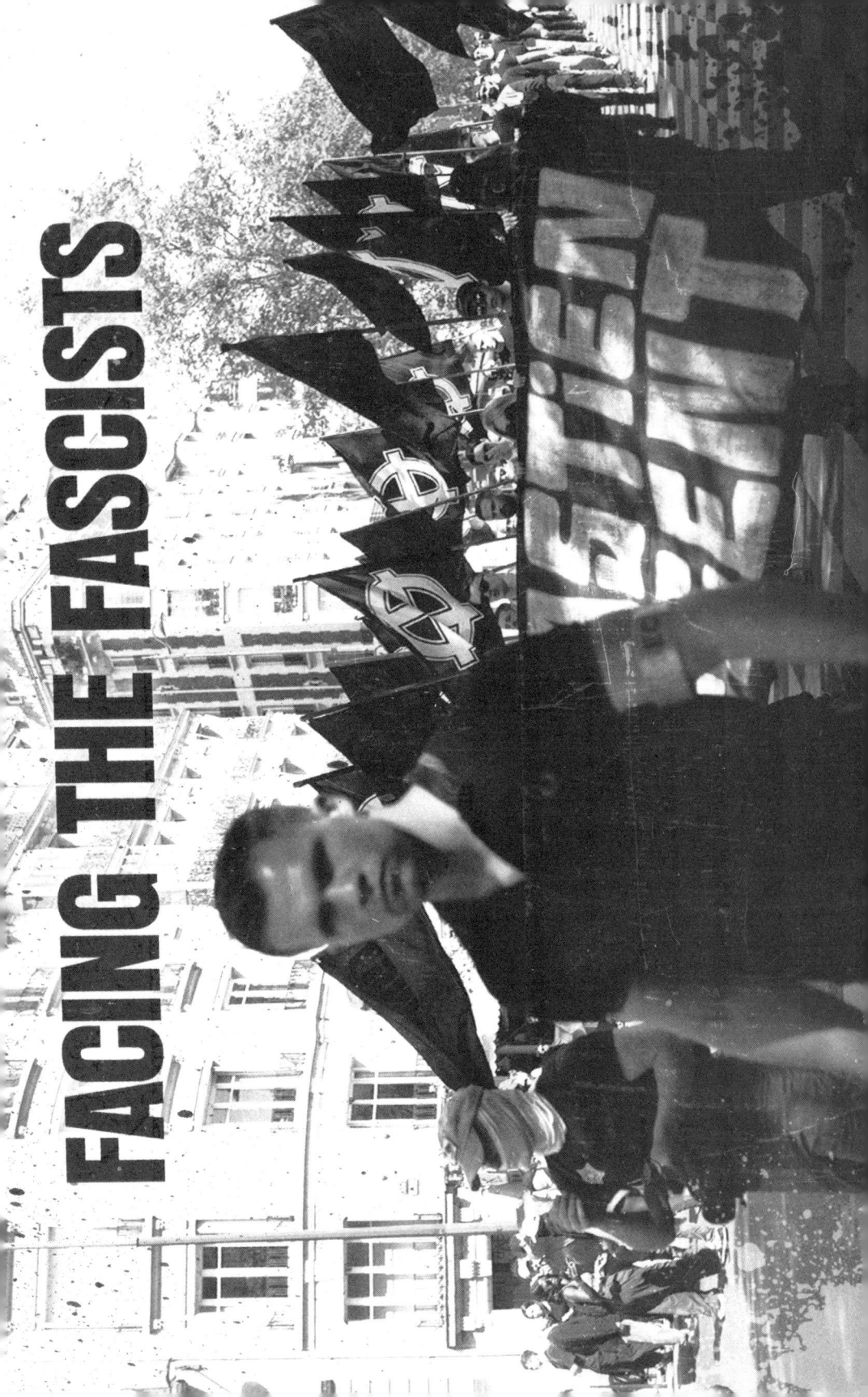

know, they have a really advanced political analysis that as far as I could understand went something like, "Anybody who kills Jews is a friend of mine." As he spoke into his walkie-talkie, I thought to myself that he looked familiar. He could have been any one of us, except he wasn't. He was exactly the opposite. At first I didn't think too much of the group of fascists, some masked, some helmeted, and all with security service armbands, that began gathering around him and across the street from me. From the flags and stickers on their helmets, it was obvious that they were all GUD members.

The GUD, short for Groupe Union Défense, is one of France's oldest, most notorious, and most violent far-right organizations. The *rats noirs*, or "black rats," as they call themselves, are a small student organization with a long tradition, founded in the aftermath of the revolt of May '68. They see themselves as the militant youth vanguard of the French far right, and their actions and imagery reflect it. Masks, helmets, black flags with Celtic crosses, and violent attacks against left-wing students on university campuses have been their calling cards for decades.

Just keep calm, keep looking at them with mild curiosity, eat your ice cream, and everything should be fine. Just as I was trying to reassure myself by thinking that maybe I was young enough looking to not regis-ter on their radar, I had a terrible realization. The bearded one with the leather jacket. He didn't look familiar because he could be any French, bearded, university-affiliated, far-left intellectual/radical/militant in his mid-twenties but instead is obviously an important member of Paris's section of the GUD, he looked familiar because I had already stood face to face with him, unmasked!

Paris, Rue Tolbiac, Sometime Earlier That Year

When we heard that the old Catholic fascists would be protesting an abortion clinic and that the young militants of the far right would be on hand to provide "security," it was impossible to hide our excitement and enthusiasm. Our excitement was on an "Asterix and Obelix find Romans in the woods" level. Finally, fascists!

From the perspective of a young radical and militant antifascist, the Paris of the mid to late 1990s was very different from the Paris of today. While today's militant Paris is synonymous to many with confrontational demonstrations, riots, mass militance, and relatively frequent confrontations with fascists, this was not so much the case back then.[1] Sure, the movements of the *sans-papiers* ("illegal" immigrants) and *chomeurs* (unemployed) provided us with a constant stream of mass direct actions and occupations, but by and large the "public" life of the anarchist militant consisted of a seemingly endless parade of largely uneventful strolls from Nation to Bastille, Bastille to République, République to Nation, or any other combination of those three points of arrival and/or departure.

Our movement was by no means weak, and by anarchist standards around the world definitely not small. The CNT-Vignoles, an anarcho-syndicalist organization of which I was a proud member, was experiencing strong growth following the 1995 general strike, with adherents numbering in the several thousands.[2] The synthesist Anarchist Federation maintained (as it still does today) an impressive structure and propaganda presence, with numerous federated collectives who managed a bookstore in the center of Paris, a legal FM radio station, and a widely distributed weekly newspaper (as in, available for purchase at any mainstream magazine shop or kiosk). All in all, the anarchist presence in movements and demonstrations was impressively large, with anarchist blocs often numbering well into the thousands. Not only that, but anarchists were often successful in obtaining concrete, if partial, victories on the terrains of conflict of the time, whether it was using direct action to accompany a strike or using mass militance to disrupt or even impede a deportation.

But by and large it was the anarchism of "established organizations," and hence its methods of organization, chosen forms of action, and how it presented itself in public were naturally a reflection of this. This is by no means a criticism of organized anarchism or classic anarchist structures. I still believe firmly in the importance of explicitly anarchist organizations, and in solid and lasting structures of our own. But I also believe, as I always have, that organization, education, workplace organizing, and propaganda need to be complemented by militance, direct action, and confrontation. Certain tactics are effective in some situations, while others are not. Some people will identify with and understand a message delivered one way, while others will identify with something different. Some things I do unmasked and with a CNT sticker on my chest, and others I do all in black and with a helmet on. If we want to raise awareness of and show the depth of support for the struggle of undocumented immigrants, we organize a massive and peaceful demonstration with tens of thousands of people. If we want to stop a deportation, we put on our masks, occupy the train tracks, and attack the cops when they come to clear it. The anarchist toolbox is varied, and it's important to make good use of all of its instruments.

But as far as the excitement that a young teenage anarchist and antifascist might be looking for, Paris then wasn't really wildly exciting. Besides the rather uneventful demonstrations, our day-to-day work consisted mainly of sitting at meetings, attending debates, or handing out flyers at neighborhood markets.

Even the fascists were hard to come by. The typical street-level young Nazi and bonehead that had been a staple of the streets of Paris in the 1980s and early '90s had been essentially wiped out by the previous generation of militant Parisian antifascists (many of them closely linked to the Red Warriors and other politicized redskin subculture gangs). The Front National, then an electoral force of an alarming approximately 15 percent, was strong mainly in other parts of the country, and anyway consisted primarily of angry old men, not militants with street presence.[3]

We had become bored and powerful enough that the militant aspect of our antifascism mainly consisted of confronting and terrifying "apolitical" skinheads who we ran into at Brigada Flores Magon concerts or bars because of their French flag patches. Absent full-blown fascists and racists to oppose, we took to opposing any form of nationalism in our youth subculture, essentially hunting for anyone fitting that description at concerts. Matéo, the lead singer of Brigada Flores Magon, summed it up pretty well: "We didn't accept running into nationalists without starting something. Either they disappeared discreetly, or they got a few punches.... If they had a patch of a fascist Oi! band, or even just a French flag, it was the end of them. If their attitude made us suspect something, we would go and ask them a few questions. We had a bit of a reputation, so clearly a lot of them suddenly discovered their antiracist convictions when confronted."[4]

So there we were, not at a concert or outside of a bar, but on the actual streets of Paris. Not at night, but in the middle of the day. And most importantly, the enemy approaching down the street was not some young idiot with a French flag, but a perfectly representative cross-section of all the elements of the rancid French ultra-right milieu. Rich monarchist snobs with the preppy forest-green hunting jacket and

Catholic fundamentalists and young fascists being pelted with eggs by antifascists.

moccasins look, ultra-conservative Catholic old ladies, university-age GUD-style militants with leather jackets and sunglasses, a few stereo-typical shaved-head and bomber jacket boneheads, and a couple of huge bouncer types who were probably Front National security. Whatever fascist clique of the time you were looking for, you could find one or two of them in this crowd of thirty or forty people.

What there wasn't, at least not in any kind of direct line between the fascists and the more or less equal number of us, was cops. Our side, made up primarily of Anarchist Federation, SCALP (Section Carrément Anti-Le Pen, or "Absolutely Anti-Le Pen Group"), and probably most significantly CNT security service activists, formed a compact line across from the fascists. Eggs began flying in their direction as they—I guess not unsurprisingly, considering the Catholic fundamentalist motivations for this particular gathering of Vichy-era nostalgics, but for us still an odd sight to behold—began to pray. In the middle of the street, some even on their actual knees. Poor fools, apparently unaware that the praying was unlikely to help them. We hated them enough that we didn't need specific incentives to attack them, but they were gathered here today to attack abortion rights and harass and intimidate women as they went in for care, which made us a little extra unforgiving. As the saying goes, "God forgives, the proletariat does not."

It was precisely then, during the customary moment of dramatic calm before the storm, as I was pondering whether being routed directly following prayer might affect the strength of their belief in a higher power, that I briefly locked eyes with who I am now pretty sure was the same GUD fascist from the beginning of our story. I may or may not have taken a moment to wink and blow a kiss in his direction, knowing how fond the fascist nuts were of homoeroticism.

On cue, we charged, and the fascists had no chance. They took a good beating, and the only worrying moment really was when I found myself facing off against one of the Front National security giants in what was clearly a very uneven matchup. Too young to know my limits yet or let a solid hundred-pound weight difference get in the way of my self-confidence, I swiftly delivered what I expected to be a crippling kick to his knee. I might as well have kicked a tree trunk, as my opponent didn't even flinch, and I concluded now was as good a time as any to back away and maybe pick on somebody my own size.

We were forced into an unexpected retreat, not by the appearance of the cops, but because one of ours inexplicably busted out the CS gas and sprayed it generously across the front line, only to have the wind push the cloud of gas directly into our faces. Aside from the unfortunate tactical error of the unnecessary deployment of CS gas (we usually kept one or two people with CS gas, not the pocket-sized ones but the large canisters with a longer range, toward the back to spray the enemy should a retreat be necessary), God striking down the antifascist resistance with tear-gas-poisoned headwinds meant that the prayers of our enemies might have indeed been answered.[5]

Further proof that Bakunin was right and God, if he exists, might be a fascist sympathizer and needs abolishing.

Return to Rue des Chartreux: May 9, 1998

It is safe now to assume that he had had the same realization as I. The difference being that while I had been connecting the dots in my head, he had been connecting the dots on his walkie-talkie and summoning more than a few angry and well-armed friends! I no longer recall which hit me first: the realization of how much danger I was in, the cry of "on charge!" as they sprinted at me, or my reaching the conclusion that as far as fight-or-flight decisions go, this was about as clear-cut as they come.

Antifascists moments before charging the antiabortion demonstrators.

Run. Run like you've never run before. Run like the wind, do not stop, do not look back. Run. Let the adrenaline give you wings, and if you feel tired or out of breath, think of the beating these people will give you if they catch you. I don't know how long I ran for before stopping or even daring to look back. A comically absurd distance and for probably five or ten actual, not rhetorical, minutes. I also recall the feeling of intense fear, something I was pretty unfamiliar with at the time, and evidently managed to again suppress a short time after my inglorious but speedy escape.

You're looking for context. You have questions that need answering, and this is making it difficult to fully appreciate the story. I know. Why are hundreds of militant fascists marching in the streets of Paris on a beautiful Saturday afternoon in May? And most importantly, you're concerned for my safety. Why was I, a teenage antifascist, standing alone in front of them, moments before setting off on the longest and fastest sprint of my short life?

The short answer to why I was there is simple: because I was a young and arrogant idiot who did not listen to the advice of older and more experienced comrades and put my safety needlessly into consid-erable danger.

On this day, the GUD and the rest of France's far-right and fascist scene were assembled to commemorate the death of Sébastien Deyzieu.

Deyzieu was a member of the royalist organization L'Oeuvre Française who perished, tragically, as he fell from the fifth floor of an apartment building while escaping from police who had broken up an unauthorized demonstration, jointly organized by the GUD and the Jeunesses Nationalistes Révolutionnaires (Revolutionary Nationalist Youth) on this same day in 1994. The death of their martyr was still fresh in their collective memory, and the intensity of their anger at "the enemies of Europe," a category in which we anarchists fit comfortably, meant that I probably wasn't wrong to be concerned about having inadvertently volunteered myself as an outlet for their fury.

As opposed to the fascists, who had gathered by way of a public national mobilization, the anarchist and antifascist scene had mobilized locally via word of mouth to oppose them. We had a meeting point a safe distance away from the fascists, and about sixty of us had shown up. It was the usual crowd, mainly people from different anarchist groups and organizations, some from the autonome spectrum, and a pretty decent CNT contingent, which is whom I was usually to be found with. When word came back from our scouts that the fascists numbered comfortably into the several hundreds, the decision from the CNT group was clear, and everybody else was pretty much in agreement: "This is crazy, there's way too many of them. We're going to get killed, or arrested. Maybe even both! We're out of here."

It was a perfectly logical, easy-to-arrive-at, and tactically sound decision. Everybody there was solidly and militantly antifascist, and the group had more than its fair share of veterans of years of confrontations. If all the different strains of Parisian anarchism, so often at odds with each other, were able to agree that we needed to cancel and go home, it's because it was painfully obvious that we needed to cancel and go home. Obvious to everyone except me.

I have no idea what it was that I hoped to achieve, but I was desperate to see them. Hundreds of real live, militant fascists. It was like something out of a horror movie, and I needed to witness it. And who knows, maybe I could identify one, or follow some home and get an address. Maybe I could jump a straggler. These are all possibilities that crossed my mind, most likely simply to justify my unjustifiable risk-taking, but none of them was anywhere near the vicinity of a good or intelligent idea. Which of course didn't stop me from thrusting my jacket onto a friend, since it had a patch or two that would have been a dead giveaway, trading it for a plain black sweatshirt, buying an ice cream to "enhance my disguise," and heading off alone, like an idiot, to stare at the mob of enraged fascists.

And that's the short answer. But there is a long answer, and it contains some important life lessons for any militant antifascist.

33 Rue des Vignoles, CNT Offices, Sometime the Following Week

I met up with Victor a few days later at the 33 and told him about my little solo adventure. Victor is originally from Mexico (though he is also a fluent French speaker), was a member of the CNT's university organ- ization, and also happened to be guitar player for Brigada Flores Magon, a band who through their lyrics, image, and militancy both as a band and as individuals offstage would quickly become a point of reference for young anarchists and antifascists in France and beyond. He and the rest of the band and crew around BFM were a few years older than me, and they had taken me under their wing as a young mascot. But Victor also spoke Spanish, which made me feel most at home interacting with him.

"What kind of fucking idiot are you? That was incredibly stupid." It seems Victor was not terribly impressed by my, um, fast running. And yes, being briefly cast into the unfortunate role of prey had already made clear to me that my choice of action was less than brilliant. But this seemed like a little much, and it was putting a bit of a damper on my peaceful enjoyment of the kebab with fries I had just bought while basking in the springtime Parisian afternoon sun. He was visibly angry at me. "Do you realize how much you're putting everybody at risk when you do these things?" Whether I wanted to hear it or not, he went on to outline it for me. I felt embarrassed and a little humiliated, half expect- ing his talk to end with, "... and that's why you're grounded for a month." It seemed rude to eat while being angrily lectured, so my fries got cold, which I very much resented. But I never forgot his words and, while not always succeeding, at least always made a conscious effort not only to abide by them as best I could, but also to share them with other friends and comrades over the years. It was history lesson, tactical advice, and scolding all conveniently rolled into one.

"You know this city used to be full of violent bonehead gangs, right?" I didn't know the details of it, but I was vaguely aware that the Paris of the mid-1980s to early '90s had boasted more than its fair

The late '90s Brigada Flores Magon, including ex–Red Warrior Julien Terzics, second from left.

share of violent Nazi skinhead gangs.[6] They terrorized marginalized communities, immigrants, and just about anybody who didn't fit their worldview of a France for the French, white, and Christian. Young alternative-looking *gauchistes*, which literally means "leftists" in French but is usually a term reserved for the far left, were one of their favored targets. "They didn't disappear by accident. A lot of people worked very hard and took some huge risks to make that happen. Rico and Julien, for example, are two of those people. You know they're both ex–Red Warriors, right?"

Rico and Julien were two comrades who were a good ten or so years older than us, probably in their mid-thirties while the rest of BFM was in their early twenties, and I was, well, a few years younger than that. Rico was part of the BFM crew as well as a CNT member, while Julien was not only a CNT member but also played a central role in the CNT security service, as well as giving self-defense and martial arts classes for CNT members and other anarchists and antifascists. Finally, he was the drummer of Brigada Flores Magon. Rico and Julien were already solidly in the category of older and more experienced comrades who we looked up to and respected, but for me, finding out they were at the "we were Red Warriors back in the '80s and rid this city of Nazis" level of experience put them in a category not far removed from veteran of May '68 in my head.

The Red Warriors were a Parisian antifascist street gang, formed in 1985, that while small in numbers—four at their inception and fourteen at their peak—has taken on an almost mythical character not only in the French antifascist movement but also internationally, thanks to a 2008 documentary titled *Antifa: Chasseurs de skins* (Antifa: Skinhead hunters). Faced with a Paris filled with numerous skinhead gangs, whose wide spectrum of politics ranged from national socialist to, um, just nationalist, Julien and Rico decided that "it was time for us to organize as a gang. A gang whose doctrine is radical antifascism and whose objective is to instill fear in the opposing camp.... The streets are a political space ... and we are people from those streets, with no intention of abandoning them to the far right."[7]

They quickly got to work with striking efficacy despite their small numbers, although it definitely didn't hurt their success that each Red Warrior practiced a martial art, with several of them even being national champions in their respective disciplines. "We started patrolling the city in cars, to find and beat these guys down. Given what the fascists skinhead gangs had already done to a lot of us, given what they stood for, and the crazy stories we would hear about them, stories of rapes, assaults, lynchings, and so forth, striking back for us was an act of public safety," as Julien recalls it.[8] They, together with several other less explicitly political but multiracial and militantly antiracist and antifascist gangs, fought a successful yearslong campaign against the fascists, becoming known for their daring raids. They were identifiable to themselves and others by their inside-out bomber jackets, revealing the neon-orange side. As a positive side effect, their actions inspired the creation of even more copycat antifascist gangs and gave birth to the French redskin subculture.[9]

Their action changed the political landscape of Paris's streets arguably for decades, and inarguably created the Paris I experienced in the late '90s. "Immediately, with our attacks, a lot of the less politically committed Nazis and racists disappeared. They were there for the gang experience, the feeling of power, the drinking and walking around on the streets with impunity. When it suddenly became an activity involving the risk of being seriously beaten on a regular basis, the mass of them disappeared forever, leaving only the hardcore politically motivated ones." In the span of a few years, Paris went from a city filled with militantly violent racist skinhead street gangs—a place in which, as Julien puts it, "if you were any kind of visibly alternative or left-leaning youth you had to go to the extreme of carefully planning your subway trips because there were areas of the city you knew perfectly well you could under no circumstances travel through"—to a city where antifascists couldn't even find a visibly identifiable Nazi when we tried. And on the extremely rare occasions when we did run into some—as occurred to me once or twice on my commute home from school as I was calmly putting up Anarchist Federation stickers on the subway and older-looking men probably in their thirties made disapproving comments that gave away their far-right leanings—they were so terrified of antifascist repercussions that all I, a young teenager of not particularly imposing stature, had to do was calmly remind them of the realities of late 1990s Parisian life: "If I see you touching that sticker, or God forbid you do something insane like touching me, I'd like to remind you that this seems to be your daily commute as well, and you will never ever be safe in this city again, so for your own safety why don't you move along quietly?" And that was usually the end of it.

Back to the story. Victor continued speaking about our older, more experienced comrades: "They know very well what they're doing. So if they said we should get out of there, it's probably what you should have done. We're anarchists, so I'm not going to be telling you what to do, but if you are just looking for excitement, I'm sure there's a lot of soccer gangs who'd love to have you. If you are going to be with us, you need to get it through your head, and quickly, that your safety and our safety are tied to each other, and that what you do or don't do has practical collective consequences for all of us. Do I need to explain this to you?"

I would have felt comfortable saying that no, I didn't need it explained to me, but the question was clearly rhetorical and, still much like a parent scolding a child, he had already launched into said explanation.

"This landscape in Paris that you benefit from, that everybody benefits from—where fascists don't show their faces, don't run around in groups attacking immigrants or people of color, don't attack demos, don't attack our spaces, and so forth—exists because people who came before you had a strategy. Part of that strategy was that absolutely no aggression would go unresponded to. Now, this might seem like ancient history to you because you're young, but you'll see quickly why it's important: Do you know who called for the demonstration in 1994 at which that fascist Deyzieu who they were commemorating last weekend died?"

Knowing the answer, the Jeunesses Nationalistes Révolutionnaires, I chimed in excitedly, trying to prove to the teacher that I wasn't after all that bad of a student. Unfortunately for me, the question was a rhetorical trap.

"Yes, exactly. But do you know who founded that organization and why?"

That I did not. As I was about to learn, the JNR were founded in 1987 by Serge Ayoub, alias Batskin (and no, the "bat" is not a comic-book reference), one of the aforementioned more committed and violent fascist skinheads who did not disappear when faced with antifascist opposition but rather went on to unify other likeminded fascists into an almost paramilitary organization. They were famed for posing masked and with baseball bats, and even appeared in formation at Front National rallies until the party realized that brute-with-shaved-head was maybe not the best look for it. A particularly violent group of racists, their most infamous crime was the 1994 murder of Mauritian immigrant James Dindoyal, whom they forced to swallow a mix of beer and chemical cleaner before throwing him off a dike and to his death.[10]

"That rally last weekend was basically a national family meeting of GUD, ex-JNR, L'Oeuvre Française, and the sort. Many of them, probably most actually, aren't even from Paris. Some might even be remnants from the '80s, and the others probably consider themselves their political heirs. Can you imagine what they might have done to you if they had caught you? And you're telling me you think they recognized you from a previous action with us? You could have easily gotten stabbed, and they could have killed you, either on purpose or by accident. And you know, that's not great for you, but it's a problem for all of us, no matter how much it's a result of your stupidity.

"First of all, it's fodder for their propaganda, both internally and publicly. They'll feel emboldened, making more attacks more likely, and so you are putting everybody else in danger. They will use the incident to present themselves as the resurgence of militant fascism, and they are desperate to be able to present that image in order to attract new people. If they indeed realized you are one of us, more or less identified with

Brigada Flores Magon's farewell concert in Paris, September 27, 2024, in memory of the life of Julien Terzics, beloved friend and comrade who passed away from cancer on July 1 of that year, age fifty-five. Attended by over a thousand people, the concert was a testament to the life of Julien, the many people he touched, and the legacy he leaves behind. His roles as anarchist organizer, antifascist militant, Nazi hunter, and one of the many motors behind the growth of a militant anarchist and antifascist subculture in the Paris of the 1990s and 2000s is well documented. But if he was able to fill those roles successfully and to be remembered with so much love by so many across the world, it's because he was above all a comrade and friend. A comrade who despite his trajectory or "scene status" was never above lending a helping hand, listening, or, as in my case, taking in a young anarchist and making him feel needed and welcomed. I have no doubt that my experience with him was replicated numerous times in his interactions with comrades throughout the decades. I, along with many others, have Julien, Brigada, and the crew to thank for shaping and cementing my antifascism, in both theory and practice: uncompromising in defense of our ideas and comrades, unforgiving with our enemies.

Mural in memory of Julien by Vinci of Black Lines. "Ranx, Red Warrior, hunter of fascist skinheads, remain in the struggle, rest in peace."

Cover of the Brigada Flores Magon LP *Anges Gardiens* (Guardian Angels).

ex-Red Warriors, BFM, CNT, et cetera, they would definitely have made a point of that. And so, we would be obligated to respond forcefully. This puts all of us in danger. In physical danger, since confrontations are always a risk, as well as in legal danger of possible arrest. Are you starting to get the point now?"

Indeed I was. And I was also extremely lucky. I learned my lesson with next to no consequences, and with the support of a network of antifascists with not only the experience but also the dedication (and sometimes patience) to take the time to explain to me the dangers of my youthful mistakes, both to me as well as others. I was fortunate not only that I lived in a city with an experienced cadre of still-active older antifascists, but also that they took the time and effort to take younger comrades under their wing and make sure experience gained and lessons learned were not lost to new generation of militants.

From that day, and over the years to come, I learned that though it is sometimes hard for people on the outside to discern, the militant antifascist struggle is much more than a conflict between "rival youth gangs," as the media often likes to frame the issue. From streets free of fascist violence comes the space for dissident youth subcultures, for open spaces and social centers, for demonstrations and rallies, and generally for the broader world of anarchist agitation, free of fascist threat. This keeps us safe as anarchists and antifascists and allows us to concentrate our efforts elsewhere, but it just as importantly, if not more importantly, keeps individuals and communities targeted by fascists safe.

Madrid, Legazpi Metro Station, November 11, 2007

Approximately ten years later, in the different but similar European metropolis of Madrid, another teenage antifascist, Carlos Palomino, age sixteen, was much less fortunate. His error was significantly smaller than mine, but he was not afforded the luxury of learning from it and continuing with his life. He would not have the benefit of a crew of more experienced friends and comrades sitting him down and explaining after the fact what he could and should do differently next time. Carlos Palomino was killed in a subway car on November 11, 2007, stabbed in the heart by a fascist's knife.

The video footage of his death is essential viewing for all militant antifascists. It is of course painful to watch, despite not being at all graphic.[11] It happens in the blink of an eye, so fast that if you are unaware of the context of what you are seeing you probably wouldn't realize or understand that something tragic just happened. But it is painful and heartbreaking to watch, because his actions are those of any young antifascist. It's something many of us have done once, ten times, dozens of times. Just as Alexis Grigoropoulos in Athens was and could have been any one of us, a young anarchist directing unfiltered rage at cops, any one of us could have been Carlos Palomino, instinctively confronting a fascist.

On that day, Carlos is with a group of about fifty antifascists, headed to oppose an anti-immigration demonstration of the far-right Democracia Nacional. As they enter the Legazpi subway station, twenty-three-year-old Josué Estébanez de la Hija, a neo-Nazi and professional soldier who is already in one of the subway cars, notices the large group of antifascists. He is wearing a sweatshirt from the brand Three Stroke, known for its popularity among the militant far right, and realizes he is likely to be identified and confronted. He pulls out a knife and conceals it from view with his hand behind his back.

When I first saw the video footage, I already knew that an anti-fascist had been killed in this incident. But it was still heartbreaking to immediately recognize how a young comrade walks so needlessly into his death. As Carlos enters the subway car where the fascist is, I was reminded of all the things I had learned in my youth in Paris as he immediately breaks several self-preservation-related rules of engagement with fascists. I discuss them here not to criticize a fallen comrade but, on the contrary, because we all have a responsibility to share our knowledge and collectively keep each other safe.

Carlos enters the subway car and places himself within significantly less than arm's length from the Nazi. In places where firearms are uncommon, such as most of Europe, staying beyond striking distance until *you* choose to engage is the first means of ensuring you are not caught off guard by your opponent. It becomes even more critical if, as was the case here, your opponent has his hands hidden from view, potentially concealing a weapon. If his hands are hidden strategically from view, it means not only that your opponent might be armed but also that, if so, he has already taken strategic action to prepare for a potential confrontation. It is an indicator of a potential imminent aggression.

As he places himself within striking distance, Carlos does what so many of us are likely to have done instinctively in our lives when faced with a Nazi. Even I and other well-trained comrades have on occasion done it while distracted or in the heat of the moment. With his guard potentially lowered by the overwhelming numerical advantage, he casually gestures to the Three Stroke logo emblazoned across the chest of the Nazi's sweater, giving him a mild poke as he does so, while gesturing and clearly saying something to the effect of, "What the fuck is this shit?" By doing so, he gives his opponent prior warning, completely unnecessarily, that a confrontation is about to ensue. That is his third, final, and tragically fatal mistake. Being within striking distance, having ceded the element of surprise, and acting individually rather than collectively despite overwhelming numerical superiority, Carlos unfortunately broke the cardinal rule of engagement with the fascist or Nazi enemy: Treat every interaction as a potentially mortal one, and act accordingly.

In the blink of an eye, Estébanez plunges his knife into Carlos's heart and pulls it back out. Carlos, stunned, stumbles back out of the subway car as his comrades scatter. The entire sequence, from Carlos entering the subway car until retreating after being stabbed, lasts exactly five whole seconds.

Carlos's mistakes are common, and he was simply unlucky to have them cost him his life. Unlucky that the Nazi he encountered was a trained soldier, by definition a professionally trained killer taught to think strategically about confrontation and not hesitate at the notion of taking a life. Unlucky that this training, compounded with Estébanez's belief in a genocidal ideology that does not see inherent value in all human life, was the unfortunate combination that cost Carlos his. There is obviously inherent risk in militant antifascism, and no matter what we do or how we prepare, the chance of injury or death will always exist. But that is precisely the purpose of thinking strategically about our actions and taking all relevant precautions: to minimize the role of luck and create the best possible odds for ourselves and those around us.

The principal consideration here, the one to always keep in mind and from which all else flows: Every fascist and Nazi you encounter is a potential murderer. It is inherent in their ideology, and it is not a coincidence that incidences of mortal violence caused by militant antifascists internationally over the decades are negligible, while the far right has tallied thousands upon thousands of deaths. You need to treat your safety in that encounter in accordance with that understanding. The rules of engagement with fascists and Nazis for us should be clear: Treat every encounter as potentially deadly. Be on your highest level of situational awareness at all times. Stay outside of striking distance until you choose to engage. If you are going to attack, maintain the element of surprise as much as possible. Do not give prior warning, leave the macho posturing out of it, and when you do attack, prioritize collective action over individual confrontation.

From the time of that talk with Victor in 1998 until the death of Carlos in 2007, I had numerous confrontations with Nazis and fascists, the vast majority of which, in proud "Nazi hunter" tradition, my friends, comrades, and I explicitly sought out. I was incredibly fortunate to always leave these confrontations relatively unscathed, despite being neither particularly large nor having had any kind of relevant combat sport or martial arts training. I was armed with a healthy dose of sincere conviction in the indispensable importance of what we were doing as an act of public safety and collective self-defense, the occasional blunt force weapon, and the words of Victor on that afternoon at the CNT, as well as Julien, Mathieu, and many others whom I'd had the opportunity to learn from and who helped keep me safe.

As I thought about Carlos's death, I remembered again how Victor concluded his blend of scolding, history lesson, and motivational speech all wrapped into one that spring afternoon in Paris. The man is a professor now, so maybe it's not such a surprise that he was able to reach an arrogant young anarchist who had next to no notion of the concepts of danger or consequences in a way effective enough for me to still more or less recall decades later. If Carlos had been so fortunate, he might still be with us today.

"No random fascist on the street is worth your life. This is not a negation of the importance of militant antifascism, but an affirmation of its necessity, while at the same time being conscious of the importance of protecting, defending, and valuing our own lives. When you do something, know why you're doing it, and do it right. You need to think tactically in terms of personal safety, as well as strategy. Even when we go after the little kids with the French flag patches on their jackets, it's not a game and it's not for fun. It's because we got fascists

NOSOTRXS NO OLVIDAMOS

ANTIFASCISTA
ASESINADO
POR UN MILITAR
NEONAZI EL 11.11.07

DIEZ AÑOS SIN TI
DIEZ AÑOS CONTIGO

EL MEJOR HOMENAJE
CONTINUAR LA LUCHA
CARLOS VIVE

 2007
2017

A sticker made in remembrance of Carlos Palomino, ten years after his death. "Antifascist murdered by a neo-Nazi soldier. Ten years without you, ten years at your side. The best homage: to continue the struggle!"

out of our scenes and off our streets with a lot of effort, and we aren't going to allow the nationalism and racism that breeds them back in.

"We won't change their minds, and that's not the point. The battle of ideas is the work of political education and anarchist agitation. Our work as militant antifascists is to deprive them of platforms, and of power. There's a quote about racism from some ex–Black Panther that's just as true in this case about fascists. The fascist's ideas are his problem. If he obtains the power or confidence to act on them, that's when they become our problem.[12] Fortunately, we can control this through our actions, but never forget that while antifascism for us is an unfortunate necessity, something ideally relegated to secondary consideration, eliminating people like us is central to their ideology and politics. You need to never ever forget that they can and will kill you if you give them that chance."

Epilogue: Paris, May 9, 2006

It's another 9th of May, and again the GUD and assorted fascists from all over France have converged on Paris. But Parisian anarchists and antifascists have learned the lessons of the late '90s and gotten serious about elevating the political and physical costs the fascists have to pay to parade themselves around Paris.

No longer limited to just a semi-clandestine meetup of people, this is now the fourth year of what is a well-structured and relatively broad antifascist mobilization, powered by "the continued joint organizational participation of the SCALP-Reflex network, the CNT, and Ras l'Front Noisy-Le-Grand," according to an account appearing in French antifascist magazine *REFLEXes* three days after the event.[13] This year, the antifascist numbers are boosted by the participation of "SUD-students section, the JCR, and Alternative Libertaire." (SUD is a rank-and-file trade union, the JCR is a Trotskyist, but large, organization by the name of Revolutionary Communist Youth, and Alternative Libertaire is a platformist anarcho-communist organization.)

In order to mobilize as many people as possible, as well as to ensure a safe and legal gathering spot as close as possible to the fascists, the antifascist rally "was officially registered and an agit-prop activity had been prepared." Some three hundred antifascists answer the call, making their way up the Boulevard Saint-Michel to position themselves at the Port-Royal train station "less than fifty meters away from the fascists." Immediately, there's a "tense face-to-face with the police," who quickly give up on the idea of pushing the determined antifascist crowd farther back. The first isolated fascist "tourists" fall upon the antifascists and get "the pleasure of tasting the vigilance and determination of the activists securing the gathering."[14]

The main group of organized fascists make their appearance. While their march went off without too much incident from departure until now, they've already had a difficult day thanks to an "incursion of antifa activists at 8 p.m., which helps to empty the bar that they used as a meeting point" for their rally. They number just over two hundred. "The antifascist security service secures the plaza and organizes the departure of the sound truck" while others head in the direction of the fascists. "The first exchanges are very violent and take place in the most total confusion."[15]

The *REFLEXes* write-up concludes:

The situation deteriorates very quickly. While the fascist organizers take up position in front of the building, the most audacious among them go to take a look at the end of the street, where they realize very quickly that the police protection is less than imposing. A weak cordon of mobile gendarmes is supposed to prevent the antifas from accessing the street, but instead the first projectiles give the signal for confrontation. A group largely dominated by hooligans from Boulogne tries to charge to the sound of "France for the French!" or "PSG, PSG!" ...

The fascists taking cover behind the cops' buses throw smoke bombs, while the mobile gendarmes pepper the antifas with tear-gas grenades. Objects fly in all directions over the heads of the cops. Bolts, petanque balls, cobblestones, smoke, anything goes. After a few minutes, we retreat to the public park of the Place Ernest Denis, from where again a maximum of projectiles are being fired. The mobile gendarmes attempt an incursion into the park, but hesitate to enter and prefer to continue to throw tear-gas grenades at us, now leveling straight head shots in our direction. In the meantime, the cop vans, accompanied by water cannons, advance on the Boulevard Saint-Michel to try to take us from the rear. BAC inspectors [groups of cops who act also as arrest squads, dressed in civilian clothing], equipped with helmets and retractable batons, burst in at the corner of the plaza to arrest isolated antifas....

We've made a mess of things in the neighborhood and raised the pressure around this event by several notches.... The standoff against the cops and the fascists has only just begun. We will be there again next year.[16]

AGAINST
DEPORTATION
RAILWAYS

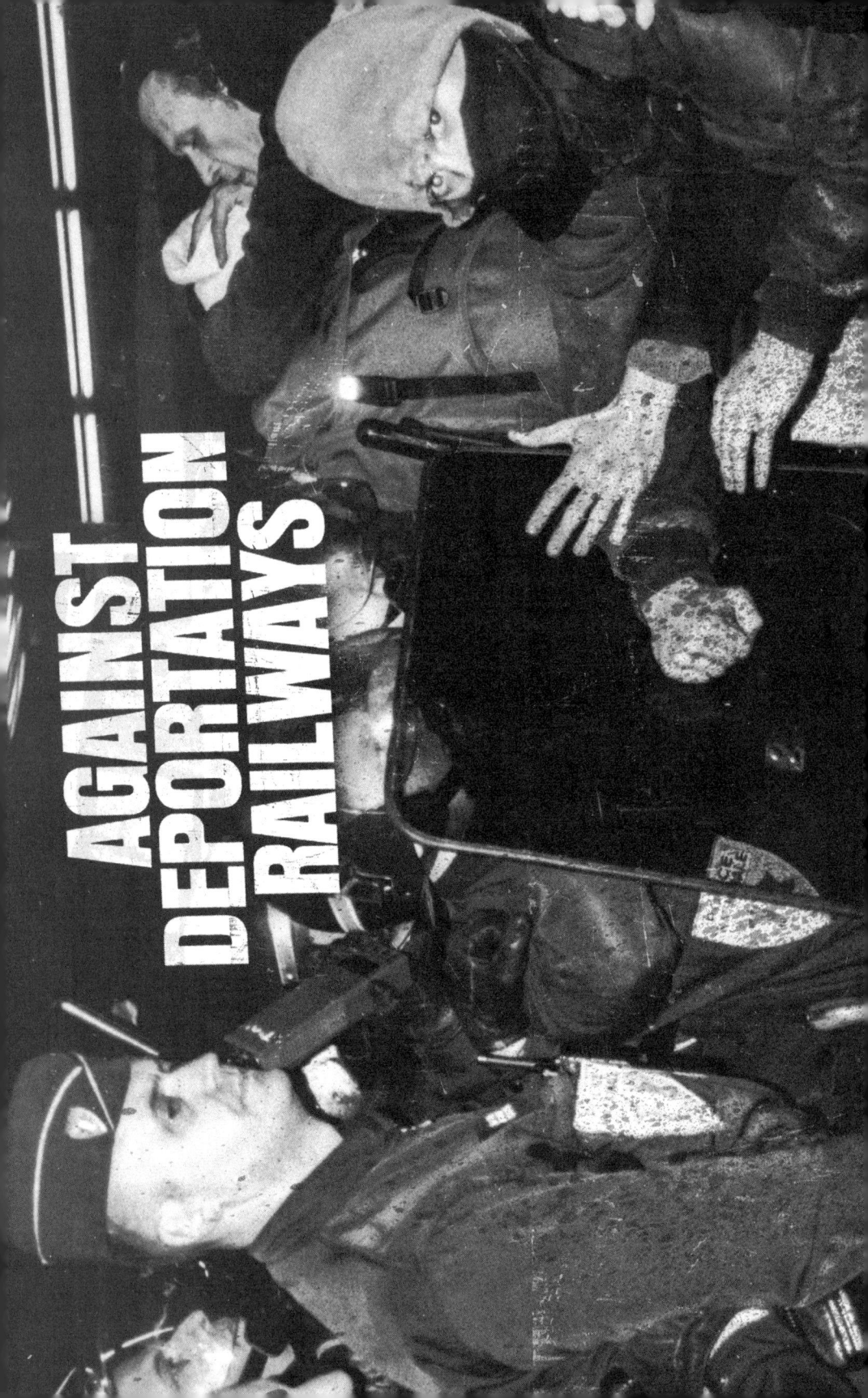

4
THE 21:03 TO MARSEILLE
Paris, May 5, 1998

Gare de Lyon

It's early evening and Sophie and I are sitting in the long-distance-train waiting area of Paris's Gare de Lyon, one of Europe's busiest train stations. All around us are travelers scurrying to and fro. Stressed-out tourist families, cameras still flung around Dad's neck, rushing their kids through the station mix with tired-looking businessmen waiting to get back home. "You did a great job with your outfit," she says to me as she looks me over from head to toe. I met Sophie at an action (or demonstration, or concert, or something of the sort) about a year ago, and we have been inseparable at political events since. She is my age, a student at Paris's Lycée Autogéré (Self-Managed High School), and if I didn't know very well the context in which she's making this comment, I might think she's flirting with me.[1] "You're looking pretty good yourself," I respond in kind.

    She stands out because she's naturally good-looking, but aside from that she's managed to transform herself into the spitting image of your perfectly forgettable average French teenage girl. Which in this day and age basically means she looks like a younger Sporty Spice in her Adidas tracksuit and sneakers. I, on the other hand, went with a significantly preppier look: khaki pants, polo shirt, nondescript jacket, and moccasins. She looks at me again, pauses, and slightly withdraws her compliment: "It's not the most functional wardrobe, though. The khakis stand out and the moccasins probably aren't great for running."

I shrug. "I did what I could, I was mainly concerned with getting this far."

While we may be sitting among the tourists and businessmen, doing our best to look like a somewhat mismatched young teenage couple waiting for a train back to their city, we are in fact not travelers, and the correct term for our attire is not "outfit" but "disguise." We are not here to take a train, but to stop one. One that every single night transports imprisoned human beings against their will. The 21:03 to Marseille, otherwise known to us as the deportation train.

Our objective is to stop the Paris-to-Marseille overnight train, which the French National Railway Company, better known for its French initials SNCF, allows the French government to use to transport North African immigrants, usually of Algerian or Moroccan origin, by rail to Marseille. Once in the port city, their expulsion from French territory is completed by boat. The attempt to block this train is an idea born of the Collectif Anti-Expulsions (Anti-Deportation Collective), and it was decided that if we were to have any chance of success, we should disguise ourselves as best as possible and infiltrate the station in small groups, since trying to march in there as a demonstration probably wasn't going to get us very far.

The CAE, officially formed only a few weeks before in early April, is an autonomous collective born in the heat of the movement of the *sans-papiers* of the mid-'90s, a French term literally meaning "without papers" and referring to the movement against the deportation of undocumented immigrants and for their "legalization." The collective's broadly accepted guiding principles are as simple as they are clearly steeped in anarchist modes of organization, thought, and action:

- Practical opposition to deportations.
- We are not allies to the sans-papiers, we struggle with them out of motivations and convictions that are our own.
- These motivations vary among individuals, but are in all cases rooted in anticapitalism.
- The collective is autonomous and collaborates with sans-papiers collectives that are autonomous not merely in theory, but in practice.

– Decisions are made by way of general assembly.[2]

The plight of the sans-papiers had exploded into the public consciousness following a series of highly publicized church occupations in 1996 by undocumented immigrants themselves, which culminated in the raid by almost two thousand police officers on the Saint-Bernard church on August 23, 1996, at the end of which 210 undocumented immigrants were detained.

Since then, solidarity demonstrations with the sans-papiers in Paris regularly numbered in the tens of thousands, with participants—as well as their demands and methods of action—representing the broad spectrum of the French center left to radical left. From the Communist Party and the CGT union to the sizable anarchist blocs of CNT, Anarchist Federation, Alternative Libertaire, SCALP, and everything in between. Importantly, the sans-papiers themselves were organized into several collectives and structures and were active and leading participants in their own struggles. As with all communities, they were not a monolith, and within the sans-papiers organizations there was also a broad spectrum of ideas and strategies as to demands, objectives, and methods of action.

While the sans-papiers organizations, regardless of their politics, were limited in their methodology by the logical constraints of their situation, namely that an arrest or identity control could quickly lead to a possible deportation and have devastating, even deadly, potential consequences for them, the reformist organizations were bound by the unsurprising constraints of their respect for legality and their acceptance of the basic premises of states and borders and the idea that a human being should in some way or another be bound by the possession of a particular piece of paper, or lack thereof, based on their place of birth. Or even more absurdly, as is the case in France, their bloodline.

We anarchists, on the other hand, had no such constraints. Our solidarity with what are clearly some of the most oppressed and marginalized groups in society—workers, people of color, many of them women, escaping from some of the most horrendous conflicts in the world at the time—was immediate and instinctive. But through our position of unconditional solidarity with the sans-papiers and the assertion that in the world we are fighting for no human will ever be illegal and freedom of movement will be for people and not just for commodities, we articulated a position of necessary rupture with the concepts of states and borders. If our position could not be granted by the state and our objective could not be realized within the framework of its existence, then it only naturally follows that we would not look to the state to grant it. A concrete struggle, then, to prevent deportations and make it possible for people to live where they choose and how they choose, in which the same stance toward the state applies as in our abstract analysis: that it is our enemy, that we are to wage war against it within the appropriate context of the time and situation we are in, and through that struggle prevent it from carrying out its objectives. The greater our success, hand in hand with those sans-papiers who were open to our solidarity and methods, the greater the growth of our collective power as a movement and the greater the degree of agency, autonomy, and freedom we could realize. We don't make demands, we force concessions and create realities. Concretely: that deportations are for stopping. To do so, we would attack the state's machinery of deportation, its infrastructure, and the enterprises that not only collaborated with it but also benefited economically from their collaboration in the literal hunting, caging, and displacing of human beings.

We do so out of solidarity, out of anti-state conviction, but also with the explicit understanding that despite our privileges and different realities, our struggle is the same as theirs and in fighting alongside the sans-papiers, as accomplices not allies, we are also fighting for ourselves: "Their situation makes us all more precarious in labor relations, the repression and control developed against them will affect us eventually as well, the hardening of borders is also a barrier to our freedom of movement, because we are also foreigners to this world and we will be pushed further and further into clandestinity (by choice but also by necessity if we are to live our desires) by the constant evolution of the law and the states."[3]

Our first attempt, then, at a practical application of this perspective on a mass scale has led us to this moment. Sitting under the elegant industrial-era steel and glass roof so typical of venerable European train stations. It seems a fittingly dramatic setting for the impending confrontation. We are waiting anxiously for the moment when an unknown number of cops will appear, escorting what I expect will be a handcuffed individual through the hall, at which point we are to spring into action and form a human chain to prevent them from being able to load him onto the train. Failing that, we are to do everything we can to prevent the train from departing. We are no pacifists, and while there was a general consensus that our side would avoid unnecessary escalations, there was an equally clear agreement that the priority here is not optics, but the accomplishing of this very concrete and tangible objective. But I'm anxious and less than convinced about our chances of success here. "Do you see any familiar-looking faces?" I worriedly ask. I'm scanning the hall as best I can and don't like what I see.

"No, I can't even see Alan or Mary. I wonder if they made it in." Mary is another Lycée Autogéré student and Sophie's best friend, while Alan is slightly older and the token cliché-looking punk—complete with mohawk and faux leather jacket—among our little youth affinity group.

Not one of us is old enough to be a legal adult, yet the four of us already have a fair amount of experience as far as getting into trouble with the state. We met at a Comité d'Action Lycéen (CAL, or "High School Action Committee") meeting, a place that can only be described as a breeding ground for high-school-age anarchists. We don't know it yet, but in a few months it'll blow up and become (in)famous during a wave of high school actions and strikes, during which groups of immigrant youths will join the large demonstrations against high school reform to attack cops and engage in widespread proletarian shopping. The mainstream student unions will fall over themselves to denounce "the violence and looting" and even ask for the cop unions to provide "security" at the demonstrations. The CAL, on the other hand, will enthusiastically participate in and welcome the developments and after the fact be the only voice articulating an opinion that commends the youth for their instinctive rejection of cops and authorities, as well as their practical and effective measures of wealth redistribution.

We're young, fanatical, and still unencumbered by wage slavery enough that we enjoy having ample free time, which we use to be regulars at every demonstration, action, occupation, political squat, concert, debate, and confrontation within the greater Paris area. And when we're not doing that, we're spending our nights together drinking, getting stoned, and listening to Ska-P's *El vals del obrero* in the catacombs under the streets of Paris. Or at least the others are, as I've discovered Sergei Nechayev's *Catechism of the Revolutionist* and interpret that my mind and body are both weapons for revolutionary struggle, and thus to best care for them I should keep them free of drugs and alcohol. (I was lots of fun at parties …)

Which is wonderful and all, but no matter how combative we may be or how sharp I keep my proverbial weapons, if there are twenty of us when the cops show up, this is probably not going to go well. "Fucking unions," Sophie mutters under her breath. "What are they good for if they can't even bring out fifty people for something like this?" Her complaint is directed at SUD, short for Solidaire, Unitaire, Démocratique (In Solidarity, United, Democratic), a small leftist union born in the aftermath of the 1995 general strike, whose railway branch had promised to mobilize for this action.

I shrug. "Who knows, it's not like we know what they look like. Maybe it'll work out."

I'm trying to be positive, because this is the route we have chosen, and if we're at the ball we might as well dance. And anyway, it didn't seem like there were too many viable alternatives available. Our previous efforts at this a couple of weeks earlier, through quieter and essentially anarchist-only word-of-mouth mobilizations, were successful in delaying the train for a few hours, as we were able to occupy the tracks. Cops eventually cleared them through liberal use of batons and CS gas, and when we returned a few days later we found an army of police guarding the tracks to avoid a repeat performance.

"Look, look, right there!" Sophie points to one of the entrances to the hall, her voice trembling with a mix of excitement and anger. I'm just spotting what she is pointing at, a young man probably in his twenties being led by an escort of seven or eight cops, when immediately my concerns about our numbers today are erased. From every corner of the hall comes a loud burst of disapproving whistling, followed immediately by what seems like the entire crowded hall erupting in thunderous chants of, "Non, non, non … aux expulsions!" amplified and rendered even more urgent by the echoes generated by the partially closed space in which we find ourselves.

The first few get up from their seats, sprint over to where the line of CRS riot police are guarding access to the platform and the train, and link arms. A few more join them. Then dozens more. Friends and comrades appear from everywhere among the crowd. The chants declaring that no human being is illegal ring loud and constant as we too join the human chain. There are hundreds of us! There are so many of us that we form two lines across the opening to the platform—one face to face with the cops who were already stationed there and seem concerned with preventing us from attempting to get access to the tracks, the line in which Sophie and I find ourselves, and another facing back toward the hall, preventing the cops escorting the sans-papier from reaching the train, as well as any other passenger for that matter.

The next few minutes go by in an adrenaline-fueled blur. The sight of the person we are trying to protect from deportation right in front of us illustrates poignantly the immediacy of what's at stake, and the discon-certed looks of his police escort only embolden us. Clearly, they aren't sure whether to push through or abort. They're not unfamiliar with resistance to deportations. We regularly show up at airports, informing passengers as well as airline workers of what's happening on their flights and what their employers are making them unwilling accomplices to, urging passengers to refuse to fly on flights that are simultaneously pris-oner transports, with varying degrees of success. We've tried to disrupt and prevent deportations too, as we did a few weeks ago at this same spot.

But never like this.

Never by the hundreds, and with the palpable feeling that we might actually succeed—and I think the cops sense it too.

The next scene is of an extreme and almost intimate violence. Clearly the order has been given to clear access to the train. CS gas and batons fly all around us. We are not armed. We have no flagpoles, no helmets, not even the cloth of a banner to protect ourselves with. Masks cover our face while linked arms keep us together but leave us practically defenseless against the baton blows. Suddenly, with neither word nor warning, the riot cop directly to my right pulls out a metal retractable baton from the inside pocket of his jacket, and in one swift motion he extends it and brings it down with a thud against the head of a comrade next to me. I hear the crack and immediately see blood gushing from the wound at the top of his forehead. His arms go limp, and the best I can do is kind of release my arm, which I have linked around his, and push him backward as he slumps, so that he falls toward the line of comrades facing the station and not at the feet of the unhinged cops.

Before I can make any kind of assessment as to the wisdom or practicality of my actions, I'm already instinctively launching a swift kick at the stomach area of the guilty cop. The same one who had been sneering at us since the beginning, and evidently had been waiting for his moment to injure a *"gauchiste de merde,"* French for "piece-of-shit leftist," which is exactly what nationalists, reactionaries, and fascists like to call us in Argentina. Sophie yells for me to get back, but her voice barely registers on my radar. Comrades break the line to carry away the injured friend, I have broken ranks with my kick, and still others, blinded or unable to breathe due to the CS gas, also break ranks and retreat.

The young Algerian is boarded onto the train, which, as the following week's edition of *Le Monde Libertaire*, weekly newspaper of the francophone Anarchist Federation, reports, "departed with a delay of thirty minutes.... The train would stop several kilometers farther, in Melun, waiting for another train transporting approximately half of its original passengers," who had been unable to board due to the clashes between demonstrators and police. "The train was again stopped at the Lyon-Perrache station around 2:30 a.m. by activists there, but not before having made an unscheduled stop at L'Estaque station to disembark the prisoners and place them in the detention center at Arenc, as the cops were concerned about the possible actions of further demonstrators in Marseille."[4]

The final scene inside the hall feels like the blink of an eye, but that same article in *Le Monde Libertaire* confirms that it indeed took place over half an hour. There are still two clearly defined fronts inside the waiting area. On one side, now about twenty meters or so away from the trains, we stand. A small group of people, about twenty wearing high-visibility vests, start to leave. I notice that they are SUD railway trade unionists, who it turns out had shown up to the action only to promptly declare that with the departure of the train their "participation was now over." We still number solidly in the couple of hundreds. In the grand scheme of things, it's nothing. It's poor attendance even at a third-division football match, barely enough people to fill a subway car, and even your strictly anarchist demonstration in Paris could comfortably number into the thousands. But in my eyes and at that moment, these people were the whole world. Who cares about numbers, optics, or the opinion of sheep? I feel at home among these two hundred who have put their bodies behind the conviction that no human being is illegal and who have stated with their actions that the state and its agents are to be confronted head-on. Rather two hundred ultra-leftists, adventurists, extremists, or whatever else they may call us, than two thousand who will stand idly by because party or union discipline says

After finally leaving Paris, the 21:03 to Marseille is again blockaded, this time in Perrache.

now is not the moment and this is not the way—or twenty thousand who march down the street with us proclaiming that no human being is illegal, only to then placidly continue with their day while others are dragged, often drugged and bound, to prisoner transports. I'm grateful for the existence of the sympathizer, the unionist, the party member, the reformist. I understand we need them, to exert political pressure and if nothing else then merely as cover. But my place is with the militants and the fighters, no matter the numbers.

In front of us, now at a distance that shields us from the gas and truncheons, is a wall of riot cops. The theoretical understanding of police as the armed guards in place to enforce the dictatorship of capital through the state-sanctioned monopoly of violence gives way to a much more practical and urgent feeling of rejection. An immediate and burning hatred of those who not only hurt my friends but did so to protect and enable the perpetration of injustice against individuals. The practical realization that whether beyond the uniform they wear and the role they play they are good people, kind, fathers or mothers, or whether they are abusive and violent partners or individuals, is irrelevant. Whoever wears that uniform is the vehicle of our oppression and my enemy, to be regarded only from that perspective.

Somebody has come back from another track with a backpack full of stones. As the chants against deportation continue to roar, a few dozen of us attack the cops. There's sadness and frustration still, because we failed, but there is also joy. There's a feeling of collective refusal and liberation.

Too Much and Never Enough

As we finally begin to make our retreat from the station, smashing security cameras, advertisement panels, and automated ticket counters on our way, I am already thinking about him: the young Algerian whose deportation we were trying to stop. Tonight wasn't about making an abstract political statement against deportations. It wasn't a militant yet still-symbolic action against the machinery of expulsion and the barbarism that categorizes human beings based on what spot on a map they happen to have been born on. Maybe it was all that as well, but those were by-products. The priority, the tangible objective, was to stop a deportation. And while there is still some distant hope that comrades farther down the line, in Lyon or in Marseille, might still succeed, we at least have failed, and my mind is already busy thinking how I, or we collectively, can do more.

Despite my concerns that we didn't do enough, by the very next day I'm confronted with the press and the good citizens of Paris howling that we did too much. I pick up a newspaper on the way to school and find articles pontificating about the extremists at the train station, outraged at the disorder, condemning the supposed outbreak of violence. Too much disorder, too much violence—words coming from exasperated good citizens of Paris as they walk past me at the very same train station and see the smashed ticket-vending machines. I've seen this movie before, and the constant hand-wringing about "the extreme left, emboldened, becoming increasingly aggressive, violent, and dangerous" has only intensified since the election of the socialist and communist center-left government coalition last year. The outrage would concentrate around the innocent people just trying to go about their day, inconvenienced and maybe even frightened by these masked ultras. And the beautiful Gare de Lyon, damaged by these vandals bent on chaos and disorder.

What was damaged? As I make my way through the station, probably headed either to the CNT or soccer practice, I take note of the "damage." The only damage to the station is to the machines that hinder our freedom of movement and convert the need to get from one place to another into an economic consideration. To the advertising panels that pollute public space and turn any place where the human eye might rest its gaze into propaganda for the constant consumption of goods we don't need. And finally to the increasingly ever-present security cameras, so that anyone who rejects this system of consumption and control can be more efficiently surveilled and criminalized.

What precious order did we disrupt? If the order they are referring to is the superficial peace and tranquility that those so slavishly obsessed only with order (but not with justice) revere, then the problem is not that we were violent or disorderly but that we effectively disrupted the orderly procedures of oppression. The order of those who prefer the continuation of oppression as long as they can turn a blind eye to it—or worse, celebrate it in the name of nationalism or racism—to the turbulence of the struggle to end it.

Violence? We threw some stones, probably injured nobody. If anything, the injured were on our side, those who faced the armed forces of the state with not much more than our bodies and the occasional flying object. A few smashed ticketing machines and advertisements? What is that compared to the momentous violence we witnessed? One that takes place constantly, unceasingly, in every immigrant neighborhood swept by human hunters. During every ticket control in the subway that begins a domino effect that ends in deportation. On flights leaving constantly with prisoners, often drugged and handcuffed, transported as human cargo against their will. With the life of this man, who may or may not face persecution, hardship, or death if returned to his place of birth. I don't need to shock or traumatize you or myself with what his fate might or might not be, what his circumstances were, whether he was torn from a family, a partner, a project, his dreams. It doesn't matter. I assert his freedom to live as he chooses and where he chooses because my anarchism demands it. As a matter of human dignity and as a rejection of the system of states and borders that I seek to destroy. This violence, this war on individuals in the name of states and nations, is the only relevant violence, the violence carried out in the defense of oppression.

A machine of violence built to protect and perpetuate the system of exploitation and human suffering that pits human against human in a needless struggle for survival. A machine that has so colonized the minds of people that they see violence as something occurring only at the point of impact. The fist striking a face, the rock landing against the policeman's shield. That predicates a false nonviolence that ignores the constant barrage of unspeakable violence that flows from the system of nations, capital, and class society: of death due to lack of access to health care, of famine and hunger created by artificial scarcity, of workplace accident deaths caused by the drive to skimp on safety measures in order to maximize profits, of endless religious and nationalist wars. Of immigrants drowning in the seas around Fortress Europe and falling in the heat of the Arizona desert in desperate attempts to escape poverty and improve their lives. This systemic violence, the violence of oppression and of its guardians, barely even registers to most as such. The violence of normality, because oppression itself is a violent act, a reality that does not change regardless of how orderly or accepted its perpetration may be.

I make my way through the city, still lost in my thoughts as I exit the subway into the largely immigrant neighborhood where the CNT offices are. Two cops are parked outside the subway, nonchalantly and randomly checking people for ID. "Papers, please." The normality of everyday violence.

Faced with this reality, who cares about legality? Who cares about popular opinion? When there were few of us and we occupied the tracks, our action was completely peaceful. Yet the state came and beat us without hesitation in order to carry out its objective. And though they were able to accomplish it in a relatively orderly manner, due to our small numbers and tactical avoidance of violence, was it not the victory of an immeasurably more violent act? Would a greater violence on our end, the application of a liberatory violence, not be justified? In what thought process does it fit that nonviolence is somehow the moral high ground, when adherence to it is actually what makes the perpetuation of human suffering and oppression possible?

I'll never forget the image or the moment, a few weeks earlier, as we were being beaten off the tracks. I can barely see him through the glass, his dark complexion and the reflection of the station lights against the train's windows making it difficult to distinguish his features and facial expressions. Two cops are moving him through the train, one holding each arm from behind him, his hands cuffed together in front. Suddenly, as they pass an open window we can clearly see as he turns to us. He lifts his hands and displays a victory sign with each, as he mouths "thank you" to us. There is sadness, dignity, and gratitude in his face. I don't know anything about him, where he is from, what brought him here, or what he is being sent back to. But I know that violence, life-changing and potentially fatal violence, is not what is happening outside the train, but rather what is being done to him inside it.

As I thought about that moment, a different, more urgent question concerned me. It's not that we are too violent, but exactly the opposite. If we didn't employ the full arsenal of our capacity for collective, revolutionary, and liberatory violence, not only to stop these situations but to be a force against this system of control that oppresses all of us, are we not as complicit as those who see it but choose to turn away? How could I justify not employing the full capacity of our arsenal of collective, revolutionary, and liberatory violence?

What we are doing is not too much, it's not nearly enough.

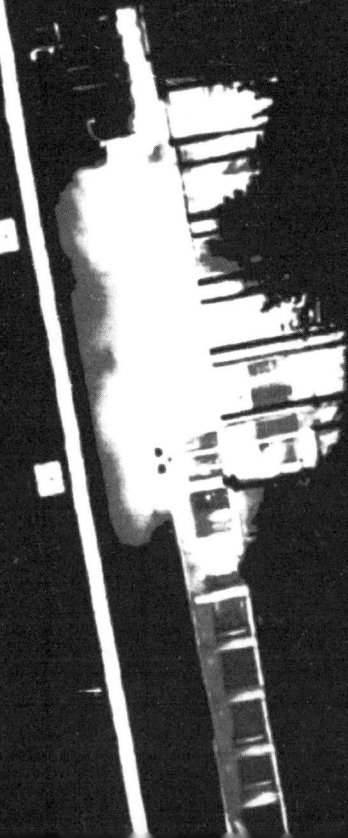

BEAU COMME

DES CENTRES DE RÉTENTION

QUI FLAMBENT

"BEAUTIFUL LIKE DETENTION
CENTERS IN FLAMES"

5

STORMING THE ~~BASTILLE~~ POLICE STATION

Paris, June 12, 1998

Gare du Nord Train Station

The casual observer could be forgiven for thinking that the mob of three hundred people, many of them masked, rapidly streaming out of the Gare du Nord train station on this Friday afternoon is a horde of feared Dutch football hooligans. It is, after all, June 1998 in central Paris, and we are in the midst of the FIFA World Cup. France is the host country, and thousands of Dutch hooligans are expected to arrive by train today for tomorrow's match versus Belgium, to be held only a few kilometers away.

But we are not football hooligans (or at least we aren't here in the capacity of football hooligans today), as the chants of "No border! No nation! Stop deportation!" that ring out through the crowd make abundantly clear. "Come on, come on, speed it up. Jog if you can!" is the exhortation from some in the crowd. As we round the corner, our objective comes into view and the crowd breaks into a sprint. It is not a rival football gang we are speeding toward, but rather a perfectly nondescript office building farther down the street. Indistinguishable from any other building on the block if not for the SNCF sign above the entrance, short for French National Railway Company. The crowd of three hundred has been gathered by the Parisian Collectif Anti-Expulsions, and although the vast majority of us were previously

87

unaware as to the precise target of today's action, the sight of the SNCF building, and finally of two comrades holding the doors and waving us in, has given away the surprise.

The SNCF is essential to the French government's deportation infrastructure, as it is on their trains that North African immigrants, usually of Algerian or Moroccan origin, are transported from Paris to Marseille, prior to their deportation being completed by boat. Since the actions at the point of deportation (airports, train stations, and so forth) were becoming increasingly difficult and less successful, we have decided to expand our strategy, broadening it to include not only attacking the moment of deportation itself, but the entire architecture and infrastructure of deportation as a whole. Not just the French state that carried them out, but the collaborationist corporations and companies that made it possible. Collaborationist. A term loaded with historical significance in France, as *collabos* (short for "collaborationists") was the derogatory term used to refer to those who collaborated with the German occupation and its French puppet regime during World War II. These modern-day collaborationists, instrumental to the process of hunting, documenting, and deporting human beings, weren't much better than their historical counterparts in our mind.

Knowing what we know, which is that today's action is aimed at the infrastructure of deportation and involves illegality and risk of arrest, the sight of the SNCF building, coupled with the two comrades placed strategically at the entrance holding open the doors to the traditional Parisian five-story structure, seems to answer any remaining questions as to what we are doing and where we are heading. For these kinds of mobilizations, the CAE uses a strictly need-to-know basis to mobilize. We make public the issue, a meeting point and time, and the approximate level of risk. Nothing more. The collective and its organizing meetings are after all essentially open and public, so for obvious reasons not even all collective members know more than that. There is an "action group" tasked with planning these actions, and as a protection against both infiltrators and the creation of "action hierarchies" its participants are (at least in theory, although I can no longer remember how much this was the case in practice) routinely alternated and rotated.

It is, of course, somewhat of a compromise on anarchist methods of organization and action, yet one we feel is acceptable in the pursuit of our objectives. If the aim were simply a meandering anarchist riot or militant demonstration, such measures might not be necessary, but clearly if the aim is to attack and disrupt very specific aspects of the state apparatus or its collaborationist machinery, then a certain degree of conspiratorial precaution is inevitable if we are to have any chance of success, though we are at the same time still employing methods of mass militance and in a constellation that allows just about anybody to participate. It's an action form that we would for similar reasons a few years later try to export to the United States with Barricada and friends, not without controversy. But that's a story for another day.

On this day and as far as this story is concerned, a few hundred of us meet up outside the Châtelet metro station in central Paris, promptly enter the subway, and begin the dance of constantly changing subway lines and directions so as to throw off the numerous cop vans that have accompanied us aboveground on the streets, before exiting at Gare du Nord to finally find ourselves in this moment.

We storm in, rushing up the stairs. I'm among the first to reach the fourth floor. A sign outside the door to the left of the stairway reads prominently, POLICE NATIONALE—DICCILEC. The first part is obvious in any language, French National Police. But DICCILEC? The acronym stands for Direction Centrale du Contrôle de l'Immigration et de la lutte contre l'Emploi des Clandestins (Central Department for the Control of Immigration and Against Employment of Illegals). Until 1994, this same agency had been called Police de l'Air et des Frontières (Airspace and Border Police), and as of early 1999 it would come to be the Direction Centrale de la Police aux Frontières (Central Department of Border Policing). A lot of acronyms, initials, and long names for one simple and incredible reality. That hidden inside an SNCF building is a literal police station, and not just any police: the border cops.

The doors are thrown open, and we begin to pour in. At another place and time, I think we can all agree anything could have happened. Not to give away the suspense, but there are no gunshots, no hand-to-hand confrontation with the few plainclothes desk cops inside. The floor is essentially one long, relatively narrow corridor with offices off to both sides. As we advance and begin to fill the space, cops almost immediately rise from their desks and make their way through us wordlessly as they head toward the exit we are entering from. Aside from some mandatory insults, nobody on our side touches them. Interestingly, and rather worryingly, we notice that the staircase we came up through and which they are now descending seems to be the only way up or down through the building and its only exit.

This relatively peaceful, and to the international observer probably more than a little surprising, choreography between the cops and us probably has something to do with a few very specifically French historical traits and present-day realities. First, there is a very strong tradition of students, leftists, anarchists, trade unions, unemployed groups, and immigrant groups using the occupation of offices, churches, public buildings, and so forth as a tool of political struggle that is relatively broadly accepted in society. So while occupying a literal police station was probably a bridge further than usual, even for the generally demonstration-friendly French society, it wasn't wholly out of context.

Secondly, and probably just as importantly if not more, France in 1998 was governed by the newly minted *gauche plurielle* coalition. Having come to power in legislative elections in mid-1997, the "plural left" is a center-left coalition comprising the Socialist Party as majority partner and the French Communist Party and the Greens as its junior partners, with the French Communist Party at the time still attracting a solid 10 percent of the vote.[1] Much like the more recent and, for radicals, probably more well-known case of Syriza in Greece, its electoral success is probably very much a consequence of the social struggles of the preceding years, which culminated in the 1995 general strike. The French right and conservatives are up in arms, trying to convince society that we now live in a light version of a reformed USSR. Because on the one hand there is a cabinet that includes three Communist Party members, and on the other because the gauche plurielle campaigned on, and followed through with, the promise of reducing the labor week from thirty-nine to thirty-five hours with no reduction in salaries.

A reform measure pushed with the explicit acknowledgment that as productivity rose, a reduction in labor hours with no corresponding reduction in pay is a measure toward sharing these gains among all workers. Terrifying for the right and sympathy-worthy for us, and indeed at the CNT and Anarchist Federation we fought for the thirty-five-hour reform, understanding that it was a reform that carried within it the de facto acceptance of an implicitly anticapitalist reality. That by reducing work hours across the board while maintaining salaries, we are accepting that the general increase in productivity is the result of the organization and progress of all of society (in education, technology, infrastructure, and so forth), that all of this progress and wealth is the result of the labor of workers, and that those workers are entitled to a redistribution of that wealth. Capitalists probably wouldn't like what the logical conclusion of that chain of thought is.

This was all well and good. But to we young fanatics and incorrigible extremists, the gauche plurielle coalition represented little more than a much-needed escape valve for the pressures created in society by the contradictions of capitalism, a lighter and less aggressive version of a capitalist society and authoritarian state. A mirage of social progress, a black hole of parliamentary opportunism that would draw in scores of idealistic young people and organizers to put a human face on the same dynamics of exploitation and oppression. A '90s version of what would be the Greek Syriza experience in the 2010s, poised to disarm and weaken radical social movements and betray our hopes and aspirations.

If we were more than suspicious to begin with, just three weeks after assuming power, the gauche plurielle released the Chevènement circular, a government memorandum indicating new conditions for the so-called legalization of sans-papiers immigrants, at a time when the solidarity movement with them was at its peak. While we were advocating for a blanket amnesty, the memo indicated a progressive legalization after an immigrant could demonstrate ten years of uninterrupted presence in France, and in some cases fifteen years. A condemnation of hundreds of thousands to a minimum of a decade of living in fear of deportation, and a gift to capitalist exploiters eager not to lose their base of easily exploitable and vulnerable cheap labor. All this while arrests and deportations continued at a steady clip. So for us, nothing had changed. Hunt the Socialist Party youth out of demonstrations where they dared show up, and continue and intensify the mobilizations and actions against the deportation system in all its forms. Confrontation and conflict.

So while we had as healthy an appetite for conflict with the state as ever, and of course the on-the-ground representatives of its repressive apparatus were the same as always and just as eager to beat *gauchistes* as before (*gauchiste* being the derogatory term used to refer to ultra-leftists in France, which literally means "leftists" but is used even by the Communist Party to refer to anarchists and other "adventurists"), there did seem to be a general directive given somewhere in the halls of the state to "take it easy on the radicals." Being too young to have experienced organizing or militancy during the time of the right-wing government, I lacked the context to understand just how out of the ordinary the political reality in which we were operating was, or how beneficial it was to keeping my criminal record sparkling clean. But apparently, the governing coalition had reached the not-so-surprising conclusion that gassing, beating, arresting, and harshly prosecuting hundreds of young radicals on a regular basis might not be a good look for a government of supposed socialists and communists. Much like the Greek anarchists of the Syriza times in the 2010s who would later describe nostalgia for the smell and burning sensation of tear gas, and to the certainly exasperated outrage of the Andy Ngos and Tucker Carlsons of this world, we were apparently living in a political reality that gave us more space to maneuver than usual.

I'm aware of all this now. But on June 12, 1998, standing inside a police station with a hundred or so comrades as I watched the rapidly amassing police presence on the street and heard the sounds of sirens blaring from what seemed like every imaginable direction, I couldn't help feeling simultaneously exhilarated and very much concerned. Joy at what at least in my mind seemed like a momentous act of rebellion and disobedience, and a gnawing fear that the immediate future would involve a lot of police violence, while the midterm future would be rich in court visits.

Inside the Police Station

"Well, this is a new one" is the best political and practical analysis of the situation I'm able to provide. Sophie, Mary, Alan, and I are all leaning out of the fourth-floor window, staring at the scene on the street below. Sophie matter-of-factly states, "It's definitely not a scenario I have ever imagined." Fair enough, although when I think of it, I have imagined it. Only it was in the course of momentous social upheaval, on the eve of revolution. Then, maybe, just maybe, storming the goddamned police station would be a logical part of the choreography of events. As it currently stood, as the work of three hundred ultra-leftists on a sunny World Cup–crazed Friday afternoon in Paris, not so much.

On the street below us, what can only be described as a small army of cops is gathering in front of our eyes. And we can still hear sirens blaring from … honestly, they seem to be coming from every direction. Aside from the growing horde of cops, there are also a couple hundred comrades, which is great, but really not as great as it sounds. As it turns out, as those of us to the front were entering the building, the cops on our tail reached it as well and promptly took advantage of the ensuing bottleneck at the entrance to prevent half of us from even entering. Some others, having just barely made it inside, quickly assessed the situation and were still able to exit before the cops solidified their lines. As I will learn the next day from the article in the right-wing newspaper *Le Parisien*, there are no more than sixty-four of us in the police station by this point.[2]

"So does this count as a modern-day storming of the Bastille?" I half jokingly ask. I'm definitely young, pretty fanatical, and not too familiarized with fear. I am also, however, not stupid, or at least not stupid enough to not realize that we seem to be in one hell of a dilemma. I'm worried and anxious, which usually motivates my bad jokes and sarcastic comments.

Though we are all underage, we have plenty of experience getting out of trouble without significant injury or so much as an arrest. Yet this situation is new and concerning. Alan helpfully points it out by blurting out his wholly unsolicited opinion that "we're all going to jail."

"Maybe," I say, "but we will forever be those who stormed the police station to attack the deportation system. When we win, when society looks back at deportations and borders the same way it now thinks of slavery and serfdom, statues will be built."

Sophie looks at me, annoyed. "I never thought I'd say this to anybody, but you really need to read less. It's making you crazy. In two days, nobody will remember this except for the prosecutors and judges handling our trials."

"Okay, maybe. But we'll definitely have one hell of a story to tell when we're older."

At least I was right on that count.

La Java des Bons Enfants

I can't remember exactly how this played out. There definitely wasn't the monumental violence on behalf of the cops that we feared, because, well, I would remember that. The riot squad, or some sort of SWAT team, never stormed the place with batons or guns or whatever blazing, as we at one point feared. We weren't drowned in tear gas as we cowered behind desks while waiting for cops to invade and beat us senseless. There was none of that. Instead, we somehow managed to negotiate a collective exit, descending the stairs with arms linked in lines of five or six, as many as the narrow stairway would permit side by side. The relatively dark and windowless stairway prompted some cops to try to take advantage of the situation to shove us down the stairs, which in turn led to some confrontations.

As we exited the building, we found a police bus waiting to transport us to our next destination, with thick lines of CRS riot cops on both sides to keep us in. We refused to enter the bus, and once everybody was outside between the cordons, we made a last-ditch attempt to avoid arrest by trying to break out of the kettle, as the comrades who had never made it in clashed with more cops across the street. Our breakout attempts failed; there were simply way too few of us and way too many cops, and we promptly found ourselves shoved onto the cop bus. And then we rode across the city, probably on our way to the next stop on our impromptu tour of Parisian police stations. Despite our precarious situation and somewhat uncertain immediate future, spirits were surprisingly high, and the mood became almost rebelliously festive as the first verses of the classic anarchist song "La Java des Bons Enfants" began to echo through the bus. For years misattributed as having been written and composed by the infamous Bonnot Gang's Raymond Callemin, better known as Raymond la Science, as early as the 1910s, this particular timeless hit anarcho-folk song was actually composed in 1973 by none other than Situationist Guy Debord.[3] Most often belted out loudly and wildly out of tune at gatherings of francophone anarchists once the wine begins flowing, the song celebrates the bombing of the Rue des Bons Enfants police station by a young anarchist and propagandist by the name of Émile Henry on November 8, 1892, which claimed the lives of five police officers, and goes something like this:

Dans la rue des Bons Enfants	In the Rue des Bons Enfants
On vend tout au plus offrant	Everything is sold to the highest
Y'avait un commissariat	bidder
Et maintenant il n'est plus là	There used to be a police station
	And now it's no longer there
Une explosion fantastique	A fantastic explosion
N'en a pas laissé une brique	Left not one single brick standing
On crut qu'c'était Fantômas	We thought it was a ghost
Mais c'était la lutte des classes	But it was the class struggle

Epilogue: Third Division of the Judicial Police, Second Police Station of the Day

"Last name?" the cop behind the desk inquires without so much as looking up in my direction.

"Rothaus."

He begins rifling through an impressively thick stack of IDs. He goes through the entire stack, stops, takes a brief pause, and begins going through the stack again. He goes through all the IDs one more time, takes another annoyed pause, and finally announces to me that "there's no Rothaus here." I'm carefully trying to weigh my words and measure my facial expressions as I wonder how to argue my case that I am, despite the lack of government-issued evidence in his hands, very much here. Combative as I may be, it's nighttime, its been a pretty long day, and I am after all now inside the second police station of the day. Unlike the first one, I was brought to this one very much against my will. Not only that, I am on the verge of what is to me a monumental personal victory within the context of this broader, somewhat less-than-stellar turn of events: I, a minor, am about to be released from the police station with my parents neither picking me up nor having been successfully notified of my presence there, something that is actually the law in France.

It seems my well-rehearsed and purposefully convoluted stories as to where they might be, why nobody can come get me, the series of guaranteed dead-end phone numbers I have provided, and my stoic resistance to the "Well, then we're just going to have to keep you here until they appear" bluffs is, against all odds, about to pay off.

So I'm thinking I might want to be a little less argumentative and witty than usual. "I gave it to one of your colleagues when we got off the bus. Mine was a passport." It seems like a fine response, fact-based and nonconfrontational.

For the first time, he bothers to gaze up in my direction. "Would you like us to keep you here until we can find it?" While first storming a police station and then later volunteering to continue being held at another would certainly make for an epic anecdote, I don't need much convincing. Continuing to conceal my contempt for this bureaucrat of repression as best I can, I nod politely and turn to make my way out. I have seen enough of police stations for one day, and without another word I am out of there, minus my passport, which will never be recovered.

Once outside, I run into Stephane, an acquaintance from the CNT who is doing legal support. I ask him if he's seen Alan. "Alan wasn't released," he says. "Apparently they're charging him and a few others. They claim Alan tried to steal one of those orange police armbands that the plainclothes use."

"Oh, shit. Yeah, it seemed they were looking at him a bit much during the lineup, but I thought it was just because he looks more punk rock than the others." We were indeed lined up in the police station's courtyard on arrival, while a few important-looking cop types stared at us and conferred among each other. As I will later learn, it was to decide who to press charges against, for the stolen police armband as well as for the "five police officers who sustained minor injuries during the occupation of the DICCILEC offices (ex–air and railway police)," as *Le Parisien* reported the following day.[4] Apparently, while blanket charges were too much for the "socialist" government, individual troublemakers were still acceptable targets.

As I'm leaving, Stephane turns to me and says, "You know you geniuses went into the wrong place, right? Whoever planned this action is an idiot."

I look at him quizzically. I know Stephane, who is solidly in his thirties, and some of the more traditional anarcho-syndicalists in the CNT aren't big fans of the CAE and its very autonomist and "action-oriented" forms of struggle, but this seems not only a little harsh but poor timing as well for a critique. I am, after all, literally just getting out of jail. "What are you talking about? There was nothing there except that SNCF building."

"Right, but you all went to the wrong floor. The fourth floor, which you crazies invaded, is the cop shop. The fifth floor, which you never made it to, is a space the SNCF has ceded to the cops to use as a holding area for sans-papiers. That was the target, and the organizers really messed up not having somebody signal that clearly once inside the building."

That explains the odd-sounding press release, clearly written prior to the action, which I will discover online once I get home and which will be reprinted a few days later in the newest edition of the Anarchist Federation's weekly *Le Monde Libertaire*:

> As part of the countrywide day of action against deportations, we take responsibility for the occupation of the Gare du Nord holding area, this June 12, 1998.

Created to imprison foreigners denied entrance to the French territory, this veritable rights-free space is a further obstacle to the free movement of individuals. Asylum seekers, sometimes gravely threatened in their country of origin, can be held here for a period of up to twenty days before finally, in most cases, being deported back to their country of origin.

Situated as a further piece of the security arsenal, this holding area participates fully in the program of the democratic state to instill a climate of terror among their foreign populations:

—The closure of borders

—Refusal of right of residence

—Deportations

We likewise denounce the active collaboration of the SNCF with the institutionalized xenophobia carried out by the French state. The SNCF lends its trains to deport sans-papiers, as well as its properties to host these sinister holding areas.

At the airports, the train stations, and the ports, resistance has been organizing. Thanks to the cooperation of passengers, some deportations by airplane have been successfully prevented. Workers of transport companies complicit in these operations should likewise be able to refuse this collaboration. We must extend our solidarity to all sans-papiers—those whose regularization has been rejected, the asylum seekers, the victims of double jeopardy, and all others—by opposing, whenever possible, the police procedures and authoritarian maneuvers of this government.

—Immediate stop to deportations

—Immediate closure of detention camps

—Right of return for deported individuals

—Regularization of all sans-papiers via a ten-year residence card

—Abrogation of all racist laws, including the 1945 ordinance

—Abolition of double jeopardy

—Freedom of movement and residence

Collectif Anti-Expulsions—Ile de France[5]

Excited as I am about having stormed a police station, even if apparently inadvertently, the gears begin slowly turning in my head.

Stephane says it clearly before it finishes fully dawning on me. "You're all very lucky all the Rambo cops were probably busy with the hooligans coming into the city for the football matches and there was just a skeleton crew of desk types and pencil pushers, or that could have gotten very dangerous very quickly. I'm amazed, honestly, they aren't even charging all of you. Probably because you didn't trash the place."

We indeed neglected to trash the place. To this day, I don't really understand how or why. Maybe because the precarious nature of our situation dawned on us quickly after having entered the place. Either way, while beneficial that particular day, it was a courtesy that wouldn't be extended during our future incursions. Three people were eventually charged for their participation in the day's events, with charges including "outrage, rebellion, and destruction of a police vehicle." Almost a year later, one was sentenced to a relatively stiff, for French standards, ten-month prison sentence.[6] Apparently even under the government of the "plural left," a police station is still a police station and this was possibly a little much.

Oh well, one more reason to fight all governments, no matter how socially conscious they pretend to be. And at least I was right about getting a great anecdote out of our little adventure.

Stephane's last words to me that night are something in the vein of "I even heard you idiots singing 'La Java des Bons Enfants' when the bus arrived. Were you trying to get beaten up at the police station?" While I don't much appreciate the lecturing tone, I do have to admit that while I reveled in the rebellious rush at the moment, it did in fact cross my mind that maybe singing a song celebrating cops exploding in a police station probably wasn't the greatest way to enter one as a prisoner. "You're like a bunch of modern-day, less dangerous but much more stupid Émile Henrys."

Clearly, it is meant as an insult, and I'm also well aware that there is no comparison between a twenty-year-old Émile Henry risking his life, and eventually facing the guillotine, in the course of the turn-of-the-nineteenth-century social war between the bourgeoisie and "propaganda by the deed" anarchists and our possibly daring but still relatively tame occupation of a police station in modern-day left-of-center Paris.[7] But my keen, or overactive (depending on how you want to look at it), sense of history can't help being immediately drawn to two parallels. First, the obvious and constant tension within anarchism, in

France as well as elsewhere, between the more established and organ-izational strands of anarchism and those of more insurrectionary and action-oriented ones. There were, back then as today, those who thought both sides were necessary, complementing and strengthening anarchism as a whole, as I always did, which explained my active and simultaneous participation in the CNT as well as in groupings like the CAE. But there were those, again on both sides, who believed that the actions of the others were detrimental to the advancement of the anar-chist idea, or sometimes that they were even contrary to it.

The second parallel is much less important, but it is the one that captures my imagination as I walk home on this night. It's a little-known fact, but much like our, as it turns out, accidental occupation of the police station, Émile Henry's 1892 bombing of a police station was just as much accidental. The original target was the offices of the Carmaux Mining Company, a company that was at that time engaged in a labor struggle with its workers. Henry intended his bomb to go off there, as he defiantly proclaimed in the closing statement of his trial, "to demonstrate to the miners that there is but one category of man, the anarchists, who feel sincerely their suffering and who are ready to avenge them."[8] The bomb only exploded at the police station because it was discovered at the Carmaux offices and subsequently transported to the Rue des Bons Enfants station. Had he been successful in his original intent, it might have very well been forgotten soon after as just another episode in the dynamite- and blood-fueled era of the class struggle between anarchists and bosses. But from his accident, as from ours, came not only a much more memorable story, but a direct attack against the state and its repressive arm.

I can't help thinking about times past, in this very city and on these same streets, when without regard to the possible consequences or necessary sacrifices, anarchists were merciless with the enemies of freedom and human dignity. As Henry said in the conclusion of his state-ment before the court, on April 27, 1894, and less than a month before being guillotined, "You have hung in Chicago, decapitated in Germany, tortured in Jerez, shot in Barcelona, and guillotined in Montbrison and Paris. But what you can never destroy is anarchy. Its roots are too deep; it is born at the heart of a rotting society as it collapses, it is a violent reaction to the established order. It represents the aspirations that have arrived to beat back the current order. It is everywhere and therefore it is impossible to capture. It will do away with you." His last words before the court were addressed to his comrades. "Comrades, courage! And long live anarchy!"

It was obviously different times, and Émile Henry, who justified indiscriminate bombings with the idea that "there are no innocents among the bourgeoisie," was certainly not an example to blindly follow, but I can't help wondering to what extent we modern exponents of this movement were doing it justice with our efforts—to the sacrifices of those who came before us and to the ideas we carry forward. But as I stroll home, I find myself humming the remaining verses of the timeless anarchist song:

Voilà bien ce qu'il fallait
Pour faire la guerre au palais
Sache que ta meilleure amie,
Prolétaire, c'est la chimie

Here is what was needed
To bring the war to the palaces
Know well that your best friend,
Proletarian, is chemistry!

Les socialos n'ont rien fait
Pour abréger les forfaits
De l'infamie capitaliste
Mais heureusement vint
l'anarchiste

The socialists have done nothing
To correct the failings
Of capitalist infamy
But luckily arrives the anarchist

Il n'a pas de préjugés
Les curés seront mangés
Plus d'patrie, plus d'colonies
Et tout pouvoir, il le nie

He has no prejudices
The priests will be devoured
No more countries, no more
colonies
And all power, he rejects it

. . .

. . .

Dans la rue des Bons Enfants
Viande à vendre au plus offrant
L'avenir radieux prend place
Et le vieux monde est à la casse!

In the Rue des Bons Enfants
Meat is sold to the highest bidder
The radiant future takes its place
And the old world lies in ruins

6

THIS HOTEL IS A DETENTION CENTER

From Paris, January 1999, to Strasbourg, April 2009

"Release Our Comrades": Central Paris, Some Ibis Hotel, January 23, 1999, Nighttime

"Get on the fucking phone and call your boss. Now. Tell him this isn't going to stop until our comrades are freed without charges." The masked person speaking is calm and collected, but forceful. He is also flanked by another ten or so people. In the background, another eighty are streaming through the doors, knocking over furniture and helping themselves to the buffet.

The friendly-looking twentysomething woman behind the hotel check-in counter stutters and has visible difficulty speaking, until she finally whimpers, "I have no idea what you're talking about, please."

She looks understandably terrified, and it's unfortunate. She is, after all, just a worker at this central Paris Ibis hotel and most likely has not the slightest idea why a mob of people is ransacking the hotel lobby, nor who these comrades are who should be freed, nor why a huge graffito is currently being spray-painted on the other side of the glass behind her. It's unfortunate, and obviously nobody intends to do her any harm. But if she didn't know before, she'll be aware after today: Her employer is collaborating with the French government to deport immigrants, and is profiting from the deportation system.

FIRE AND FLAMES
FOR THE DEPORTATION MACHINE

We aren't here to win friends or make public relations; if anything, that's what the demonstrations are for. We're here to stop deportations or, failing that, make them as difficult and costly as possible. And the corporation that owns this hotel, Accor, is a central player in the French state's deportation infrastructure. The Accor corporation owns several hundred hotels throughout France, divided into various brands across a few different price categories. It's this hotel infrastructure that they have chosen to place at the service of the French state, renting out rooms at airport hotels for the state to hold immigrants until the moment of their deportation by airplane.

The particular Ibis hotel that is currently being ransacked on this dramatically rainy Parisian night is actually the third to be targeted in the last couple of hours. At each one, the procedure is more or less the same. Storm in, some tag the outside while others ransack the lobby. The only variable, really, is how many frightened tourists scatter away as they see us, and just how flustered or frightened the person at reception is when encountering us. At each stop, the same request is made: "Free our comrades, don't press charges, stop renting rooms to the government. Please understand, this won't stop until you stop."

And then we disappear into the night as suddenly as we appeared.

Just as I'm beginning to worry that there are less and less of us after each hit, that discipline may be lagging, and that sooner rather than later cops will begin to catch up with us, we get the word: "The seven arrested comrades have been released. No charges." As we withdraw from the hotel and disperse, I take a moment to observe the trail of destroyed furniture and flyers against deportation strewn everywhere across the lobby. Behind us, the literal writing on the wall (or glass, to be perfectly literal) is eloquent in its simplicity: ACCOR COLLABO. STOP AUX EXPULSIONS. "Accor Collabo, Stop Deportations!" It's the end of a long day that began some ten hours earlier, at the Roissy Ibis Airport Hotel.

Charles de Gaulle Airport Ibis Hotel, January 23, 1999, Noon

The Ibis hotel at Paris's Charles de Gaulle airport is about what one would expect for a two- or three-star airport satellite hotel. Drab and wholly unspectacular office-building-like architecture on the outside, sullen-looking businessmen and perfectly stereotypical stressed-out families with 2.3 children running around the lobby on the inside. If anything, the lobby is its one and only immediately noticeable

Graffito outside a Parisian Ibis hotel: "Accor collaborates to deport the sans-papiers. Let's attack Ibis, Mercure... —CAE."

particularity. It's a ground-floor-only structure with a flat roof that connects the significantly taller buildings where the actual rooms are located.

What makes this particular hotel unique, and the reason two hundred people are about to storm through the main doors, access one of the towers where the rooms are located (with the help of a comrade who previously entered incognito and holds open a strategically important access door), head up a flight of stairs, smash a window, and take command of the rooftop area above the lobby, is inside one of the room towers. The one on the other side of the lobby our two hundred protagonists are about to enter.

It's a testament to the mundane, banal, and, I would venture to say, outright evil nature of human suffering and oppression in consumer capitalist society. In this hotel, side by side with the hustle and bustle of the businessmen and the joy of the vacationing white European families, is the despair of other humans who are being held here against their will.

An entire wing of this Ibis hotel is literally a prison, where sans-papiers are held before their definitive deportation on an Air

Afrique or Air France plane. A prison made possible by the collaboration of the Accor hotel group with the French state's deportation machinery.

As we pour out onto the first-floor rooftop through the busted-out window, a few comrades unfurl a large banner reading "Stop Deportations!" and hang it over the front of the building, covering the Ibis logo, to the loud cheers of the few dozen supporters who remain outside the building. Sophie and I make it outside onto the roof, where we are immediately struck by something. The prison, or "temporary detention center" as the supposedly human-rights-conscious socialist government prefers to refer to it, is apparently on the same floor, just opposite from where we entered onto the roof! We can make out shadows through the windows of people throwing peace signs and can see them banging against the windows.

Our reaction is visceral and instinctive. Fifteen or twenty of us break into a run toward the other side. We've barely reached the windows, and the first kicks and elbows are flying against them, when we start hearing people yelling, "Stop! Stop!" It's a couple of the people from the action group who planned this action. "I know what you're thinking, but it probably won't work, and most importantly, the immigrants themselves asked us not to do it." What we are thinking is, obviously … prison break! There are still no cops here to speak of, so what would it take to pull the plug on the largely symbolic action and just flee here while giving cover to whoever wanted to try to use it to escape? And if they were to succeed, then the action would be an all-around success anyway. Accor publicly shamed, their detention center breached, and some individuals given another concrete chance at freedom.

The CAE was explicit that our support for the sans-papiers was intrinsically linked to our anarchist principles, that our interests were linked to theirs in our desire for the abolition of states and borders, for the end of capitalist labor exploitation, and for the freedom and autonomy of human beings. At the same time, we worked hand in hand with the collectives of sans-papiers that were largely autonomous from party or NGO structures and who were most welcoming of solidarity by way of direct action. In this case, the action group was in touch with a collective who was in contact with these detainees. "We explained to them that the chances of a successful escape are low." This is objectively sadly true, since we are outside the city and at an airport of all places. Only one train in, a few buses, and a highway, rendering it almost impossible to escape as a mob. "They know if they try to escape and fail, they'll be subjected to penalties, it will allow for a legal extension of their detention time, and it'll possibly earn them a ban from the French territory. They said they'd rather take their chances with the passengers on the plane."

I, uncharacteristically, take a deep breath and quietly process my feelings of anger, frustration, and sadness. The point isn't lost on me, and there's a good chance they're not wrong. He was referring to the strategy of appealing to passenger solidarity in order to get deportees deplaned, a tool we have often used successfully to prevent deportations and run out the clock on a person's detainment.[1] But it doesn't make it feel any less counterintuitive or frustrating.

Other comrades, though, are much less introverted with their thoughts, and a bit of a shouting match breaks out. "What the fuck is this shit? This isn't supposed to be a lobby group! We're standing in front of the windows of a fucking unguarded prison and you're telling me I shouldn't touch them because some people I don't know and who I've never spoken to are against it? What kind of process is that? You think this is autonomy?! If I wanted to be told what to do without being asked my opinion about it, I would have joined a party or become a cop."

The comrade speaking, Alice, is one of the more classic *totos* among us, "totos" being the either loving or derogatory francophone shorthand for anarchist autonomes—depending on the context and tone used to say it. She and the affinity group around her are, to put it mildly, no fans of delegation or of tempering messaging or tactics to account for optics or appease others, regardless of who they may be. Her last words are, "If they don't want to escape through the open windows, nobody is going to force them, but I don't see what that has to do with me breaking them or not," before turning around furiously and walking away. The tension between collective members subsides for the rest of the day, but it's very much indicative of a growing strategic rift inside the group, a rift that would only deepen a few months later in the aftermath of the CAE's next mass action.

The middle-aged man leaning through the shattered window and trying to interact with us is a walking, living stereotype of a French detective. Flannel shirt over a notable beer belly, light-brown suede jacket, balding, and a prominent mustache. He seems to be missing the

CAE demonstrators occupy the roof of the airport Ibis hotel. A plainclothes police officer can be seen at the window.

obligatory aviator glasses to complete the look, but I guess sunglasses might be a bit much since it is after all past 4 p.m. on a cloudy and rainy afternoon in the dead of Parisian winter, or, in other words, basically nighttime.

Which is also probably why, even more so than his unconvincing promises that there will be no arrests if we leave soon and peacefully, we're about ready to make our exit. We've been on this roof for a few hours now, and once the initial excitement of being out here (and yelling at each other!) wore off, we've basically spent the last few hours milling around and chatting with each other in the freezing cold. The monotony has only really been breached, mercifully, when some comrades in solidarity arrived with drinks and sandwiches, which they threw up to us. There is no further practical or symbolic objective to be attained by our continued presence here, unless the objective is to die as wet and frozen martyrs in the rain on this windswept roof.

The only way off the roof is through the same broken window we used to get onto it in the first place. It's barely wide enough to fit one person at a time, so any kind of concerted mass attempt to get out of here is completely off the table. Worryingly, as we peer our heads through the window to look down the hotel corridor, we see that there is quite the welcoming committee waiting for us. The hall is packed on both sides with a veritable gauntlet of riot cops. We confer among each other, determined not to let them split us up so as to guard against targeted arrests. It's quickly decided that we'll all enter the corridor through the window and begin massing there, in order to then head down the corridor and stairs as a compact group.

As the first brave souls climb through the window and into the cop-riddled hallway, it becomes clear that the cops have other plans. They begin to push and shove people, trying to muscle them down the hallway and toward the stairs. Immediately, baton swings are met with kicks and blows. We hesitate, unsure if it's best to use the threat of our continued presence here as leverage (after all, I have no idea to this day how they would have evacuated us from there if we had decided to stay indefinitely) or if we should speed up and get as many people into the hallway as possible to defend our comrades.

Somebody yells at the mustached detective that either he gets the other cops to back off and allow everybody into the hallway or we'll just stay on the roof. Incredibly, the move works and the cops retreat partially, allowing for all of us to get into the hallway, together and untouched. We begin heading down the stairway, again flanked by riot cops. As most of us reach the ground floor and begin exiting the building, I hear shouting and almost immediately feel a football-stadium-like human avalanche of people pushing from behind. We pour out into the street in a disorganized blob.

"They started hitting us with batons from behind and arresting people in the middle of the stairs." It's Sophie, who for some reason was one of the last people off the roof.

In the middle of nowhere, and with cops everywhere, it's clear there is nothing more to be done here. As we hastily head to the train station, somebody proposes the usual, that "we should go to the police station until they release them." A woman speaks up. It's Alice, the toto from the argument at the beginning of the occupation. "Yes, we could go to the police station and beg for their release. Or, we could pay some of the other Ibises in the city a visit until they beg us to stop, and force their release."

With that, the remaining hundred of us head into the city under cover of night, minutes later erupting into the first of the evening's three

Ibis hotels, where a masked crew of ten corners a frightened-looking concierge. "Get on the fucking phone and call your boss. Now. Tell him this isn't going to stop until our comrades are freed without charges."

Epilogue: Strasbourg, April 4, 2009

We're in the heat of battle in the midst of the annual NATO summit. A black bloc of about a thousand, mainly people from Germany and France, has fought intense battles with the cops all day. The bloc has just fought the cops back off a railway overpass, and we now have an endless arsenal of rocks from the tracks at our disposal. The clearly overwhelmed cops retreat under the ferocity of the attack. Fifteen thousand robocops have been assigned to protect this summit, with the goal of rendering militant resistance impossible and futile. For the second day in a row, they are failing spectacularly.

As we advance into the Port du Rhin neighborhood, a pharmacy is looted by both revolutionaries and local residents together, before being set aflame. Just the day before, local immigrant youths were guiding black bloc activists around the neighborhood as they erected barricades, fought running battles with the riot cops, and attacked a military jeep, prompting one of the soldiers inside to draw his handgun. In turn, black blockers aided local youths in prying open the gates of a police storage space where seized scooters were stored, returning them to the community.

We have now arrived at the border with Germany, separated by only a river and a bridge. German riot cops line the other end, and the bloc is content with building barricades to prevent them from crossing while lobbing the occasional stone in their direction. I walk back from the front line for a well-deserved break and take in the scene behind us.

The first thing I notice is the now-abandoned border police station, completely ablaze. Schengen may have rendered this border mainly obsolete, but the symbolic value of a burning border crossing is enormous.

Not far behind the border crossing, flames are starting to emerge from a five-story building. Just a few minutes earlier, a solid bloc of about one hundred black-clad militants ransacked the lobby and used its insides to erect flaming barricades in the street. It's a sign that our movement does not easily forget, and a reminder that collaboration does not pay. Strasbourg's Ibis hotel is engulfed in flames.

If the Ibis hotel had to burn, it was not as an act of senseless destruction, but a concrete protest against the Accor brand (which owns, amongst others, the Ibis chain) and its complicity in the deportation of "illegal" immigrants through the rental of its rooms to the State as a last "housing" location for immigrants before their deportation.
—Antifascist Left International, "Riots, Destruction, and Senseless Violence", Göttingen, Germany, April 2009

offensiv
militant
erfolgreich

Strasbourg
„über Randale, Zerstörung und sinnlose Gewalt"

Cover of the Antifascistische Linke International's post–NATO summit text reading: "Offensive. Militant. Successful." (Note: "Offensive" is used in the attacking sense.) "On riots, destruction, and senseless violence."

Fight Fortress Europe!

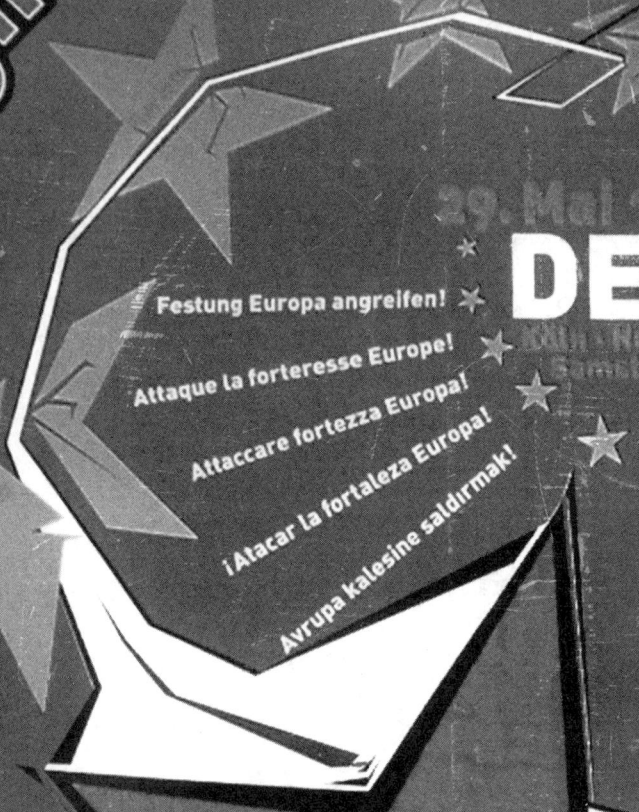

29. Mai 1999
DEMO
Köln · Hohenzollernring
Samstag · 13 Uhr

Festung Europa angreifen!

Attaque la forteresse Europe!

Attaccare fortezza Europa!

¡Atacar la fortaleza Europa!

Avrupa kalesine saldırmak!

Join the antifascist block!

antifaschistischer Kampf
ist international!

7

EVERY AIRPORT AND TRAIN STATION A BATTLEFIELD

At the Dawn of the Antiglobalization Movement

The "Socialist" State Closes Its Borders: France, March 1999
In its May 1999 issue, the French political and cultural journal *Vacarme*
published this detailed account of the thwarted efforts by Italians
and immigrants to reach the European demonstration for freedom
of movement that spring, the title of which translates to "We Are All
Underground." The account begins:

> On March 26 and 27, responding to a call by the social centers
> adhering to the Milan Charter, the Ya Basta! association, and the
> Movimiento delle Tute Bianche–Gli Invisibili [Movement of the
> White Overalls–The Invisibles], 3,500 Italians accompanied by
> 150 Albanian, Kosovar, North African, Ukrainian, and Moldovan
> undocumented immigrants tried to reach Paris to participate in
> the European demonstration for freedom of movement and the
> regularization of undocumented immigrants. To prevent them
> from doing so, the French government has not hesitated to close
> its borders....

> *Paris, Week of March 21*
> The arrival of the Italians was eagerly awaited. The French demon-
> strators were excited about the reinforcements and admiring of

their reputation: At a time when the sans-papiers movement is no longer able to bring out more than a few thousand people in the best of cases, the Italians provide a guarantee of numbers, the prestige of their exiled or imprisoned theorists, and precious experience in case of confrontations with the police. The police are well aware of this, of these "autonomes" who have turned the armed struggle of the 1970s into a creative and broadly established movement, but the police are focused only on their past. By the admission of their own minister of the interior, they have been preparing for a week prior to their arrival. Between the hopes of the demonstrators and the fears of the police, between their categories and ours, the press will hesitate until the end: Are these "left-wing extremist militants" or "pacifist organizations"? Are they defenders of the sans-papiers or smugglers of illegal immigrants?[1]

Unaware of the nuances of Italian inter-autonome or post-autonome politics, we were indeed deathly excited about the imminent arrival of the Tute Bianche reinforcements from Italy for the European-wide demonstration for freedom of movement, to be held in Paris that coming weekend.

We had been captivated by the images from a few months earlier, October 24, 1998, to be precise, during a Europe-wide day of action in protest of the death of Semira Adamu, a young Nigerian woman killed by Belgian police. While we in Paris were busy getting kettled outside the Belgian embassy and I was perfecting my wildly successful "But officer, I am but an innocent young tourist here to gaze in awe at the beauty of the Arc de Triomphe, why on earth would you hold me here together with these frightening criminals?" routine, the White Overalls were holding a march against an immigrant detention center in Trieste. Keir Milburn describes the scene:

> The white overalls on the front lines had crash helmets and home-made Plexiglas shields. To the amazement of the police the shield-bearers started to group together, a line of chalky white demonstrators overlapping their shields, the rows behind raising their shields above their heads as protection from rubber bullets and tear gas. The demonstration was attacked by police and customs officers, but the front line was able to resist and

advance to the fences of the detention camp. There, after hours of alternate clashes and negotiations, a number of people were allowed to enter the camp for the first time and document the inhuman conditions of the prisoners. A month later on the 15th of November the camp was closed.[2]

This was all that we knew and cared about. Lost on us, partly due to the language barrier and partly because international communication wasn't quite as fluid back then as it is now, thanks to the internet, was the process by which the White Overalls phenomenon had come into being: an attempt by some sectors, in the tradition of the autonomist and far-left armed and militant struggles of the 1970s and the social centers of the '80s and '90s, to break what they saw as the "losing loop of 'conflict—repression—struggle against repression.' The aim was to enter a different scene; where social conflict can bring positiveness and start a new loop of 'conflict—projects—broadening of the sphere of rights.'"[3]

In the pursuit of this objective, they adopted a set of positions, compromises, and new forms of struggle, mainly agreed on by a segment of the social centers movement in the "Milan Charter," which were deeply controversial within the Italian movement and led to a serious and often polemic split. The position that the nature of labor relations had changed, from the *tute blu* (Italian equivalent of "blue-collar") lifetime factory employment at which the youth of the '70s had revolted against, to a labor landscape of precarity and unemployment that rendered many youth segments of society, and other oppressed and marginalized populations of the world, invisible and expendable—and thus the adoption of the white overalls and the Tute Bianche name—was one we could share. But the positions and compromises included, for example, attempts at developing working relationships with mainstream media and at times reaching out to established political parties and elected politicians—for many an unforgivable break with the practice of political autonomy and the objective of forcing concessions from the state and capital not through any kind of collaboration or cooperation but through the construction of dual power. Further, on the tactical front, we had assumed that the White Overalls had avoided offensive tactics in their recent actions as a simple matter of strategy, when in fact many of them held a pseudo-pacifist line of "no violence is initiated by us," both as a matter of political principle as well as a tool to be better represented in media coverage.

These political and tactical differences not only split the movement inside Italy but would have serious practical and on-the-ground consequences in the heat of the antiglobalization movement's high-water mark of summer 2001, some of which we would vividly experience firsthand in both Gothenburg and Genoa.

But for now, as far as we were concerned, we had big things planned and the cavalry was coming—assuming they could get past the French socialist deportation state's border blockade.

The *Vacarme* account continues:

Paris, Place Beauvau, March 26, 1999, 4 p.m.

Even before their departure, the French police announced their intentions: the train [transporting the Italian demonstrators] will be stopped at Menton, its passengers subjected to identity controls.... Greens and Communists, signatories of the March 27 demonstration, call "for the legalization of the sans-papiers" and "for freedom of movement" and would like, at least for a weekend, to not be ashamed of their government. A delegation of parliamentarians from both parties obtains a meeting with [Minister of the Interior] Jean-Pierre Chevènement. The Minister promises "calm and cordial" identity controls.... He also states that the non-EU foreigners among the demonstrators ... will be refused entry at the border, not to be arrested by the French police, but rather entrusted to Italian customs. The representatives object, citing the Schengen Agreement and the freedom of movement within Europe. They are mistaken. If the Minister of the Interior can with ease entrust these sans-papiers to his colleagues from across the Alps it is precisely because Schengen is also, and above all, a transnational policing accord. The representatives become angry ... and threaten to take a hard stance should the train be blocked. Chevènement doesn't give a damn, but he has saved face.... *L'Humanité* [daily newspaper of the Communist Party] congratulates itself: "The Communist Party of France intervened with the Prime Minister to ensure that the freedom of movement of the demonstrators is guaranteed."

Vintimille/Vintimiglia [French/Italian Border], March 26, 1999, 6 p.m.

The tension mounts. The failure of this attempt at internal concili-
ation among the French left renders the conflict at the same time
more local and less national. The dispute is now carried out on the
ground: the ground being in this case a train station at the French
border. Italy has at least allowed its trains to run, requisitioned
as they were by demonstrators advocating for free public transportation. The railway workers' general strike that paralyzed Italy
that day didn't even stop them—the COMU (a grassroots railway
workers' union) allowed "in a completely exceptional manner,
for the essential services necessary to be rendered so that the
demonstration in Paris is a success." France, on the other hand,
decides to make use of its railway apparatus differently, by refusing to equip its trains with motors. Reversal of roles, reversal of
techniques: this time, it's neither railway workers on strike, nor
enraged farmers, nor antideportation activists who are blocking
the tracks, but rather the SNCF itself. A kind of state lockout in
which a state-owned enterprise, instrumental actor in the deportation of sans-papiers, takes on the role of zealous guardian of
order at the border....

Saint-Ludovic [French/Italian Border Crossing], March 26, 1999, 11 p.m.

Around 9 p.m., the demonstrators decide to cross the border
regardless, by their own means, walking through the town of
Saint-Ludovic to take the train to Paris at Menton that they
had previously been refused at Vintimille. The plan is for those
with papers to refuse to show them to the border police, to the
customs officers, or to the CRS waiting for them at Menton: "We
refuse any discrimination between demonstrators, or the denial
of entry of the Albanians, Kosovars, North Africans, Ukrainians,
and Moldovans among us by the French authorities" (statement by Ya Basta!, March 26, 1999, 11:30 p.m.). The endeavor is
somewhat epic, and so is the weather: torrential rain. Jean-Pierre
Chevènement completes the dramatic scene: At Saint-Ludovic,
spread out over eighty meters, ten cordons of CRS block the road,

supported by members of the French Foreign Legion. Even journalists are not allowed to pass. France has closed its borders.[4]

Paris, Place d'Italie, March 27, 1999

We're at the starting point of the demo and word is spreading fast
among the anarchist bloc. Anger and frustration are very much palpable.
The Italians have not made it over the border. "You think we're still
doing this?" Sophie asks me, concern in her voice, although I can't
quite make out if the concern is due to the disappointing possibility of
us not carrying out the planned action or because we may still carry it
out despite our greatly diminished numbers. I shrug and reply with a
less-than-convincing "I hope so."

There's maybe ten thousand of us at the demonstration. It's a
decent but not great number. Especially considering we had billed it as
a Europe-wide mobilization, and aside from a pretty symbolic delegation from the Portuguese Communist Party, there is nobody except the
usual Parisians. The anarchist and autonome bloc is strengthened by
some comrades from other French cities, but next to no internationals.
There's maybe a thousand of us, but a solid half of those are from the
CNT, Anarchist Federation, or Alternative Libertaire. As fond as I am
of all of those organizations (and even a member of one of them), we
know perfectly well that most of their militants will not be joining us
for post-demonstration action. It's just how it is.

And so, much like Sophie, I'm fluctuating wildly between anxiety
at the potential risk of what is to come and excitement at the prospect
of us being successful. Unlike past actions, today I know not just the
level of risk (high) and the political target (another one of the pillars of
the logistical infrastructure of deportation) but also the precise target.
One of the French state's preferred deportation airlines: Air France.

Today's action might be of a spectacular nature, but our struggle
against Air France's collaboration with deportations not only actually
dates back several years, as far back as prior to the creation of the CAE,
but also was instrumental to its birth. "The collective was born ... out
of a practice: intervening directly against deportations by going to speak
to the passengers at the airport and inform them of the presence of
deportees on their flights and trying to convince them to refuse to travel
under those conditions. The first results were encouraging, and many
sans-papiers were deplaned."[5]

CAE members block the Air France counter at one of Paris's airports.

In fact, the presence at the airports of different activists and militants in attempts to prevent specific deportations wasn't just a large part of what brought the CAE to life, it was also a practice that continued regularly for years afterward. While this narrative may be, in the interest of keeping you, the dear reader, entertained, largely limited to our most spectacular moments of mass action, the reality is that the overwhelming majority of the work and time invested by us in the CAE was of a much more mundane and monotonous nature and involved a lot of long train rides from the city to the airport.

Sometimes, although rarely, those airport visits included more visible forms of action—such as blockading the Air France check-in counters. But our most common function, and by far the most effective in the actual prevention of deportations, involved being regularly present at the airport, speaking to passengers boarding flights that carried a person being deported, making them aware of the situation, and attempting to persuade them to refuse to fly under these conditions—either by refusing to sit down once boarded or by other means. We worked diligently to destroy the impression that for potential deportees the airport marked a point of no return. As some comrades explained in an interview with the French periodical *L'Oeil Électrique*,

"If we chose ... to intervene at the moment of deportation, it's because it's the most visible but also the most fragile in the process of an arrested sans-papier's deportation process: to carry out the deportation the state requires at the very least the passive complicity of the flight crew and the passengers. If somebody manifests their disapproval, then this fragile machine breaks and the sans-papier is taken off the plane."[6]

CAE members had been employing this much less spectacular but often effective strategy for almost two years now: being present at the airport, often in groups of as little as two or three and sometimes on a daily basis for weeks on end, to inform passengers of what was happening on their flights. The reason was that if a boarded passenger were to act in solidarity with the deportee, for example by refusing to sit down, the pilot would have the authority to demand the deplaning of the deportee if he were of the opinion that the conditions were not suitable for a safe takeoff and flight. This strategy was effective and beneficial in several crucial respects. French law at the time limited the length of an immigrant's predeportation detention to not more than ten days. In practice, this meant that if their deportation was prevented for long enough, and if the cause of that delay was not an action on behalf of the deportee that could lead to a criminal charge of some kind but rather due to circumstances outside of their control (like the actions of a conscientious passenger), then that person would eventually be released. Release, while obviously meaning clandestinity, still offered a second chance at remaining in the country.

A much more famous example of this form of action took place in July 2018, when Elin Ersson, a young activist from Sweden, refused to take her seat on a Turkish Airlines flight from Gothenburg to Istanbul that carried a person being deported to Afghanistan on board. Unlike the actions of passengers during the time of the CAE in the late 1990s, she was solidly in the social media era and live-streamed her efforts and the entire situation.

While she focuses the camera solely on herself, her video begins with a member of the flight crew trying to snatch the phone from her hands, while others yell at her, "Sit down, we want to go home!" Shortly after she clearly states that "a person is going to be deported to Afghanistan, where there is war and he is going to be killed," a man with a British accent can clearly be heard saying, "What about all these children here that you are frightening?" right before he snatches the phone from her hands. When a Turkish voice can be heard saying, "We are with you," and telling her that what she is doing is right, while others can be heard applauding her actions, she begins to cry.[7] Eventually, both she and the intended Afghan deportee are removed from the flight.

For those of us who had lived these experiences two decades earlier, Ersson's live stream was not just a window into a situation we had constantly worked to create but never witnessed with our own eyes, it was also incredibly illustrative of a reality we had already become acutely aware of during our hundreds of conversations with passengers. The reality that those passengers who themselves had so-called immigration backgrounds, or who were from colonized or ex-colonized countries, were significantly more open and receptive, identifying and empathizing with the situation of the potential deportee, and were much more liable to openly show solidarity. Just as in her case it was the European families headed for vacation in Turkey or Turkish people returning home who were least receptive, in our case, "We had difficulty intervening at the airports when the passengers were European. Tourists or businesspeople, they tended to prioritize their fear of being delayed. So what worked perfectly on an Air Afrique flight became much more difficult on a lot of other airlines."[8]

While her actions were regarded as heroic and courageous in the eyes of many, and she was indeed successful in getting the detained person off the plane, the Swedish state intended to make an example out of her. Although she was finally sentenced to a fine, Swedish prosecutors had originally called for "Ersson to serve a six-month prison sentence for violating Sweden's air traffic regulations."[9] This was precisely what the French government had begun doing in this situation in the late 1990s, rendering this strategy much more difficult and less successful, as the government began actually prosecuting passengers for "interfering with air traffic," "public disturbance," and things of this nature for refusing to take their seats.

Partly due to this changing reality—but also because while there was a general consensus that the immediate moment of deportation might be the most fragile, many of us didn't share the opinion of some in the collective that the moment of deportation was also the most visible—we took the collective decision to broaden the struggle against Air France. While the immediate moment of deportation was very visible

Police stand guard outside during the occupation of the Air France headquarters at the Esplanade des Invalides in Paris.

and poignant to those who happened to be its direct eyewitnesses, those were very few people. It was a conflict largely visible only to us, the cops, Air France, and the few passengers who happened to witness our efforts at the airport, but it was completely hidden from the eyes of the rest of society.

We intended to shift the center of the conflict, taking it out of their terrain of airports and city outskirts and into the heart of Paris. Into the city's most affluent and iconic areas, taking a battle that takes place on the periphery and giving it an impossible-to-ignore dimension in the heart of the city. It was time for a spectacular blow, to strike against both the heart of Air France as well as the government, and to do so in massive numbers. At the end of the demonstration, ending squarely in the center of bourgeois Paris, meters away from the Louvre, the Champs-Élysées, and the French National Assembly, we would continue as a bloc and invade Air France's flagship location at the historic Esplanade des Invalides. This time, we had no intention of staying long. We would enter, strike, and be gone again. Or at least that was the plan.

Inside Air France, Paris, Esplanade des Invalides, March 27, 1999, 5 p.m.

The glass doors of the venerable and elegant Parisian building host-ing Air France's central city offices, a traditional and flagship location for the airline, swing open. I can't remember the logistics of how we avoided security locking them as they saw us approach, but it's safe to assume there was probably an affinity group somewhere acting as advance crew that prevented them from doing so. But what I do remem-ber is that this time was … let's just call it different.

Whereas before there was some restraint during these actions, particularly during the police station action, there is none of that today. Many hundreds of us pour into the lobby area. It's a wide and very open floor plan, with counters and offices all around the perimeter of the lobby. While some set to work destroying the computers and telephones at the counters, others make a beeline to the offices. It's an almost carni-valesque image, as papers and documents fly everywhere and turn the floor white. I imagine this is what it looks like when a finance company knows it's about to be raided by the feds, only with more shredding of papers and less throwing around of computers.

It's an explosion of pent-up rage. Despite the masks, I can clearly recognize a great many of the participants. People who have spent day after day after day speaking to people at airports and being harassed by cops and security for giving out flyers. Comrades who have invested endless hours plotting, scheming, and organizing to be the most effective wrench possible in the gears of the deportation machine. People who for years have been fighting fascists in defense of immigrants, who stand in solidarity with them on all the terrains of social war, and who state clearly that our destinies and fates are inseparably intertwined. That our freedoms are on the line in their struggle. We've disrupted airports, stopped trains, raided hotels, and stormed police stations.

But most of all we've seen up close and in person the devastating human toll of the deportation system. As anarchists we already understood its adverse effects on the rest of society and therefore our own lives directly—the use of undocumented immigrants to drive down wages and frighten "legal" workers into accepting worse labor conditions, the use of discourse around "illegals" and "invasions" to strengthen systems of control and domination throughout society, and so forth. But we have now for years been eyewitnesses of its direct consequences in the form of human suffering—heartbroken souls sobbing at the destruction of their dreams in life, shaking at the prospect of a return to places they fled, fearing for their lives. People driven to desperate acts, sometimes choosing to take their own lives rather than be taken from the place they have chosen to call home and separated from their loved ones. Anarchists most of us, we already have a clear intellectual comprehension of the horrors of borders, but no matter how much you might believe you understand something like this, no amount of intellectual comprehension compares to experiencing the pain and damage firsthand.

And then we were told that with this government things would be different. That with supposed socialists and communists in power things would be better. Much like in the Trump era, we were told that we should be quiet and vote for this "lesser evil" in the interest of harm reduction. And while it is true that many immigrants were granted amnesty and regularized, and that this was therefore a better reality than the one offered by a right-wing government, for us it was not a question of reducing the quantity of human suffering but rather a matter of principle. Our goal was not to keep unnecessary human suffering caused at the altar of nationalism, racism, and borders to a socially acceptable level but to eradicate it.

So here we are. And here I am. In the most luxurious area of Paris, standing ankle-deep in a pool of assorted office debris as I look out the window. Vans full of riot cops are flying toward us, cops pouring out of them constantly. In the excitement of the moment, I think we may have stuck around longer than we intended to. Alice, Sophie, and I contemplate making a run for it. But the mass of the crowd doesn't seem to be going anywhere. It's around this point that we notice still other comrades barricading the doors. They are also CAE comrades. Alice yells at them, "What are you doing? We can still fight them, look how many they are, they can't arrest everybody!" There are in fact hundreds of us comfortably in the building, well over three hundred at least. One of the comrades dragging furniture to the front door retorts, "It'll be a massacre, and they'll pick people up all over the neighborhood. There aren't a million places to hide here. We're better off negotiating an exit like at Ibis."

I squint at him with my best confused and disapproving look. "Um, have you seen what this place looks like? I'm pretty sure we aren't just walking out of here." If some of us were already growing increasingly concerned about what seemed to be transpiring—a de facto decision by some in the collective to again more or less willfully subject hundreds of us to potential arrest—his next words marked the beginning of what would eventually become a noticeable split. It was something to the effect of, "Even if they do arrest us all, it will make for great press repercussions."

For us, mass direct actions and the acceptance of the possibility of arrest were one thing, solidly aligned with our anarchist principles and the understanding that direct action in solidarity with immigrants would necessarily put us outside of the bounds of legality. But to purposefully, or at least passively, expose ourselves to arrest and identification was not only strategically unsound but also closer to liberal and reformist concepts of nonviolent morality disguised as politics ("I suffer and let myself be victimized by the state, and therefore am correct in my political position").

It soon becomes clear that in this case, we young radicals are in the minority position. The collective is split, but most of all the mass of participants seems content to more or less passively await

The international anarcho-syndicalist bloc during the G8 summit, Cologne, June 1999.

developments. One comrade who reached his breaking point with the collective due to this situation complains that "the objective of this occupation seemed to be simply to gather as many people around the CAE as possible after the demonstration, with no other goal than to stay inside the building waiting for the cops: a completely symbolic action that played on the consumerist aspect of many of its participants."[10]

Not much later, sitting inside one of the numerous police buses that carried the 369 of us who were detained that day and thinking about how much this was not what I had signed up for or how I expected this day to end, I swore to myself to no longer put my safety and freedom in the hands of those who were willing to barter it away or endanger it for the purpose of political profit or mediation.

The Rising Tide

The observant reader might notice what is brewing here. The increasing collaboration between cross-border networks of radical activists on a mass scale, or in this case at least the attempt at it. The weaving of networks on the basis of joint ideas as catalyst for collective action in the form of transnational convergences, often with a certain degree

"Terrorists are not those who blow up detention centers, but those that build them!" Cologne, June 1999.

of illegality and mass action as common denominators. The explicit articulation of the intersection of issues of capitalist trade and labor needs with the increased policing of borders and repression of those critical of them as the first stages of a new neoliberal order in which goods and consumerism are unrestrictedly free but humans are not. The convergence of the struggles born of this new reality—struggles of labor, of freedom of movement, and against techno-repression and state terror—were the currents that pushed the antiglobalization tide forward. We don't know it yet either, but what we are witnessing are the first manifestations of the incredible rising tide that would come to be known soon after as the antiglobalization movement.

It's been largely forgotten today, but the antiglobalization movement and the struggle for freedom of movement were intricately linked from day one. The No Border network, Europe-wide networks of struggle, solidarity, and agitation against the border regime and for freedom of movement, predate the large antiglobalization mobilizations and integrated themselves seamlessly into the larger wave of protest. In fact, the first day of demonstrations at the high-water mark of the antiglobalization movement, the G8 summit in Genoa of 2001, was exclusively dedicated to freedom of movement and solidarity with immigrants.[11]

And it shouldn't come as a surprise. One of the most evident contra-dictions of the neoliberal free trade agreements was the creation of a system promoting freedom of movement for goods in order to weaken workers' power, strengthen consumerism, and increase the accumu-lation of capital—while at the same time enforcing a border regime responsible for thousands of deaths at its gates.

Not three months after our mobilization in Paris, the G8 summit was held in the German city of Cologne. The mobilization of the radical left was spearheaded by the Antifaschistische Aktion/Bundesweite Organisation (Antifascist Action/Countrywide Organization). It may have turned out to mark "a low point for the radical left in Germany" that presaged the splits and divisions that were to follow a few short years later and eventually lead to the demise of the AA/BO, but on the international level it was another surge in the growing wave that was the antiglobalization movement.[12] Although an army of thousands of cops ensured the demonstration remained symbolic and free of open conflict, this time thousands upon thousands traveled from different points of Europe to participate. In fact, the CNT together with some Parisian unemployed workers' organizations had negotiated a train from Paris to Cologne, and this one did indeed arrive, transporting thousands. That day, both the red and black anarcho-syndicalist bloc and the antifa bloc each numbered comfortably in the several thou-sands. Chants and banners in numerous languages were everywhere amid seas of red and black and antifascist action flags, illustrating the truly internationalist character of the crowd and hinting at the enor-mous mobilizations of the anarchist and radical left to come in the next few years as the tide of the antiglobalization movement reached its peak.

Ministerial Summit of the World Trade Organization, Seattle, November 30, 1999

Thick clouds of tear gas fill the downtown air. Thousands of protesters sit and blockade strategic streets, while others prevent delegates from entering buildings, sometimes chasing them away. Behind the front lines, largely inaccessible to the cops, a small but determined group of anarchists—according to those who were there, never numbering much more than one or two hundred—are systematically targeting banks, corporate property, and police vehicles while erecting small barricades.

Delegates are unable to move from their hotels to the convention site. Besieged by tens of thousands of activists employing a diversity of complementary tactics, police lose control of the situation.

The next morning, a continent away in Argentina, where I briefly find myself, I drag myself out of bed and head to do something or other against my will at an ungodly early hour. The a.m. hours not being exactly my strong point in life, I am still comfortably more than half asleep and not terribly lucid as I stumble to the kiosk to buy the day's newspaper to read on my commute. But one quick glance at the front page of the papers stacked in front of me jolts me awake. There is an image of a person surrounded by a cloud of tear gas, throwing a canister toward the cops. Below it, the caption blares:

> **Stormy Summit:** The summit of the World Trade Organization was slated to begin yesterday in Seattle, USA. But some fifty thousand militants from trade union and environmentalist groups impeded it with their protests. The police repression resulted in a pitched battle and the declaration of a state of emergency.[13]

The article inside describes the scenes illustrated above and, if I remember correctly, shows the image seen around the world of a robocop aiming his less-lethal weapon directly at the heads of sitting demonstrators, as tear gas swirls around them. Excuse the use of a phrase drawn into ill repute by its unfortunate application to the actions of the US military in Iraq, but I read the article in shock and awe. We knew of the summit, and we knew that protests were planned. But honestly, we expected permitted marches, tame parades, and hippies with puppets. To see this kind of militance on a mass scale, in the heart of the empire, was a powerful inspiration. To illustrate the potential power and importance of so-called symbolic action—as the attacks, whether against the infrastructure of the summit or the symbols of capital, remained largely in the sphere of the symbolic regardless of how affecting or inspiring they may have been—for those of us outside the United States they represented an unmistakable message. But the message wasn't only in the militance, it was also in the fact that in nothing less than the core of the empire, not only had comrades dared to challenge the state, but with a variety of tactics they had in fact succeeded (if only temporarily) at successfully disrupting the normal operations of state and capital.

Clarín

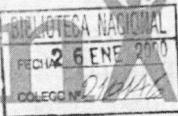

UN TOQUE DE ATENCIÓN PARA LA SOLUCIÓN ARGENTINA DE LOS PROBLEMAS ARGENTINOS

Miércoles 1° de diciembre de 1999

Buenos Aires República Argentina Año LV Nº 19.343

Precio en Capital Federal y GBA: $ 1,00 • Recargo envío al interior: $ 0,20 Uruguay: $ 20 • Brasil: R$ 3,90 • Paraguay: G$ 4.000 • Chile: $ 1.200

Precios con opcionales, en el índice de la página 2

INFORMACION GENERAL PAG. 55
Península Valdés ya es mundial
La UNESCO declaró al paraíso de las ballenas patrimonio de la humanidad.

SUPLEMENTO ESPECTACULOS
Dady Brieva, agrandadito
Triunfó en TV con los chicos y ni piensa en los Midachi.

POLICIA PAG. 58
El chico de la picada fatal, preso
Tenía prohibido manejar pero lo hacía igual. Por eso ayer lo detuvieron.

EL PLAN DE LA ALIANZA PARA AUMENTAR LA RECAUDACION

Fuerte impuesto a los que ganan más de $ 2.750

De la Rúa aumentará la tasa de Ganancias • Y eliminará gastos que se pueden deducir para pagar menos • La presión será mayor para los ingresos superiores a $ 5.000 • En este caso, la suba representa 9% más de lo que se paga hoy • Así esperan recaudar 920 millones extra. **PAGS. 22 Y 23**

La Alianza y el peronismo, en pie de guerra por el Presupuesto PAGS. 24 Y 25

CUMBRE BORRASCOSA Ayer debía comenzar en Seattle, EE.UU., la cumbre de la Organización Mundial de Comercio. Pero unos 50 mil militantes de grupos sindicales y ecologistas lo impidieron con sus protestas. La represión policial derivó en una batalla campal y en la imposición del toque de queda. **PAGS. 34 Y 35**

DATOS OFICIALES

En EE.UU. los errores médicos matan más que los accidentes

Mueren por año casi cien mil personas, la mayoría por drogas mal recetadas • Otra causa son los diagnósticos equívocos • En cambio, los accidentes del tránsito provocan 44 mil muertes. **PAG. 46**

LA QUINTA CAUSA DE MUERTE	Cifras en miles
Corazón	727
Cáncer	540
Apoplejía	160
Pulmón	109
Mala praxis	98

SECRETARIA DE PROMOCION SOCIAL

Pinky tendrá un puesto en el Gobierno porteño

Fue candidata a intendenta de La Matanza y perdió • Piensa aplicar el plan que había elaborado en la zona más postergada de la ciudad. **PAG. 48**

AFECTO A CASI 2 MILLONES DE USUARIOS Y DURO CERCA DE UNA HORA

Enorme apagón en la Capital y el GBA

El corte empezó poco después de las 21 y abarcó más de media ciudad y gran parte del conurbano • Llegó incluso a Bahía Blanca y a zonas de Neuquén y Río Negro • Edenor y Edesur dicen que no tuvieron la culpa • Y adjudicaron el problema a fallas en el sistema que transporta la energía desde el Comahue. **PAG. 49**

FRASE DEL DIA EDUARDO DUHALDE: "DESDE EL 10 DE DICIEMBRE NO HABRA UN SOLO REFERENTE JUSTICIALISTA: NI LO SERE YO NI TAMPOCO MENEM". PAG. 19

Cover of Argentine newspaper *Clarín*, December 1, 1999.

I wasn't there personally, but the conclusion I reached can probably be multiplied by tens of thousands or hundreds of thousands across the world. For us, the first generation of radicals to come of age after the fall of the Eastern bloc, there was only one possible conclusion to be drawn as we began to see the tide of the antiglobalization movement rise: that the lesson of the collapse of the Eastern bloc was not that we had reached the "end of history" and that capitalism is inevitable and inescapable, it was that empires can and do fall—and often do so with shocking suddenness. That if the Eastern bloc proved that "socialism without freedom is tyranny" and bound to fail, then the growing discontent with the unfettered capitalism we were living in proved that "freedom without socialism is privilege" and was likewise vulnerable. That collapse and revolution can and do happen, and that if we organize intensely enough, fight bravely enough, and push hard enough we might just be able to topple this thing. The wave is coming, and we intend to ride it.

PART 2

2001, FROM THE INAUGURATION TO THE SUMMER OF RESISTANCE

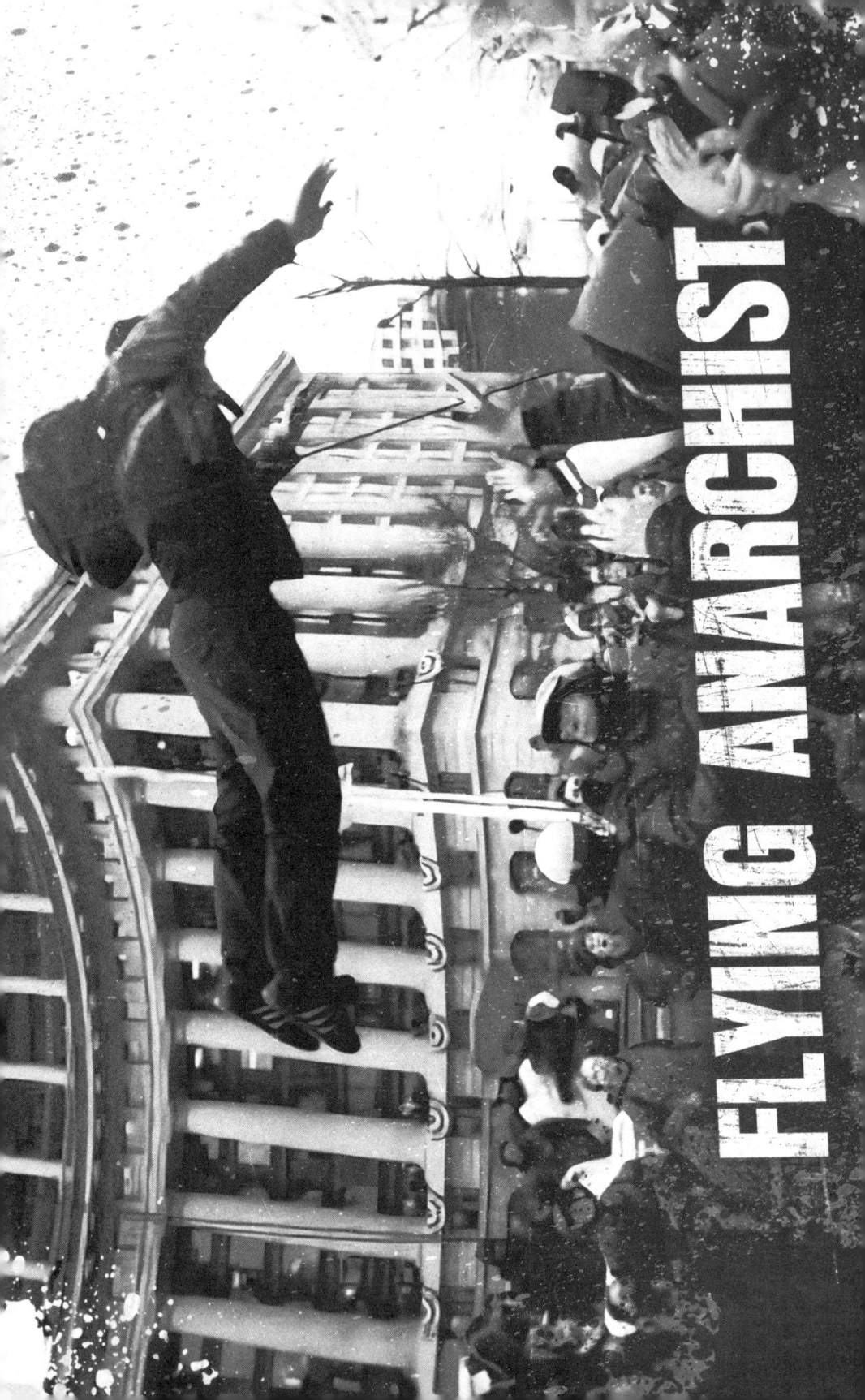

FLYING ANARCHIST

8

THE INAUGURATION
Washington, DC, January 2001

What better way to kick off the year could there possibly be than by visiting our good friend George Dubya in Washington, DC, on the day of His Majesty's coronation. We had gotten word that a small army of liberals was headed in that direction, displeased at the results of an electoral spectacle that had gotten, well, a little too spectacular for their tastes. I can't personally say that I quite cared which farm animal ruled the barn, but the collective and I and a few hundred close personal associates had a bit of an axe to grind with Mr. Dubya.

You see, we had very politely gone to meet with him at the presidential debates in Boston a few months earlier, in order to present a reasonable list of what we liked to call "sensible, progress-oriented reforms." Namely, the abolition of private property, class society, the concept of the modern state, and so forth. Great was our shock and outrage when we weren't allowed to participate in this debate. I mean, Mr. Nader we could understand, the man was rich and boring, but us? Young and exciting revolutionaries … suburbia deserved to see us on TV! Long story short: Cops were hit, pepper spray flew, barricades were thrown, innocent pacifists were arrested, and we vowed we'd meet again!

Neither I nor my associates take such promises lightly. So, with much more than a little help from some comrades in Washington, DC, we wrote a call to action and organized a little something called the RAAB (Revolutionary Anti-Authoritarian Bloc), inviting six hundred or so of our best friends to join us. We told them there would be liberals to radicalize or, failing that, to use as cover. The idea was wild and exciting, not having been tried since hundreds of radicals rampaged during the '69 Nixon inauguration. Nothing less than wrecking the inauguration parade of the president of the United States of America. The kind of pipe dream only the young, naive, and overly enthusiastic anarcho-folk could possibly conceive. We would stop the damned thing, and the whole world would be watching on TV. Personally, I couldn't think of a more inspiring way to communicate to all those others fighting US imperialism (the good old-fashioned military kind as well as the new, "more effective, longer-lasting" economic version) around the world that even in the heart of the beast, the belly of the empire, the brain of the machine, the ... (Note to self: Keep overly rhetorical pamphleteer-speak to a minimum!) Anyhow, we would stop it, and the whole world would watch with the same mix of shock and inspiration they had on the morning they awoke to find pictures of thousands of demonstrators shutting down Seattle on the front page of their morning newspapers.

★

Having survived a double-digit-hour drive in the middle of an epic blizzard, as well as a closed yet seemingly endless and huge organizing meeting the night before, there we stood. Cadger, Alan, myself, and a ragged bunch of a couple hundred young (and some not so young) mischief makers, in the very heart of the empire. All in black, milling around in a park at 9 a.m. Given the numbers, I was a bit uneasy.

First of all, where were the millions? The thousands upon thousands of raging, ideologically driven young hooligans? Well, okay, maybe they simply didn't exist in such numbers. Whatever. But where were the angry liberals? The "Gore Won" crowd, Voter March and NOW and so on. There may be a lot of things I don't know, but I do know that a few hundred black bloc folks running around a Washington that boasted agents out on the streets from over forty different federal agencies without any cover was not likely to go well or last long.

Most discomforting, however, was exactly the opposite of that: There were no police around. What kind of sick joke was this? It must be a death trap. There were over four thousand cops on duty for this event. This whole happening had been made very public; there was no way they didn't know. The meeting place had been changed a few days earlier due to security concerns, but still, they do pay people to keep up on this stuff. My mind kept racing back to "must be a death trap." They're parked on every side street. Hundreds of robocops, waiting for the order to spring, surround us, beat everybody to a pulp, arrest us, and end our glorious incursion before it even begins. Whatever the case, it was too late to let such trivial worries stop us now.

A life without the feeling of suicidal daring is a life not lived.

At 9:15 sharp, with that familiar yet lovable feeling of walking, albeit proudly and excitedly, into certain defeat, we moved out. Banners were unfurled, reading beautiful messages like "Class War: For a Classless, Stateless Society" and other such poetic masterpieces. Lines were formed, hoods went up, ski masks went down, and we took the streets at the pleasantly brisk pace that black blocs seem to often have. No cops came flying at us. Not immediately anyway.

Before that happened, we marched around for a while, knocked over some barricades, chanted some slogans, threw some paintballs, and kicked a few limos. During this time, an unexpected and memorable thing happened. I looked backward at some point — and there were very, very many of us! Comfortably over five hundred. Especially the front sections of the bloc looked impressive, as we had made a concerted effort to march in lines of affinity groups and make use of banners down the front and sides to keep it all cohesive and protect from police attack and snatch squads. To us this was standard, but it was a relatively new development apparently for the US anarchists, one that was much commented on afterward, mainly positively.

At that point, feeling newly emboldened despite having already developed a rather interesting police escort, we took a quick right turn and stumbled right into ... the headquarters of *The Washington Post*. (Accident? Or were we actually headed there all along? You, my friend, will never know.)

I am not of the school that believes in pandering to the media line. The mainstream media are, and will always be, our enemies. This is, in my most humble of opinions, one of the very simple facts that for some reason a large part of the anarcho-world is either unwilling or unable to grasp.

So, let's take a short break from our exciting recap of the action to break it down once and for all: You, as a committed and dedicated anarchist militant, are opposed to many things. Among them capitalism and corporations and such. Just about all relevant media is owned by said corporations. Do you really expect corporate journalists to write honest, meaningful, and positive pieces about the people and movements that seek to eliminate the source of their money and influence? No, beloved comrade, you don't. Because it doesn't make any sense! Further, they are paid to sell newspapers. Sensationalism sells newspapers. Stories about dangerous criminals, hooligans with no message or purpose other than chaos and destruction, bent on blood and mayhem and so forth, is what sells newspapers. Stories about kind-hearted young idealists trying to create a better world through infoshops and mutual aid, and kissing trees, and not eating bunnies, and whatever other nonsense you may be feeling like feeding the journalist in front of you in order to try to "clear the name of anarchism" are not quite as big hits, unfortunately. So, to recap: A journalist is more or less on the same level as a cop. The cop represents the repression of the state; the journalist creates social repression of our movement through lies and misrepresentation. Therefore, we need to bypass and challenge the mainstream media and create our own alternative forms of communicating our message. As for dealing with the journalists, I am an advocate of the Greek style. Smash their cameras, light their vehicles on fire, and if they still don't get it, smash them. Neither we nor our struggle are a spectacle provided for their newspaper sales.

With this in mind, I could appreciate the sound of the glass shattering as a mob of hundreds stormed in, terrorizing the journalist scum who tried to run and hide for their pathetic lives. If ever there was a bastion of lies and corporate propaganda, this was it! Whatever harm came to them, they deserved. Let's see them ignore this in tomorrow's paper, if they still have offices from which to write their stories, that is!

Sadly, all this madness and mayhem existed solely in the overly excited creative spaces of my mind. The reality was significantly less exciting. The black bloc mob, acting on the commonly utilized and always troubling "sheep model," mainly just stood there chanting. Eyes met as everybody looked at everybody else, waiting for somebody to do something. Precious seconds were wasted. The building was spray-painted, a paint bomb flew, and time was up. The police had caught on, and they started moving us on. And just as that "No Parking" sign was about to be launched through the window. Maybe next time!

★

Soon after, they came. Pouring out of red vans and white vans and assorted other unmarked police vehicles, a sizable horde of cops flying out toward the front and the back of the bloc and trying to pen us in. It was a sad and demoralizing sight. Here we were, numbering a good six hundred by this point, faced with what couldn't be more than a hundred cops, who weren't even in riot gear, and panic ruled the mob, especially toward the back of the bloc. Some noble examples of resist-ance were to be seen, like Moose, our very own Big Friendly Giant who, when threatened by a cop's baton, simply yanked it out of his hand and threw it away. Or the quick-thinking folks who entered the alleyway conveniently situated at the point of conflict and attempted to ram the line of cops with a huge dumpster. When that failed to break the line, this quick-thinking group of daredevils, among which I counted myself, got divided from the larger bloc, which now found itself surrounded and was quickly penned in on the sidewalk. Given that we in the alley were a group of about twenty or so, we had to face the reality that there was nothing to be done. It is an odd feeling, that of leaving your comrades behind, turning around and walking away, knowing that the fate that awaits them is most likely an arrest and a few days of unpleasant jail time, followed by a host of trumped-up charges, thousands of dollars in legal fees, and other pleasantries.

However, in militant actions, as in life, it is important to know when to change into yuppie wear and walk away. The concept of the moral martyr is one of the many facets of the victim mentality complex that plagues anarchism and leftist movements, one we desperately need to break. We are in this struggle to win, not to prove ourselves via some strange conception of honor, or pride, or other such social construc-tions. We do what we do because we have an objective, a project, and a vision that we would like to see become reality. Let's leave the fair play for sporting events, please.

There are, for example, few things more frustrating than having to listen to a "revolutionary anarchist" raise a whiny complaint about how it is okay to fight fascists but not okay to fight them ten to one. What would you prefer, that we fight "one on one, man, just you and me, and see whose balls are bigger," or some other macho competition? Sorry, I'm not interested. The enemy is the enemy, and all advantages we can take, we take. Fight dirty and fight to win. If you are going to last in your dangerous life of living beyond the boundaries of the law, it is important to learn to use all advantages to your benefit, including knowing when to just walk away.

★

Part of the magic and excitement of lawbreaking is that seconds are stretched into minutes, and hours into days. So much can be compressed into so little time. Or maybe this is simply the way it was supposed to be, before our lives were emptied of danger and uncertainty, back in some imaginary existence in which our days did not consist of dull routines of obedience and alienation. But probably not. Most likely, it is just the illusion created by being overly aware of your every action and your surroundings for extended periods of time. The necessary consequence of living experiences that could land you in jail or seriously injure you, and then just moving on, realizing that the whole ordeal lasted mere seconds.

Such a feeling came to me while I was standing across the street from the surrounded portions of the black bloc on 14th and K. We were a group of fifty or so, who had regrouped outside the cop trap and were trying to push the cops around, break into the street, and generally create enough chaos to provide opportunities for the others to escape the imminent mass arrest. We had devised a fun little game in which we would charge the cop lines every time the sign said "Walk" and stop every time it said "Don't Walk." It was going fairly uneventfully (relatively speaking, as trying to break through police lines is rarely an uneventful happening) until the wiseass in front of me decided to take a cop's badge. Buddy, they will *shoot* you for that! It's one of the most basic laws of nature: Don't fuck with the cop's badge! They get in serious trouble if they lose that, so, consequently, you get in serious trouble if you try to take it.

Good sense notwithstanding, I was down with it. That is, until he decided to toss it behind him and straight at me. It was a cartoon cliché moment, in every sense. Like when a bomb or any other exploding artifact is thrown and the character in question can't stop themselves from catching it. The badge arced into my stomach. I executed a perfect catch, worthy of the "Play of the Day." The world froze. I recall so much happening in the few seconds that followed. I remember the opening up of the line of sight between the big, bull-like cop and myself. I remember the vicious look of shock, anger, and outrage in his eyes. And, much like in our favorite Saturday morning cartoons, nothing seemed to happen during the time it took me to process what was coming. The world just stopped. It's animation law. You can't start falling until you realize there is no ground below you.

Then it hit me. Quite literally. A zillion pounds of furious pork in blue, impacting my midsection in an American-football-style tackle worthy of the greats. I hit the pavement, flat on my back, completely winded, and with this huge but much-more-agile-than-he-looked hulk still on top of me. "Give it back, give it back, motherfucker, give it back!" he thundered. The man had turned a worrying shade of purple. It was like I had angered the biggest bully in the yard. This was a rather odd feeling. I was afraid.

I can think of precious few moments in the course of my "adventures in mass militance" when I genuinely, as opposed to strategically, sucked up my pride and begged like a desperate child, even when in hindsight it often would have been a much more beneficial course of action than playing tough. This, however, was one of those memorable (memorable?) moments when the self-preservation instinct overpowered the arrogance. I recall a rush of winded begging, pleading, endlessly repeating that I didn't have his precious badge, that I was sorry, that I'd never come back to Washington again, that I'd give it all up, that cops were my friends, that—

That he was no longer on me! He was retreating, a dozen or so fellow black blockers pushing him back. Pffft ... obviously, I'd shown him! I got up slowly and looked arrogantly around. "Had it all under control, folks." I think I also muttered something like "Thanks." It was over.

★

Once I recovered from my first, last, and not-so-glorious American football experience, it was time to analyze what steps were to be taken from here. Playing Red Rover, Red Rover with the cops at the crosswalk was, aside from being rather monotonous, proving to be a painfully frustrating exercise in futility. And it soon became clear that this was in no way, shape, or form enough of a disturbance to provide the necessary cover for the escape of the surrounded comrades. As we stood there, desperately trying to think of something groundbreaking to save our mobilization from a pathetic defeat, the most wondrous and unexpected of miracles took place.

Ahead in the distance, beyond our couple of hundred cornered comrades, beyond the rows of police, and beyond the din of the idling arrest buses, we started hearing voices. Lots of voices. Hundreds of voices. Eventually they came into view, as did their signs. It was nothing less than a mob of demonstrators, several thousand strong. Liberal demonstrators. It was the Voter March and NOW crowd, the "Gore Won" and "What have they done to our democracy?" crowd. It was the mob of the outraged SUV-driving upper-middle-class white mother from suburban Boston angered because "her vote was not counted" (when in fact, though not that I care much, it was mainly the working-poor African American single mother from Florida whose vote was not counted).

Now, I like to think of myself as a person with a lot of faith in humanity. I believe that to be an anarchist in the time and age in which we live requires this. I do not, however, have much faith in the US liberal crowd. I stood there, dazed, confused, and distrusting, probably looking like some sort of perturbed masked stoner completely unable to comprehend the events around him. Was this good? Was this bad? Would they walk by and free the comrades? Or would they see the raggedy-looking bunch of young kids dressed in black, think of how horrible it would be if their Timmy, John, Joanna, or Suzanne turned out like this, and break into cries of, "Shame! Shame!" at us?

Much as it pains me, time unfortunately does not stop while I have my little philosophical moments, and I was suddenly snapped out of my ponderings by the sight of this mob catching up to where the police had the majority of the black bloc trapped. As they merged, demonstrators on both sides of the police line pressed against each other, and there was yelling and shouting, pushing and shoving—and then the police lines dissolved. It was like a much less dramatic and much less exciting modern-day version of Moses parting the seas. They were parted, and our people were set free!

★

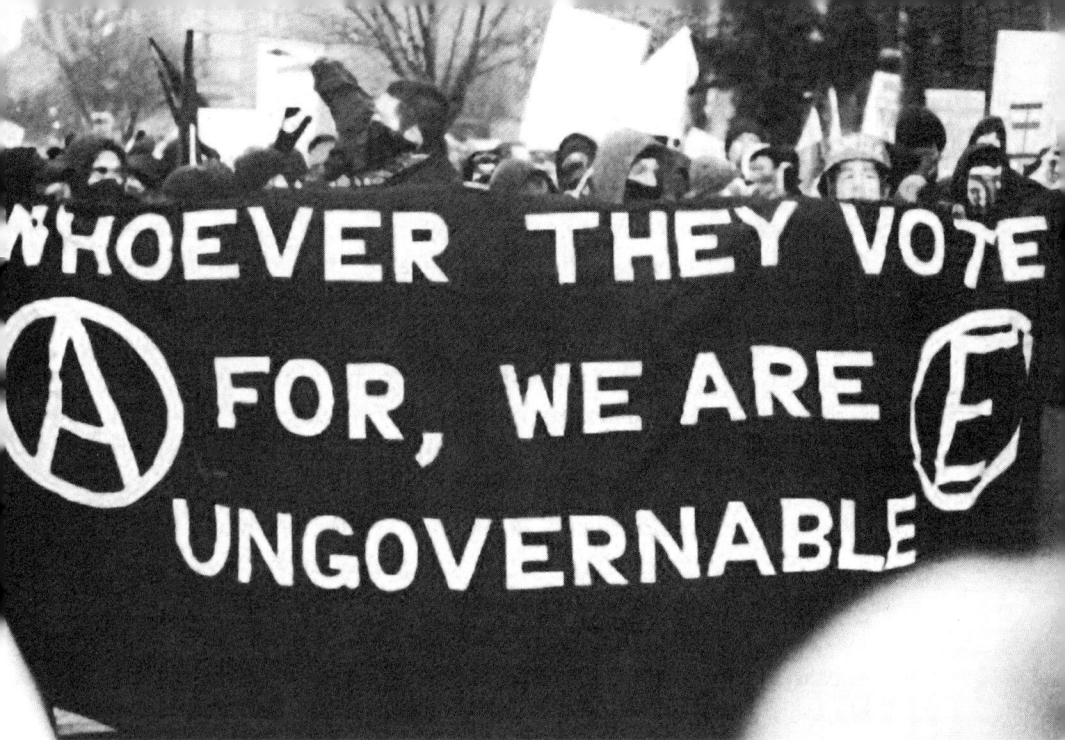

"Whoever they vote for, we are ungovernable." Washington, DC, 2001.

Ten minutes had now passed since this momentous event, and it was on again! The trapped bloc was now no more than an unfortunate footnote in what was certain to be a day filled with glory. Behind the beautiful "Whoever They Vote For, We Are Ungovernable" banner, we were now on the march again! Minus the police escort, and with our numbers down from six hundred to two hundred, but I viewed this as a positive turn of events. You see, in order to properly assess the strength of the bloc and our capabilities and to make sound judgments as to what was feasible or not, our affinity group followed a tactical rule of thumb in black blocs that I like to call the "divide by three" rule. We have stuck with it through the years, as it has proven more or less true just about everywhere. But it was especially true then. In the post-Seattle period, the black bloc attracted a whole lot of new people. It was one of the fragile points of what was then a growing movement, as the reality was that you were probably marching side by side with a fair amount of inexperienced people. As such, when matters became serious, many people were not necessarily prepared for the, let's call it "higher level of risk" that was suddenly involved, and disappeared. Which is perfectly fine, as everybody can and should participate up to the extent they feel comfortable. But between this and the natural rate of losing people when situations become volatile, it was usually the case that when trouble broke out, you were generally left with about one-third the number of people you had when you started. We viewed it as a positive development, though, because we noticed that although the cover of the larger blocs was of course nice, the character of the "post-skirmish" blocs was usually noticeably different. Tighter, more compact, and significantly more combative! (We would experience the same phenomenon just a few months later on day two in Quebec City.)

This was exactly the case here. We looked around and saw a mob definitely lower on banners and numbers but composed mainly of affinity groups we knew and trusted. Veterans of Seattle, Washington A16, Philly RNC, Cincinnati TABD, antifa actions, you name it. No more worrying about stragglers or undercovers, just two hundred determined close friends and associates from across the Midwest, Atlantic, and Northeast. Free of our police escort and with the guidance of our trusty scouts, we set off to try to access the parade route.

Determined not to repeat the mistakes of earlier in the morning, we quickly set about arming ourselves for the confrontation to come: attacking the checkpoints! You see, anticipating massive protests, the Secret Service had for the first time in history established checkpoints all along the parade route. Not believing we could actually successfully storm them, we had decided at the previous night's meeting that our objective would be to systematically attack and disrupt them. Our scouts guided us to a construction area where the bloc commandeered a large and heavy construction wagon. It was promptly filled with signs, cones, wooden poles, and the like, then placed in the middle of the bloc and surrounded with the few banners that remained, in order to avoid losing it if there were another clash with the cops on the way. Not soon after, we reached the first checkpoint. Just as we began turning toward it, the voice of a breathless and very excited scout came crackling over the comms: "Do not charge that checkpoint. Continue two blocks farther. The one here is ridiculously weak."

We stood there, about a half a block away from the checkpoint, and I remember giving myself a moment to take in the beautiful scenery in front of us and the magnitude of what was about to take place. Here we were, the anarchist youth, not only confident and determined, but now also equipped with nothing less than a mobile battering ram! In front of us was what I can only call a weakly set up checkpoint, consisting of a

The reconstituted black bloc on its way to the Secret Service checkpoint.

metal detector, some metal barricades, and maybe ten police officers. To top it all off, the street was on an incline leading down toward the checkpoint. Being the conscientious young people that we were, we even took the time to call out warnings to the bystanders between us and the checkpoint. We moved the banner out of the way and led the battering ram to the front. I'll never forget the faces of the cops and Secret Service agents as what was about to happen dawned on them. There is a popular French anarchist saying, "*Que la peur change de camp*," which translates roughly to "Let fear switch sides." As in, let's lose our fear and let the fascists, cops, and the state be afraid of us. And this was pure fear in their eyes. If only they could see the joy and broad smiles under our hoods and masks!

"Five ... four ... three ... two ... one ... *charge!*" And charge we did! I think the Barricada Collective recap of the day still describes the following scenes best: "Police and secret service scattered for their lives and the metal barricades of the state were toppled by the power and determination of the RAAB as hundreds of anarchists and revolutionaries, not 30 as the corporate press reported, as well as newly empowered and emboldened reformists, surged past the no longer existent checkpoint."[1] Beyond the checkpoint, it was only one short block or so to the parade route, and this was guarded by one row of metal barricades and maybe a dozen officers. There was no way they could stop us, and the delusions of grandeur about the upcoming headline "Anarchists Force Cancellation of Presidential Inauguration" were already running wildly through my head. In my defense, confessions later extracted from several friends and comrades reveal I wasn't alone in my megalomania. We were pretty sure this was the definition of "protagonist of history," as opposed to "spectator."

And had it not been for the Hollywood-like appearance of this anecdote's villain, I suspect we would have barreled straight into the parade route. Whatever would have followed is likely to have been memorable. Or tragic. Or most likely both—it's a fine line. But just as all of his colleagues were scattering, one quick-thinking and honestly courageous Secret Service agent came screeching out of the side street with his car, straight into the trajectory of the bloc's battering ram. A window shattered on impact, and the side of the car took a thundering hit. But the battering ram had been stopped. The agent sprung out of the car and then even tried to arrest individual anarchists who were flying past the checkpoint. If you are familiar with the genre "early twenty-first-century anarchist riot porn," you will be familiar with the first of the day's several heartwarming images: An unfortunate black bloc participant, bent over with hands behind his back, faces an obviously imminent arrest at the hands of the Secret Service. Directly behind the unsuspecting agent, another courageous friend holds a huge orange traffic barrel above his head, about to launch it at the agent. I'm happy to tell you that both comrades made it away safely.

As we stood there, a group of maybe 150 or so anarchists and another dozen young Revolutionary Communist Party members (for historical accuracy and fairness, the RCP youth were never very many, but back then they always had your back, at least as far as the action on the streets was concerned, though they might publish polemics with horrors about your politics after the fact), I couldn't help thinking about my unfortunate famous last words. Flashback to the night before, an eternal spokes council meeting. "Shouldn't we discuss what to do if we make it past the checkpoints?" asked one audacious and optimistic comrade. I quickly responded that it was impossible, and most people nodded or wiggled their fingers. Not wanting to waste time, we just kind of dismissively moved on. Now, I believe audacity

A black bloc participant charges a Secret Service agent, successfully un-arresting a comrade.

and unbridled optimism are essential tools of any anarchist organizer and militant. On an organizing level, a lot of our achievements would have been impossible without more than a bit of insane optimism. On a mass militance level, the many, as we lovingly termed them, "anarchist suicide missions" we embarked on that then turned out to be wildly empowering victories were nothing more than collective acts of optimism in the face of not-so-promising realities and conditions. And on a personal level, more than a few imminent arrests were avoided by sheer audacity. So, faced with what had just transpired, I was regretting my comments. Not only because they would lead to me being mercilessly bullied for several years for my lack of faith, but also because they played no small part in the absurd spectacle we were now experiencing.

Anarchists, being sweet and cute as we are, will often do things that to the casual observer will seem unexpected and crazy. Taking a quick time-out to have a general assembly with the presidential parade route to one side and some irate Secret Service agents to the other is probably high on the list of "things you don't expect to see right after demonstration smashes through security checkpoint." And yet, this is exactly what we did. Because, you know, decisions needed to be made and we wanted to be inclusive about it. How could anyone not love us? While a couple of people kept watch, we calmly discussed the merits of trying to storm the parade route. At this point, the discussion no longer revolved around "Is it possible or not?" but rather "I'm not so sure it's worth it, I'm pretty sure they'll shoot us." Today, years later, I'm somewhat ashamed by my words back then. This is maybe a good time to extend apologies on behalf of myself and my collective to those friends and comrades who felt pressured by us to lay down their lives for what would certainly be a symbolic and powerful moment but really not much more. I like to think that I now value human life just a tad more, and especially the lives of my comrades! Our bad. But at the moment, we couldn't believe what we were hearing.

"If this isn't worth taking a bullet for, then what is?" We were outraged and disappointed. And if anybody has read *Barricada*, you will remember that nuance and diplomacy were not necessarily our strengths. I can now also safely say that as a general rule I would prefer to just not take a bullet in general, but if there were no alternative, then I can think of more than a few better and more productive causes for which to take one. But, as this anecdote demonstrates, this was not the mindset at the time. All we could think of were the potential international headlines about anarchists forcing the cancellation of the presidential parade and what that could do in terms of growth and confidence for our movement. More importantly, it seemed like the most powerful message of practical solidarity with our comrades over-seas and in the so-called Global South. "You are not alone, even in the center of empire, look at what is happening!" But, fortunately I suppose, cooler heads prevailed and the bloc settled on a bit of symbolic kicking the barricades. After a few minutes of this, the other side brought in more riot cops as reinforcements, and we moved merrily along.

★

"You see, I told you all the basement shows, stage-diving, and crowd-surfing would be useful!" We were in the van on our way back, and Alan was trying to convince us that his daring escape had been possible only due to the "unique skill set" afforded him by his love of obscure punk rock and basement shows. We were all guilty of being "subculture kids," but Alan took it to a whole different level. If there were three guys in a basement somewhere in a small town in Uzbekistan banging two pots together while a third screamed into a can, and they somehow managed to put it on a tape and call it punk rock, Alan had that tape, knew the lyrics despite not speaking the language, and looked forward to the bootleg recordings of their upcoming shows in rural Hungary and small-town Romania. Cadger, the much less famous but clearly more aware of his surroundings "first jumper," wasn't having it. "What the hell are you talking about? The shows you go to don't even have stages, let alone ten feet of vertical space, much less enough people for landing on. Don't try to bullshit us," he retorted. "We had to coax you to jump like a scared dog from a burning building." This was par for the course as far as the kind of deeply stimulating conversations that were usually had in the hours and days directly following mass mobilizations or actions. Apparently it took some time for our neurons to regroup from the insane hours we kept in the weeks and months prior, as well as from the adrenaline and stress of the actions themselves. But inane arguments aside, and be it panic, punk rock skills, or just plain good timing, jump he did, and the rest, as they say, is history.

It's one of the more iconic images that the anarchist wave of those days has left us. Over the years, I've seen it on mobilization materials, magazines, and punk rock posters both in North America and Europe. I'm talking, of course, about the famous "Flying Anarchist." Suspended perfectly parallel to the ground, a good ten feet in the air, "Flying Anarchist" is forever immortalized in his Superman pose, flying off of the Navy Memorial, arms outstretched, soaring directly over what is a very surprised-looking robocop, directly into the arms of the loving masses and into safety. It was definitely quite the sight.

It was the culmination of the last series of battles of the day. Anarchists and other revolutionaries had successfully commandeered the Navy Memorial and surrounding space, directly on the inaugural parade route. While some fought the repeated charges of both robo-cops and plainclothes pigs, others scaled the monument, removing the flags of militarism and hoisting black and red-and-black flags. The sight of the wildly energized and confident bloc ripping down the US Navy flags and replacing them with the flag of anarchy, in the middle of Washington, DC, and directly on the parade route, was simply beautiful. As we fought off the now third wave of cops, both plainclothes and

A Secret Service agent stands among what's left of the parade route checkpoint.

uniformed, who tried to push us back, I suddenly heard, "What's impossible now, huh?" It was none other than the optimistic comrade from the night before, teasing me one more time. I could see him laughing under his mask, but rarely have I been so happy to be proven dead wrong.

★

"La suerte solo rie a los audaces": "Fortune only smiles on the bold." So goes a famous Argentine rock song. I'm definitely no poet, so symbolism and metaphors aren't necessarily my strength, but I feel like precisely that point was illustrated to us that day in an unusually poetic manner. How much more clearly could we expect the principles of solidarity, individual courage, and collective strength to be portrayed in practice? For individual courage, we had the image of a lone anarchist taking on a Secret Service agent in defense of his comrade. For solidarity and audacity, of Alan literally flying through the air into the safety of the bloc. And for collective strength, of destroying a Secret Service checkpoint with what can only be described as shocking ease.

We took these lessons and experiences to heart and used them as stepping stones for the greater and bolder adventures that were soon to come, as our confrontations with the state are nothing if not adventurous. We now knew that when we believe in our capacity, as courageous individuals and as a collective fighting force, we can achieve unimaginable feats. Sixteen years later to the day, I saw similar acts of individual and collective courage on the same streets of Washington during the Donald Trump inauguration. And many comrades now owe their freedom to the courageous charge that allowed them to escape the police kettle. I don't need to have been there to know that it was the quick-thinking audacity of the optimists among us that created that moment. And I know that what we discovered back then is just as true now. That circumstances are something we can create, and that "lucky" is often just another word for daring. That when we are bold, audacious, and wildly optimistic, we become truly ungovernable. "Fortune only smiles on the bold."

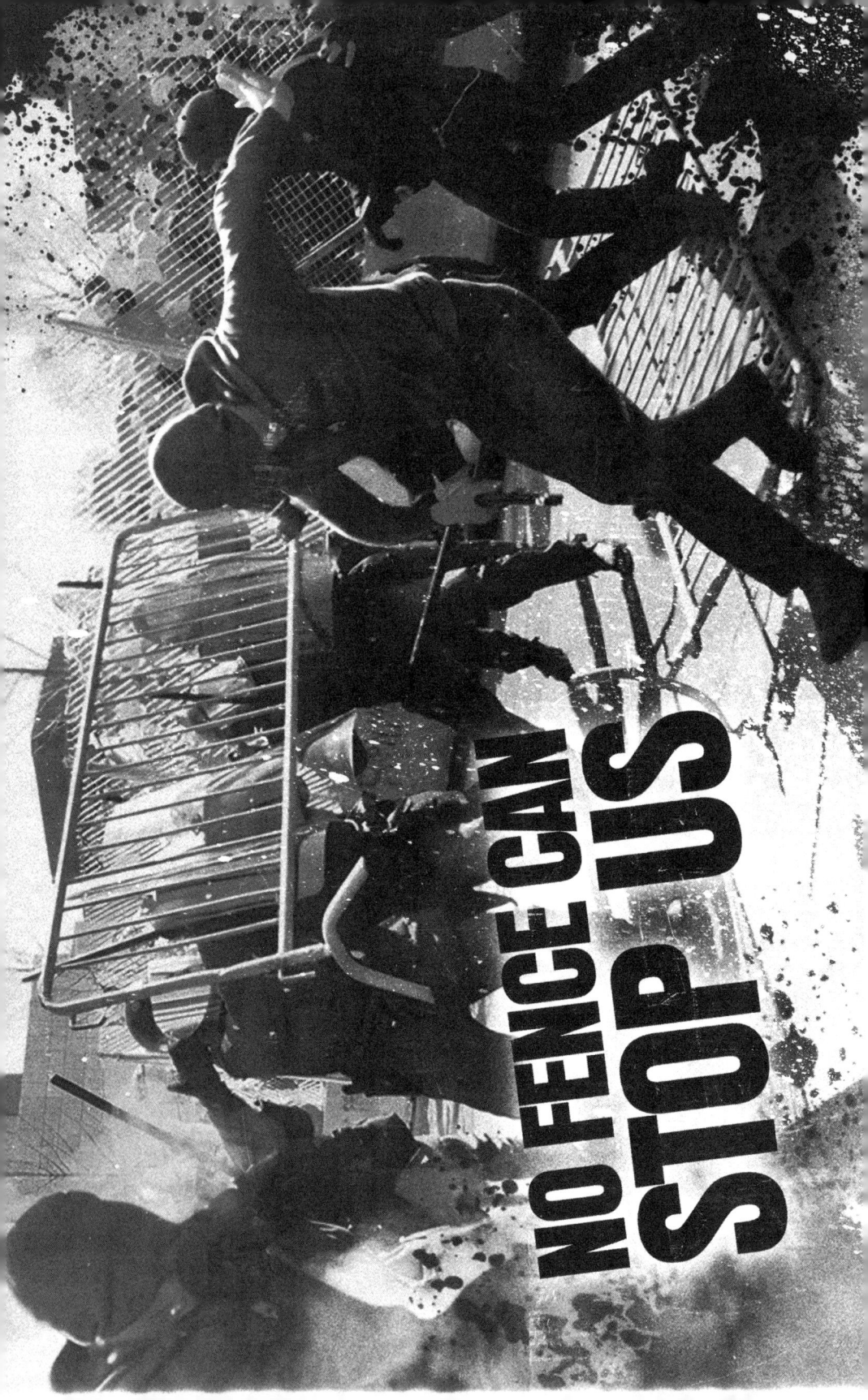

NO FENCE CAN STOP US

9

"WE HAVE NOTHING, DESTROY EVERYTHING! EVERYBODY TO QUEBEC CITY!"

The Summit of the Americas, Quebec City, April 2001

The Call

The following call to action was originally published in the March 2001 issue of the anarchist publication *Barricada*, the mouthpiece of Boston's unabashedly confrontational Barricada Collective:

> On the weekend of April 20th to 22nd the ruling elites of the Americas will gather in Quebec City to discuss the implementation of the FTAA (Free Trade Area of the Americas) and, to a large extent, the future of us all. The FTAA represents essentially an expansion of NAFTA to include the entire Americas region. The objective? To further clear the way for laws allowing corporations to sue member nations when they feel a government measure impedes "free trade," to further attack the already fragile social safety systems we have, to pave the way for possible privatization of schools, hospitals, and all other social services, and to further consolidate the dictatorship of capital in the Americas.
>
> It is the lives of everyone in the Americas they will be playing with at the summit in Quebec City, the lives of every American (Northern, Southern, or Central) worker, peasant, unemployed, retiree or student. Yet, for some reason, the "democratic" leaders that govern us have neglected to invite us to this summit, or even

to show us the texts they will be discussing for that matter. They have even gone as far as to build an enormous fence around a large part of Quebec City to keep us out. All this has prompted many reformist organizations to protest, and they will be in Quebec City to demand a "place at the table."

Yet we, anti-statists, anti-authoritarians, anti-capitalists, and revolutionaries, will be converging on Quebec City for a different reason. We are not interested in a place at the table of capitalism, or in providing a more humane and friendly face for what we know to be an inherently flawed system. We have a different vision, one of a society based on mutual aid and solidarity, where people are not robbed of the fruits of their labor, and where decisions that affect everybody are made by everybody, rather than by a select few. And, just as importantly, a society where people know who their enemies are, and are ready to stand up to them. We are interested in nothing less than the destruction of the "table of capitalism."

The Summit of the Americas is an attack on all of us and must be treated as such. We must show the ruling elites of the Americas that we are ready to resist their attacks and fight back. We must show them that we are ungovernable and that no amount of police can keep them safe from the anger of those they oppress.

Friday April 20th is the day of action called by the Anti-Capitalist Convergence and the Summit of the Americas Welcoming Committee. Actions on this day will be divided into three "blocs." A green bloc with no, or minimal, risk of arrest; a yellow bloc, for people planning to do civil disobedience; and a red bloc, for the "disturbance oriented" crowd.

We are thus calling on all militant revolutionaries to converge on Quebec City on April 20th in the red bloc to show the ruling elites that no fence is strong enough to withstand the force of the people when class anger erupts. It's time for the Revolutionary Anti-Capitalist Offensive!!

IT DIDN'T START IN SEATTLE, IT WON'T END IN QUEBEC

Revolutionary Anti-Capitalist Offensive
Spring 2001[1]

"We Have Nothing, Destroy Everything! Everybody to Quebec City!"
From the March 2001 issue of *Barricada*.

Into the Great White North: Remote Border Crossing, Eastern Maine, Sometime in April 2001

Months of scheming, plotting, and planning, and it all boiled down to this one most momentous of moments. I slouched back in my seat, opened my mouth gaping wide, let my tongue hang out just enough to be believable, tried to drool a bit, and generally did my best to look as pathetically fast asleep as possible.

We rolled in. "Where you boys headed?" she asked us. I cracked open an eyelid; the curiosity was too much for me to handle. She looked old, friendly, and innocent. It was 3 a.m., and she was alone. Good signs. "Newfoundland, ma'am. Ski trip, ma'am," answered our driver, decked out, as we all were, in his finest yuppie wear. I personally was sporting khaki pants, a Carhartt vest, and sunglasses around the collar of my shirt, despite it being the dead of night, in the middle of the winter, and in the great sunless north. I'd seen yuppies in the wild before, and apparently they did these things! A printed-out map of the ski area where we had made reservations, as well as two pairs of skis in the middle of the car, completed our disguise.

"All US citizens? Any criminal records?" Both together. The tension was unbearable. We knew this routine, and these were exactly the questions we had hoped to avoid. The entire reason for this somewhat complex operation to enter Canada was precisely that we were the *dirty car*. As in, the one filled with all the problem kids, traveling as one group so as not to compromise anybody in the next shipment of anarchists across the border, all of whom were still legally *clean*. We weren't all US citizens, and yes, there were some pretty exciting criminal records among the gang.

In my personal case, it was even worse. A couple of months earlier, on our way to a planning meeting in Quebec City, we had been stopped at the border. In finest international-drug-smuggler style, our car carried its contraband stuffed inside the lining of its doors. Only in our case, instead of drugs what we were trafficking was the March issue of *Barricada*. And while the customs officials didn't find the ones stuffed in the doors, they did manage to find the small stack that some absolute imbecile (possibly myself, I honestly can't remember) left under the driver's seat. And this was unfortunate. Because while *Barricada* was never the most subtle of publications, that particular issue was particularly direct. The cover was a full-color fold-out poster of a couple of cops on fire, with the headline "Fire and Flames for Capitalism!" Not necessarily the calling card you want to present at customs and immigration, you think? Maybe not, but still pretty good if you consider that the last page of the magazine, featuring an extensive list of creative ways one might cross the border into Canada, ends with a graphic of a mob of armed people screaming, "We Have Nothing, Destroy Everything! Everybody to Quebec City!"

"Yeah, I don't know how these got here, officer," I answered. "Honestly, I just volunteer at a bookstore and they asked us to take these for them. I didn't even think to look through them, I don't know anything about politics myself. This is crazy. I'm personally offended by this content, and believe you me, I'll be having some harsh words with the people who gave me these. What's that? Are we headed to Quebec City? No, of course not. We're just young college students on our way to Montreal to drink alcohol." It was the most unconvincing story I'd ever tried to sell, and I felt almost embarrassed to be pitching it out loud. Which is why I still can't believe that, despite essentially announcing in writing that the purpose of our visit was how to best organize to burn one of their cities to the ground, these people actually still let us into their country! Yes, there was an attempted interrogation, as well as a lecture from Canadian border police on the virtues of Canada as a democratic country that was interested only in keeping troublemakers out, along with the signing of a document stating that we were allowed only to the Montreal area and if found in Quebec City would be subject to arrest and deportation—which I promptly threw in the first trash can I found once we had arrived safely in Quebec City.

Back to the scene of my second attempt to cross the border, the "ski trip." After a brief but in my mind seemingly eternal silence, the rest of the car laughed and responded with a pretty confident "No." I drooled intelligently. What a preposterous concept. Us? Criminals or foreigners? Rich, white yuppie college students, headed to a ski resort in a brand-new golden rental car, made possible by the kind financial contribution of an aging radical leftist professor? Of course not!

"Can I see your ID, please?" This was bad. ID checks we certainly couldn't stand up to. The whole purpose of this charade was that we had no doubts that, despite being allowed into Canada after the incident with the incendiary reading materials, we had at the very least landed ourselves on a no-entry list and would be denied crossing at summit

BARRICADA

REVOLUTIONARY LEFTIST PUBLICATION OF THE BARRICADA COLLECTIVE

Front and back cover of the March 2001 issue of *Barricada*.

time. My dreams of days and nights of fire and brimstone on the streets of Quebec were slipping through my fingers.

She took the IDs, glanced at them halfheartedly, and started to give them back. One of us had an odd name. She commented on the fact. "Yes, ma'am, you see, ma'am, my parents are from _____, ma'am, and the name is traditional _____, ma'am." This was tragic. He was rambling. I liked him, but I would be forced to kill him as soon as we got out of this place, regardless in what direction we ended up heading. It's a golden rule: When telling imaginary tales, say as little as possible while seeming like a perfectly normal person holding a conversation. The more you talk, the more room for error. And furthermore, absolutely refrain from saying "ma'am" every damned second word!

Mercifully, he stopped. She started to wave us through, then paused. "Oh, what about him? He American? Arrests?" She was referring to me. I drooled defiantly. Silence ruled the vehicle. Why the hell weren't any of the idiots I call my comrades opening their mouths? Finally, somebody answered, "No." "Should we wake him?" they asked her. The moment of truth had arrived. If I was awoken, I would have to answer. If she asked to see ID, chances are she would then proceed to run it through the computer, and that would be the end of that. We could go home and watch it all on TV. Or perhaps the temptation would draw a bald-faced lie out of me and we would spend the summit sitting in a cell, not even having the privilege of watching it on TV.

"Nah, let 'im sleep." I drooled victoriously, an evil grin spreading on my imaginary internal face. Glorious achievement was written all over the insides of my yuppie mask. She waved us through. It was there, on that forgotten Maine road, directly on the way to Newfoundland and several hundred miles east of Quebec, that we scored the first of what would be a week of many victories. We were safely over the border.

Just Because You're Paranoid …

My memory being a pretty weak muscle, and these events being several years in the past, I have to admit that between my moment of victorious drooling and the actual arrival in Quebec City, I don't recall much of anything. The next image stored in my brain is of driving into Quebec City. We even took the extra effort to drive *around* the entire city and enter it from the north, just in case police were controlling the directions from the US and western Canada. We really didn't want to miss this!

I have scattered memories of driving past the convergence center in our fancy, good-looking rental car, and of quite a few pairs of eyes intently set on us, clearly thinking to themselves, "These are obvious undercovers, try to remember their faces, this may be useful to you in the days to come." I have to admit, for some reason I found myself mildly amused and entertained by this. (Note to you young ones out there: Never, ever go to the convergence center. They are death traps for the innocent, gullible, and helpless, crawling with surveillance, cops, wackos, and every other danger imaginable. Avoid them at all costs. I knew this in Quebec, although it seems I had forgotten it during some events later that year, which you will read about in the chapters ahead, and while this had no noticeable negative consequences for me—quite the contrary, actually—I'm sure the poor comrade who accompanied me there regrets ever setting foot in one.)

I recall our courageous and to this day much-admired driver, who despite my frustrations at the quality of his verbal border-guard-finessing skills not only was forced by us to take history's longest route from Boston to Quebec City but then immediately undertook the drive back to Boston, only to return with another car full of crazed anarchists a few days later. An unsung hero if there ever was one!

I recall sitting in meetings conspiring with people I'd never met, with a ski mask on the whole time because you never know who's there and you can never be too cautious, as well as refusing to attend what turned out to be a pleasant nighttime warm-up demo, out of fear of preemptive arrests, as had occurred at a few prior mass mobilizations. But mainly, I recall staying cooped up in the "safe house" and waiting for the days of action to begin, with a growing sense of paranoia.

I felt like the world's most wanted fugitive, even though I was guilty of no other crime than a whole helluva lot of fantasizing about smashing glass, panicked cops, tumbling fences, and humiliated and shamed politicians. Well, I guess we were all pretty guilty of some kind of conspiracy, and it was probably less than completely normal to be living in a house with enough helmets and hockey sticks to equip several professional ice hockey teams—but those details aside, we were model citizens. I was so paranoid that every time I made the intrepid voyage across the street to the supermarket (lest one find oneself in the midst of an involuntary hunger strike due to the fear of going outside in the days leading up to the action) I was half expecting the cashier to take one look at me and order the doors of the store be locked as she called the police, nervously muttering, "Uh, we got one here, pretty sure he's here for the riot"—in French and with a strange Quebecois accent of course! No amount of acid or other expensive designer drug shit will get you these delusions.

It paralleled some of the less outstandingly militant moments of my youth, standing in line at the Argentine equivalent of a Store 24 or 7-Eleven at 4 a.m., stoned beyond any and all sense of judgment and loaded with absurd amounts of chips, chocolate bars, sugary kiddie cereal, candy, popcorn, soft drinks, and whatnot, eyes darting nervously as I muttered to Jorge, "Dude, man, are you *suuuure* this is allowed? I think the cashier is looking at us all weird." (Yeah, I was straight edge for many years of my youth, but not all of them. I can feel some of you judgmentally snorting, "Pfff, if you're not now you never were" as you read this. Spare me.)

"Yes, genius, she probably *is* looking at you weird. Because it's 4 a.m., you're spending your life savings on junk food, and your eyes look like you lightly sandpapered them."

"But are you *suuuure* it's allowed to just blatantly buy so much food? I mean, you don't think it's too much and we'll get arrested?"

"Yes, Tomas, I'm sure."

"Okay, but if I get arrested because of this shit, I'll kick your fucking ass, man. I'm a fucking serious deadly revolutionary, I can't get arrested for this kinda shit."

"If we get arrested for *buying food*, you can feel free to kick the living shit out of me and never speak to me again," he said in a tone usually reserved for one's seven-year-old sibling.

"Okay, deal."

Of course, what inevitably happened was that this tension, the tension existing exclusively in my head, that is, inevitably reached its boiling point as soon as it was my turn to interact with the cashier. At which point, and without managing to say a single coherent word, I burst into uncontrollable laughter, unable to breathe or communicate, and Jorge had to both pay and escort me out.

I felt more or less like this when I arrived in Quebec City, but without being stoned out of my mind. Only a healthy addiction to adrenaline, the revolutionary's best friend, mixed with the fear of it being taken away from you, can do that.

Short story long, I was in bad shape here. Mind you, this wasn't the fear of the inexperienced, or frightened, or what have you. It was the fear of the compulsive troublemaker, sensing himself lucky enough to have arrived at what was, up to that point in his life, the biggest prescheduled political disturbance he was to have the pleasure and privilege of partaking in. Many others just as deserving as me (if not more) had suffered the misfortune of being turned back at the border and had been relegated to following the events on TV as a sort of anarchist version of the Super Bowl. For us, though, everything was going perfectly, and all that was left to do was to wait patiently ... and it was killing me!

We weren't just parachuting in for the fun here, however, and to be fair to ourselves, our being safely in Quebec City and in a relatively safe and secluded place had little to do with luck and much to do with the extensive and intensive effort, organizing, and planning we had invested into making this mobilization a success. Together with comrades from other cities, we had written up both of the "Revolutionary Anti-Capitalist Offensive" calls that were then subsequently published in *Barricada* as being written by an "Autonomous Organizing Collective of Anti-Authoritarians from the Midwest, Northeast, Montreal, and Quebec," together with the not very believable disclaimer that we had "received these texts anonymously" and were "printing this call and providing space in our publication in order to ensure the success of this initiative."[2] Never ones for armchair quarterbacking, we had been up to the city several times in the months prior and took a very active hand in ensuring that the right elements would be mobilized into town, that they would have the logistical elements necessary for their safe arrival, and that once arrived they would be well cared for and well equipped. Just as importantly, we attempted to provide the political coordination and cohesion necessary to ensure that ours would be an effective fighting force on the streets of Quebec, not just tactically but also politically.

... Doesn't Mean They're Not After You: The Germinal Affair

Which is exactly why when François, one of the Quebecois comrades, breathlessly entered the house on April 17, just three days before the start of the summit, to inform us that six individuals from Montreal had been arrested "with an arsenal of smoke grenades, shields and baseball bats that police say were to be used at the summit" as they drove to Quebec City, the saying that "just because you're paranoid doesn't mean they're not after you" took on a vibrant new degree of urgency for us.[3] While the arrest of some comrades was unfortunate, a preemptive arrest of comrades on the way to a summit — especially well-equipped ones — didn't seem out of the ordinary or like a particularly concerning turn of events at first, even if the loss of a small arsenal of shields, bats, and smoke bombs was a setback. Yet François seemed extraordinarily concerned. Our Quebecois friend, temporarily losing his grip on the English language in his agitation, struggled to find the words. "No, no. You're not understanding. *Germinal!* It's the people from Germinal. One of them was a cop!"

Backs arched, heads shot up, and urgent and worried looks flashed across the room as we began to understand what he was saying and the implications it would have on us. The "Montreal" part of the Autonomous Organizing Collective of Anti-Authoritarians from the Midwest, Northeast, Montreal, and Quebec was, among others, comrades from Germinal with whom we had met on more than one occasion. Germinal was a small but politically heterogeneous group that "doesn't make a claim to having a precise ideology: different political tendencies cohabit in its bosom, from communism to Quebec independentism by way of anti-authoritarianism and feminism."[4] In a press release a few days following the arrests, they described themselves as a "political self-defense movement based on the principle of facing the force of police on equal footing." In their words, "Our struggle has pitted us against the thugs of the state" and "to effectively resist … organized force, it's necessary to also organize civil self-defense."[5] This was a sentiment and spirit we firmly identified with, focused as we were on making sure that our side arrived at the impending clash with the best possible materials as well as making political preparations so as to not be mere punching bags for the thugs of the state. It was unsurprising that we had drifted toward each other in the course of our preparations for the summit.

Someone said the obvious thing we were all thinking: "We need to get the fuck out of here, right now!"

Jorge remained silent, though, assessing the situation. "Who did you say this place belongs to?" he asked François. "You said they weren't political, right?"

"Right, it belongs to a nonpolitical friend of a nonpolitical friend."

"Okay, so we're safe on that side. We entered Canada without our passports or IDs being run, with a car whose plates don't trace back to any of us and which is already back in the US anyway. So there's no names to look for or any car that can lead them here either." He looked at François, then at Cadger, then at me. "Our safety here depends on every-body being honest and admitting mistakes if they made them. Whatever embarrassment you might feel, trust me, that will be better than us all getting picked up because somebody was too ashamed to be honest."

He continued his comradely but determined interrogation. "Did either of you use your real names during any of these meetings or at the consultas?" He was looking at Cadger and me, as we were the only two Barricada members who had attended the consultas—large, open general assemblies attended by hundreds of activists of all stripes, which we had also taken advantage of to hold private meetings with other militant elements. We had made an art of having a new and wholly unremarkable name for each one of us at every mobilization, meeting, or city we found ourselves in, the only downside being the numerous awkward moments when, in the course of a meeting or event, someone would address one of us by our supposed name and we would completely fail to react until it dawned on us that we were being spoken to. "Oh right, right, *Joe!* Yes, it's me you're talking to, because Joe is in fact my name and has been so since I was born."

I was almost offended by Jorge's question, and my face showed it. I responded with something unnecessarily arrogant and dismissive. "François, besides your affinity group and us, does anybody else know we're here? Because that's really the only weak link I can think of."

François shook his head with conviction, and Jorge reached his conclusion. "I think we're safest here. Any comrade's house will be worse, we definitely can't check into a hotel, and even just walking down the street exposes us to getting stopped. Finally, if they were going to do a wave of arrests, they would have done it simultaneously, to avoid us scattering and disappearing. I know it seems counterintuitive, but I don't think they're after us and I think we're safest here."

While Cadger and I were basically already halfway out the window while Jorge spoke, he made some solid points. I looked lovingly at our mountain of helmets, hockey sticks, and pucks and pondered the sad fact that if we were to leave, we would be forced to abandon our arsenal. Combat folklore and misplaced romanticism aside, abandoning our materials would be a serious setback to the larger bloc, as we had stockpiled materials for a good forty or fifty people. We took the necessary precautions, such as setting up a twenty-four-hour watch, and made the political decision that if they came, we would resist in the hopes of creating a standoff that would last long enough for more activists to gather and create a visible conflict out of our situation. But we chose to stay.

Had we known then what we would learn soon after, we would not only have immediately scattered to the four winds, but we probably would have made our way out of Canada as discreetly as possible. Our assumption, which seemed a reasonable one, was that there had been an informant in the immediate social vicinity of Germinal, a trusted sympathizer to whom somebody had said too much, leading the cops to a relatively lucky strike. The reality, however, was not only solidly out of a spy novel, but also illustrated that while we might have sometimes underestimated ourselves, our capacities, and the danger we represented to the state, they were deadly serious about us and more than willing to invest large amounts of funds, man-hours, and energy in order to neutralize us.

As Mario Bertoncini, one of the arrested Germinal members, explained in an interview a few months later, "The police discovered our movement following a tip in November [of the year 2000]."[6] In early December, a thirty-four-page report prepared on the basis of information delivered by a police informant, in which it was stated that "a group of leftist and anarchist militants was organizing for demonstrations around the summit ... with the objective of de-stabilizing it," marked the beginning of the monthslong operation.[7]

After several months of twenty-four-hour surveillance and monitoring of all incoming and outgoing phone calls made by Germinal members known to them, the authorities devised a plan to infiltrate the group. The Royal Canadian Mounted Police (RCMP) mounted a joint operation together with the Sûreté du Québec, provincial police service for Quebec, in which they "created a fake transportation company between Montreal and Quebec, seeking to employ one of our members."[8] Knowing that Jean-François Dufresne, one of the Germinal members, was looking for work, they posted "notices around his apartment. Jean-François in fact turned out to be the first person to apply for the job," which offered what was at the time an attractive pay of seventy-five

Canadian dollars per trip.[9] "Jean-François was immediately hired by
Andre Viel, a police officer in the RCMP since 1991. Eventually, Alex
Boissonneault, another Germinal member, was hired as well. Some
time later, the police officer Viel introduced a new 'employee': Nicolas
Tremblay, RCMP police officer since 1997."[10]

The police officers used the repeated long drives between Montreal
and Quebec, fifteen of them in total, to gain the trust of their targets.
The police infiltration strategy was as much effective as it was classic
in the infiltration of radical movements: "First, begin lightly with an
employer-employee relationship; proceed to fabricate a false relationship of friendship based on supposed common interests or opinions;
finally, develop a bond of camaraderie uniting militants in struggle
against a common adversary."[11] In likewise classic informer/infiltrator
fashion, the two policemen who eventually became new members of the
group were extremely rich in material resources, eager to share them,
and unusually enthusiastic, often attempting to push other members
of the group to more radical and violent plans.[12]

Fearing infiltration and at times suspicious of their new "comrades,"
Mario explained that they concluded that "there didn't seem to be any
risk, since it was inconceivable that they would have created a business,
mobilized numerous vehicles, hired us, and invested all this energy just
for our little group."[13] Not only did it turn out not to be inconceivable,
but according to a police source the entire operation ended up costing
nearly one million Canadian dollars.

The end result? Seven arrests and charges of "conspiracy to commit
mischief that could present a real danger to the lives of people," "possession of explosives with dangerous intent," "theft and concealment of
military equipment of a value less than $5,000," and a dramatically
produced press conference on April 18 in which police presented to
the media and general public the formidable arsenal of the so-called
Germinal Commando.[14] The media were all too eager to present the story
of dangerous armed anarchist extremists plotting to lay siege to the city
of Quebec, blaring information about the arrests and their footage from
the police press conference on the front pages of all the main newspapers.

According to *Le Soleil*, the arrested "had at their disposal a formidable military arsenal" and were preparing to "cause serious damage with
stolen military materials.... The activists also had gas masks, slingshots,
two bags of steel bearings, homemade shields, baseball bats, motorcycle

helmets, chains, a hammer, pliers, and several thousand antiglobaliza-tion flyers."[15] The theatrics of state repression were completed by the display, alongside the mostly defensive weapons, of assorted dissident literature, "including copies of the anarchist newspaper *Le Trouble*."[16] While the *Journal de Montréal* speaks of the "perfect rioter's kit," *Le Devoir* takes the police discourse one step further and writes of "bombs" being found among the Germinal group's materials.[17]

We watched the television coverage of the police press conference in concerned silence, then took in the sensationalist newspaper cover-age on the morning of April 19. If their plan was to dissuade us, it failed spectacularly. We were already in this dance, and at this point, we had no intentions of abandoning it. If anything, these events strengthened our conviction and drew into even clearer focus the importance of the battle that lay ahead. And if their objective was to turn public opinion against anarchists and militant resistance to the hated fence and the FTAA summit, the events of the coming days would prove that they had failed, just as spectacularly.

"What If Nobody Throws the First Stone?": Laval University, Friday, April 20, Noon

Finally, mercifully, the glorious day arrived. After a long night of star-ing worriedly out the windows, plotting, pointlessly wearing helmets around the house, and finally getting around to the last-minute detail of, you know, painting the banner we had told every anarchist in North America the bloc was supposed to converge around, it came time to move on out.

Jorge was there, anxious to get his first real taste of action after having been unable to participate in our inauguration adventures. He had also had the misfortune to be out of town when we'd had our "discussion" with Nazis in Wallingford, Connecticut, the month before. Alan, now our in-house anarcho-celebrity better known as the Flying Anarchist thanks to his inauguration feat at the Navy Memorial, had likewise missed Wallingford and was itching to get back in the fray. Our grizzled veteran of the protests at the World Trade Organization summit in Seattle, Steve, was geared up to relive those days, and Moose, who had also had his fun in DC, was ready to go.

Last but certainly not least, there was Cadger. Cadger had invested just as much time and energy as I had into making sure the FTAA summit would *not* run smoothly, and, always being a trusted partner in all things related to danger and criminality (and in the boring shitwork as well), he was to be my partner for the day. I'm sometimes averse to having partners during actions, which I'm aware is not a positive character trait, but if there is one person I can work with, he's definitely the one. The whole trusted crew had assembled, with the remaining members having arrived late that night, and we were ready to thrust ourselves into the battle to come.

The walk from our home base to the starting point of the demo was one of those experiences one would be sure to never, ever forget. It had all the hallmarks of a strange, disconnected, and surreal dream. There we were, a group of about a dozen people (us, plus our local connection), walking down the street on a perfectly sunny and surprisingly warm morning in Quebec, dressed in black from head to toe. Among us, we carried a neatly folded and unbelievably heavy banner. Wrapped inside it were a good forty or fifty hockey sticks with their blades sawed off. Another two comrades tried their absurd best to look like ordinary citizens while lugging a bag filled with hockey pucks. There were crowbars, there were poles, there were helmets, and there were hammers. You name it, we had it.

As civilians walked by us, I made it a point to smile and nod politely as if we were nothing more than a bunch of young locals out for a morning stroll. This is a common psychological trick I use while blatantly partaking in illegal activities. Act like it is the most normal thing in the world while doing it, and most people will react like it *is* the most normal thing in the world while watching it. Of course, this tactic only works within the limits of reason and common sense, and we were pushing these as far as they could possibly go. And just when it seemed this walk would never end—we truly, sadly, incredibly got lost on the way—the university campus dawned over the horizon.

We stood around in the relative safety of the university campus, lost among the gathering black-clad mob. *The Northeastern Anarchist*, publication of the Northeastern Federation of Anarcho-Communists (NEFAC), would go on to describe this mob as "one of the most well-equipped and broadly supported (not to mention, the most gender-diverse) black bloc mobilizations in recent activist history."[18] It was then and there that I was struck by a recurring irrational fear: that the expected and anticipated riot would magically fail to materialize.

Front banner of the Revolutionary Anti-Capitalist Offensive as the black bloc march departs the university campus.

This fear was especially ridiculous because we were now in a group of at least several hundred, in which "many people came prepared with padded body armor, helmets, batons and shields (to counter police attacks); gas masks, vinegar-soaked masks and heavy gloves (to defend against tear gas); ropes, grappling hooks and bolt-cutters (to tear down sections of the security fence); and slingshots, hockey pucks, rocks, paint bombs and Molotov cocktails (to take offensive actions when necessary)."[19]

As we started walking down an avenue devoid of shops or officers of the law, the terrible fear that nothing would happen, that it just wouldn't get started, refused to subside. Here I was, among thousands and thousands of demonstrators, a good thousand or so of whom were dressed in black and armed in one way or another, panicked that nothing would happen. I nervously asked Cadger, "What if nothing happens? What if it just doesn't kick off? What if nobody throws the first stone?"

Wisely, sensing my fear and despair, he answered, "Of course it will. Of course somebody will throw the first stone."

"But how can you be so damned sure?" I pleaded, on the verge of tears.

"Because if nobody else does, one of us will. And if we do, the rest of our cluster will too. And then the rest of the mob will follow." Alas, truer words had never been spoken.

The walk into town reminded me of Chairman Mao's Long March. In other words, a death march! We trudged for a solid two hours, wearing helmets and jackets in the unseasonable heat. The road was lined with nothing but trees, small houses, and residential apartments. There was not a cop to be seen anywhere, nor anything really worth lashing out at. (Well, there was one traffic cop, who, when the tires of his vehicle were punctured, clearly lacked the tact or experience with militant demonstrations to know to just sit peacefully in his vehicle and let it go, and he almost paid for the mistake with his life.)[20] This scenario did not help my "nothing's gonna happen" complex. But finally, just as I was expecting victims of heat exhaustion to start dropping from the march, we reached the first symbol of international capitalism that would have the misfortune of crossing our route: a Shell gas station.

Immediately, individual bodies surged out of the crowd and hockey pucks glided gracefully through the air, shattering windows and starting the beautiful music that marks the entrance to the "other reality" of riots and disturbances. The soothing sound melted the anxiety, and the power of numbers and determination roared through the bloc. Not far ahead lay the fence of shame, behind which cowered the rich and powerful of our continent, deciding our fate, trading our resources, and, curiously, having forgotten to invite us to the party!

Red, Yellow, Green: The Colors of Resistance

Our march now numbered comfortably in the five digits. Needless to say, anarchists—whether in bloc or otherwise—represented nowhere near the majority of demonstrators on this day. The broad spectrum of the antiglobalization movement was represented there. There was the traditional hard left, represented by the entire alphabet soup of authoritarian Marxist organizations, including a surprisingly large and well-equipped contingent of Quebecois Maoists. There was a fair amount of older antiwar and pacifist types, whose activism seemed to have found a second wind inside the spectrum of the antiglobalization movement. Among them were some of the more dogmatic types, traditionally of the "peace police" and "parade marshal" variety. Their commitment to pacifism was so authoritarian and odd that they would at the drop of a hat resort to both violence and conspiracy theories to justify attacking people involved in property destruction and handing them over to the cops. We'd had issues with them in the past and, at risk of giving away the world's least surprising plot twist, would have issues with them in the future. Finally, there were locals. These locals were to greater or lesser extents politically aware or active, but they had all been drawn here by an effective combination of the intense anarchist and anticapitalist outreach work done in the lead-up to the summit, as well as by the several unforced errors on the side of the police and authorities.

The authorities had no better idea as a security concept than to erect a miles-long "security perimeter" around the area of the convention center. This perimeter fence quickly became known as the "Wall of Shame" and was despised by both activists and locals. Intended to be erected almost a full month before the start of the summit, the fence not only significantly impacted the daily lives of the many area residents, but its almost medieval nature also presented antiglobalization activists with a simple and effective messaging opportunity: "Which side are you on?"

As Cindy Barukh Milstein put it:

> The contrasts could not have been sharper. Closed meetings and secret documents inside; open teach-ins and publicly distributed literature outside. The cynical co-optation of "democracy" via a gratuitous "clause" as a cover for free-floating economic exploitation versus genuine demands for popular control and mutual aid in matters such as economics, ecology, politics, and culture. The raising of glasses for champagne toasts versus the rinsing of eyes from chemical burns.[21]

Our message was clear and resonated with the local communities: *They aren't here for you, and we are not the invading "anarchist hooligans" you have been told to fear. The real invaders, of your city, your lives, and your well-being, are those building fences to hide behind an army of fifteen thousand cops while they decide our future.*

While the political makeup and traditions of the crowd may have been wildly diverse, there was near consensus on two crucial aspects of the mobilization: anticapitalism and a respect for diversity of tactics. There was an explicit understanding that it was not only this latest iteration of free trade agreements that was problematic, but that capitalism in and of itself needed to be confronted and abolished — and that all forms of struggle are valid and necessary in that pursuit. These positions might seem self-evident today, but at the time the adoption of explicitly anticapitalist and pro-direct action positions by what was essentially a mass movement was a testament to the galvanizing effect that the Seattle black bloc had on the larger antiglobalization move- ment — and in this case, of the excellent work of the two large coalitions of anticapitalists, the Convergence des Luttes Anticapitalistes (CLAC, or "Convergence of Anticapitalist Struggles") in Montreal and the Comité d'Accueil du Sommet des Amériques (CASA, or "Summit of the Americas Welcoming Committee") in Quebec City.

Milstein continues, "It was a brilliant stroke to stake out a non- reformist posture not only in CLAC's name but in the very theme for the summit weekend as well: the Carnival against Capitalism. An opposition to capitalism was openly front and center, both during the many months of organizing leading up to April and at the convergence itself."[22] Most importantly, from our perspective as anarchists, both organizations upheld and practiced a deeply anarchist and antiauthoritarian vision of both anticapitalist struggles and what the world of resistance against it, as well as the one that would replace it, should look like. "CLAC/CASA's short lists of organizational principles ... included a refusal of hierarchy, authoritarianism, and patriarchy, along with the proactive assertion of such values as decentralization and direct democracy."[23]

Together with a vocal and vibrant rejection of capitalism steeped in antiauthoritarianism, both CLAC and CASA boldly and unequivo- cally embraced the concept of diversity of tactics. This was particularly effective in the run-up to the summit in defusing the eternal movement debates about "violence" and stifling media-driven narratives about "good" protesters versus "bad" protesters. Just as importantly, CLAC and CASA adopted the "Prague model," which had been used with great success by demonstrators just a few months before at the summit of the International Monetary Fund in the Czech Republic. By implementing a color-coded and geographically separate action concept (red for high- risk actions, yellow for nonviolent direct actions with risk of arrest, and green for actions with low or no risk of arrest), organizers were able to create clearly defined and announced spaces for people with all kinds of different comfort levels for risk as well as varying tactical preferences.

This maximized mobilization by "making everyone comfortable setting their own level of involvement and risk."[24]

The diversity of tactics stance succeeded in creating what Milstein calls a "welcoming space for those many more anti-authoritarians who perceive themselves as less militant. It widened the margins not of militancy, in other words, but of what it means to reject capitalism as an anti-authoritarian."[25] In practice, "What the diversity of tactics principle translated into was a diversity of people."[26]

A few blocks before we reached the hated fence, the sound system announced, "Turn to the left to go to the green zone if you would like to participate in a safe, nonconfrontational carnival against capitalism."[27] Hundreds, maybe thousands, broke off from the march and headed into the neighborhood of St. Jean-Baptiste, a working-class area located in the urban core of Quebec City whose residents had been greatly affected by the security perimeter that ran through the heart of their community. We didn't go there, but as Nicolas Phebus, local member of NEFAC and member of the neighborhood's Comité Populaire, writes, "The 'green zone' on Saint-Jean was a smashing success."[28] A smashing success made possible only by the deep ties between local anarchists and the community. Phebus continues:

> Years of involvement in the neighborhood, working around various issues with all kinds of people — single moms, working poor, artists, youths, merchants, etc. — proved to be essential. In less than two weeks, we mobilized a new group to organize our "green zone" activities. The response was inspiring: dozens of people took it upon themselves to organize and staff a free food table, an infoshop, a place for kids, different musical events, and so on. On the other hand we were able to produce a special 16-page issue of the Comité Populaire's newspaper, and distribute 9,000 copies of it door-to-door the weekend before the Summit. In this newspaper we tried to explain everything we thought was important to understand the opposition to the Summit. We had articles explaining "diversity of tactics" and the system of three color zones, the non-reformist approach, the links between globalization and welfare reform, the Black Bloc, and so on. And of course a front-page article urging people to take to the streets and "occupy the neighborhood." ...

The scene at the toppled fence on April 20, 2001.

Thousands of locals showed up, many feeling so safe they even came with their kids. It was also used by at least three different affinity groups to carry non-violent symbolic actions (which probably wouldn't have happened otherwise).... This said, we did make a few compromises while organizing it. The biggest is that we felt that, as organizers, we had a responsibility to do whatever was possible to ensure that it was a safe place for everyone. Although we knew that in reality this wouldn't necessarily make the place any safer, we did communicate to the police that this was a "green zone" where trouble was not expected. We didn't ask for a permit, but they gave us one anyway. We also organized a "security team" which scouted the whole city to know where the riot squads were all day. One compromise was that, although it was an anti-capitalist day of actions, we did collaborate with the merchants on the street and tried to ensure their collaboration. This way, many boarded storefronts became free expression billboards. The action wasn't "pure," but we think all of it was worth the price.[29]

Back on the Boulevard René-Lévesque, the voice on the sound system continued: "For those of you who wish to continue the fight, the fence is straight ahead!"[30] This was our cue.

"This Fence Can Stop a Vehicle Traveling 90 Miles per Hour"— But It Can't Stop Our Movement: Boulevard René-Lévesque, Friday, April 20, Approximately 3:00 p.m.

I can affirm with all the conviction in my heart that the scenes that followed were some of the most beautiful moments I have had the fortune to experience. Moments blessed with a singular feeling of power and liberation. The sublime instant when the logic that is force-fed us from birth—such as that streets are for cars and that cops are for obeying—is thrown out the window, leaving as final fleeting mark the sound of shattering glass, or in this case crashing fences. It is the time when all other concerns leave one's mind, when the body becomes invincible, physical pain is never more than a small nuisance, and desire and conviction shape realities. It is the moment when ordinary rebels, filled with rage and hope, can act in accordance with the urgency of their yearning. When the adrenaline courses through the veins and nothing else matters beyond the experience at hand.

I felt it in the moment, as "thousands continued on towards the fence, touching off the first of the weekend's protracted street battles," and I can't deny it now.[31] Battle makes me happy. It makes me feel alive. The acrid smell of tear gas makes me feel nostalgic, and I can't put vinegar on my salad without thinking of the relief it so often gave me from the blinding and choking effects of chemical warfare. But I will argue until I turn blue in the face with whomever believes that this is somehow because I enjoy violence. From a tabloid NEFAC distributed in Quebec City: "The truly violent are those who prepare for the summit by accumulating tear gas, plastic bullets and pepper spray. Those who enact laws and measures that will put hundreds of thousands of poor in the street, those who let pharmaceutical corporations make billions on sickness, causing the death of millions of people, those who are copyrighting life and creating dependence and hunger. In a word, those who put their profits before our lives."[32]

Battle against the state is the fulfillment of my convictions. It is the realization, however stupidly and fleetingly, of my ideas. It is completely natural and normal to take pride and pleasure in those moments and those acts. And so it is with exhilaration and joy that I enter into battle for what I believe in. That moment represents, at the very least, an opportunity for the advancement of my ideas and the retreat of those forces diametrically opposed to them. In the spaces we create, be they

A lone demonstrator throws a tear gas canister back toward police.

permanent in structures of dual power or temporary as we beat back the forces of the state on the streets of Quebec City, there is the realization of the world I aspire to help build and live in. It is joyous work in the advancement of the end of violence. How could we carry it out with anything other than broad smiles under our masks?

Risks are forgotten, consequences irrelevant, and your power is beyond limits.

It was this power that provided the beautiful and unforgettable scenes of ordinary people becoming fire-hurling superheroes, of rather small people hurling enormous chunks of pavement with shocking ease, and of red and black flags flying high amid clouds of tear gas. Above all, it allowed us to topple the fence that could "stop a vehicle traveling 90 miles per hour" in a matter of minutes and put us face to face with the riot police, who watched in a state of awe, wondering uncomfortably what would come next.

What came next was a sea of people swarming into the "red zone" and throwing themselves, armed with only some helmets and hockey sticks, directly at the lines of riot police, who retreated slowly, surprised as they were by the conviction and virulence of the crowd. Small groups

Police shoot tear gas at demonstrators from behind the toppled fence.

charged them with metal barricades in hand as others continued the aerial bombardment of cement, golf balls, and hockey pucks. There were even a few teddy bears, launched by way of a rolling catapult![33] I happily allowed myself to be overcome by "riot tunnel vision," in which the only direction to look was forward, and threw myself at the cops. Barricades flew, arms and legs swung, and I picked a tear gas shooter to concentrate on. Unfortunately for me, at more or less the same instant that my hockey stick impacted his body, the line of cops parted directly to his left. From behind came yet another cop armed with a tear gas shooter. He pointed directly at my chest and, leaving me time only to grimace, fired straight into me.

First, the air left my body. Immediately after, a cloud of white powder exploded onto my jacket and flew straight into my face. The two-dollar goggles and the vinegar-drenched ski mask I was wearing allowed me to take note of the situation around me a bit in the moments before I became completely blind.

In my mind, the toppling of the fence was to be followed by a mass invasion of the "red zone." Battle-crazed fire-throwers up front and the rest of the mob following behind—not out of any sort of vanguardist concepts, just because, you know, throwing the mollies from behind is neither safe nor elegant!—as the police scum slowly edged backward. This was precisely the task I had thrown myself into, and I assumed others were on the same page. Sadly, the reality was quite different.

I looked back and beheld a scene reminiscent of a Roman gladiator battle. The deafening roar of the cheering crowd was not accompanied by action but rather was coming from a huge mass of people at a safe distance behind the fallen front section of the fence, or worse, lined up like spectators at a marathon, behind the still-standing sections of fence and on the sides of the street. Perhaps this was due to simple fear, or perhaps it was because the anarchist movement has done a rather good job of breaking the myth that "violence" against property or inanimate objects is unacceptable but a significantly poorer job of deconstructing the state's monopoly on violence against people (under which I grudgingly classify cops). Those who had actually crossed the now imaginary line between "our" zone and "their" zone didn't seem to number much more than a few dozen, at most fifty.

Reality—the one outside of my mind at least—is unfortunately not painted exclusively in brushstrokes of glory and heroism. Amid the beauty and power of the scene were mixed some rather unpleasant sights. Some misguided genius threw a Molotov from within the crowd and almost hit one of our own. Another did more or less the same, grazing my helmeted head and sending a rather unpleasant whoosh of heat in through the side of my helmet. A few other brilliant bulbs placed themselves smack in the middle of the conflict area in a nonviolent sitting protest, creating a significant risk to themselves of someone throwing a stone and injuring or killing one of them.

Granted, this text is an account of a whole lot of rioting, lawbreaking, and assorted violent actions. However, I have nothing against pacifists, and by no means do I view violent action and mass disturbance as the only way to achieve any sort of revolutionary social change. Far from it. They are but a single tool among an array of many others. Further, these actions can even be counterproductive when not complementing the much more tedious but important day-to-day work of building structures of popular power and resistance. There is a time and place for everything, and hypocritical as it may sound sandwiched in what is essentially a several-hundred-page-long chronicle of rioting, I say it regardless: It is very important not to allow ourselves to be sucked in by the more glamorous aspects of our work. A wide and diverse movement with room for all to participate in it—in the way they best see fit and to the extent of their abilities—is the only kind of movement we should seek to build. That said, while those who prepared the groundwork that created a local population favorable to us, as well as all who provided logistical support (medics, movement journalists, housing organizers, and so on), were just as important, if not more, as those who took part in the actual frontline fighting, that was not my role and this is but one person's account.

That disclaimer now behind us: Authoritarian and ultra-ideological pacifists are also not to my liking. Dogmatists who believe they have the right to impose their tactical and philosophical concepts on others have no place in a healthy antiauthoritarian movement. Particularly vile are those who believe that the heat of battle is somehow the moment to try to prove their point. Those who interfere during actions, who try to grab militants during fights, and who put out fires in banks (fires set with much love and care!) are simply making already dangerous tasks more dangerous and putting others, as well as themselves, at extra risk. Among ourselves, we made the stern decision that those who purposefully interfered during actions, and by doing so endangered us or others, exposing us to risk of arrest and injury, were essentially doing the job of the police. As such, they would be extended the same treatment that is normally reserved by us only for the repressive agents of the state. In short, they were fair game in our book.

So it was about time to go and lob one of these fools into the nearest cop (two birds, one stone) and out of our way. Sadly, by this point I was damn near blind from the tear gas wafting from my jacket, so instead I staggered back out of the gladiator cage and into the crowd. Nick of time, too, because shortly after that I just could not, for the life of me, open my eyes. Blind as a bat in the middle of a momentous battle. I don't recommend it!

Fortunately, one of the many golden-souled activist medics came to my assistance. "Okay, okay, just open your eyes," she said in a voice that sounded as if she were asking me to do the simplest task imaginable.

I insisted, "I can't, I can't, there's no way."

Through my blindness, I sensed her looking at me with pity. I could hear it in her voice. There wasn't much doubt in my mind that I wouldn't like what she would say next. "Don't be afraid, it's okay, just open your eyes," she cooed gently.

Grateful as I was, my thoughts were something to the effect of, "God fucking dammit, what in the hell is wrong with you. Here I am blind in a riot and you want to talk to me about abstract and philosophical concepts like fear. I fucking hate leftists." (For the record: I consider myself a leftist, of the antiauthoritarian brand, I am proud of that heritage, and I don't tend to appreciate it when people try to convince me that a social anarchist is any other sort of creature.) "Don't you get it, I'm quite simply physically incapable of opening them."

Thinking it unwise to say that out loud to the kind woman, but not knowing how to express the problem more diplomatically, I stammered and ended up whimpering something incomprehensible, akin to the sounds a frightened puppy might emit. I sighed internally and braced myself for the next round of condolences and pity. Before she had finished the next sentence, my patience was up and I blurted, "No, you don't get it. I am not capable of opening my eyes. You need to grab them with your fingers, open them, and squirt whatever magic potion you intend to squirt in them."

Aside from the sounds of crashing objects, diverse screams and yells, and tear gas canisters flying overhead, nothing much happened. Finally, she said something again. It wasn't good. "Yeah, the powder from your jacket is starting to get to me as well. I can't see very well either, we need to get somebody else to take care of you." And with that, she thrust me in some direction or other and eventually into the hands of someone else. This next person thankfully wasted no time, pried my eyes open, squirted me with something, dragged me away from the action, and sternly told me to stay put for a few minutes. It was like being a small child on time-out, but they were clearly the voice of reason here.

Sitting there, on my relatively comfortable and distanced grassy hill, taking in the panoramic view of the action while enjoying the bitter smell and tingly sensation of tear-gas-drenched air, my eyesight slowly returned to normal, allowing me a welcome opportunity to assess the general situation and plan my next steps. The riot cops, having noticed that the crowd would not surge forward and eat them alive, had reorganized themselves and begun slowly advancing—although not before suffering the comical humiliation of sending their brand-new

Anarchists ruin the water cannon's debut, quickly putting it out of action for the day.

ultra-expensive toy, a water cannon truck, charging from behind the crowd into a mass of black bloc anarchists. Apparently the user's manual didn't explain that these things are best used from behind the safety of police lines to keep crowds at a distance, and not as a sort of massive and pretty slow iron horse to run through crowds. Unfazed and unimpressed, we promptly tabled the turns and charged at the water cannon! Great was our surprise when, in one of the summit's most iconic David versus Goliath scenes, a lone anarchist was able to approach the driver's side window and shatter it with nothing more than a wooden hockey stick. The water cannon beat a hasty retreat, not to be seen again that day.

Water cannon debacle aside, the cops had meanwhile quickly figured out that tear-gas canisters were not meant to be used as rubber bullets and were more effective if lobbed into the middle and back of the crowd rather than aimed at the chests of those in the front. Thus, they had managed to split the crowd into more and more clusters, creating a fair bit of panic as people retreated from clouds of gas only to find more clouds of gas still farther behind. It was clear that this battle was lost. We had lost the element of surprise and there was no possibility of reorganizing our forces in this atmosphere. And slowly, sure enough,

The aftermath of the April 20 clashes in Quebec City.

the fighting did die down, as people were pushed into the intersecting streets, down in the direction of the cliffs.

I soon found myself drifting with the mob in that same direction, and it was not long before I was comfortably lounging on the steps of some building, helmet and hockey stick at my side, enjoying a warm soup provided free of charge by one of the many activist support groups and pondering the perfectly sunny day, with nary a cloud in the sky. It was a pleasant interlude of calm, of chatting with friends and comrades from faraway cities, and of wondering what the rest of the still young day would bring.

Play Stupid Games, Win Stupid Prizes, Benefit from Mutual Aid and Solidarity

So there I was. I had long since lost both my affinity group and Cadger. Riot tunnel vision provides me with a strong sense of direction and purpose, as well as making me acutely aware of my surroundings and the dangers they could bring, but it also makes me sometimes forget about anyone who does not pose a danger to me. Like I said, I can be a bit averse to partners and affinity groups during actions anyway. I trust my judgment and know I can look after myself and make correct decisions, and I fear being held back by the sheep mentality of militant spectators, a particularly North American phenomenon, at least at the time. Also, to be honest, a lot of us Barricada kids were also pretty well networked thanks to our roles with the magazine, the federation, in mobilizations, and within antifascist circles—which allowed us to relatively safely affinity-group-hop even in the midst of actions, since there was often at least one person whom we could identify and who could vouch for us.

That said, about four hours later, I managed to find myself standing around, alone, on the same avenue where the fence had once stood, having lost about one hundred meters or so to the advancing cops, looking with muted interest at the situation. It reminded me of the typical drunken college riot or chaos punk riot: The cops stand there, not doing much of anything aside from firing the occasional tear gas canister, and we also play our assigned role in the mini-spectacle by having some drunken punk/college kid throw the occasional stone or beer bottle.

Suddenly, I felt an incredibly powerful and painful blunt force impact my upper thigh. Clearly, somebody had hit me with a baseball bat, as my leg gave way and I instantly fell to the ground. But how—and why?—had anybody hit me with a bat when there wasn't really anybody near me? As medics swarmed around me and an affinity group with shields and helmets rushed in to give them cover, it dawned on me that what had taken me down was not a bat but, unsurprisingly, a plastic bullet. Not a rubber bullet, mind you, a plastic bullet. These are much wider, which is why I didn't associate the pain with what one might expect from a rubber bullet.

As the old adage goes: Play stupid games, win stupid prizes. For some reason, I had decided to throw a stone at the cops. It was a stupid, pointless, futile act. Nothing at all was to be gained strategically from it, and there wasn't any kind of significant cover of people from which to do it or into which one could retreat. It was a prime example of: I'm doing this because I can. I was playing "drunken punk aimlessly throws rock," although I was neither drunk nor a punk, and I definitely knew better. Which isn't to say there always has to be a strategic end to an action of this kind. It can be an expression of personal rage, a moment of anger, a way to gain confidence in one's own abilities. And if you aren't needlessly putting others in danger, there is a solid chance that neither I nor my comrades will be policing your actions at a protest, since we, you know, generally frown upon that.

But this was just dumb, and I can picture the cop on the other side going, "Yeah, I think I'll just shoot the jackass with the helmet who's standing there alone and just lobbed a stone at us." Fortunately for me, I managed once again to straddle the line between learning a painful lesson and then moving merrily along, and suffering lifelong and life-changing consequences from my actions. I was shot in the thigh. Upper thigh. Inner upper thigh. Do you see where I'm going with this? Maybe three or four inches from my groin. Judging from the explosion of black, red, and blue bruising that wrapped around the entire circumference of my thigh for well over a month, I'm pretty confident that had the impact been on my groin, it would have resulted in hospitalization and potential lifelong consequences.

As it turned out, the medical treatment I received was somewhat different. "Open your mouth, open your mouth," one of the medics commanded. As I pulled up my mask and complied, one of them stuck something under my tongue. I assumed it would be some kind of medicine, some magical painkiller, but being of a curious nature I asked what it was. "Vegan chocolate, to help keep you calm." I'm not sure this was quite the intended medicinal effect, but it did make me laugh, which temporarily distracted me from the blinding pain, so I guess I can't exactly call it ineffective.

One of the formless, trash-bag-wearing, helmeted, goggle-sporting, shield-wielding creatures that were protecting us turned to me and asked if I could walk. This was an excellent and rather terrifying question. Honestly, I wasn't too eager to find out. Just as how in cartoons you don't start falling until you notice there is no ground below you, likewise you aren't injured until you try to use the affected part of your body and it fails to comply with your commands. Having been seriously injured one, two, or a dozen times, I know this to be undeniable. So, as long as I just lay here peacefully enjoying my vegan chocolate, I would be perfectly fine aside from the pain, and I wouldn't in fact have a broken leg or any kind of sharp, stabbing pain that might hinder my walking or running.

Because, trust me, being out of action due to a broken bone had absolutely not been in my planned schedule of events, much less if the cause of injury were to be noted as "is apparently an idiot." Reluctantly, I began to get up, since when you are not actually a drunken punk or college kid, how long can you really lie in the middle of the street before it becomes unseemly?

Fast-forward fifteen minutes. I was off the streets and in some-body's apartment. Two of the previously formless masked and shielded creatures were caring for me, except that they were now revealed to be friendly-looking young people, a man and a woman. It was the same two who had successfully peeled me off the pavement and, despite my insistence that I was just fine, were adamant about taking me back to their place for a short break to make certain that I wasn't seriously injured. Going home with strangers you've just met and whose names you don't even know? Questionable even under the most normal of circumstances. Definitely not best practice when playing "lone injured rioter in foreign country." But the alternative of limping around alone, possibly grievously injured and soon unable to walk, didn't seem much better. And honestly, if they were cops, then they were the most thor-oughly equipped and best-disguised infiltrators imaginable and would almost deserve the right to arrest me for their efforts.

So there we were. John, as we'll call him, although I never knew any of their names, was icing my inner thigh in what I can only describe as an unexpectedly and uncomfortably intimate moment. The other, let's call her Megan, was providing me with painkillers in the form of drugs apparently more powerful than vegan chocolate. She seemed to have some medical training, and I was receiving some first-rate, personalized medical attention, free of charge, courtesy of one of the world's finest insurance policies: anarchist solidarity and mutual aid. Megan gave me her prognosis: "You got very, very lucky. First of all, just a little farther toward the middle and you would be in an ambu-lance or emergency room right now. But as it is, it's just a really bad contusion."

"Can I … ?"

"It'll probably hurt like hell, but you're fine to keep going. Or you can stay here if you want, that's fine too, but we're going to head back out in a few minutes. Where you from?"

Usually I would hesitate, or respond with the go-to lie, "Springfield." But I was feeling a bit vulnerable, yet comfortable in the hands of these strangers. I was lying on a sofa, being cared for and fed by street fighters who had cast off their armor and weapons—a small stack of shields, helmets, and slingshots sat by the entrance—to reveal the friendly and caring personalities of unknown comrades. In a moment of rare candor, I responded honestly. "Boston."

Megan raised her eyebrows, and her reply was almost immediate. "Do you know the Barricada kids?"

I shouldn't have, and I'm embarrassed to admit it, but I again responded honestly. "Um, kind of. I'm in the collective." As it turned out, they were very much familiar with our fine publication.

That broke the ice, and for a few minutes we forgot that outside a battle was raging. They told me that they were from Prince Edward Island, a place I hadn't known existed and which honestly sounded made up. As we spoke, even for that short moment, I was amazed at the extent to which although we came from what I would eventually learn are polar opposite places, both geographically and culturally, the bonds of the anarchist idea—the belief in the principles of solidarity and mutual aid, in class over country—could make comrades of us in a matter of minutes, even in the most adverse of circumstances.

In that apartment and thanks to a random collective of kids from some far-off place, I was given a practical lesson in a concept that the me of my youth had for years refused to grasp: There isn't just an entire network of support and solidarity behind every fighter. First of all, there is no behind and no in front. There are equal positions on different fronts of struggle, and everywhere is a front line. Every fighter depends on their network of support and solidarity, just like any healthy network of support and solidarity needs its fighters. But as those PEI kids showed me—well-equipped, fearless, and militant as they were, as I would learn while sharing barricades with them over the course of the weekend—every fighter is ideally much more than just a fighter, and we would do well to not allow the role of combatant to take over the entirety of our personas.

First Interlude: Seattle, April 20, Sometime Late Evening

That evening, FBI agents "raided the offices of the Independent Media Center in downtown Seattle, seizing computer-log records, according to federal sources."[34]

Just a few hours earlier, on the other side of the continent, a group of intrepid anarchists in Quebec City had broken into a police vehicle, which was either unwisely parked or abandoned by fleeing officers. They liberated shields, helmets, communications equipment, and, most importantly, a binder full of documents. After quick reading and quick thinking, they rapidly determined that these particular documents were for sharing. They headed to what we can only assume was a safe location with anonymous internet access and logged on to Indymedia—the activist Twitter of the antiglobalization era.

As the *Seattle Post-Intelligencer* would later report, "Security plans intended to protect Western leaders attending a trade summit in Quebec City were stolen from a car there over the weekend and posted, hours later, on a Seattle-based Web site."[35] The wording is unfortunately deceiving, giving the impression that the uploaded documents, posted on Seattle Indymedia, have to do with protecting "Western leaders" from assassination attempts or murderous terrorists. In fact, they were primarily focused on antiglobalization demonstrators and different crowd-control strategies and contingencies to be employed against them—such as which directions to steer unruly crowds toward, where to call police backup from depending on the location of disturbances, and so forth.

Most importantly for us, the documents included a list of "high risk" individuals and groups to be monitored and targeted—and, it's safe to assume, to be arrested if identified. It's not the longest of lists. If we had seen it or been made aware of it before leaving the house on Saturday morning, one particular line would have caused us great concern: "Unnamed individuals from the *Barricada Collective*."[36]

But we didn't see the list, just as we were blissfully unaware at the time that a cop had infiltrated NEFAC as well. As we would later learn in the Coalition Against Repression and Police Abuse's report "The Germinal Affair: The Art of Infiltrating and Manipulating a Militant Group":

> On April 18, Sergeant Detective Robert Lessard instructed his undercover agent to attend a joint general assembly of the CASA

The black bloc on the move on Saturday, April 21.

(Summit of the Americas Welcoming Committee) and CLAC (Convergence of Anticapitalist Struggles)....

The list of targeted individuals of this surveillance operation was composed of three militants of the Quebecois Émile-Henry group, three militants of the CLAC Montreal, one individual from the Boston anarchist group Barricada, and one individual from the US anarchist group Sabate (also from Boston).[37]

Still blissfully unaware of the extent to which we found ourselves in the crosshairs of state repression and surveillance, we set out the next morning with joyful determination for a second day of confrontation in the streets of Quebec City.

The Anarchists Are Coming: St. Jean-Baptiste, Saturday, April 21, Approximately 4:00 p.m.

The day began with a permitted march composed primarily of "Canadian unions, progressive organizations, and assorted activists" that drew close to forty thousand people and made its way "through the lower part of the city, far away from the FTAA meetings and the security perimeter," where it "ended in an empty lot."[38] One Canadian Auto Workers union member was clearly upset and could be heard asking,

"Why was the 'legal protest' conducted miles away from the security perimeter? Had I known I was marching toward a parking lot, I would have stayed home and done that at the fucking mall."[39]

The Northeastern Anarchist continues the description: "Of course, not everyone followed the march to its final (non)destination. About halfway through the march, a de facto coalition of wobblies, Canadian Union of Public Employees (CUPE), Canadian Auto Workers (CAW), black bloc anarchists, and radical cheerleaders" broke off from the official protest march of the more mainstream organizations, mainly Canadian unions, and headed toward the fence on Boulevard René-Lévesque. "Along the way, a couple of bank windows got smashed in, and at one point several anarchists ran down a side street and returned rolling a dumpster full of long wooden sticks and projectiles."[40]

On the way toward the fence the bloc entered, for the first time that weekend in such an organized and collective fashion, the neighborhood of St. Jean-Baptiste. The reception we received was incredible and moving: "In a scene reminiscent of troops going off to fight a popular war, battle-ready militants marched up the hill and through the St-Jean Baptiste neighborhood while hundreds of people lined the streets and hung out of windows to greet them with loud cheers of support."[41]

CrimethInc. provides the sentiment of a resident on that day: "As one middle-aged mother observed while members of the Quebec Black Bloc hugged each other before going off to battle the cops, 'I always thought this was going to be sinister, but these are just brave kids.'"[42]

History was on our side in St. Jean-Baptiste, in a much more immediate and literal sense than usual. The neighborhood we were entering—adjacent to where the summit congress center was located, and through which a significant part of the security perimeter's despised "Wall of Shame" ran—was one of North America's few remaining working-class areas located in what are otherwise yuppified and corporate urban cores. St. Jean-Baptiste also happens to be, in the words of Nicolas Phebus, "for various historical, social and political reasons ... for the last 30 years a hotbed of radical activism."[43]

But while the immediate history of the neighborhood has made the terrain that much more fertile, and the actions and security strategies of cops and authorities have allowed anarchists to present a clear and simple alternative to locals, none of this would be enough without the principled and committed day-to-day effort of local anarchists.

Phebus continues:

Some local anarchists and radicals have been active for a few
years in the organization that is responsible for most of this
local activism: the Comité Populaire Saint-Jean-Baptiste. The
Comité Populaire is a 25-year-old community group that is part
anti-poverty group, part citizens committee, and part popular
education group. Although it is by no means "well funded," the
organization still has a few valuable resources, including a widely
read free quarterly newspaper, *l'Infobourg*, a weekly lecture
program, l'Université Populaire, an office in the middle of the
neighborhood with computers, fax and telephone, and a little
bit of money.[44]

Today, Phebus remains unequivocal about his opinion, one
shared by many local class-struggle anarchists and Comité Populaire
members, that "most of the antiglobalization activists, and most anarchists for that matter, were middle class and bourgeois and didn't give
a fuck about working-class people and lumpen people," while the
Comité Populaire was precisely a community organization of poor
and working-class people whose task it was to defend their material
and class interests. "We were interested in fighting the local effects of
neoliberalism," Phebus says in a 2021 interview. "We were into fighting
for tuition freezes at the university, for social housing, against welfare
reform, against unemployment insurance reform, and so forth. We
were basically fighting against the concrete application of neoliberal
policies in the national social system. Of course we know that there
is a link between globalization treaties and those policies. But we felt
that the real issue was poor people's conditions, not how the market
operates. In our view, activists were more interested in the conditions
of the Indigenous in Chiapas than of their neighbors in the inner city."[45]

Despite this original position, the Comité Populaire stopped seeing
the impending summit as a distraction when "it began to clash with the
daily lives of the people in Quebec City. When it became obvious that it
would impact everyone in the city for months. That it would make life
miserable for everyone downtown."[46] A situation that became abundantly clear when police announced their plans to erect the security
perimeter a full month prior to the beginning of the summit and to allow
only those with "resident cards" into the security zone. It was from this

point forward that the Comité Populaire took the lead in an impressive community outreach campaign. Organizing autonomously and outside of any broader coalitions, the Comité Populaire refused to enter into any violence versus nonviolence debates. And while "everyone was talking about the FTAA," the Comité Populaire "decided to talk about the summit, the cops, and the fence."[47]

Phebus continues:

We felt that globalization was way beyond anyone's interests. That the way to reach people was to discuss the security measures and organize against the fence. So in addition to the general agitation against the FTAA and anticapitalism, we developed a campaign around the security measures. We formed a group in the neighborhood with the Comité Populaire, an unemployed workers' union, CASA, and one other community group. We held a general assembly open to anybody, we drew up a leaflet, and decided on a plan of action. Instead of having a flurry of little actions, we decided to focus on two main things: a demonstration and a public assembly in the neighborhood about the fence.... We drew up a leaflet and printed about 4,500 copies, which is a little bit more than the number of doors in the neighborhood. We distributed them to everyone, and the cops made a terrible mistake. They arrested one of our crew who was distributing flyers, simply for refusing to identify themselves, which made national news and front pages of local dailies.

We approached the issue from a civil rights perspective, and the cops gave us the argument on a platter. Afterward, everyone knew that we were distributing leaflets, and it became kind of a fad to have the leaflet. The forbidden leaflet which the cops didn't want people to see. So it helped a lot, and when we held the public assembly there were like 150 local people there. We had invited the cops, the politicians, the mayor, the civil rights union, and none of them came. So in the end what you had was basically a panel of five anarchists talking with the locals. And the people, instead of having the impression of being duped into listening to anarchist propaganda, had the impression that the authorities were laughing at them. The cops didn't want to talk to the people or talk about the fence. They simply didn't want to discuss security measures with the locals. When they didn't show up it was a huge publicity stunt for us, because it showed that they had something to hide and disrespected people. The cops were basically saying that the fence was there to protect people from the anarchists, but in the end the shops were outside of the security perimeter, so this was a lie.[48]

The cops were trying to play on the local community's fear of a repeat of the 1996 clashes in the area, when during a huge riot "everything in the neighborhood was smashed." There was a fearmongering campaign from the cops and media for months, showing images anytime a window was broken anywhere around the world. "People were expecting Prague or Seattle. They were expecting every shop window smashed, every dumpster burned, every car overturned. That was the expectation and people were scared, especially because there were still vivid memories of riots, which frightened people."[49]

Fast-forward to the afternoon of Saturday, April 21. The much-anticipated anarchists have arrived in St. Jean-Baptiste. But thanks to the work of the Comité Populaire—which had even distributed another nine thousand copies of its newspaper on the weekend before the summit with "articles explaining 'diversity of tactics' and the system of three color zones, the non-reformist approach, the links between globalization and welfare reform, the Black Bloc, and so on"—we were received with open arms.[50] In the rarest of sights for an antiglobalization mobilization, the windows of the local shops were not even boarded up. It was clear to the neighborhood that we were not there to destroy their community—no matter what we may have thought of businesses and business owners, big or small—but rather to fight, for them and with them, against those who had been invading their community and affecting their day-to-day life: the cops and their fence.

The latest edition of the Comité Populaire's newspaper ended with an exhortation for "people to take to the streets and occupy the neighborhood."[51] The neighborhood responded, taking to the streets en masse to cheer on the "brave kids" and offering food and water. As time went by, more and more joined us in the streets. Their presence rendered the terrain all the more fertile for our resistance, and as word spread of the intensity and nature of the clashes, more and more locals

The black bloc makes its way toward Quebec City's Old Town after the union march on April 21.

switched from curious and supportive spectators to active participants. When all was said and done in St. Jean-Baptiste, in the eyes of
the neighborhood, "it's the anarchists who saved the day."[52]

Second Interlude: St. Jean-Baptiste, Saturday, April 21, Sometime in the Early Evening

The setting, from a participant's account in *Barricada*:

> Eventually the black bloc arrived at Rue St. Jean in the St. Jean
> Baptiste neighborhood. As was overwhelmingly the norm
> throughout the weekend, cheers and encouragement from almost
> everybody in the area met the bloc. At this point the bloc entered
> a rather narrow alley that led to a section of the perimeter fence
> which was largely unguarded. Immediately people went to work
> on it with bolt cutters, grappling hooks, and tying ropes. At this
> point a bulldozer was driven right up to the fence, presumably
> to prevent the black bloc from rocking it back and forth until
> toppling it in the fashion seen on Friday. The driver quickly
> pressed the bulldozer up against the fence and jumped out.
>
>   However, the bulldozer did not do much good, as people
> quickly cut a wide hole through the fence (and also smashed the

windows of the bulldozer). Once again, there was not the massive rush into the perimeter that would have been hoped for, but at least 30 people entered to face what was definitely not more than about 15 policemen. Upon seeing the masked intruders, many of the policemen decided to turn tail and run. Unbeknownst at the time, the next building down the street where the invasion had taken place, was the congress center where the delegates were located.[53]

It's a Wild West showdown in the Great White North. In my head I can hear the spaghetti western music playing, and I'm expecting a tumbleweed to come dramatically rolling across our scene at any minute. It's unfortunate to find myself playing this particular role, disapproving as I am of macho *mano a mano*, *hombre a hombre* posing. Had I had ten comrades with me, I would have gladly accepted their help, with no qualms about the unfairness of our numerical superiority. But in this moment, as I steal a quick glance behind me, I realize that as I continued to blindly push forward farther into the security zone, my comrades have retreated. I am very much alone, as is my opponent.

So alas, this is the role I have been cast to play, and I have no intentions of disappointing the spectators. (Narrator's voice: *There are, in fact, no spectators*.) We face off about ten to fifteen meters from each other. My opponent, modern-day sheriff of this town and guardian of the unjust existing order, has traded in the traditional sheriff's badge, cowboy hat, and boots for the look of the mid-level guardian of the status quo: suit and tie, badge clipped to his belt. His outfit is completed, fittingly for a scene in this movie, with a gas mask.

Nemesis of the Wild West sheriff, I am cast in the role of anarchist desperado. Lone, somewhat reluctant antihero, thrust into the fight against the isolated representative of the state's oppression. Or at least my mask allows me to decently play that role, hiding as it does that I ride gleefully and with a smile on my face into battle against our enemies. My outfit is likewise a classic of the outlaw anarchist desperado genre, just as effective at protecting anonymity as it is at resisting flowery descriptions. Black sneakers, black pants, black jacket, black ski mask, black motorcycle helmet. Vintage, if you will.

We pause for dramatic effect. Possibly speculating as to who will flinch first. We both stand our ground. The tension mounts.

Draw.

My opponent reaches around to the small of his back. To my surprise, he doesn't produce a gun. Having already been shot the day before (if "only" with a plastic bullet), discovering that I am not about to be shot again, this time with live ammunition, is a pleasant surprise. Instead, he snaps out an expandable baton. It's a cunning move. The weapon of choice of many a Parisian anarchist and antifascist, it hurts me to see it wielded by my enemy.

Little does he know, though, that I hold an ace up my sleeve. Or in this case, inside my jacket. I unzip it and reach inside. It doesn't cross my mind that this action could very well cause him to indeed draw his sidearm and thus be my last. What I produce is a gem even more beloved and mystically revered than the expandable baton. This diamond in the anarchist toolkit is more unwieldy and difficult to conceal, hence it is reserved for only the most special of occasions.

The crowbar.

What a beloved and versatile tool. We depict it lovingly in pictures and images in our media and publications, but has anyone ever really written prose in honor of its glory? Probably not. And honestly, hopefully not, as that might be going too far. Militancy fetishism and whatnot. But it is indeed one of the finest articles of militant practicality we possess. It is all things at all times. Tool with which to open doors, hammer with which to deconstruct capitalist landscapes, and, as in this moment, practical weapon of self-defense should one find oneself alone and in danger.

Crowbar in hand, and following yet another obligatory brief pause for dramatic effect, I sprint toward my suited opponent. This turn of events clearly is not in the script he was handed when signing up for this job, and he promptly turns tail and runs. As I chase him around the corner, an enormous building comes into view. The convention center, maybe all of fifty meters away. We've not only breached the perimeter, we've actually reached the convention center. Except there is no we, for I am alone. Alone, except for what is now an entire posse of suited men with gas masks between me and the building. This time, one of them does draw a firearm, and, driven as I may be but still not eager to make being shot a daily occurrence, I sprint back toward the safety of my comrades.

End scene.

The Wrong Three Way Fight—The Black Bloc Versus the Pacifists Versus the Locals: Offices of the Canadian Imperial Bank of Commerce, Saturday, April 21, Late Afternoon

The Northeastern Anarchist states: "In an effort to draw fire away from the frontlines on Rene-Levesque, the black bloc attempted to open up a new battle front against the security perimeter a few blocks to the east of the boulevard. Along a small side street off of Rene-Levesque, about 50–60 well-equipped militants were surprised to find the unguarded headquarters of the Canadian Imperial Bank of Commerce (CIBC) directly in their path."[54]

Not a word was said or a moment wasted as we encountered this blemish of a building in our path. It was almost perfectly square, all glass, gray and black—perfectly representative of the soulless architecture of corporate capitalism. Promptly "every ground-level window was smashed to shards by a frenzy of projectiles, and a Molotov cocktail was lobbed through the damaged exterior."[55] As *Barricada* describes it, "Crowbars, wooden barricades, rocks, batons, and anything else was used to send the capitalists a message."[56]

Aside from the principled "we destroy banks on site" position we were diligent about upholding, this unguarded property-destruction target was also a welcome reprieve from what was at this point going on thirty-six hours of nearly constant pitched battles with the cops. In contrast to much of the rest of the weekend, attacking the building was an almost calm and soothing activity to be taking part in, especially since it seemed unlikely that the building would shoot at us or fight back.

While the building may not have fought back, we were surprised to find ourselves promptly under attack. Not from cops, but from the "ultra-dogmatic pacifists affiliated with Operation SalAMI," a reformist coalition that had not only "refused to work with CLAC/CASA due to the diversity of tactics issue" but had even gone as far as to organize "workshops on how to interfere with property destruction and perform arrests" in the interest of "de-escalation" and "neutralizing potential vandals."[57]

What began as loud boos coming from the SalAMI crowd quickly escalated when "a Molotov cocktail was lobbed through the damaged exterior" and a group of pacifists extinguished the incipient fire. We didn't take kindly to this, and "the situation degenerated rapidly into a series of minor altercations. Supposedly 'non-violent' activists tried to physically attack the black bloc. People were shoved around, punches were thrown, and in one instance, an individual was maced after trying to defend himself."[58]

While we were focused on the pacifists, we at first failed to notice that they weren't the only ones looking on disapprovingly as we disassembled the CIBC building. We were also being observed, and not with loving and admiring eyes, by "a large number of local street kids" who had "congregated, not as protesters, but simply to watch the unfolding events," as one CrimethInc. eyewitness account puts it.[59] This was a demographic whose opinion we cared about significantly more, sympathetic as they were to "foreigners fighting the police, simply because they were fighting the natural enemy of street kids everywhere, while still being suspicious of them on the grounds that, like the delegates and the pigs, they were foreign invaders. Nothing the protesters had done until this moment raised their wrath—but, having no prior experience with the rationale of property destruction, the sight of a bunch of foreigners smashing up windows in their city enraged them."[60]

The yelling and screaming quickly became more intense, and the group in front of us became increasingly aggressive—following us, picking up weapons, threatening us with them, and yelling at us about "destroying their city." I couldn't help but sneer under my mask and think, "Bro, it's a cookie-cutter corporate box of a building housing a bank. It's not exactly the grocery store on the corner of your block." But aside from the immediate security risk the situation was developing into, we were acutely aware of the delicate political situation we were spiraling into, so I kept my constructive feedback to myself.

Until now our relationship with the locals had been stellar. They had identified the cops and the wall as the invaders into their city and the nuisance negatively affecting their lives, not the invading "anarchist hooligans" that the press and police had told them to fear. Our attacks on the fence and the police hordes had been met by supportive cheers and material support from locals, and as the confrontations persisted and became more and more widespread, more of them lost their fear and enthusiastically joined in.

News of a pitched battle between black bloc anarchists and local youths was guaranteed to spread like wildfire, leading to further conflicts between militants and locals. Not only would it destroy the dynamic of joint resistance that we had experienced so far, but it would also allow press and police to present the clashes as the work of isolated radicals, confirming the narrative of invading anarchist hooligans at war with the working-class population with whom they claim to be in solidarity.

What comes next is illustrative of the political maturity, tactical flexibility, and collective discipline with which the Quebec bloc, particularly in its Saturday iteration, handled itself.

From CrimethInc.'s journal *Inside Front*:

> A couple 'Bloc members tried to reason with them—the language barrier proved insurmountable, as did the machismo barrier, and both of them got punched in the face.
>
> These two kids are the ones most responsible for the success of the demonstration, though nobody knows it. They had the humility and focus to simply turn and walk away when this happened, which is fucking amazing, especially considering the reputation the Black Bloc itself has for machismo. If they had not done this, the whole weekend would have been ruined, and direct action activism would have been set back a decade—for the visiting activists would have ended up in a riot with the locals, and every possibility of something positive happening would have been lost.
>
> Given some time to cool off, the locals sent a couple of their number to speak to kids from the 'Bloc. It turned out they really wanted to fight the pigs together with these foreigners, and they respected what they [we] were doing, but needed an assurance that these kids weren't just here to trash their city. This given, on the conditional terms which any anarchist has to speak in when "representing" a larger group, the episode was over and everyone could focus again on the real enemy.
>
> I'm not opposed to property destruction, of course—if it were up to me, every corporate store, office, and factory would be burned to the ground by tomorrow morning—but it was critical that the 'Bloc kids recognize that, under these circumstances, it was an ineffective tactic, because the locals did not understand what it was intended to do. Had they insisted on sticking to 'Bloc dogma, catastrophe would have resulted. Instead,

everyone returned to the front lines, and the action reached its heart-quickening climax.[61]

We opted for a strategic withdrawal from the area—I prefer to not call it a retreat—and headed back into St. Jean-Baptiste.

An Exercise in Anarchist Self-Discipline and a Punitive Expedition: Somewhere in St. Jean-Baptiste, Saturday, April 21, Approximately 6:00 p.m.

From the participant's account in *Barricada*:

> The final offensive of the small but determined black bloc in the St. Jean neighborhood was carried out in conjunction with another affinity group which was carrying at least a dozen molotov cocktails. The general consensus seemed to be that, although the perimeter was too heavily guarded to break into in the immediate area, this particular action was about re-paying the class traitors in blue with a "warm" salute.[62]

We huddled and someone spoke. "They're confident that they're safe behind the fence. They won't move and they won't back away from it. All weekend we've been trying to breach it, they'll never expect this." There was no debate or hesitation, just quiet determination and logistics. "Shields to the front, slingshots right behind them, Molotovs third. Make sure to spread out the Molotovs on both sides."

There were maybe fifty of us, but we made up the core of that day's bloc. Almost all were either directly affiliated or loosely aligned with NEFAC or ARA collectives from the Northeast or Midwest (as well as some CrimethInc. people). A cluster of affinity groups composed solidly of people well prepared "both mentally and materially for the risks associated with being in a black bloc."[63] This was to be, in theory, the final hurrah of the day's small and disciplined bloc. As a final act we'd planned a sort of punitive expedition, with the intent of showing both to the cops and to ourselves that fear can and will change sides—and indeed is changing sides in real time before us.

One of the affinity groups had collected their remaining reserves of Molotov cocktails, and we had moved to a small side street, relatively shielded from the prying eyes of cameras and with the spectators' gaze at a safe distance. It was an almost private affair. Fifty of us and twenty or thirty cops about two blocks down, guarding a fence on a small and otherwise deserted side street. "The bloc formed up into lines with the shields at the front and advanced the two blocks up a narrow street. As the bloc neared the lines of police, tear gas canisters and rubber bullets began flying."[64]

At this point, I had been shot so many times already. (Okay, two times. But numbers are relative. Two Skittles for lunch: not a lot. Twice shot with different less-lethal munitions in thirty-six hours: a lot.) But there was no pain and no fear. There was no retreat. I was safe among my comrades. Nobody flinched, nobody retreated. We fed off of each other's confidence. Comrades who had previously shared an affinity of ideas with each other now strengthened their ties as they forged bonds of combat. Bonds no amount of meetings and discussions alone can replicate. Not a single person broke their line. We continued to advance, crouching behind shields and makeshift barricades. We met bullets with slingshots, and tear gas with cobblestones.

We inched closer and closer. Close enough that had I not been so concentrated on the task at hand, I'm sure I would have been able to identify the looks of worried surprise on the faces of our enemies. They had unleashed a veritable storm of munitions at us, and yet we continued our approach undaunted. A voice rang out from the heart of our bloc: "Now!" And "a hail of molotov cocktails was released onto the police lines, causing more than one to retreat, and drawing a loud cheer from the crowd."[65]

Satisfied with the weekend's activity, and concerned about such a militant group becoming isolated and vulnerable to targeted arrests as there were less and less people on the streets (or so we thought), we began to withdraw from the neighborhood and head toward the highway overpass at the Côte d'Abraham. There, we could grab a bite to eat—which some of us hadn't done for over twenty-four hours—and use the cover of the larger green zone crowd to safely disperse.

As we walked through the main commercial street of the neighborhood, I couldn't help but notice that despite two days of near constant clashes, many of which took place in the heart of St. Jean-Baptiste, not a window had been touched. While there was indeed property damage during the course of the weekend, targeting "several banks, a Shell gas station, a Subway restaurant, quite a few media vehicles, and at least one police vehicle," not a single shop was attacked or window broken in the neighborhood of St. Jean-Baptiste—and that was a good thing.[66]

This is not an uncontroversial statement, I'm well aware. It touches on issues of respectability politics and on the question of to what extent it is appropriate or even favorable to moderate our politics or forms of action in order to appease others or present ourselves as less intimidating or more appealing to broader sectors of society. In my eyes, it borders on anarcho-populism and brings up one of the political tensions I feel most vibrantly as an anarchist: the tension between waging war to the acutest extent possible against our enemies and acting strategically in the pursuit of amplifying the real possibilities of actually defeating those enemies and achieving our long-term constructive goals, as opposed to the more immediate and destructive ones.

Of course, as CrimethInc. wrote in regard to the situation at the CIBC building, if it were up to us "every corporate store, office, and factory would be burned to the ground by tomorrow morning."[67] But that we didn't in this case—although we certainly would have loved to and likely could have—is indicative of the deeply significant process that took place both in the run-up to the FTAA summit and, even more incredibly, in the streets during those two days.

Anarchists, broadly speaking, had successfully constituted themselves into a cohesive and coherent fighting force, both politically and on the streets. In the months preceding the summit—through the intensive efforts of anarchists within the CLAC and CASA, through anarchist influence and participation in community organizations like the Comité Populaire, through the extensive outreach and propaganda efforts of NEFAC both locally and as a regional structure, and through the efforts of dozens of anarchist groups and collectives across the continent—we had managed to articulate our political positions with enough coherence and reach a wide enough audience that we successfully defeated the narratives of the state and cops. Not only that, but anarchists were able to frame the political questions about the summit in a way that was favorable to radicalization and the advancement of anticapitalist and anti-state struggle. Public discourse centered more around the perimeter fence as a metaphor for the undemocratic nature of capitalism, while the unprecedented police mobilization was seen as the state acting in defense of the interests of the powerful, undercutting the state propaganda that the fence and cops served as barriers against the invading "anarchist hooligans." Anarchists successfully turned the state into the invader, and themselves into welcome allies of the local community.

As NEFAC members and platformists, our perspectives and objectives regarding these types of mobilizations were oriented toward the objective of, as Nicolas Phebus puts it, "involvement in the class struggle, to push for the autonomy of the class, and to radicalize—in the sense of going to the root of problems—social movements."[68] But this is a perspective that isn't terribly controversial among anarchists more widely. Anarchist "involvement in CASA and the Comité Populaire helped popularize anarchist principles and methods."[69] These organizations also successfully created a positive relationship between anarchists and the local community, the results of which were palpable during our time in the city, and which benefited local radicals for years afterward.

Had we chosen simply to act out our impulses and "adhere to bloc dogma, catastrophe would have resulted."[70] Instead, anarchists in Quebec City displayed shocking discipline—shocking, sadly, because in numerous instances in the years that followed, this wasn't the case. Of course, in this case, state surveillance and repression may have unknowingly aided in making this possible, as the obstacle of the Canadian border kept out a lot of the comrades who were less organized or plugged in or who had less access to material resources. This made for not only a numerically smaller bloc than at most mass mobilizations, but also a bloc that was, as I mentioned, quite politically cohesive, particularly after the first clashes had shrunk it to its most organized and prepared core.

Whatever the cause—whether it was fate, luck, political coherence, collective discipline, or a combination of them all—the fact remains: Despite the probably unfortunate, and at the time widely criticized, editorial decision in *Barricada* to go with a graphic screaming, "We Have Nothing, Destroy Everything! Everybody to Quebec City!" we didn't go on an anarchist rampage there. Not because there is anything inherently wrong with an anarchist rampage. I yearn to see every bank, office, and shop—every single physical manifestation of capital and its hold on our lives—razed. Phebus, too, is clear about this:

> There was a time when I also would have said fuck it and smashed the windows. Because I was young, poor, marginalized and felt no

Demonstrators take cover during clashes in the afternoon of the April 21.

connection to the community. But now I realize it's also more of a strategic question. Its about the larger goal and what you want to accomplish.... In order to win the argument for diversity of tactics, to be able to organize our own things, to be able to be part of the larger movement and not be totally marginalized—and to be able to be protected by the larger movement and the locals, we had to be able to demonstrate a certain political maturity and strategic thinking.[71]

In other words: Some moments are for living our desires, whether in small groups in the night or as five hundred like-minded folks in a militant demonstration, alone against the world, constrained only by the limits of our courage and capabilities.

But at other times, we have to know how to think strategically, to operate politically, to win over hearts and minds, to gain allies, and so to defeat our opponents. Because while we may desire to see the world of oppression, capital, and states burn down tomorrow, it's unlikely we will achieve that goal as an isolated invading horde—and if we do attempt to burn down this world on our own, it's even less likely that what replaces it will be something better.

Reaping What We Sowed: Côte d'Abraham Overpass, Saturday, April 21, Evening into Night

Very rarely in the life of an anarchist does the reaping come so immediately after the sowing, if it ever comes at all. (And if it does come immediately after, chances are it's not a good thing.) But as we made our exit from St. Jean-Baptiste, we were treated like heroes, "receiving cheers, water, and vinegar from local residents."[72] Before we knew it, we began to pick up stray black blockers as well as enthusiastic local youth, and our numbers swelled to a comfortable 150 people.

As we headed in the direction of the highway overpass at the Côte d'Abraham, we could clearly see clouds of tear gas rising in the air. We assumed that, at best, other similarly small groups might be engaged in confrontation with the cops. At worst, we feared it was pacifists getting gassed for sitting in the street, on a highway overpass that was closed anyway, in front of a fence. As we walked closer, we began to make out rhythmic drumming sounds. We rounded the corner and the Côte d'Abraham overpass came into full view. As I took in the incredible sight before me, I couldn't help but feel vindicated. We had been diligent in our organization and preparation. We had been disciplined in our work and messaging beforehand. We had shown restraint at the CIBC building and flawless collective self-discipline while in St. Jean-Baptiste. And now, we were seeing the results in real time. The scene was breathtaking, awe inspiring, and generally demanding of flowery language and prose beyond my literary skill. Luckily, the report-backs from *Barricada* and *Inside Front* capture the moment well:

> The perimeter fence is to our right with the water cannon spraying from behind, several rubber bullet shooters posted behind it and to their left a line of shielded riot police blocking a side street. In front of them, and all the way down the highway, thousands of people are assembled.[73]

> Quebec youths and street kids man the front lines, throwing back tear gas canisters and rocks as they had seen the activists doing, thrilling in the feeling of reclaiming their city from the powers of police and capital. They hide behind makeshift barricades, running up close to the police line to throw molotov cocktails into it, showing superhuman courage in the face of the

Demonstrators wear gas masks while contributing to the cacophony of rebellion during the evening of April 21.

once intimidating riot troops. Behind them, over three thousand people, of all ages and class backgrounds, stand on the freeway, beating out a deafening rhythm on every surface available in support of the street warriors.[74]

If our objectives were to create the conditions for revolt—to generalize resistance to the cops, the state, and the summit, and to normalize mass militance and confrontation—the scene in front of us was the practical confirmation of all our efforts. Militant resistance was now the collective practice of thousands, and courage had become contagious. Again, *Barricada* followed by *Inside Front*:

> 20 black blockers … took up positions behind a small staircase against a building near the line of riot police. They constantly fired their slingshots at the police and made advances, despite the rubber bullet firing riot cop that would periodically take runs at them.… When the policeman with the rubber bullet gun

would run out to shoot at someone, rather than retreat, dozens of people would run towards him, forcing him to beat a hasty retreat.... Every once in a while police would launch concerted teargas attacks, launching about 10 simultaneously. Yet, instead of retreating, people would rush forward, almost competing to get at the teargas canisters and launch them back to the police lines. As a result the police would be completely blinded. Dozens of fighters would take advantage of this to rush forward, take up positions, launch molotovs, and generally lay siege to the line of police.[75]

A piece of North America had been transformed into Palestine, a white man's Intifada now raging such as only the most idealistic punks and radicals had dared dream of—and immediately comprehensible and desirable to all present.... Below the freeway, in the activist camp that had once been part of the green zone, free food was shared, hundreds danced joyously in circles, spirits were higher than they've ever been for parades or holidays. People who had not been exposed to the d.i.y. values of sharing and self-determination immediately comprehended what was going on.[76]

At that moment in time, in that place in history, we could be forgiven if in our youthful enthusiasm and exuberance it really did seem to us that maybe, as the report in Inside Front put it, "the entirety of the old world was about to puncture and collapse."[77]

Epilogue: "Uproar Is Our Only Music"

There's a lot to be said about the events of Quebec City by way of conclusion. The simplest of them would be to quote the raw numbers given in "The Germinal Affair," which tell us that there were "463 arrests, 181 injured, of which 162 were demonstrators and 19 were police officers, and an estimated $50,000 in damages."[78] The security measures themselves had the astronomical price tag of $156,000,000. The intense tear-gassing of demonstrators alone set the Canadian state back "almost a quarter of a million dollars."[79] The mass tear-gassing was so unprecedented in Canadian history, with "police officers launching over 5,000 tear gas cartridges in forty-eight hours," that on Saturday, during the events, Canadian authorities were forced to order more stock from their US supplier, Wyoming's Armor Holdings. Nine hundred rubber bullets were also fired at demonstrators during the two days of clashes.[80]

While the hard numbers give us a feel for the enormity and intensity of the clashes, a political analysis can be found in the opening paragraph of an article published in *The Northeastern Anarchist* in the immediate aftermath of the summit. The article captures the spirit of hope and optimism of militant anarchism of the day while succinctly describing the importance of such mobilizations for the broader anarchist movement, as well as noting the encouraging trends of ever-greater acceptance and adoption of anarchist ideas and tactics by the broader antiglobalization movement:

> Despite the largest security operation in Canadian history, the best efforts of the Canadian authorities proved to be a complete failure in preventing demonstrations of "Seattle-like" proportions. For three days, defiant protesters destroyed large sections of the security fence perimeter, clashed with riot police, and were responsible for the delay and cancellation of a number of high-level trade meetings....
>
> Beyond the dramatic images of tear gas and street battles, the Quebec protests mark an important evolution in the anti-globalization movement in terms of tactics, militancy, organization and a radical departure from liberal-reformist politics. Despite the increasing popularity of direct action, decentralization and directly democratic forms of decision-making within the anti-globalization movement, the mobilization around the Summit of the Americas is the first time that these methods of organization were used to reinforce explicitly revolutionary anti-capitalist politics on a mass scale. Additionally, the wide support for a "diversity of tactics" managed to raise the level of confrontation and militancy during these protests, forcing the terms of struggle beyond the narrow confines of passive symbolic action and in the direction of revolutionary resistance.
>
> Indeed, for anarchists these developments point towards exciting possibilities for the movement, and instill great hope for the future of revolutionary struggle here in North America.[81]

If *The Northeastern Anarchist* offers us a window into the value of these mobilizations for the broader North American as well as international anarchist movement, the words of Nicolas Phebus are particularly valuable to understanding the immense and lasting positive impact that the actions against the Summit of the Americas had on the anarchist movement locally. Phebus, then a Quebec City–based member of both NEFAC and St. Jean-Baptiste's Comité Populaire, was generally of the position that so-called summit hopping was "a distraction" that drained the limited resources and energy of local radicals away from other, more substantive, class-struggle-oriented and day-to-day forms of organizing and struggle.[82] As Phebus puts it bluntly, he "had no interest in the antiglobalization movement before we learned that the summit was going to be in Quebec City. I was skeptical of people starting to organize for it two years in advance, and probably looked down on them. I also expected it to be mainly Trots and nonviolent types."[83] While he recognizes that Seattle and then Prague definitely caught his attention, he maintains, "We did not want the summit and did not choose the summit. And I've never been to another antiglobalization mobilization, either before or after the FTAA. To me it was a distraction."[84]

I make mention of his initial stance in order to qualify his remarks about the effect of the summit — and more concretely, the period of organizing to oppose it — on local radicals. Phebus is clearly not a cheerleader of summit mobilizations, nor particularly invested in the antiglobalization movement, nor a mindless cheerleader of militant black bloc anarchist orthodoxy. Far from it. He comes from one of the staunchest class-struggle-oriented and organizational traditions within anarchism. When asked twenty years later if the time, energy, and effort spent organizing to oppose the summit was worth it, his response is categorical:

> Yes, absolutely! The simple answer is that the summit increased the repertoire of action. It increased the scope of what's possible. The years before the summit, the late 1990s, there was a core of maybe thirty leftist youths in Quebec City. Those youths could mobilize maybe 100 or 150 people, and to do so you had to form crazy coalitions with Trotskyists, communists, anarchists, and all sorts of weird people. You had to compromise on everything, just to get maybe 100 people in the streets.
>
> After the summit, there wasn't just more of us. We had a new savoir faire and boldness in terms of direct action, not just in the

anarchist movement but in the community groups and social movements where anarchists were involved. This lasted for a decade, maybe even fifteen years, following the summit.

We learned a lot during the summit about organizing things and about starting from where we are and figuring out the steps needed to go where we need to go. We developed a more practical and concrete understanding of how things are done. Instead of pipe dreams, we had dreams and figured out what steps were needed to make them a reality. Of course the summit grew NEFAC, which reached fifteen or so activists in Quebec City post-summit, but not that much. The anarchist movement, though, the number of active anarchists of every persuasion, grew exponentially. And we were able to work primarily with them, which meant that the compromises needed in order to effectively be able to pull off larger actions, campaigns, or projects were way easier to make than the compromises needed to work with reformists. After the summit, for a couple of years, we had maybe fifty anarchist activists, with the ability to mobilize two or three hundred people.

This effect wasn't so much due to the riot. What propelled the anarchist left in Quebec wasn't the three days of the summit. Of course they helped. They galvanized people. But it was really the year beforehand. For most anarchists in North America, including Quebec, we have no movement to draw from. There's no one older than us. Every generation is faced with a situation where there is nobody who came before them and they need to reinvent everything from scratch. It's not like in France or Germany. For us, a black bloc was a dream. It was something you would see on the news. Squats were a dream. How on earth do you do that? How do you manage such a thing? We had a bit of experience with the student movement and some small direct actions related to it which were cool. But the summit helped us see how to do these things in our size. A year afterward we were able to fool the cops with a demonstration of 400 people and open a squat which lasted four months. We never had to defend it, but we were politically strong enough and organized enough that we were able to open a squat and put the city in a position where they couldn't just come and close it down. And that was, for the me of 1996, a pipe dream. It was impossible, you had to be in Paris to do things like that. It was unthinkable in Quebec City. The summit taught us that we could do that. That we could open an infoshop and keep it open for fifteen years. We could open a bar if we wanted to. We could organize a Reclaim the Streets. We learned that when we dreamed bigger than we thought we could, it often turned out well.[85]

The enthusiasm of NEFAC illustrates the optimism and boldness of the anarchist movement at the time. While Phebus's testimony speaks to the potential of these kinds of mass mobilizations to have long-lasting positive effects on local anarchist movements, this is far from a given, as we would soon discover in Gothenburg in the aftermath of the summit of the European Union.

Which is why we'll conclude with the most timeless of aspects, a poetic rendition of the spirit of the times, the conclusion to the *Inside Front* scene report, a piece fittingly preceded by the phrase "Uproar Is Our Only Music." With what one would hope is what those reading more than twenty years later will identify with and work to experience in their own adventures in rebellion. The experience of collective strength in battle, of rebellion even in the crosshairs of repression, and, most of all, of unbridled hope, bordering on deluded optimism. It requires optimism to believe that it isn't just the demise of the world of states, capital, and oppression against which we fight that is imminent, but that so too is the birth of the world of our dreams and desires, which will replace it. A world free from oppressions, states, and classes and filled with solidarity and mutual aid. The world of anarchy and communism.

As the sun set over Quebec City on the second day of action against the Free Trade Area of the Americas talks in April of 2001, the police slowly pushed forward to the north, until they were stopped in a standoff at the foot of a freeway overpass. At this point everyone else, rioters and reporters alike, had their faces covered for protection from the tear gas that filled the air; at the same time, those who had been timid before had lost their fear—from two days of watching bullying police hit in the head with bottles, of seeing supposedly impregnable walls torn down with ropes, of breathing tear gas until it lost all power to impress. It was impossible to tell now who had been from the Black Bloc and who had just joined the struggle: formerly apolitical Quebec street youth held the front lines, throwing back gas canisters and rocks as they had seen activists doing, thrilling in the feeling of reclaiming their city from the powers of police and capital. They hid behind makeshift barricades, running up close to the police line to pitch molotov cocktails, showing superhuman courage in the face of the riot troops that had terrified them twenty-four hours earlier.

Behind them, over three thousand people of all ages and backgrounds stood on the freeway, beating out a deafening rhythm on every surface available. The street signs, which only two days before had told them where to go and how fast, became sounding boards for their frustration and their conviction that this conflict was worth fighting; the concrete, which had cut them off from the soil beneath their feet and reinforced the propaganda on every corner proclaiming that the only possible condition was capitalism, competition and cultural standardization and mind-numbing work—that very concrete was torn up to become hammers to play that music of revolt, or else to be thrown, carried on the echoes of that percussion, into the faces of the forces of repression.

Below the freeway, in the activist camp that had once been part of the safe zone, free food was shared, hundreds danced joyously around fires; spirits were higher than they'd ever been for parades or holidays. People who had never been exposed to the anarchic values of sharing and self-determination immediately comprehended and embraced them. It seemed the entirety of the old world was about to puncture and collapse.

Who among us has not spent hours, weeks, whole years of life that, at the end, left nothing to show but the physical fact that we survived, that we lived through them? This moment justified even those sad, squandered years. Even the weary ones who had slogged through decades of tedium and absurdity were vindicated: we had finally arrived at this, the first threshold of childhood. The past behind us that had seemed so senseless, the future ahead unknowable and more menacing by the minute, all

Front and back covers of the May 2001 issue of *Barricada*.

this was worth it, justified into eternity, so we could live this danger, this freedom, this feeling of breaking through the skin of the world.

There is another world, a secret one made up of all our unlived dreams and unacted impulses, all those parts of ourselves which find no point of entry into the one that is—it waits, simmering, ready to boil over at six billion different pressure points. When it did that afternoon, we drank tear gas with gratitude and abandon, we were energized as people only are during great catastrophes or triumphs—neither plastic bullets nor water cannons could daunt us, for we were living as we had always known we should. The music we made together, beating out our own cadences on the sheet metal of the city, was the eruption of our individual longings into the material world; united in their singularities, they formed a symphony no composer could have authored. It surrounded us, deafening, greater than ourselves; when we closed our eyes, it sounded like singing, like a vast unearthly choir above us.

I would have liked for that song to have gone on forever, for it to have been our lives.[86]

WE MUST DEVASTATE
THE AVENUES WHERE THE
WEALTHY LIVE

LUCY PARSONS

10

DAYS OF WAR, NIGHTS OF LOVE

The EU Summit in Gothenburg, June 2001

The Siege of Hvitfeldtska: Thursday, June 14, Sometime in the Morning

"Wake up, wake up! You have to see this!" The Old Man was clearly agitated, which, given his usually calm demeanor, was already alarming. He seemed more amused and surprised than concerned, though. On the other hand, as I would soon learn, anytime that in the context of some international mass mobilization a comrade comes to rouse you with urgency from your sleep, chances are nothing good is happening. This might actually be a fair justification for my chronic insomnia, as while I am no scholar of hip-hop, maybe Nas was right and "sleep is the cousin of death," at least for activists. The Old Man insisted, "Get up now! They trapped us with containers."

"Eh? What?" This was about as articulate a response as I could muster. I wasn't quite sure if I was having trouble processing this because I was still groggy or because it really did sound incomprehensibly crazy.

We had arrived in Gothenburg the night before, on the eve of the first demonstration against the summit of the European Union and coinciding with the arrival of US President George W. Bush. We spent our first night sleeping at Hvitfeldtska school, one of several schools around the city that activists had negotiated with the local government

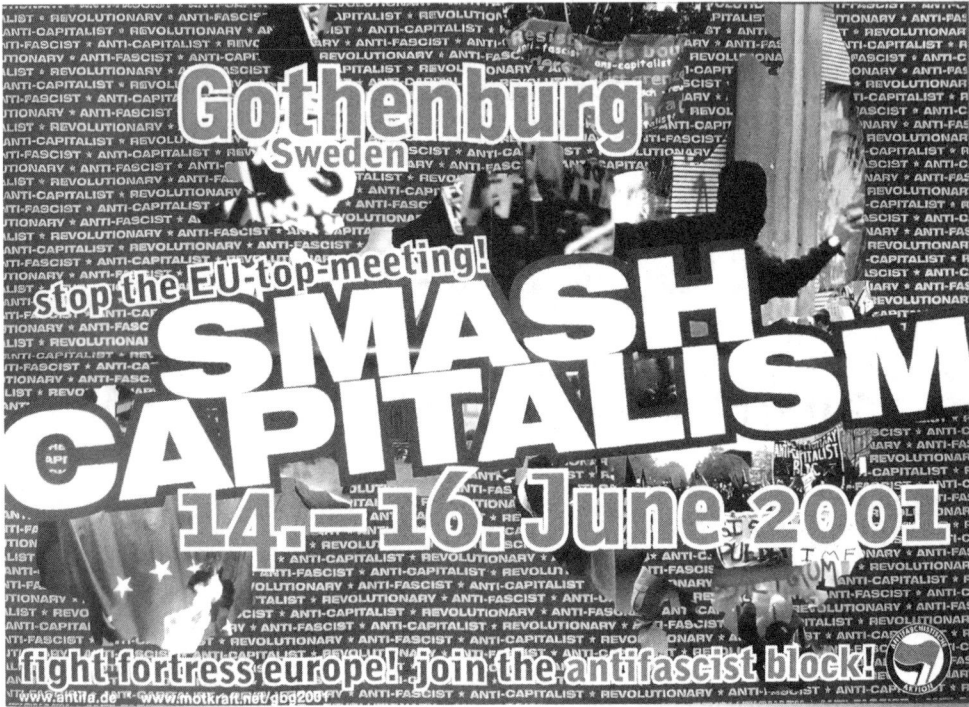

AFA mobilization poster for the opposition to the EU summit in Gothenburg, Sweden, June 2001.

to use as convergence centers and sleeping spaces. Hvitfeldtska was a castle-like three-story building located on a small hill not far from the center of Gothenburg, with a typical schoolyard-type open space in front of it. The main access to the school was a one-lane road on a slight incline, with a medieval-style stone wall on one side and thick shrubbery on the other. On all other sides the school was surrounded by about a city block's worth of forest, with the occasional pedestrian walkway and stairs leading to the school or yard.

"How could the people on lookout not notice when they entered the yard? How come nobody heard them? Why didn't they sound the alarm?" I asked as I got dressed and slowly became more lucid. We had arrived late and exhausted the night before. It had been a long train ride, uneventful aside from the brief panic the moment we woke up from our nap, peered out the window, and saw that the train was in some kind of gigantic metal contraption. Being the *sudakas* that we were, we arrived at the only possible conclusion: that our entire train had been abducted by aliens, since we were clearly inside some kind of loud and massive spaceship.[1] The other passengers seemed to be taking it in stride, though, so the alien-abduction theory seemed unlikely, and we soon learned that our train was actually now on a boat, an advance in modern travel and technology we had been unaware existed. We hadn't yet seen or talked to too many comrades, but we had been assured on arrival by the kind people at the welcome table that all the usual security precautions were in place and that we could feel free to rest for the night and plug ourselves into the infrastructure the next morning. We had reached out through the collective to AFA Stockholm beforehand and had been informed that Hvitfeldtska was to be the meeting point for organized antifascists and anarchists from Sweden and abroad. The role of the Swedish antifa network in organizing and mobilizing for the opposition to the EU summit was one of the main reasons we were particularly excited about being there.

While the German antifa and autonome tradition might have more of a mystique and be more well known internationally, the Swedish Antifascist Action network was probably closer to us, politically and tactically, than most of the present-day German antifa groups. First, the network seemed to be composed primarily of anarchists, identified by the small yet revealing detail that most, if not all, local groups chose to represent themselves with the classic Antifascist Action emblem with black flag in front, red behind. This contrasted with the ideologically heterogeneous German antifa and autonome scene and was probably due to the strong and active anarchist tradition in Sweden, a country that to this day still boasts one of the world's largest anarchosyndicalist unions, the Central Organization of the Workers of Sweden, more commonly known by its Swedish acronym, SAC. Second, their organizing structure was more akin to ours, with most groups organized within the framework of the national Antifascist Action network. The AFA network convened regular congresses, functioned through commonly defined main points of unity as well as action, operated a website, and was generally organized in a manner that allowed revolutionary antifascism to present a louder and more cohesive voice to those around it than isolated antifa groups otherwise might.[2] This was in stark contrast to the situation in Germany, where since the recent demise of AA/BO (Antifaschistische Aktion/Bundesweite Organisation, or "Antifascist Action/Federal Organization"), for reasons I would a few years later experience painfully firsthand, nothing similar of relevance existed.[3] Finally, and importantly for the immediate purposes of why we were all there, thanks to the absence of repressive laws such as those in Germany forbidding the wearing of masks or even elements of personal self-defense (helmets, padding, etc.), Swedish antifascism on the streets looked more like Germany in the late 1980s and early '90s than anything else, although it was not nearly as massive of a phenomenon. In short, trying to disturb the summit of the European Union (with the added bonus of our friend George W. Bush attending), together with anarchist and antifascist friends, while parading around a Scandinavian never-never land with masks and helmets on seemed like a pretty good first stop on our European tour.

"You're still not understanding," the Old Man insisted. "It's much worse than that. I don't know how to explain it. You need to come to the scaffolding and see this." I finished getting dressed and followed him up the stairs and out onto the scaffolding that the city of Gothenburg had set up around the entire back of the school building. From there, we had a perfect elevated vantage point providing us with an overview of our surroundings for several blocks, a place to visualize potential "troop movements," both friendly and enemy.

From our perch at the "anarcho-command center," I couldn't believe my eyes. In my youthful bliss, I wasn't aware that such a thing was possible. The police had built what was essentially a giant open-air prison around the school. Gothenburg is a port city, and evidently the police had commandeered a large amount of cargo containers from the port and placed them end to end around the perimeter of the school overnight, constructing a seemingly insurmountable wall around us. And all of this without anybody becoming aware of what was happening as it was being erected. A little later, we learned that it had not been built overnight, but rather during the morning, after police had already cordoned off the area—but sleeping placidly, and alone, as we were in a classroom inside the school, we had missed the whole thing. Even so, it was both insane and, I have to admit, quite impressive. I commented to the Old Man, "Yesterday we learned you can put a train on a boat. Now we learn you can build an open-air prison with containers. What a time to be alive." He wasn't terribly impressed with my observation, retorting with, "I'm glad you're amused, but what now?"

We had abandoned our perch on the scaffolding and gone out to the schoolyard to look for comrades and get a better sense of the situation and what our options might be. As we stood there trying to decide which

A segment of the container ring around Hvitfeldtska school, pictured in the background.

comrades from AFA we could speak to, our first, superficial, judgmental, and probably very prejudiced impression of our situation, and for which we both to this day owe a lot of the northern European comrades an apology, was that we had quite a problem on our hands. The cops and the prison corral around us were one thing, and bad enough. But looking around the schoolyard we saw primarily young, decently dressed, often blond and blue-eyed kids. Obviously judging activists on their age, dress, or physical characteristics is wrong and unfair on every level; I know it now and we both knew it then. Oscar blurted out under his breath, "But these are all children!" I nodded in quiet agreement, even though this was especially stupid, because, well, we were just as young as the rest of the "children." But they didn't convince us, because they didn't look "scraggly." Neither did we! Both the Old Man and I consciously avoided looking too subcultural or punk rock, as did most of our collective and friends, but we were used to this being the exception rather than the norm in the anarcho-crowd. We didn't yet know that northern European antifas tend to have a low-key look. Long story short, as far as we could tell we had somehow ended up not among militants but surrounded by innocent-looking, young, blond do-gooder activists.

Luckily, our superficial first impressions proved to be comically incorrect—a surprisingly quick life lesson in not judging a book by its cover. Discreetly, and over just a half hour or so, the innocent-looking, well-dressed blonds were disappearing, and black-clad comrades in ski masks would magically reappear in their place. Like the collective hive mind of a bee colony, the aimless chatter in small groups rapidly gave way to enterprising worker bees erecting barricades and stockpiling weapons, enthusiastically encouraging others to join in and do the same, with multilingual mutterings of, "Come on, come on, we need to barricade everywhere." Some scurried to and fro with construction materials to erect or fortify barricades, while others began disassembling the pavement to stockpile stones.

"This feels weird and out of place." Oscar pointed it out, and indeed it was. It felt like the most out-of-context pre-riot atmosphere ever. On the one hand, well over a hundred black-clad anarchists, autonomes, and antifascists were intently erecting barricades and stockpiling ammunition. On the other, a beautiful sunny day with not a cloud in the sky, the lush green of our surroundings, the elegant old-world schoolyard, and even the cops, who just seemed to stand around leisurely while calmly observing our preparations.

Not having connected with others yet, the Old Man and I had taken to constructing what we lovingly came to refer to as "the private barricade." Through the woods was a pedestrian walkway that led to a small entrance to the school's courtyard, right next to the actual building. On that walkway, maybe fifteen or twenty meters away from us among the trees, two riot cops had been stationed. We declared this our battle station and got to work building a beautifully organized and elegant barricade: a solid foundation of wooden boards reinforced with stones for weight on both sides, wooden planks set over the top as forward-facing spikes, capped off by an arsenal of stones and bottles carefully placed next to the barricade along the schoolyard's stone wall— easy to reach for us, and in prominent view of the cops in front of us. You know, so they didn't get confused and think coming through here might be easy. Finally pleased with our handiwork, we pulled out two chairs from a classroom to relax on while we waited. Every once in a while we would be motivated enough to yell random insults at the cops, and if they seemed to be either getting closer or relaxing too much, we used the universal language of stone-throwing, in which we were fluent,

Oscar and Tomas's personal barricade at Hvitfeldtska.

and unenthusiastically lobbed a stone in their direction to convey the message "Please maintain a respectful distance."

If I had been a smoker, I would have taken the opportunity to smoke a cigarette dramatically while sitting behind our glorious barricade. But as smoking is an unhealthy and disgusting habit, I unsurprisingly didn't have one on me. I let my mind wander and began romanticizing. "Hey, Oscar, you know what this reminds me of?"

"No, but I'll bet anything it's something stupid and exaggerated."

Clearly, the Old Man knew me well.

"Doesn't this kind of remind you of how you imagine the stalemates at the front during the Spanish Civil War? Just sitting around, bored despite the imminent danger, trading insults with the fascists, and every once in a while firing random aimless shots?"

The Old Man sighed, let out a mild laugh, and responded, "I'm starting to think it's a good thing we have our private front here, so nobody can hear the stupid shit you say. This isn't a war, nobody will be shooting at us anytime soon, and it certainly isn't, you know, one of the most momentous events in the history of anarchism."

This seemed fair, and I brought the epicness down a notch, although unfortunately the comment about nobody shooting at us would not age well. "Fine, fair enough. Hafenstrasse?"

"Better," Oscar responded, "although they were thousands, and I don't think we are two hundred, but whatever makes you happy." I was indeed happy. A little concerned about our situation, but happy nonetheless.

★

Anarchists are nothing if not democratic, at least in our intentions. In yet another display of the beautiful nature of anarchist methods of organization put into practice, indeed preserved, under more than trying circumstances, a general assembly had been called. I wouldn't place this one quite on the level of the "post–Secret Service checkpoint demolishment at the side of the presidential parade route" assembly we had held in DC during the inauguration, but it was definitely a sight. Some find this endearing, while other more authoritarian tendencies find it infuriating and incomprehensible. Yet here we were. While skeleton crews of volunteers stayed behind at the different barricades, including the massive one constructed on the main road leading to the school, several hundred of us, a little less than half of us masked, sat in the schoolyard, surrounded by cops and barricades, holding an open-air general assembly.

A friendly-looking hippie type with a megaphone presented himself. He was involved in the coordinating group and had information from the cops, as well as from outside the school. "The police are saying that illegal and violent acts are being planned from inside the school." A few of us laughed. I thought to myself that that sounded about right, although I did wish I was a little more plugged in as to the specifics of those illegal and violent acts. He continued, "They will not allow anybody to leave without being searched and identified. Anybody willing to be searched and present identification they say is free to leave. Also, the anti-Bush demonstration has started, they know about the situation here. A lot of them are trying to get here with the demonstration in solidarity. There have also been clashes with the police at the demonstration." A lot of murmuring immediately ensued. Safe to assume we were all wondering the same things. Are we really going to allow the cops to individualize us like that? Have they gone insane? What if we wait for the other demonstrators and try to exert pressure from both sides to break the siege? Should we attempt to break out?

General assembly at Hvitfeldtska discussing how to respond to the police siege.

It quickly became clear, via a quick show of hands, if I recall correctly and at the risk of offending anarchist orthodoxy, that we would not accept any "solution" based on individualization and control that involved submitting ourselves willingly to the police. By the same token, we would under no circumstances allow ourselves to be searched. We weren't about to hold anybody prisoner, though, so those who wanted or needed to leave were free to do so, but after that we would respond collectively. We would wait as long as possible for support from outside to arrive in the vicinity, and then we would attempt a collective breakout. The discussion quickly turned to the logistics of how exactly to best stage our breakout attempt.

A man with a British accent spoke next, presenting himself as a representative of the Wombles, short for "White Overalls Movement Building Libertarian Effective Struggles." While the two were not organically or organizationally related, the Wombles were essentially the UK variation of the Tute Bianche/Ya Basta! movement, primarily an Italian phenomenon that had grown out of a post-autonome tendency in the country, oriented around Italy's more moderate social centers and, as the name indicates, heavily influenced by the Zapatista uprising in Chiapas. The Tute Bianche were internationally well known and much idealized within the antiglobalization movement at the time. Politically they argued that the "autonomia" experience of the 1970s and '80s had reached the end of its road and that new forms of organization, struggle, and communication were necessary. They sought to make mass militance, both in terms of participation and broader acceptance, more accessible by refraining from the use of "aggressive weapons" against the police, usually summed up in the "no sticks, no stones, no fire" guidelines they sought to establish in mobilizations (or impose, depending on the mobilization and how you experienced them). Instead, they generally wore helmets and foam padding along with their trademark white overalls, and their shields were often painted with inspiring slogans or depicted scenes of capitalist devastation across the globe, as they attempted to collectively break through police lines. The idea was to use their body as a tool to articulate a particular conflict in society, while engaging in struggle in a way that could, in their eyes, better communicate their message to society at large than the more traditional forms of confrontation.

In the British man's opinion, because there was only one way out of the school as a group—the main road with the stone wall on the one side and the thick bushes on the other—the geography wouldn't accommodate a diversity of tactics here. If we attempted to break out using "any means necessary," it would mean de facto that those who preferred or intended to do so otherwise and with less confrontational means would find themselves subsumed by that tactic. Doing so would force them to bear both the political ramifications of a method of mass action that did not represent them as well as the potential concrete physical consequences of such a confrontation with the police. The solution the man proposed was to attempt to break out in "escalating waves." The White Overalls would go first and would attempt to push their way through the police lines. The black bloc would be farther behind and would refrain from offensive action until it was clear a nonviolent breakthrough was not possible.

As he finished, another round of agitated murmuring ensued. After a lengthy and controversial discussion, the White Overalls' proposal was accepted. I can't remember if this happened by consensus or majority vote, just as I still don't understand how this issue didn't devolve into an hours-long shouting match disguised as debate in which the minority opinion announces regardless that they never agreed to delegation of their will of any kind and intends to do as they please, as a few of these high-stress-situation general assemblies with different participating political traditions sometimes did. Maybe because the summer was still young and some of the contradictions and divisions weren't quite as pronounced as they would become in Genoa. Or, at the risk of blatant and almost nationalist generalization: The cultural background of mainly British, German, and Swedish activists hashing out political differences is very different from when, for example, mainly Italian and Greek activists are doing so. Let's just say one is more intense than the other. And I mean this in the best possible way, as if anything—and as usual with the "for better or worse" disclaimer—I am socialized by the latter and feel much more comfortable in political spaces where content trumps form and heated and polemic discussion is neither shied away from nor frowned upon.

In any case, Oscar and I weren't convinced, and judging from the interventions neither was a fair amount of the mask-wearing crowd. A few of the speakers had expressed their principled disagreement with any concept of staged or mediated conflict with the authorities, as well as with the idea of purposefully "restricting" ourselves in the face of a police force that would most certainly not be extending us that same courtesy. Another, from the accent clearly an Eastern European comrade, expressed her disapproval of reducing this impending and apparently inevitable clash to a ritualized confrontation, a spectacle of sorts, toned down in its intensity for the purpose of making it more palatable to the media or some imaginary "civil society."

Barricada had vigorously defended a similar position in its pages, both before and after the "Summer of Resistance," so I happily joined in. Not because I believed we could win the argument, but because it seemed positive to be able to have such a frank and open discussion of the motivations for militant struggle and confrontation with the state in such a large setting. We viewed these mass mobilizations as an opportunity for budding activists or "random discontents" to be radicalized through exposure to our praxis, and clearly a decent cross-section of varied "antiglobalization activists" was present here. Not only that, but the nature of many of these forums and debates makes it so that they skew toward the more conciliatory positions, due to the simple fact that standing up in front of hundreds of people and announcing yourself to be enthusiastically in favor of violent revolution and throwing fire at agents of the state, not just theoretically but right here and right now, is a good way to draw unwanted attention to yourself. But here, we were as close to anonymous as you can be in real life, with no names and with masks on.

Security culture conscious as I was, though, I still took the trouble of removing the Antifaschistische Aktion pin from my jacket and using it to clip shut the space between my eyes on my ski mask. When I spoke, I took care to speak English with an accent neither American nor Spanish, to further confuse any possible prying eyes or ears. I don't think I brought anything particularly groundbreaking to the conversation. Quite honestly, I don't recall what I said, though it was probably some variation of the arguments mentioned above.

However, I do remember the collective surprise and outrage from "our camp" at what came next. One of the fortifications we had built, indeed the main one, was an imposing and sturdy barricade composed of assorted school furniture and construction materials at the main entrance to the schoolyard. It was a straight shot from there down the main road where the police lines were, through which we would attempt to break out. The White Overalls argued that the optics of leaving the barricade intact and assembling once past it were somehow unacceptable. They wanted to march as a group, collectively, from the school, through the courtyard, and toward the police line. "What are these people talking about? There's no media here, no bystanders, nothing. Just cops and us." Oscar was right, it was indeed absurd. And it was the first of several experiences we would have over the years with some elements of the post-autonome left disarming and endangering their own spaces, people, or allies to fit the narrative they had decided was correct.

Twenty years later, I have absolutely no recollection of how they succeeded in either convincing us to dismantle that barricade or imposing the idea on us. I know it's a pretty big hole in the plot, and I apologize, but just as I don't understand how we let it happen, I remember perfectly that it did indeed happen. I suppose the summer was young and the frictions with the Ya Basta! movement were still in their infancy. Simply being in the same venue and having a joint discussion about politics and strategy is a clear indication of this, as by the time Genoa came around a month later, the reality would be radically different. But this time we acquiesced, and dismantled it was.

What came next was a fiasco. Ya Basta! would release a communiqué later that day, describing the events as follows:

> On Thursday the police intruded our community's area in Gothenburg. The riot squad besieged our area with riot shields, dogs, horses, helicopters and containers. The police threatened to attack the rooms where we lived.
>
> Our aim was to defend our area with methods that are as nonviolent as possible. After a long discussion with other people living in the Hvitfeldtska area, we strived to break out from the besieged area. We used only defensive equipment like personal armour, helmets and shields.
>
> We did 8 attempts to break through the police lines. No violence was committed from our side. But the police attacked us with open violence. They rode horses at full speed into our crowd and beat people up with batons. They even used dogs, and one person was bitten on his face.
>
> We cannot judge people who threw stones at the police, because they were defending their own lives.
>
> We have seen the same happen in Chiapas, Malaysia, Columbia and numerous other countries, where army and the police are at war with people. Now we see this also in Europe. We cannot consider this as anything else than a declaration of war from European Union against its own citizens.
>
> We accuse the police of rioting, brutal violence, repression of citizens' basic rights like the freedom to express their opinions. The police who are responsible of all these crimes must be made accountable of their action.
>
> Ya Basta—for humanity against neoliberalism
> Gothenburg 14/06/2001[4]

Obviously, I'm not exactly a neutral and objective commentator here, as my and many other anarchists' experiences with Ya Basta! both that day and later in Genoa were less than ideal. They could be forgiven for the dramatic language and hyperbole, as we were often guilty of the same. But other than that, I don't think we ever found so much to object to in such a short text. This was a condensed prime example of just about everything we found problematic in post-autonome tendencies that veered from autonomy into hard-line reformism (or liberalism, for the US crowd).

Who is it that you are saying should hold the police accountable for their actions? The state? This implies that police violence, or quite simply the state making use of its legal monopoly on violence to further its interests, is not intrinsic to the nature of state power but is rather an unfortunate deviation from its benevolent nature, requiring nothing more than a course correction.

What are these rights they are talking about? The concept of "rights" is already not without controversy. Who grants them? What rights do we have and why? But the phrase "citizens' basic rights" excludes immigrants, both with and without papers, human beings who are very much not citizens in the countries in which they reside. So apparently, since you need to be a citizen to possess these rights, they are granted by the state and thus constrained by legality. An anarchist position would argue that, if anything, we should separate the concept of rights from legality. That it is the power of social movements and their successes, both past and present, that have achieved concessions from both state and capital that are now deemed "rights." That rights under capitalism are nothing more than concessions that a broad enough segment of society would no longer allow the deprivation of, and that we should be constantly attacking the boundaries of legality and the framework of capitalist rights until we reach a place where the demands of the mass of society are no longer compatible with the framework of private property and state rule.

Finally, there was the equation of repression in places like Chiapas and Colombia—places where the state works hand in hand with paramilitary death squads to murder its opponents—with a police attack on a school in social democratic Sweden, in which the police used dogs and batons … and nothing more. No less-than-lethal munitions, no tear gas, no pepper spray, and certainly no live ammunition. The subtext of this absurd exaggeration was the need to prepare the ground for the evergreen classic of reformist victimization, now parroted by a supposedly radical movement: that the violence of the state is an inevitability, and that being brutally victimized by it is somehow an argument in favor of our ideas. The more of us who are beaten and jailed, the more virtuous and morally superior our movement. A position we wholeheartedly rejected, and it is no coincidence that *Barricada*'s Summer/

WE ARE NOT VICTIMS, WE ARE VICTORS: THE EU SUMMIT IN GOTHENBURG

We will not enter into the details of what happened in Gothenburg, as it has been three months now since these events and most people should already be familiar with what took place.

As a short summary though, we would like to remind everybody that the police surrounded and eventually raided a convergence center that was given to the demonstrators by the city itself and guaranteed as a demilitarized zone. This took place before absolutely anything had happened.

The next day, the police fired into a crowd of demonstrators (mostly black bloc) wounding three, one seriously.

Still not content, on the evening of the sixteenth they surrounded and retained for hours an anti-police brutality demonstration, before sending the anti-terrorist squad armed with automatic weapons into another school were demonstrators were sleeping. Here they proceeded to beat people, throw them down flights of stairs, torture them (for example, twisting noses in order to get people to "talk," and making them lie in the rain in their underwear while periodically kicking and beating them).

This is all indeed quite unfortunate. However, we at Barricada do not believe in posing as victims in order to appeal to popular sympathy. That moralistic argument we reserve for pacifists. There was indeed a strong repression, but only because the organized radical resistance was powerful enough to scare the Swedish state into dropping the mask of benevolence.

Every time there was police repression, the resistance was even stronger.

As the police surrounded Hvitfeldska school, hundreds inside masked up and took to building barricades. Those who were at the Bush demonstration redirected themselves and fought pitched battles with police in order to aide in the escape of those trapped inside.

Those inside tried to fight there way out as a group, only to be thwarted, not only by the police, but by the delays caused by the media whoring of the White Overalls and their many tactical blunders.

Despite this, many fought their way out of the school, escaping in full black bloc gear through a line of police, a small forest, a ring of steel containers, and yet another line of police.

On the next day, June 15, police yet again provoked, surrounding the black bloc on three sides and charging into it with dogs and on horseback.

Yet again, the response of the almost one thousand person black bloc was ferocious. Hundreds charged the police, repeatedly forcing them to retreat, while others erected barricades and dug up cobblestones on Gothenburg's most exclusive avenue, the Avenyn.

After several hours of pitched battle, the bloc began to disperse, but not before completely destroying (and often looting) the avenue of the rich. Banks, exclusive stores, McDonalds and Burger Kings, elite cafes, exchange stores. Furthermore, hundreds repeatedly attacked and destroyed police vehicles.

At night the battle raged once more, as police attacked a Reclaim the Streets, trying to disperse it, only to find themselves surrounded on all sides by an angry black bloc and local youths. Repeatedly they were charged and forced to retreat, several receiving direct cobblestone hits to the head.

There can be no doubt about it. Gothenburg was a clear victory for all of those who seek a total rupture with the established system. Our enemies received a loud and clear message. They are afraid that the message will spread, and it is for that reason that the media campaign of disinformation has been so intense and the repression so heavy.

Unfortunately for them, the writing was already on the wall, "When will they ever learn... When Police Attack, We Fight Back"

The Battle of Gothenburg is not yet over, and it is now time to support those who are bearing the brunt of the repression (not only the prisoners, but AFA as well).

The spray painting on the outside of Hvitfeldska school could not have been more eloquent, "...But in the End, *We* Will Win!"

The Barricada Collective

BARRICADA #8. SUMMER/SEP. 2001

"We Are Not Victims, We Are Victors." A news brief on the EU summit in Gothenburg in the Summer/September 2001 issue of *Barricada*.

The Ya Basta! bloc and the black bloc preparing the attempt to break the siege of Hvitfeldtska.

September 2001 piece on Gothenburg was titled "We Are Not Victims, We Are Victors."

Fortunately for us, they were kind enough to not "judge people who threw stones at the police, because they were defending their own lives." How gracious of them. I suppose this was good, because there is a special place where we anarchists keep our disdain for judges—and it's the same one otherwise reserved for cops and soldiers.

In any case, the breakout attempt described in the communiqué consisted of about thirty people divided into three or four lines, which were for some reason formed across the width of the street but left the sidewalk completely unoccupied. It was, by any definition, a fiasco.

I want to say that we resisted valiantly when the literal cavalry came charging, especially considering the idiotically exposed situation we found ourselves in thanks to Ya Basta!'s ridiculous demand that we dismantle the central barricade, along with the wide-open sidewalks that offered free passage to the cops on horseback, which they then used to flank us and attack from three sides at once. It felt like a fifteen- or twenty-minute battle, although I'm sure in reality it was no more than five minutes.

Ya Basta! and the police face off outside Hvitfeldtska school.

But it was intense, and nothing if not picturesque. A schoolyard version of Cowboys and Indians, played by adults and modified to Cops and Autonomes, yet still taking place on an actual schoolyard. The backdrop of the schoolyard, an elegant Scandinavian building, stone walls, and a lush green forest made it at times seem like a surreal rendition of the world's most chaotic ballet performance. Like one of those videos of riot scenes set to classical music, but in real time. I won't be providing a play-by-play here, but two elegant moments are etched into my memory among the chaos of the intense, and ultimately futile, attempts to keep the cops at bay and out of the schoolyard. First, a particularly aggressive cop who, channeling his inner Viking, charged far ahead of his colleagues into us, snarling and roaring like an actual plundering warrior and waving his baton wildly as he imagined a sword in its place. We were momentarily impressed, this being our first live Viking sighting, but we were up to the challenge, and the next scene was of that very same Viking beating a hasty retreat, a look of surprise and possibly fear on his face, under a hail of rocks. It was the first clue that maybe, just maybe, the Swedish police didn't quite know what they had gotten themselves into.

Police attack the Ya Basta! bloc during the attempt to break the siege of Hvitfeldtska.

The second took place during a brief lull in the confrontation, shortly before we were definitively pushed into the school building itself. We were retreating into the building, the cops temporarily at bay, when suddenly I heard a strong German accent yell, "But what about the horse?" As I turned to look, I saw a horse, one of those same police horses that had just been used to charge us during Ya Basta!'s spectacularly ineffective escape attempt, being led gently across the schoolyard by a friendly masked gentleman. If it wasn't for the horse's distinctive police visor and his companion's ski mask, one could have been forgiven for thinking this was just a young man taking his horse out to pasture on a lovely and peaceful Thursday afternoon.

Alas, while it was indeed a lovely sunny afternoon, it was anything but peaceful, and the next cop attack was coming. Somebody yelled, "Fuck the horse, come on," as we held the doors to the school open and let as many people in as possible before shutting them.

I don't know how long we were in that school for, but it was a while. We were a group of fifteen or twenty, composed of one or two big-city Swedish AFA affinity groups, a few Germans, Oscar, and me. We had quickly gotten to the first floor of the building, where we dissuaded the

232

Police on horseback charge demonstrators on the main road leading to Hvitfeldtska school.

cops from entering by showering them with furniture. It all still had a quaint romantic charm to it. Here we were, young and glorious heroes on the side of freedom and justice, defending our little fortress from the faceless Viking hordes of evil, resisting under siege with whatever tools we had as the enemy, again literally, tried to storm the gates. And it was entertaining at first, too, but the cops eventually retreated to a safe distance and we grew bored of launching chairs through the windows. It was a lot of effort for us, and not much reward, as the cops just took a small step out of the way if one got near them. And anyway, we had decided that the furniture was probably best put to use barricading stairways and hallways. Which we promptly did, with a surprising degree of silent diligence. The work ethic of our newly formed international antifa brigade was commendable, and soon there were veritable ceiling-high mountain barricades on the stairways and in the hallways, with fire extinguishers parked behind them should it come to that.

Content with our fortifications, we surveyed the surroundings. As we looked out the windows on the back side of the building, it became painfully apparent that the mood on the ground floor was radically different from the one on the first. Whereas we had been busy fortifying

233

and preparing to resist as long as possible, we could see people on the ground floor surrendering to the cops. Voluntarily. A constant stream of people, walking out the door with their hands above their heads and then sitting themselves in a police kettle. Today, with the maturity that allows for a more nuanced and understanding perspective on things, I see that there are reasons an individual might choose this course of action. Maybe their personal situation means they can't expose themselves to the possible physical and legal ramifications of this kind of action. Or things have escalated in a way they weren't prepared for, and they are simply not comfortable with this degree of violence or risk. I would still argue that ideally, one should reflect on these possibilities beforehand, as few things are more dangerous, to the person themselves and others, than being in an action with a person who has not analyzed the worst possible physical, legal, and mental consequences of their actions and is therefore not prepared to face them should they arise. And my sympathies were even more limited that day, because the cops had offered those who wanted to leave individually the chance to do so if they agreed to allow themselves to be searched, an offer almost two hundred people took them up on. We even waited for this process to end before beginning with the collective breakout attempt.

All that said, what I hopefully wouldn't do today is what I, and most others on that floor with me, did then. First, one of the Germans tried persuasion. "Come upstairs, we'll let you through. They won't come in so fast, and the people from the demonstration are on their way." It didn't seem to be working, as the stream of surrenders continued unabated. For a moment we thought they maybe didn't speak English, which seemed unlikely since in Sweden pretty much everybody speaks English. Nonetheless, one of the Swedish comrades gave it a shot. A lot of shouting back and forth in Elvish ensued; we didn't understand a single word. And while I find Swedish a pleasure to listen to even while understanding nothing, this didn't sound like people agreeing on anything. It was around then that a man from below began yelling at us, conveniently in English, "Look at you with your masks and your violence, you are just like them!" as he pointed toward the cops.

Compare anarchists to cops, while you surrender your stupid self to those same cops and demonstrate zero understanding of even the most basic principles of solidarity and mutual respect, and you can bet nothing good will happen. Especially if those same anarchists currently find themselves in a building under siege, and you and your genius friends insisted on *dismantling* barricades because you found the "optics" not ideal for your messaging. A multilingual shouting and insult match ensued, and we promptly decided to leave them to their fate and move on. Personally, I was enraged. We had made a collective decision to fight our way out, and your surrender made those of us intending to follow through with it more vulnerable, both tactically in the moment as well as legally later on. If our strength lies in collective power and action, what signal are you sending our enemies by staging a mass surrender after the first confrontation?

As we moved away, Oscar requested a translation of what the Swedes had said before all hell had broken loose, and a comrade from Gothenburg obliged. "A few of them are from the Ya Basta! people, and they say they are not comfortable with the violence. I think this part we all understood. But a lot of these are comrades from our network. They say there is no way we can get out of here anymore, or that the others will break the police perimeter. They say if they surrender now maybe there will be no charges and maybe they can be at the demonstration tomorrow."

I blurted out, "That's insane. How can there be no charges? We built barricades, fought the cops, and destroyed the school. Am I missing something here?"

He said, "Actually, it's not even certain that they will take them to the police station. Sometimes when there are disturbances they put us all on buses and disperse us on the outskirts of the city." I laughed then, and I'm laughing again now as I write this. This was the most "social democratic never-never land" thing I had heard in my life. It turns out they actually do this, or at least did, as it was not only confirmed to me by several comrades later on, but I personally experienced a version of this "Bad antifa, you can't play with your friends anymore today, go home" dispersal tactic on behalf of Stockholm's police a few years later.

Escape from Hvitfeldtska: Thursday, June 14, Sometime in the Afternoon

"Well, now what?" Oscar asked as we entered the school's computer room on the third floor. Things had died down, and some of the others were taking a break in the room next door, while a few headed back up

Police in the courtyard of Hvitfeldtska school, prior to the breakout attempts.

to the scaffolding to get a visual of the surroundings and, more importantly, see if we could see or hear the mythical solidarity demonstration that was apparently on its way to rescue us. The Swedes had phones on them and had managed to confirm that a significant portion of the anti-Bush demonstration had broken off to head toward the school and that there were constant confrontations with the cops taking place along the way. Oscar, in a moment only a Jewish activist could bring to life, was taking a moment to call his mother and assure her, "Everything is fine, Sweden is beautiful, I'll call you in a few days again." Possibly landing in jail was one thing, but landing in jail without previously checking in with Mom and being exposed to Jewish-mother guilt trips was a bridge too far. He mentioned matter-of-factly, "Just in case we end up in jail for a few days, it's better I call her now." It seemed fair enough, so I didn't argue, also because I was currently fixated on my own little wonderful discovery in that room. In the haste of the battle, somebody had either forgotten or abandoned a beautiful pitch-black motorcycle helmet. It seemed obvious that it would be confiscated by the cops if I left it there, so I made the decision to adopt it.

A short time later, we had regrouped with a few others holed up inside the school and were having the proverbial "what is to be done" debate. "If I am going to be arrested, I will not be sitting in a classroom waiting for it to happen, just as I under no circumstances was going to go willingly with my hands above my head like some sad prisoner of the world's most pathetic war. That demonstration is somewhere on the other side of the containers. The line of cops before the containers is only one cop deep, and they are pretty spread out. If we just charge them, there's no way they can stop all or even most of us. Then we just have to follow the sound to the demonstration."

I tried to be as forceful and convincing as possible in my arguments, although in hindsight it seems the group needed little convincing. We were, after all, the small group of hard-liners who had, for one reason or another, decided that surrender was not an acceptable option. I wanted to continue conveying a message of confrontation, that much is true. But Oscar and I, together with the Germans, shared another motivation: What if the Swedes were released without too many legal consequences, but us foreigners were deported, possibly from Europe?

Oscar, ever the theoretician among us, suddenly discovered his more basic interests of personal convenience. "Are you crazy? We fight our way out. This is my first time in Europe, we got here three days ago, there's no way I'm letting these people deport me." It certainly wasn't the grandest of motivations, but it was still one I could get behind. I was also in no position to judge, as my unspoken motivation was the shallow allure of giving my shiny new helmet its battle debut. As for the Swedes, a few were locals who were concerned they might be singled out after the fact for their organizing roles (spoiler alert: they were right!), but they along with the others also seemed intent on not letting the police have the last word on this day and wanted to make one more attempt to end it on a combative note and set a more optimistic tone for the days to come. After all, the actual day of action wasn't even upon us yet; that would be tomorrow.

One of the Germans, with their annoying insistence on pointing out minutiae like logic and reason while everyone is trying to concoct an audaciously half-baked plan, raised a mundane concern: "How shall we get over the containers?"

Oscar replied, "The cops are getting through somehow. Either there are openings, or stairs, or we will have to fight our way to one of the streets and try to break the line there." Safe to assume most crowds would not take this as an acceptable answer, but this was an action-oriented group and, honestly, there weren't too many different proposals on the table anyway. The Germans shrugged in acceptance, and it was so.

Yet another anarchist suicide mission was thus formalized and finalized: We would mask up (and in my case put on the shiny new black helmet whose owner I'm sure would be happy I rescued from the clutches of the police), grab as many projectiles as we could carry, jump out one of the ground-floor windows, charge straight through the police line while yelling and screaming like banshees, magically clamber over the containers, and find our way to freedom in the crowd that was somewhere on the other side.

The whole sequence took probably thirty seconds at most. But if you train yourself to manage your adrenaline well, in these situations you can slow down time and become aware of every detail as it takes place. We scrambled out the window and into the forest like the world's worst-trained commando squad. Almost immediately, though, we were met by the sounds of freedom. As we ran I could clearly hear the sound of hundreds, maybe thousands, of demonstrators roaring nearby. Just as the rush of excitement of hearing our friends on the other side hit me, the line of cops in the forest came into view, not more than ten or fifteen meters away. I can't speak to what happened to my left or my right, as I concentrated on the two cops in front of me and the space between them. I raised my stone as if to throw it, but primarily I was concentrating on running through them, bowling them over if need be. I expected them to lunge at me, to possibly break the arm I was using to shield my body and face with a baton swing as I ran past. They never moved. They may have had the authority of the state behind them, but in that moment in those woods it was just a few of them and us, a screaming mob of masked militants who flew at them from a window. We will never know if out of shock or fear, but none of them moved to stop us. It was a testament to the power of decisive collective action. If we had hesitated, doubted, or slowed down, there is no doubt it would have been the sudden and painful end of our excursion.

In yet another clear sign that fate not only smiles on the bold but often even looks carefully after them, in the following moment an anarchist miracle occurred. Straight in front of us, right where we were sprinting toward the wall of containers ahead, was a ladder perched against one of them. Clearly it was what the cops had been using to get back and forth, and now it immediately changed into a veritable stairway to, if not heaven, then at the very least freedom.

The next few moments are, as they say, history. I'll remember them forever, but should I ever begin to forget, they are conveniently captured on video.[5] As we emerged atop the containers, the crowd on the other side erupted in a welcoming roar. But there was yet another line of cops on the other side of the containers, between us and the demonstration. And at the point in the line of containers where we stood, the distance to the friendly loving arms of the demonstration was too great. And so, like a modern-day anarchist remake of the Clash's epic "Should I Stay or Should I Go" video where they dance atop a wall, we ran across the tops of five or six containers. While the memory is beautiful and I was able to appreciate the moment as it took place, like many liberating experiences in life, it was simultaneously terrifying as well. Incredibly, most of the tops of the containers were only chicken wire, and it seemed completely plausible that the weight of all of us running across could collapse them, leaving us trapped in a very real open-air prison cell, with enraged cops all around us, and possibly seriously injured from the fall. But again, fear and hesitation were not privileges we enjoyed, and so we sprinted merrily across while some in the crowd cheered and other comrades pushed closer to the police line and began to divert their attention. As the black flags of the comrades who had come in solidarity battered the police shields, we jumped off of the containers into the crowd and lived to fight another day.[6]

Having landed safely in the crowd, one would think I would value my unexpected reencounter with freedom enough to, you know, flee and regroup. Being an incurable fanatic, no such measured thought crossed my mind, and instead I turned to join the others in the assault on the police line I had just sailed over. A few moments later, though, somebody tapped me insistently on the shoulder. I turn to see a masked woman with ridiculously huge and captivating blue-green eyes speaking to me in excited, incomprehensible tones of Elvish, to which I responded with my most eloquent, "Sorry, no Swedish. English?" She obliged with, "You should probably leave. They are trying to single people out, and the pin on the mask stands out. Also, you are the only one with a helmet."

I processed several things simultaneously. First, while I could only see her eyes, I decided that this young Swedish antifascist was beautiful anyway, and that I had loved her all my life. Second, she seemed to be telling me to leave, and her words were basically a polite version of, "You stick out like a sore thumb, what are you, an idiot?" This was heartbreaking and hurtful, kind of like being rejected without even having approached the other person. A preemptive rejection. On the other hand, this kind soul was making an effort to look out for the safety of a perfect stranger. And as I looked around, I noticed that there were no longer many of us gathered, and I was definitely the only genius in a motorcycle helmet. Finally, where the hell was the Old Man? I responded with the most confident and friendly-sounding "Good point, thank you" that I could muster, since "Thanks, hey, what's your name?" clearly would be out of line given the context. Then I changed discreetly and got myself out of there.

A few hours later and thanks to the goodwill of every activist-looking type I had run into in the city and asked for help and directions, I arrived at Schillerska school. This was the other, and now only, convergence center and sleeping space available for activists in Gothenburg. I'll spare us the colorful description of the place and surroundings. It was basically exactly the same as Hvitfeldtska school, even down to the color and courtyard in the front, but it was more centrally located and had no hill or green space around it. Considering the day's experience, I would have preferred the safety of anywhere other than an activist convergence center, but we weren't exactly locals up here and options didn't abound. And anyway, I needed to find out if Oscar had made it to safety as well, and this was the best place to find him. There was also the small detail of finding out what had become of our belongings.

I was able to spot him quickly enough. Skinny guy with long red hair, made him hard to miss. He was sitting on the stoop outside the entrance to the school, and while everybody else was enjoying the free soup, the Old Man was happily working on a collection of three 7-Eleven hot dogs. While they were cheap and great (vegan dumpster-diver kids liked Odwalla bars, we liked cheap convenience-store hot dogs, please don't judge us), the Old Man was self-admittedly stingy, and it was unlike him to be "splurging" when free food was available. "You know there's free food here, right?"

"Yeah, but I decided that escaping an improvised prison by jumping out of a window at a line of cops while screaming like a conquering Viking, and then flying over an industrial container past another line of them to finally run into safety is quite the accomplishment and deserves a reward. I'm also annoyed because I messed up my ankle." He pointed to the crutches lying on the stairs next to him.

"What, those are yours?"

He nodded and explained that he had sprained his ankle after jumping off of the container, and the kind medics at the convergence center had provided him with the crutches. "They even have the school's name engraved on them, so it's a nice little souvenir, I guess." He then gave me a rundown of what he had learned since arriving at Schillerska. "First of all, once the cops left, they got some vans and vehicles to the school and took everybody's belongings. So our bags are here." What a service! Bonus points for solidarity and mutual aid. I had been a little concerned about spending the next two months in Europe with nothing but the clothes on my back. "They arrested like four hundred people, so we were pretty lucky to get out of there." I like to think that audacity and perseverance also played pretty big roles, but I guess a little luck never hurt anybody. We eventually learned that precisely 454 people were arrested that day at Hvitfeldtska. Police later spoke of an estimated 700 people inside the school: 454 were arrested, and another approximately 200 exited voluntarily after submitting themselves to individual police searches, which leaves only about 50 people unaccounted for, so all in all I think we did pretty well.

Then a problematic detail dawned on me. "Hey, Oscar, are you coming to the demonstration tomorrow?" He looked at me, as was so often the case, with mildly annoyed impatience. Considering the man was on crutches and couldn't even walk, much less run, I guess the answer should have been obvious.

And thus begins a tale of two Gothenburgs.

A Tale of Two Gothenburgs, Part 1: Friday, June 15, Around 9:00 a.m.

We must devastate the avenues where the wealthy live.
—Lucy Parsons

If the breathless accounts of both the local Swedish and international mainstream media of the time are to be believed, or even the mythology shared by a lot of the antiglobalization movement, Gothenburg was devastated by an invading horde of thousands of international anarchists, which left parts of its downtown area "in ruins."[7] Tony Blair, then British prime minister, even declared it to be the work of what "effectively is an anarchists' traveling circus that goes from summit to summit with the sole purpose of causing as much mayhem as possible" and announcing that "anarchists will not stop us."[8]

Standing around at the top end of Avenyn, Gothenburg's central and most elegant avenue for shopping and dining, as I tried to assess my surroundings and the character and potential of the still-gathering black bloc, "marauding horde of anarchists about to loot and terrorize their way through peaceful Scandinavian city" is not how I would have chosen to describe the scene. Having lost contact with the AFA comrades from the day before after the escape from Hvitfeldtska, and with Oscar out of action, I had walked here with a bunch of perfect-stranger activist types from Schillerska who "chose to express their democratic dissent" a little differently from what I was used to, and so we had parted ways on arrival at the demonstration. The scene on this Friday morning was slightly underwhelming.

A black bloc of a strong several hundred, maybe nearing a thousand if counting generously, milled around waiting for the larger coalition demonstration of antiglobalization groups and left-wing organizations toward the location of the EU summit to begin. The numbers were not huge, considering the prominent and international mobilization, and there were none of the telltale signs of a particularly combative formation. None of the buzz, energy, and anticipation of people fidgeting with protective equipment or weapons, no diligent comrades ripping up the paving stones for ammunition, no people whose backpacks made noises that gave away their contents as they walked. None of that. In fact, few people were even wearing helmets, and there weren't any flags on poles, and only a few banners. If anything, the mood could be described as relatively subdued, with people generally chatting and drifting around. At this point it wouldn't have been surprising if it all ended in a relatively harmless performative confrontation at some fence somewhere in the vicinity of the summit.

But the police apparently had other plans, and I believe that we have their actions to thank for the dynamic that developed for the remainder of the day. Thank, not blame. This distinction matters.

Liberals, reformists, and even many anarchists will attempt to justify property destruction, confrontations, or other kinds of militant resistance with the argument that it is a justified reaction to a specific act of repression, such as a police attack or escalation. This implies that a more peaceful protest is somehow inherently desirable, not just from a strategic perspective but as a matter of political and moral principle. Not to mention that it implies that capitalist order is somehow peaceful aside from moments of acute violence, when in fact it exerts a brutal, but usually orderly, constant violence on individuals and communities.

This argument also reduces our agency as a movement, contextualizing our actions as the infantile response of reckless youth who simply don't know better, rather than as the result of reasoned political analysis. For me, and for the broader "us" at the time, the anarchist analysis seemed clear and obvious: The state should always be attacked, and our political analysis made it self-evident to us that any opportunity to make a statement against the symbols of consumer society and capitalist dominance over our lives was a valid one. Violence was the state, capital, and the reality of our daily lives, not our reaction to these. This was the principle we held true, and the exceptions were what we, as individuals and as a movement, determined to be the political and tactical considerations to take into account in a specific context. As in, will we gain the solidarity and trust of potential allies with this action, or will we alienate them? Are there individuals or communities at higher risk who we are in solidarity with and who are on the streets with us for whom the potential cost of repression due to militance is too high? (We would see great examples of this collective movement discipline the very next day, as well as one month later in Genoa.) Finally, will this increase the agency, confidence, and power of our movement, or will it end in a defeat that could weaken us?

In the case of international summits such as this one, the equation seemed clear. These summits were a battle primarily of symbolism. On one side were Western capitalist democracies trying to project images of stability and power, proclaiming the collapse of the USSR and the Eastern bloc as the "end of history" and the projection of capitalist democracy as the best of all possible worlds. On the other were anarchist revolutionaries whose conclusions about the Eastern bloc collapse were not the inevitability of capitalism and the bourgeois state as the final stage in the organization of society, but very much the contrary: That if one empire could fall, then so could another. That the inevitability was not capitalism and the state, but revolution. That the collapse of socialism without freedom would only exacerbate the contradictions and inequalities of freedom without socialism. And so, these summits were to be converted into highly visible moments of total rejection of and rupture with the state. Attack the symbols of capital, attack the repressive forces of the state, and turn the celebrations of capitalist order into moments of conflict and ungovernability.

This was all well and good on paper, but it didn't change that the vibe at that moment wasn't exactly screaming, "Burn it all down." I would argue that we were relatively underprepared for the gift the police were about to give us.

The demonstration began and the bloc placed itself behind the alphabet soup of Marxist-Leninist groups. We headed straight down a side street, away from Avenyn. We hadn't even gotten fifty meters when we were stopped by a line of riot cops and out-of-control police dogs trying to separate us from the larger demonstration. I was close to the front and concerned about our rear guard, as considering what we had seen the day before, cops trying to kettle us and hold us there for hours seemed like a distinct possibility. On a narrow side street, with essentially no ammunition or protective equipment, it probably wouldn't take more than a few lines of cops on each end to success- fully trap us. In fact, the situation inspired so little confidence that my helmet wearing had me concerned about being exposed to a targeted arrest rather than feeling safe.

As the bloc began to disintegrate and retreat under baton and dog attacks, it became clear that the cops had not thought this through. Maybe overconfident from their success the day before at Hvitfeldtska, they seemed to have greatly underestimated the combative potential of this crowd. As we spilled back onto Avenyn, it seemed maybe I had done so as well. Incredibly, not only were there no cops to our rear guard, but there were also no cops down Avenyn at all. The collective hive mind came alive, as some groups tore apart the conveniently cobblestoned sidewalks, while others began using the stones to charge the police lines. The cops' batons and dogs were useless at a distance, and the horse charges were of limited effectiveness considering the amount of people and the hail of cobblestones they faced.

With the cops held at bay, others began descending Avenyn, filling the air with the joyous din of shattering glass. Avenyn was not only the only logical direction in which to retreat, it was also filled with upscale cafés, banks, corporate shops, money-changing stores, and even a McDonald's. If you are familiar with Paris's Champs-Élysées, picture a similarly wide avenue but in a somewhat less prestigious and small-town version. The place was so wildly unprepared for us that instead of the usual landscape of closed and boarded-up stores that cities during summits of the antiglobalization era usually presented, not only were the stores without protection, with the exception of the boarded-up McDonald's, but most were open for business!

Everywhere I looked I saw uplifting scenes typical of your classic anarchist riot. An Intersport (think European version of Sports Authority or Dick's Sporting Goods) had its windows smashed, and several comrades entered it, generously redistributing soccer jerseys in every direction as they exited. One determined group managed to remove the wooden boards protecting the McDonald's, and then its windows promptly came crashing down. Panicked yuppies fled as the chairs and tables of upscale outdoor cafés were repurposed for use as burning barricades, while very respectful anarchists gestured to those inside to please be so kind as to move away from the windows before they threw stones through them. Meanwhile, others set their sights on banks and money exchanges. Incredibly, the money exchange was open, allowing people to destroy it from both inside and out.

Had we been more organized and even mildly conscious of this possible development, let's just say our Summer of Resistance tour of Europe would have been significantly better funded than it was. But I didn't have so much as an affinity group with me, so sadly bank robbing was definitely off the table for the day. We soon forgot the missed opportunity for literal direct action against income inequality as we encountered a whole fleet of parked—and unmanned—police vans, which were enthusiastically taken out of commission.

There was even a somewhat elegant organic dance between individuals and affinity groups throughout this whole time. Tired from the running battles with the cops, some would retreat from the front lines and rest by way of relatively unhurried property destruction or barricade building, and others would take the initiative and replace them at the front. I felt safe and at home during all of it. Which seems like a surprising feeling to have while in the midst of a riot, in a foreign country, and by yourself. But this was the epitome of the exclusively anarchist riot. Please don't be fooled by the guy with the

"Marx-Engels-Lenin-Stalin-Mao" flag who managed to place himself in front of every camera that day; this was an almost purely anarchist and revolutionary antifascist event. And I know what you're thinking: Isn't that a bad thing? Don't we want to have other groups, other communities, and generally as many layers of society as possible on the street with us? The answer is of course an enthusiastic and unhesitant yes, absolutely. That is the political preference. But there is a personal aspect at play here as well. When we choose to participate in volatile situations like riots, we are exposing ourselves to a certain amount of personal risk. Risk of arrest, risk of injury, and even in rare cases risk of death. Fortunately, there are a host of different actions we can take, both in preparation for as well as during the riot, to minimize these risks and enhance our individual and collective safety, briefly summarized below.

In preparation, some of the hopefully obvious basics. Have a partner. You and your partner should be part of an affinity group with which you have previously established names for yourselves as well as for your group, and hand signals to help you move in an efficient and coordinated matter, not to mention being able to find each other quickly and easily should you become separated. Likewise, you should discuss with your affinity group both your intentions as well as the levels of risk you are comfortable with. Even better is if your group is part of a larger cluster of groups, who have likewise established a certain level of coordination and trust with each other. Also, take the time to familiarize yourself with the area and your surroundings before the day of action. Once the day comes, it is important to be intelligent and thorough about dressing in a way that protects your anonymity, so no patches, shirts with slogans on them, or skimpy bandannas that conceal nothing. (Pro tip: If you have an extra T-shirt with you, then you have a mask with you, so you should always have an extra T-shirt with you.) Just as important as protecting your anonymity is to be aware of context and surroundings. Ten people dressed like lost ninjas in a rainbow sea of happy colors will not increase your safety, it will only expose and endanger you. This is true as well in the case of personal protections and equipment. Do these shields, helmets, and padding increase your safety and potential scope of action, or will there be five hundred cops concentrating on the ten folks who showed up looking like they came ready for a hockey game? Finally, there is such a thing as a point of critical mass for black blocs, but it is a judgment call you need to make based on the general balance of power (i.e., how many cops and other potential enemies are you likely to encounter). We cancelled many an action or militant demonstration due to inadequate turnout on our end or an unexpectedly large turnout on the other side. It's unfortunate, but you need to be prepared to either go with a plan B or opt to wait for a more auspicious day and time.

But even when taking all possible precautions and being diligent about safety and preparations, in broad, diverse, and massive confrontations we will still have to deal with *the elements*. The elements can take many forms. Sometimes there are people from other political traditions who take issue with property damage or attacks on police or fascists. Sometimes authoritarian pacifists will not only attempt to interfere but will actively work to harm or detain us. There is good reason *Barricada* repeatedly published statements warning these people that if they continued to behave as cops and endanger militants, they would be extended the same treatment as cops. Other times, participants who don't come from the same traditions as us might use abusive, sexist, or homophobic language, or even worse engage in threatening or transgressive behavior toward us or others, forcing us to engage in order to try to defuse and disarm a potentially dangerous situation, but this sometimes leads to physical confrontations as well.

We had to deal with this problem repeatedly in Paris during high school student strikes and demonstrations in the late 1990s, when thousands of North African immigrant youths participated in attacking cops and looting stores but also sometimes engaged in sexist catcalling of women. We even had to physically intervene in a few cases of street harassment and assault. Clearly these attitudes were unacceptable, and our withdrawing from that space would have only allowed the problem to worsen, not improve. And just as in a politically diverse and large crowd you often have individuals who are politically immature, this kind of crowd is likely to have individuals who are tactically immature. These elements might throw objects from inside the middle of the crowd, seriously endangering those up front. Or they might be more liable to panic-run at the first sign of smoke or tear gas, sparking dangerous and unnecessary sudden movements. And finally, the larger and more diverse the crowd, the more difficult it is to spot potential undercover officers among and around us. Whether we like it or not, many in our movement adhere to a certain set of social codes. Some are more subtle than others, and some may be of a more conscious nature, but the fact remains: We can usually spot our own. To be clear and fair, this is often a direct negative result of the subcultural ghetto that anarchism is resigned to in many parts of the world. But in situations of danger, it allows us to use subtleties in attire, terminology, and even mannerisms to have a pretty good idea of who is one of us and who might just be a cop.[9]

So, while we should always be striving to expand our networks and engage with and be joined by diverse masses of people when taking to the streets, if when the time comes we find that it is the proverbial "just us," as on this day in Gothenburg, we can lament that failure and explore its causes after the fact. But in the moment, we might as well enjoy the safety and comfort of being "among friends" and work to make the best of it, free from many of the specific challenges and concerns we just discussed. No snatch squads to look out for, no liberals to argue with, no pacifists unironically trying to fight us.

On the contrary, it was such a family affair that, in the midst of rioting our way down Avenyn, my attention was caught by a specific, particularly prolific stone thrower on the front line. To my great surprise and joy—as well as his brief fear and then also joy as I desperately tried to catch his attention and reveal who I was through helmet and ski mask—I even ran into a long-lost Parisian friend and comrade. None other than Julien, from Brigada Flores Magon and the CNT! I was surprised to see him there, as he came from a somewhat more respectable anarcho-syndicalist tradition, but this shows that the participants in mass militant actions, or in this case summit mobilizations, were not from separate demographics but often significantly overlapping ones, of people investing their time and energy in local organizing as well as bouts of militant confrontations with the state. Case in point, Julien specifically was actually in Gothenburg as a CNT delegate at an international anarcho-syndicalist meeting. In any case, his was clearly the bigger surprise when a masked and helmeted nut in the middle of a riot ran in his direction yelling, "I know you! I know you!" In my defense, he was guilty of "inadequate masking up" (another good sign that many weren't quite expecting these developments), and I was at least able to muster the self-control to not shout out his name mid-stone throw.

This was indeed a family affair, the quintessential anarchist riot. A dazzling spectacle of performative violence. If summits of world leaders

Julien Terzics, left of police officer, during the clashes on Avenyn. Immortalized on the cover of Oi Polloi's *Total Resistance to the Fucking System* LP.

are primarily international battles of symbolism and messaging, our five hundred or so industrious press secretaries did a great job putting out a clear and concise statement and distributing it widely. A press release delivered by way of cobblestone and shattered glass to friend, potential friend, and foe alike. Greatly summarized, it read as follows: We cannot be contained and we cannot be dispersed. We are many, and our movement is growing. Despite your best efforts, we can and will turn your summits into theaters of revolt and resistance. You can throw the full power of the state and media against us, but as the writing on the wall of Hvitfeldtska said, "… in the end, we will win."

Young Love: Saturday, June 1, Sometime in the Evening

Well, this was going to be awkward. Just the idea made me feel embarrassed and uncomfortable, but I didn't see any other alternative here. It was this or, since I idiotically had no intention of parting with any of these beloved items, sleeping as a foreigner at the train station following two days of rioting with a helmet, ski mask, and gloves in his backpack, which didn't seem particularly wise. So I headed to a pay phone, pulled out the number she had written down for me, and called Lena. "Yeah, um, hi, Lena? It's Tomas, you know, from earlier."

She sounded a little surprised to hear my voice, and who could blame her? After all, we had parted ways not much longer than an hour earlier, having agreed to meet the next day.

"Yeah, look, please don't take this the wrong way. I'll explain in person and I promise it'll make sense, but do you mind if I sleep with you tonight?" Wonderful. I'm supposed to be somebody who does a fair amount of writing and public speaking, and this was my choice of words? This was before newfangled technology like Signal and WhatsApp, where you can reformulate your audio or even delete it and try again if you mess up. This was on an actual phone call, with no take two if you botch your first attempt. As Lena would later love to remind me, "Can I sleep with you?" is a bit of an unorthodox way to open a phone call with somebody you've known for all of twenty-four hours. I tried again. "Sorry, sorry. 'Sleep with you' is really not a great way to put it, that's not what I meant. Do you mind if I spend the night wherever it is that you are?" Fortunately, either because she had decided to trust me, or because she liked me, or because we came from the same political tradition and school so she understood that the subtext of my sudden urgent interest in spending the night with her probably had little to do with "creepy guy coming on too strong" and a lot to do with repression (I later learned it was actually a combination of all three), she responded with a friendly "Yes, no problem."

The repression that had rendered me temporarily homeless was the discovery that the Schillerska school, where my belongings were, not to mention the injured Old Man, was surrounded by cops.

I had arrived alone, but in the best of moods. The last three days had been kind to me. On Thursday, there was the successful and nothing if not cinematic escape from Hvitfeldtska. On Friday, we had, as the beloved Lucy Parsons urged us to do, devastated the avenues where the wealthy live, sent the cops on the run, and even went shopping with no money. My only possible gripe was that the football jersey I had so carefully picked out at Intersport was not of a Swedish team, but a British one. It also had a hole in it where the antitheft device used to be, but that I didn't mind, as I figured I could still pull it off and claim it as "anarchist chic." I had picked it because it was red and black, but now I felt as if I had visited the Eiffel Tower and brought back a souvenir statue of the Leaning Tower of Pisa. All in all, though, this seemed like a petty concern in the grand scheme of things, especially considering how my day had ended.

Once we had made our way down Avenyn, we erected some pretty impressive barricades out of portable toilets and wire fences. There, armed with a practically interminable supply of cobblestones, we waited for the inevitable massive police assault. And although it never really came, there were a series of intense confrontations with various riot cop squads, which had by then devolved into the cops throwing stones back at us. Considering this was in broad daylight and in view of all kinds of international press, this was clearly a sign of their frustration at how events had developed. Eventually, though, many of us, me included, decided it was time to change into yuppie wear and discreetly disappear. Particularly because there was another rendezvous in only a few hours at a park called Vasaplatsen for a Reclaim the Streets party.

I wasn't convinced by the scene at the Reclaim the Streets. The crowd was pretty spread out, and I was having trouble gauging just how combative it might be. By this point in my Swedish adventure, I was realizing my finger wasn't quite as firmly on the pulse of the movement as I like to think it usually is, which also made me a little uncomfortable, as I was starting to distrust my own judgment. Further, there was oddly no police presence whatsoever, which was making me a little uneasy. And finally, the days of battles and rioting had apparently begun to catch the attention of the local immigrant youth, and so the crowd had a more diverse character. Which is great, but hanging out masked and alone with a helmet and a looted shirt in your backpack in a crowd you are unfamiliar with just hours after destroying a city ... well, it seemed like a high-risk, low-reward thing to be doing. Knowing when to call it a day and disappear is a large part of staying safe and free in these kinds of environments, as most arrests tend to be toward the tail end of the action or in the hours and days following it, as this is when we are most dispersed and police have the most pressure to show repressive results.

And so, as I decided it was time to begin making my retreat, a voice from behind addressed me in English. "You again, with the antifa pin on your mask! Didn't I tell you you should probably take it off?" It was the beautiful antifascist with the ridiculously huge blue-green eyes again!

I got defensive, as I sometimes do, and babbled something or other about how I didn't have anything else on hand with which to clip the space between my eyes shut and would rather be a little more distinctive with something I could remove than more exposed with a part of my face.

"I'm kidding, relax. But I did want to say that I thought your comments yesterday at the assembly were really good, and it's good that people actually make these kinds of points publicly." Were it not for the ski mask, she would have been treated to the spectacle of my jaw cartoonishly dropping. It's a bit of a blur from there, but I mentioned that I was actually just leaving and why. To which she responded with a nonchalant, "Yeah, that sounds about right. I'll go with you, we'll be safer together." I was again thankful for the ski mask, but now even more so for the infamous antifa pin concealing the space between my eyes and my eyebrows. It helped hide the exaggerated eyebrow raise of astonishment at these developments. I made a mental note to work on my poker face once the mask came off.

We made our way to a nearby bench, not too far from Vasaplatsen but far enough for it to be plausible that we were an innocent young couple out for a stroll (just please don't look in my bag, officer). We chatted for hours, which went by in what felt like minutes. I can't remember a single word of our conversation, but I don't think that matters much. What I do remember is that we were happy enough just to be in each other's company. And even though we enjoyed a good anarchist riot just as much as the next black bloc monsters, it was clear that for both of us sharing a personal moment of tranquility and intimacy with another human being (not in the physical sense, please remove your head from the gutter) seemed like a wonderful way of winding down the day. So we sat on a park bench, under the shade of trees and surrounded by the charm of old-world European architecture, and did precisely that. We were still close enough to the Vasaplatsen to hear the sounds of confrontations, as well as what we at that time thought were fireworks, but in that moment we might as well have been in another universe. It's difficult to feel more alive than when adrenaline meets the excitement of young love.

It probably even explains the why of something I used to find somewhat odd: Most of the amorous relationships I was in began around, and sometimes literally in the midst of, major mobilizations or confrontations. It was something I was ashamed of for a while, and when my relationships fell apart, I thought that the Keanu Reeves character in the movie *Speed*, even though a cop, might have had a valid point about relationships based on intense experiences never working. Then I realized that this phenomenon was maybe not that surprising at all, and if anything was something positive. The mobilizations, riots, camps, convergence centers, and general spaces of the anarchist move- ment were where I felt at home, comfortable, confident, and generally in my element. And if you are feeling comfortable with yourself and your surroundings, and you are living intense moments that free you from the alienation so often experienced in daily life, it is only natural that you will be better able to interact with others in a manner that is respectful while also open and confident. After all, the world I'd like us to live in is one where we all feel like we can speak to the person of our dreams and think of nothing and no one as being out of our reach.

We said goodbye with a kiss, and I don't think I could possibly have been any happier. It wasn't quite on the level of *Let's kiss in the ashes of the old world*, but for a first week in Europe, *Let's kiss among the shattered glass of upscale storefronts* seemed pretty great. She wrote her number on the back of a piece of paper and suggested the most romantic second date I could possibly imagine: "Meet me tomorrow in the international antifascist bloc." I of course agreed, then responded with what is the height of anarchist black bloc monster flirting: the sharing of my real name.

The demonstration on Saturday was uneventful, as well it should have been. The cops seemed to have finally gotten the message and kept a prudent distance from us, while we refrained from any offen- sive action, respecting the common agreement that the Swedish AFA network had entered into with the larger coalition of antiglobaliza- tion organizations. My tensest moment of the day came in trying to find Lena! She had said that she would be "near the front around the Antifascistisk Aktion banner. You can't miss it, it's a huge baby- blue banner with pink letters on it." And while I had quickly located the rather large and impressive banner, the demonstration was well underway and there was still no sign of her. I had already gone through all the stages of grief and imagined a million different reasons she might have decided to not show up. Apparently I would just never see her again and she would become a mirage in my fevered head, some idealized and completely unreasonable image of a potential perfect partner in both crime and love who nobody else would ever be able to compare adequately to, when ... there she was. Never mind, it's just not that easy to find people among a mob of a thousand black-clad militants.

We marched in the large and disciplined antifa bloc alongside comrades from all over Europe, and toward the end we left to play demo tourists and visit the anarchist parallel universe of the international anarcho-syndicalist bloc. Probably the only place where black bloc folks can mingle among a sea of "normal" civilian-looking humans of all shapes, genders, and ages and yet still feel relatively comfortable and welcomed. And the bloc was impressive, not only because of its size but also thanks to the veritable sea of red and black flags—to such an extent that the cover of the March 2002 issue of *Barricada*, a significant one for us, as it was the month in which we announced our entrance into NEFAC and *Barricada* officially became the "Agitational Monthly of the Northeastern Federation of Anarcho-Communists," is an image from precisely that demonstration.

The demonstration wrapped up without further incident, and Lena and I spent the next few hours again walking around Gothenburg and enjoying some quality time with each other. We parted ways as night fell, and I made my way back to Schillerska under a summertime rain, to check on the Old Man and tell him of my glorious adventures.

I was about a block away from the school when I noticed the police vehicles. Everywhere. It seemed like the street was closed, or if it wasn't, getting through here would probably involve some kind of police control or ID check. There was no way I could imagine what was happening or about to happen inside that school, but my Spider-Sense must have tingled, because I instantly decided I wasn't in the mood to try my luck, turned around, and walked away as fast as I could.

Which brings us back to yours truly, at a pay phone, standing in the rain on a random street corner in the city, waiting like a lost child for Lena to come and rescue me. Embarrassed by my plight, I had offered to find my way to her place once she'd kindly accepted my inviting myself over, but she flat-out rejected it. "You shouldn't be going around the city alone at night, and if you get lost you'll miss the last train and won't be able to get here. Don't move, I'll be there in less than an hour."

A Tale of Two Gothenburgs, Part 2: Oscar Versus the Swedish Anti-Terror Squad

Sometimes I wonder about the possible effects on my karma of the life-style choices my anarchist convictions have inspired. (These thoughts are preciously rare, mind you, as after all, my anarchism is fairly solid.)

But on the off chance that in the modern era any kind of violence as a political tool is actually wrong and we are just antisocial nihilists who use political justifications to engage in illegal activity rather than participating civically as good citizens in the democratic process — if all that is so and capitalist democracy is actually the best of all possible worlds and the Good Lord's plan, then a lot of us would have definitely accumulated a lot of bad karma along the way. Fortunately, on the occasions when my mind wanders far enough to ponder such things, I am reminded of the very different life experiences that Oscar and I had in Gothenburg. If karma does exist, then it was rewarding my acts of rage and resistance with love, safety, and comfort while Oscar, who sat peacefully for that time at a school, was rewarded with something somewhat different.

Lena and I had spent the night in the safety of suburbia, um, "recovering" from three rather agitated days, and we had just made our way back to Schillerska to reunite with the Old Man and take him with us. On our way there, the two of us, both as guilty of all the crimes that exist as could be, were this time finally stopped by cops, who searched my bag. By this point I had "only" a ski mask on me, which I found concerning and pretty incriminating considering the whole "we tore apart the city's main and most exclusive avenue" aspect of things. Lena indicated discreetly that it wouldn't be a problem and to keep calm — I thought to myself that that was a pretty stupid assessment of our situation. With no escape route or any kind of alternative, I resigned myself to whatever my fate might be. Sweden being as Sweden is, the cop took my ski mask, looked at me, and sarcastically asked, "Are you cold?" to which I responded with a perfectly normal "Yes, sometimes," and we were free to be on our way.

The first words out of the Old Man's mouth when he saw Lena and I approaching were, "Do you have any idea what happened here yesterday?" Not, "Hey, who is this stranger?" or, "Where were you last night? I was afraid you might have died or gotten arrested."

"Yeah, the cops surrounded the school and I assumed they were checking IDs of people going in and out. So I retreated to safety. By the way, Oscar, meet Lena. She was kind enough to take me in yesterday and she will be housing us for the next few days until things calm down and we can safely take a train out of here."

"Uh, yeah, no. Not quite," was his response. Oscar loved nothing more than narrating a good story, and he launched right into it. And this is indeed a tremendous anecdote, and I have to admit it's been one of our favorites over the years. Oscar's recounting of it takes something that sounds traumatic and could have easily ended tragically and changes it into something that without fail had us in fits of breathless laughter.

How much does a written transcript of a greatly told story do justice to the original? Not only is tone lost from the verbal delivery, but in this case it's also translated from Spanish to English. Nonetheless, I will let Oscar speak here in his own words. The storytelling usually began with, "Hey, Oscar, tell us again about the day you got to meet the Swedish anti-terror squad because you hurt your ankle and didn't go out to a demonstration and destroy half of Gothenburg, while Tomas tore the city apart and then was out sleeping with his new Swedish partner!"

> *Fiiiiine. I was sitting in the schoolyard, on the steps of the entrance to the building. Happy with my new crutches, chatting with a comrade from Chile I had just met as we both enjoyed a bowl of soup. I had my back to the street, and suddenly mid-sentence the Chilean goes silent, his face turns a pale white, he drops the soup, turns, and sprints off into the building. I had a moment to wonder what the hell was going on before I turned around. When I managed to look behind me there was some kind of death squad marching straight toward us. Robocops with ski masks and automatic weapons (at least as far as I could tell), in a tight bloc formation, not quite running at us but definitely going at a pretty decent pace. It was the craziest shit I'd ever seen.*

> *I immediately turned and started running up the stairs, but you can't really call what I was doing with the crutches "running." I was going way too slow, so I threw the crutches away. The adrenaline shock magically cured me of any pain in my ankle. I sprinted as fast and far as I could, following the Chilean I had just met, reaching the fifth and last floor of the building.*

> *It was completely dark and as far as I could tell there were just us two on this floor. I started calling out to him, "Where are you? Where are you?" From somewhere in the darkness I heard this piece of shit yell back, "I don't know, man, figure it out yourself, leave me alone." Zero solidarity, this guy. And this guy had found some hiding place, but there was nowhere else left to go, nowhere to hide.*

I found basically a space between two pieces of furniture. Imagine the worst hiding spot in the world. A kid playing hide and seek would probably do better. It was basically a one-meter gap between two closets, and I found something like one of those large cardboard-type thick papers, like a school material, what kids would use for a presentation, so I put that in front of me and basically kneeled behind it. Just the worst hiding spot of all time, but I had no other choice since this other motherfucker refused to help me.

So there I was, sitting in the darkness, and I could hear the cops on the floors below. Silence. Sounds of a door being kicked in, followed by shouts of "POLICE!" as they kicked open a door. Then rumblings and cartoon-like screams of "Aaaaaarrrrghhh" and "No, no, no," and people crying.

Silence again. Next floor. Same thing. Boom boom boom. Boots kicking at doors. "POLICE!" Chaos, panicked yelling, hysteria, crying sounds. Silence. Next floor. And I'm like, "What the fuck, two more floors and it's my turn. They're going to get here and I'm fucked." Which is when I found God and started praying, and back then I was ultra-atheist, anti-religion. But I started having a conversation with God, you know, just in case. "Hey, God, you know I haven't always really necessarily been on your side, but if there was ever a good moment for you to prove to me your existence, right now would be great." I figured I needed to try to take every advantage I could get. I prayed the "Padre Nuestro" and any other prayer I could manage to remember.

Fourth floor. BAM BAM BAM. "POLICE!" Another round of the same show.

And then they got to my floor. But since it was dark, they came in silently and more in a "stealth mode." Which only made the whole thing even more terrifying and sinister. It was like some kind of SWAT team hunting people down in a dark building.

Suddenly I look up and I just see this huge glove grabbing the cardboard in front of me, and I think, "Okay, that's it. This is the end, I'm done."

He pulls away the cardboard, I look up, and there is this huge fucking Viking in front of me. Full robocop outfit, face covered,

257

pointing some kind of crazy rifle at my chest. And just a giant. He starts barking at me in Swedish and I can't understand a single word. I get so nervous I suddenly forget how to speak English and start shouting back in Spanish, "I don't know! I don't know!" He grabs me by the hair, which if you remember was pretty long back then, throws me toward the stairs, and another one pushes me again, so I roll down the stairs with so much force that I crash into the wall below.

I finish rolling down and bouncing off the wall and it's immediate. Like a perfectly synchronized one-two. Bounced off the wall and immediately had a knee on my chest and was pressed against the wall again. He figures out I don't speak Swedish and starts barking at me. "Is there anybody else up there?! Anybody else?!" All the while fully masked and pointing a rifle at me. And obviously I know that other asshole, the Chilean, is up there, but I don't snitch on him. "No, no, there's nobody, I was alone." The cop goes crazy. "TELL ME THE TRUTH! TELL ME THE TRUTH!" As I'm starting my next round of panicked "No, no, there's nobody there," he grabs my nose and starts twisting it. I didn't even know it could twist that far without breaking, but I just keep yelling, "No, no, no," like a lunatic.

The cops says to me, "We don't like immigrants like you here in Sweden. Next time you come here we are going to kill you, you piece of shit." And with that he rolls me down the stairs. I roll from the fourth floor to the third. From the third to the second, second to first, I roll like a Slinky toy all the way out the door and into the yard.

As soon as I'm done tumbling into the yard, they strip me down to my underwear, handcuff me, and throw me on the ground with their dogs barking basically inside my ear. Then, to round it out, it starts raining.

And they left us there like that on the ground for like three hours. With the dogs barking and the occasional masked cop trying to intimidate us by hitting his baton against the ground right next to our heads.

But I was calm at this point. I mean, after all, we were in Sweden. People like me had come here in the past precisely because it wasn't Chile. If this had been in Chile, I would have been shitting in my *pants. But at this point I was mainly entertaining myself thinking about what an incredible story I would have to tell.*

And this is interesting from a sociological perspective. Imagine the extent of my experience of privilege until then that even as a left-wing person I couldn't conceive that the cops could possibly just kill me in that school. Of course, I didn't know at that point that they had shot somebody just hours earlier. And if this had been after Genoa and the Diaz school craziness, I probably would have been a lot more worried. But I until then I had never had any personal problems with the law, I didn't grow up under any particularly oppressive regime beyond the usual liberal capitalist democracy. To the contrary, I grew up in a relatively comfortable sector of society and so had no personal experience of police brutality, and as a child my view of police was the typical one of a middle-class child, seeing them as good people who were there to protect us. So because of my politics I had an intellectual understanding of police brutality, but on a personal level it just didn't seem believable that a cop could just murder me in the street. And on top of it all, I'm in Sweden of all places. No matter the situation, I couldn't see them murdering, or even beating to a pulp, a handcuffed foreign university student in a schoolyard. And honestly, sometimes I forget because I miraculously escaped without any kind of real injuries, but they had already pretty much kicked my ass inside. I had my nose almost broken, was dragged by my hair, was essentially stabbed by the rifle in my chest, and then bowled down five flights of stairs. It seemed like if there was a beating to be given, I had already gotten it. So I really wasn't worried and understood that at that point it was mainly a show meant to intimidate us.

And after a few hours of this, they took all our IDs, filmed us one by one, and just like they had arrived, they left. I remember standing there in my underwear and all I could think was, "Holy shit, nobody is going to believe the story I have to tell."

And so concludes the tale of "How Oscar Met the Swedish Anti-Terror Squad." Formally, the unit that entered the Schillerska school that evening with automatic weapons drawn is known as Nationella Insatsstyrkan, which translates roughly to "National Special Elite Force," and they were ostensibly looking for an "armed German terrorist."

The operation was quite the shock to the country, as well as those seventy-eight people, primarily young students, who experienced it. One sixteen-year-old Swedish student, Elias Granath, described it as follows:

> By the schoolyard we're faced with another shock. The dark yard has become a military zone. Barking of dogs and orders fill the air, I hardly realize that I am forced down toward the ground, with the wet and rough asphalt against my face and the hands behind the neck.... None of us lying there on the asphalt was allowed to say a word, we couldn't look up or move. The boots that walked in front of my face made the rules clear for us: "Obey or be punished."[10]

Unsurprisingly, the "armed German terrorist" who was the pretext for this operation never materialized, and none of the seventy-eight individuals identified were ever charged with any crimes.

Escape to Suburbia and a Shooting in a Park

We were on our way to Lena's house, or, to be more precise, her parents' house, where in yet another example of how absurdly open a lot of Swedish society is, they allowed a couple of foreigners whose definition of demonstrating probably fit comfortably into several paragraphs of criminal law to live in their home with them for a few days, one of them sharing a room and bed with their seventeen-year-old daughter. I can imagine quite a few other scenarios in which I would have been chased away with a shotgun as opposed to graciously fed and housed. As we sat on the train taking in the beautiful Swedish summer scenery, the Old Man was still incredulous. I couldn't help being amused by his outrage, and I still am to this day. "You told me Sweden was a nice social democratic state, that things probably wouldn't be so intense here, more like a 'warm-up.'"

This is true, I had indeed said that.

"I got attacked by cops and barely escaped through a window, flew off of an industrial container and almost broke my ankle on one day, was terrorized by the anti-terror squad and used as a human bowling ball on the next, and now I'm on crutches. All this, I want to remind you again, was the price of *not* attending one single solitary demonstration or action, where if I'm understanding correctly, we could have been shot."

While the proverbial "we" had devastated the avenues of the wealthy and terrorized cops for two days, and in my case there was the added bonus of nights of romantic fervor with my newfound love interest, Oscar's entire tour of Gothenburg had consisted of escaping from one school and then limping to the next one only to be attacked again, this time by armed cops in ski masks. Still laughing, I replied, "Well, apparently I misjudged this one."

Oscar didn't let up. "Yeah, no shit. Remember when you said things would probably be more structured here?" I had indeed said that as well. That was because the geography of this mobilization made it likely to skew heavily toward autonomes, anarchists, and antifascists from the northern parts of Europe, whose traditions of black blocs and mass militance were closer to the German antifascist model. Tight formations, lines of affinity groups, bloc sealed off by banners. Compact, militant, and martial looking, but often content to transmit the message and image of collective strength without necessarily seeking out confrontation. Very effective defensive formations, but not ideal for the "chaotic riot."

Instead, we had witnessed two days of constant pitched battles, massive charges against police lines, and a level of property destruction Sweden hadn't seen for decades and likely hasn't experienced since, culminating in Sweden's first shooting of demonstrators since 1931. I was a little concerned about how I had managed to so badly misjudge what to expect from a mobilization, and for years I couldn't wrap my head around why the Swedish state, a deeply social democratic entity for which violent repression of activists as a measure of first recourse is both unusual and unexpected, had chosen to act in such a preemptively—and wildly—confrontational fashion. Not only was it unexpected, but the apparatus responsible for executing this line of preemptive repression, the police, was also wholly unprepared for the level of resistance it was to encounter. They lacked basic elements of crowd control and dispersal, such as tear gas and rubber or plastic bullets, as already discussed, but they also lacked the training and preparation, as well as experience, for dealing with mass militance on this level. And so they resorted to running at crowds with their horses, letting dogs loose on us, or throwing rocks back at us. The rock throwing wasn't just the act of one overwhelmed or overzealous cop. There is video documentation of an entire squad of riot cops, in broad daylight and in the middle of a central city boulevard, engaging in a rock-throwing face-off with a front line of protesters.[11] I should know, one of those rocks bounced off of my fortunately helmeted head. Most people that day were not helmeted, so all things considered I should be thankful it hit me and not somebody else. But even with a motorcycle helmet on, it was loud and painful. All of this was dangerous and sometimes even frightening, but from a crowd-control perspective, it was not very effective. The climax was the shooting at Friday evening's Reclaim the Streets event at Vasaplatsen.

By no means is this a justification of the shootings. Video evidence clearly shows nineteen-year-old Hannes Westberg, the most critically injured of the three people shot by the police that day and who as a consequence lost a kidney and his spleen, being shot in the back as he is running away from the police line and already at a distance of ten meters or more from them.[12] In the moment of the shooting, he was presenting no immediate danger to the physical integrity of the officer who shot him or that of any other officers, and certainly none justifying the use of deadly force.

But the shooting was an unsurprising climax when viewed in the context of the events of the past thirty-six hours, and the nature of the confrontations at and around Vasaplatsen. Demonstrators, feeling empowered by their success in repelling police attacks on Avenyn but still furious from two days of preemptive police aggressions, were attacked by a gang of about fifteen suspected neo-Nazis. The police entered Vasaplatsen, conveniently, shortly after antifascists had already repelled the Nazi attack. By now, what had begun as an almost exclusively anarchist riot had also drawn the aforementioned fair amount of local immigrant youths, who enthusiastically defended the square against the Nazis and joined in the subsequent confrontation with the cops.

The cops were coming under more and more intense attacks, from ever-closer distances. Having neither dogs nor horses on hand at that moment, police had no recourse other than a baton or a gun. In that context, and with the logic of a scared and authoritarian guardian of state power, shooting at demonstrators rather than retreating doesn't seem like an unexpected turn of events.

I was not at the scene of the shooting. Having wandered away to chat with Lena, we heard from a distance what we assumed were firecrackers. Gunshots in real life don't sound like they do in the movies, and as we were unaware of the Nazi incursion and subsequent escalation, we thought things had died down. So gunshots never crossed our mind. But Felham—a comrade from AFA Stockholm whom I met in 2005 during an antifascist mobilization in Stockholm and went on to share front lines with in several cities over the years—was there. Felham is the son of Chilean political refugees. He left Chile at the age of five and finally settled in northern Sweden with his parents. In 2001, Felham still lived in Umea and had traveled to Gothenburg with his local antifa group, who were not yet members of the AFA network, although they would join soon after. He describes the situation as follows:

> Things were pretty calm at the Reclaim the Streets, a lot of hippie types sitting around, and a lot of groups of kids dressed in black and immigrant kids just kind of hanging around. But the cops were stationed like a block away. They were blocking the road on one end of the square and not letting people pass. Suddenly a group of ten or fifteen Nazis shows up and starts attacking people. To be fair, actually, "Nazis" is maybe not the right term, as these weren't actual organized militant Nazis, they were actually right-wing hooligans from the local firm Wisemen. [The Wisemen is a right-wing hooligan firm (Swedish: *huliganfirma*) associated with the local IFK Gothenburg soccer club, and one of the most well-known hooligan groups in Sweden. The purpose of their attack was apparently to "defend Gothenburg" as the city was in ruins due to the riots.][13]
>
> The people were able to repel the attack, but the point was that the hooligans retreated toward the cops, and the cops let them pass their lines and protected them. And they did that like three times! The hooligans would come out from behind the cop lines, attack the crowd, start getting overwhelmed by the numbers because more and more antifas and immigrant kids were realizing what was happening, and then retreat into the protection of the cops. It was insane, and obviously people lost it. And that's when the real riot began and the attacks on the cops really got intense.
>
> My group and I were right there when Hannes got shot, and even though as far as we knew cops in Sweden didn't have rubber bullets, we assumed anyway that's what they were using, that they must have gotten them for the summit or something. That

they were shooting live ammunition never crossed our minds. And if you look at the videos, you can tell that this was the case to such an extent that people don't really flee in a panic after the shooting. On the contrary. We saw Hannes fall injured, assumed he had been hurt by rubber bullets, and this only made us and the rest of the crowd angrier and escalated the confrontations. We only realized after the fact, that night watching the news, that those zooming noises we heard were actual live ammunition rounds flying around us.

It was just all-around bad decision-making from the cops. It never made much sense. There were maybe a couple of dozen cops, hundreds and hundreds of us, and the only explanation I can find is that they panicked, because there was no immediate threat that would justify shooting randomly into the crowd like they did. It enraged the crowd completely, and things only got more difficult for them from then on.[14]

The Butterfly Effect

For many years I thought it was just simple miscalculation on the part of the Swedish state. Even Swedish comrades would later tell me that as a whole, they were caught completely off guard by the developments, but especially by the preemptive strikes of the police. Indeed, there was a so-called Gothenburg model of managing protest, and it was oriented around de-escalation, including forming a contact group to negotiate with the demonstrators' networks and taking actions such as making local schools available as convergence centers. The strategy was that through de-escalation they could limit any possible violence or "excesses" to a containable level. So the simplest-sounding explanation for this sudden about-face was probably the most reasonable: They had infiltrated the general assemblies that had been held the nights before we arrived, and something they heard or saw spooked them into believing that there was an imminent need for preemptive action and that not taking any would result in greater harm.

And for years that's how it remained. A small mystery that was not of much concern to us anyway. We in any case applauded and celebrated the offensive actions that resulted from this turn of events, and as a collective fighting force we were able not only to effectively defend ourselves against the state's attacks but even to promptly launch a successful counterattack of our own. It's not at all unlikely that had the police not placed Hvitfeldtska school under siege, and then the next morning immediately surrounded and attacked the antifascist bloc, confrontations might have been limited to some completely routine disturbances around the summit's security perimeter. So while we definitely made the best of it, the why of it all remained an unsolved mystery.

Years later, I ran into a translation of an article that appeared in 2006 in the Gothenburg newspaper *Göteborgs-Posten*. In it, a researcher at Gothenburg University presents evidence that "to avoid President Bush being physically threatened or politically humiliated during his visit, the police brass was supplied with threat scenarios that turned out to be wrong."[15] These incorrect threat scenarios, which included talk of firearms at Hvitfeldtska school and a plot by "400 Ya Basta activists from Italy who were allegedly planning to attack the President's hotel," were provided via US intelligence channels to the Swedish military, who in turn communicated them to the local police, along with pressure to take correspondingly appropriate action.[16] Essentially, US intelligence, spooked by the near sabotage of the Inauguration Day presidential parade and the numerous breaches of the security perimeter in Quebec City, were eager to keep any potential unrest or confrontations as far away as possible from President Bush. Whether the confrontations were larger in scope or more intense in nature was of no concern to them, as long as they were as far away as possible from the president. As the *Göteborgs-Posten* article concludes, this led to "seeing the Gothenburg model sacrificed at the security altar of President Bush" and allowing the Swedish authorities "to be used as a 'useful idiot,' and, without realizing it, put a foreign country's security interests before their own."[17]

It's a nice thought to have, if maybe a little self-absorbed: that we, not just those of us who were in Gothenburg physically, but all anarchists from around North America who took on the presidential inauguration and the FTAA, were at least partially responsible for how events unfolded in Gothenburg. The butterfly effect of chaos theory applied to mass militance. The collective "we" had flapped its wings in Washington, DC, and Quebec City and helped to brew a storm in Scandinavia!

Epilogue: Return to Vanersborg

Lena was from a small town about forty-five minutes north of Gothenburg called Vanersborg. A few weeks after Genoa, I returned there to spend a week with her as well as her ridiculously welcoming family. One night, as we were standing in line at an *imbiss* (food truck), a middle-aged, nondescript man suddenly approached me and began yelling and gesticulating in my direction. When he pointed toward the antifa flag pin on the lapel of my jacket while yelling something about *"kravall,"* which I by then knew means "riot" in Swedish, the situation seemed clear to me: older fascist harassing and threatening us, which, at risk of sounding arrogant or macho, wasn't going to end well for him. But just as I took a step toward him, I was unexpectedly stopped by Lena. Considering we were usually of similar opinions as to how to respond to these kinds of situations, this seemed surprising. She and the guy exchanged some agitated-sounding words but left it at that, and eventually he walked away. "He's not a Nazi," she explained. "Just a regular citizen who at the moment dislikes AFA and is upset because we are seen as those responsible for the 'destruction of Gothenburg.' This has actually been happening a lot over the last few months, with just 'normal citizens' harassing or threatening members of AFA and visible antifascists. I don't think we made many friends with what happened in Gothenburg."

The post-Gothenburg toll on the Swedish antifascist and anarchist movement was indeed heavy, and many comrades I spoke to in the years following the Gothenburg summit identified these events as the beginning of a couple of difficult years for radical antifascism and extraparliamentary movements in Sweden, provoked by a combination of an outcry of public opinion against the "vandals who destroyed Gothenburg" and the ensuing state repression, which for Swedish standards was particularly heavy, resulting in over fifty years of prison sentences being handed out, targeting several activists prominent in the antifascist movement. Their experience is of course no detail, and it should not be minimized. To the contrary, the Gothenburg example lay at the crux of one of the central questions regarding militant opposition to these kinds of summits: Is the symbolic message worth the real and lasting effects of burnout and repression that local structures and networks will face? But here again, the opinion of somebody like Felham is revealing, as are his perspectives on the Gothenburg events almost twenty years later. Felham, while already identifying with militant antifascism in 2001, increased his activity in the aftermath of Gothenburg, with his entire group joining the AFA network right after the riots and he then going on to join AFA Stockholm a few years later. His voice is of course only one of many, and there are indeed opinions within AFA, especially around the Gothenburg group, that are more critical of the impact of the riots on radical politics in Sweden. But his is also the voice of somebody who devoted decades of his life to militant antifascism, and he was for many years one of the central figures among a highly committed and militant generation of antifascists in Stockholm, during a time when both AFA Stockholm and the Revolutionary Front had fascists decisively on the run.[18] His verdict is clear:

> I think my, and our, experience was similar to many others. This was not only the first big demonstration for us, but it was also our first contact with the antiglobalization movement, which also meant our first exposure to radical politics that wasn't centered around small-town antifascism. In Swedish small towns, this basically means we hunt down, confront, and fight town Nazis and racists. Some of us had a background also in the animal rights movement, which was huge in Sweden in the 1990s, but this was completely different.
>
> We went there with the intention of disturbing the summit, without expecting much to happen beyond some confrontations ... because this was Sweden. But it was exactly the kind of experience that a movement needs to radicalize people and bring them toward extraparliamentary politics, and the experiences of both police violence as well as effective and successful militance and resistance in Gothenburg radicalized a lot of people. When people say it was negative for us as a movement, I understand the point they are making. On the one hand, some new repressive laws were enacted post-Gothenburg, although even then it is unfair to say they were exclusively due to Gothenburg, as for example the anti-mask laws came several years later, after we continued being successful in mass militance. And anyway, what is the enactment of laws meant to disarm militant antifascism if not a sign that we are doing something right? The other point they are usually making is that we came onto the radar of a much larger segment of society, of regular people who suddenly heard more about what AFA or antifa was and were very much opposed to us based on the sensationalism they saw in the news, like your

experience in Vanersborg. It was probably a lower-intensity version of something very similar to what is happening in the US with Trump today and antifa being labeled as terrorists in the wake of the Black Lives Matter uprising. So while that kind of attention brings the opposition of the so-called mass of society, it at the same time draws a lot of younger people, people who were already politically left of center or alternative in their lifestyles, nearer to antifascism, and that was the case with us.

Gothenburg radicalized a lot of people, myself included (it made me much crazier than I was before), and drew to us a lot of people in Sweden who skipped several steps of the so-called ladder of politicization or radicalization. Kids would basically usually first land in Ung Vänster [Young Left], which is the youth wing of the Left Party. From there they would get disillusioned with party politics and join the SUF [Swedish Anarcho-Syndicalist Youth Federation], and from there they either landed in AFA structures or did both. But that was usually the progression into anarchist politics and militant antifascism.

That process was completely shaken up by the Gothenburg riots, and I don't know if it was thousands, but definitely hundreds of people who had witnessed and lived those events skipped those steps and landed directly in the structures of the anarchist space in Sweden. Not only did the AFA network actually expand in the aftermath of Gothenburg, but the confidence that having experienced and being part of such a successful exercise in mass militance gave a lot of people was probably an important factor in the AFA network's strategy of mass mobilization and mass confrontation to oppose the Nazis' demonstrations in Salem.[19] I don't think our presence in Salem would have been nearly as massive, nor would our voice have been able to draw so many different kinds of people, were it not for the experience of Gothenburg. Salem was a protracted victory of antifascism built on the foundations of the Gothenburg riots.[20]

"We Are Not Victims, We Are Victors!"
In the aftermath of Gothenburg, just as was the case post–Quebec City, we were surprised by how many anarchist comrades, as well as other assorted radicals, chose to center their messaging around the

supposed scandal of the scope of violence used by the state to oppose us, almost always in self-victimizing tones of shock and indignation, akin to anarcho-pearl-clutching, which never ceased to surprise us. Arguing that the state resorting to violence through the use of the array of so-called less-than-lethal crowd-control weaponry at its disposal, like tear gas, rubber bullets, pepper spray, and the like—or in the case of Gothenburg its very limited arsenal of batons, dogs, and horses—is somehow an outrage or an injustice reveals a fundamental misunderstanding of the nature of state power and violence.

It implies that the capitalist state is not built upon and maintained through the exertion of a constant and systemic violence, but rather is a benevolent thing, one that only exists due to the mass acceptance of the social contract it proposes, and that this violence is somehow an aberration, a veering off course that simply needs to be corrected. Of course, the modern Western state does indeed rely primarily on the consent of its citizens, rather than the acute exertion of brute force, for stability and governance. But the underlying reality is and will always be: If its power is threatened or its order placed in existential danger, it will revert to brute force to maintain itself, regardless of how many, or few, still ascribe to its proposed social contract.

And so if we identify the state as a violent entity and an enemy to be fought against—and hopefully someday destroyed—we should not expect it to grant us any concessions when we enter into conflict with it, and by the same token, we should not be granting it any concessions either. One might think that this runs contrary to what we often see: anarchists and revolutionaries participating in, and often at the forefront of, struggles either to gain specific concessions from the state (for example, labor protections, minimum wage struggles, or unemployment benefits) or to curb its most violent aspects and excesses, such as the struggles to defund police departments or outlaw specific practices.

First, there is a political consideration. We intervene as anarchists in these specific struggles in order to "pick people up where they are standing" (as the German expression goes) and expose them to anarchist ideas and practice from a position of solidarity and support. And to push the position that the solution to the contradictions within the capitalist state can only be found from a perspective of total rupture with it, that they indeed have no possible resolution within the framework of capitalism. The example of the struggle to defund police is a good one in this case. Somebody sympathetic to issues of oppression and state violence is likely to be on board with lowering local police budgets in order to better fund education, substance abuse prevention, and the like. They understand that a society that prioritizes funding its general needs rather than its repressive forces is more likely to be a less unequal society, and a less unequal society will probably have lower rates of both property crime and violent crime, thus necessitating less resources allocated to policing itself. But they will balk at the idea of abolishing police, claiming them essential to avoid a breakdown of the societal order. And indeed, they are of course correct. Capitalist society, with its inequalities and its survival-of-the-fittest morality, would not only be an unlivable jungle without police, it would be ungovernable. Which is where anarchist agitation intervenes, to pose the question of a radical change in how society is organized. If you can agree that a society with less inequality is a safer and less violent one, imagine if we organized all of society on the basis of mutual aid and the needs of its members as a priority, rather than the seamless accumulation of capital. And imagine if instead of the state policing communities, we had communities themselves be responsible for and accountable for their collective safety and well-being.

The other side of this coin is a purely tactical one, and it was the relevant one for our situation in Gothenburg. If we are going to enter a mass militant confrontation with the state, the less armed and dangerous its agents are, the better for us. Greek police do not have (or at least don't use) rubber bullets. If they did, anarchists would be much less able to get close enough to them to effectively use Molotov cocktails as a tool. Tear gas, which Greek police make generous use of, may be unpleasant and can even temporarily blind you, but it will not, obviously, cause you sudden and unexpected blunt force trauma. And even though the university asylum in Greece is no longer law, a large enough sector of society deems state incursions into university campuses as something outrageous and controversial enough as to effectively allow for those campuses to be a relatively safe space to retreat, regroup, and either reattack or disappear. These concessions grant us greater possibilities for action and confrontation in the short term, but they also mean that in the medium or long term, in a moment of actual potential revolutionary upheaval or an insurrection, the state will still be constrained not by legality but by knowing that the use of certain tactics and weapons that have not been normalized in the eyes of large segments of society will risk provoking further sympathy with demonstrators and potentially amplify the conflict or revolt they are trying to stop.

It's why the police in Minneapolis gave up the Third Precinct even though from a purely military perspective they could have defended it. The political cost of further enflaming and spreading rebellion was too high. It's the same principle that once upon a time made it so that anarchists in Athens would sit on university campuses during violent confrontations with the state and still have their phones with them (their actual personal cell phones!), with the logic of, "If the state used our phones to track people down just for throwing rocks or occupying a university campus, it would be a scandal, and society would never allow it," while German antifascists never took their phones anywhere and had to worry about ten-person snatch squads plucking them from demonstrations for the mere act of briefly pulling a handkerchief over their nose. In short: It is a matter of power dynamics, as well as to what extent resistance to the state is normalized and accepted by society, and how effective this has been at limiting the state's range of repressive action.

ADVENTURES IN RURAL BARCELONA

11

THE CANCELLED SUMMIT: OUR ANGER IS ALWAYS JUSTIFIED

Barcelona, June 2001

Banned from the Squats—The Practical Consequences of the Anarchist Versus *Independentista* Rift on One Anarchist's Sleeping Arrangements: Unknown Squat, Sunday, June 24, Late at Night

"I'm very sorry, but we can't let you in tonight." The person standing in the doorway seemed friendly enough, maybe even a little apologetic, but the message was clear and the decision firm. It was close to midnight, and I was standing outside a squat in Barcelona, the exact location or name of which I can no longer remember, and at which I was apparently an unwelcome guest. It had already been a long day, with arrival at city, riot, desperate escape from cops, and the now traditional losing of the Old Man all rolled into one day. So what I would have loved to do was to go full Karen and ask to speak to the manager of squatting, since this was an unacceptable outrage. But that would get me nowhere, so I decided to opt for diplomacy. "But why? Hannah and her group said we should come here tonight to sleep, that the place was open for international people."

"Yes, but today there were riots and the city is full of undercover cops, so only vouched-for people are allowed in at the moment. And it's late, everybody is sleeping, and I'm not going to run around the place waking everybody up to see who it is who knows you." What a conundrum. How to react to a collective security decision that makes pretty good sense but for you personally is a small disaster that leaves you temporarily homeless after a very long day. Not to mention that the little anarcho-scenester in me was already imagining the shame and ridicule to come: "You couldn't find a place to sleep in Barcelona? The city with like a hundred squats?"

As I began my retreat and was in the process of trying to make peace with the idea of spending the night at the train station, the squat door reopened and a woman called out to me. "Hey you, stop, stop. I remember you from Hvitfeldtska!" she said with a strong German accent. "Look, they're not letting you in because one of the locals was on the metro with you and noticed your pin," she said as she pointed to an *estelada* pin on the lapel of my jacket. The estelada is the left-wing *independentista* version of the Catalan national flag, which includes a red star inside a triangle (similar to the Cuban and Puerto Rican flags).[1] It is used by independentistas to differentiate themselves from the bourgeois nationalism of other currents of the pro-independence movement. I had picked it up as we were leaving the first demonstration and had put it on my jacket as I sat bored at the train station later on in the day.

It was a little souvenir, of course, but it was also a small gesture of solidarity with progressive and revolutionary movements of national liberation. The Barricada line, which was not without controversy, was that it is right for people to organize for their own liberation along the lines of their specific oppression, which includes national oppression, and anarchists can and should extend critical solidarity to these movements. Particularly in the cases of the Basques and Catalans of the Spanish State,[2] whose national oppression until the 1970s went to the extreme of even being forbidden from speaking their native languages in public by a literal fascist dictatorship, and who took up arms as oppressed nations against an imperial and colonial construct such as the Spanish State, and on top of that did so with concepts of inclusion that were free of any trace of "blood and soil" reactionary ideas, the concept of solidarity seemed evident to me. As Edgar Partisano, a good friend from Girona, a small city about an hour outside of Barcelona, and a decades-long activist and organizer, summarized it for me one night, "Our fight is for a socialist and inclusive Catalunya, and all are welcome in it. Catalan is not who is born here or has a certain blood, but whoever chooses to come here and feels Catalan." It is not by coincidence that the now-defunct Euskadi Ta Askatasuna (ETA, or "Basque Homeland and Liberty"), as well as the lesser-known armed Catalan equivalent of Terra Lliure (Free Land), both made abundantly clear that their concepts of independence were inseparable from the struggle for socialism.

I had had a chance to meet a lot of these people in Paris during the 1990s, and to experience the open and welcoming character of their movement during the annual demonstrations held in the city in solidarity with political prisoners of the Basque struggle, as we marched together demanding amnesty and repatriation of Basque prisoners to the Basque Country. We of course came from different traditions of resistance, and theirs was markedly more Marxist and Leninist than ours, but it was clear that they were comrades with which we could share a demonstration as well as the occasional barricade.

We even attended trials of ETA militants held in Paris, to stand in solidarity with them as well as their friends and family members. Before you collapse into fits of condemnation and self-righteousness: Yes, ETA made some very poor and unacceptable military and tactical decisions. Some of those decisions took the lives of innocent people, including workers who met no definition of a valid military target. But the organization and the broad social and cultural movement around them was much more than that, and those trials were nothing if not inspiring to witness as a teenage activist. Young idealists, often no older than their mid-twenties, facing the full weight of the state and the certain prospect of decades in prison with unwavering dignity. Unfailingly they all followed the same script: refusing to stand for the judges, declaring themselves members of the military branch of ETA, and finally announcing that as Basque prisoners of war the French state had no authority to judge them and that they would now be leaving, at which point they would get up and take about one step before being either forcibly sat down again or removed from their own trial proceedings.[3]

Fortunately, relations between anarchists and independentistas in Catalunya have greatly improved over the years. "Both the anarchists and the independentistas were completely marginal, mainly youth subcultural groups in the early 2000s," as Edgar undiplomatically put it. To be precise, a 2001 article in *El País*, dramatically headlined "The Complex Web of Radical Violence," identifies the three main currents of youth radicalism in Catalunya as squatters, anarchists, and, as they term them, "separatists," placing the number of them who "regularly resort to violence" at 1,660, with another 3,980 "sporadically resorting to violence." These figures are provided by the police, who are also kind enough to provide an exact breakdown: The *habitues* of radical activism" consist of 780 in the squatters' movement, 450 "radical separatists," and 335 in anarchist collectives or groups.[4] While we can be skeptical as to the accuracy of the police intelligence work that led to these figures, it is clear that this was anything but a mass movement.

Edgar continued, "Our small numbers left us particularly open to petty squabbles and an inordinate level of importance given to sectarian infighting, the catalyst of which was more often than not some tension between cliques than content." The left wing of the pro-independence movement has grown exponentially over the last ten years, particularly since the crisis of 2008–2009, and is today even represented by several members of the radical left formation CUP (Candidatura d'Unitat Popular, or "Popular Unity Candidacy") in the Catalan Parliament, with the CUP reaching 8 percent of the vote in 2015. As a side note, one of these representatives, David Fernandez, could often be seen in parliamentary sessions with an Antifascist Action T-shirt on, which gives a bit of a clue as to what the movement background and makeup of this organization is. And so, unsurprisingly, a broader, more politically mature movement also brings with it a greater maturity as far as recognizing friend from foe. And while there are of course obvious differences within the two camps, it is evident that on social issues, immigration, antifascism, and generally most of the day-to-day, bread-and-butter issues of radical social movements, we are very much aligned. To the extent that, even though it may sound contradictory or surprising, there is actually no shortage of libertarian activists involved with the CUP on a local level. Edgar notes that they even had a joke about anarchists on election day: "If you see somebody dressed all in black looking a little lost and confused at the balloting station, help them out ... it's probably an anarchist voting for the very first time, and for us." Indeed, the CUP is a fascinating hybrid of party meets social movements, combining electoral politics with a strong municipalist practice and bottom-up, directly democratic decision-making within the party.

In summary, "The political developments, coupled with the very concrete experience of the common fight against the repressive forces of the Spanish State in the streets, have created a new generation of activists who are significantly less sectarian than what we were in the past. A great example of this were the actions of CNT dockworkers in Barcelona during the days before and after the independence referendum of October 2017 in Catalunya, who were instrumental both in warning about the arrival of ships transporting and housing Spanish police as well as in carrying out diverse actions of disruption and sabotage during their stay."[5]

But that was then and this is now. The situation on the ground in Barcelona in June 2001 was a bit different, and the very real and logical political differences between the classic anarchist movement and the independentistas were exacerbated by the unfortunate but usual sectarianism and petty squabbles of radical movements around the world. Anarchist graffiti crossing out *"Esteladas"* with circle-A's and proclaiming *"Un Patriota = Un Idiota"* ("A Patriot = An Idiot," which is actually pretty accurate, but in this context unfortunate) were common, and the provocations went both ways.

Either way, late night at the door of a squat was not a great setting for a nuanced discussion on the merits of anarchist practical solidarity with left-wing movements of national liberation, and a nonlocal or Catalan anarchist trying to lecture locals about a question that was much, much more pertinent to their daily lives than mine probably wouldn't go over too well in any scenario. In short: It's all well and great on paper, but in practice I was still currently homeless.

"Listen," said the German woman, "we can clear it up when more people are awake tomorrow. It won't be a problem. We can vouch for you, and they trust us, but tonight we can't let you in." Fair enough. "But you can sleep in our van if you want." She pointed at the yellowish Volkswagen van parked right outside. If there was a stereotype on wheels of "German autonomes driving around Europe from squat to squat," this was unmistakably it. But whatever, there was a bed in it and I was more than pleased with the option, until she dropped the punch line. "Listen, be careful, though, because Nazis came by yesterday and threw firebombs at the building." Oh, wonderful. On the one hand, if they had attacked the night before there was a good chance they wouldn't be attacking again the very next day. That said, if I were a Nazi looking to barbecue some anarchist scum, this vehicle would be the first thing I'd be setting on fire. At least my screams of terror would be a good alarm to warn the others.

I didn't have the deepest sleep of my life that night, struggling to get a decent night's rest fully dressed and with an iron bar under my pillow, which my hosts were kind enough to provide me in case I had to spring dramatically into action at a moment's notice. While I did survive the night without incident and the issue of my temporary banishment from the squat was amicably resolved the next morning, I spent a few hours sitting in the van awake, reliving the day's events and letting my anxiety run wild regarding the burning question of the moment: What in the hell had happened to the Old Man, and would he finally show up at our train station emergency rendezvous point tomorrow?

Life at the Barcelona Sants Train Station: Wednesday, June 27

This was now my third straight full day spent sitting at the train station. If you've seen Tom Hanks in *The Terminal*, you should have a general idea of my life of train-station-waiting-area limbo. In my case, it was a constant dance between extreme boredom and latent panic and terror.

Boredom because—and please, young people, hold on to your chairs here while reading in Official Grandpa Voice—when I was young, we didn't have supercomputers with all the knowledge, and stupidity, of the history of the world compressed into a magical device in our pockets. So, for entertainment, I was reduced to pouncing on people's discarded newspapers for reading material. Every once in a while a holy grail would appear in the form of an actual magazine. By the second day of this purgatory, it was clear that relying on the literary scraps discarded by the nine-to-five crowd as they came and went wasn't giving me the level of intellectual stimulation I needed, and I had to take drastic action. I began spending actual money buying mainstream media publications from the station's magazine kiosk.

By the second day in the evening, I had even fallen into a structured routine of boredom, anxiety, stress shopping, and anger, which went more or less as follows: First, arrive at the train station around 9:30 a.m., hoping that Oscar will magically appear at the meeting time we had arranged in case we got separated. "If we lose each other, we come back here to meet, every day at 10 a.m. and 10 p.m. until we find each other," was his indication to me when we arrived in Barcelona three days earlier, left our bags at the train station locker, and rushed straight to the riot, er, I mean demonstration. When 10 a.m. came and went and he was still nowhere to be found, proceed to step two, make the telephone rounds: Call CNT. Call legal support. "No, sorry, still nobody by that name. Not on the arrest lists, not in any of the hospitals. We even called the morgue just in case. Nobody has ever heard of him." Step three: Become genuinely concerned, spend money on mainstream media like *The New York Times* or *Time* magazine to distract myself and try to speed up the time until next rendezvous at 10 p.m. Followed closely by step four: Be outraged by content of mainstream media, perform youngster rendering of "Old Man Yells at Television," interpreted as "Teenager Shakes Fist at Newspaper." Which quickly leads to pangs of self-awareness as the voice in my head reminds me, "Uh, you know people can see you, right?" The final step in the process was: Spend even more money stress-eating at international fast food chain, feel fat and ashamed, sit quietly for a few hours, and start the process all over again.

As the third day began to run its course, I was concerning myself more and more with the question of how to explain to Oscar's parents that, in a shocking twist of fate, their Chilean son had mysteriously disappeared not at the hands of some South American military junta's death squad, but in the broad daylight of a supposedly democratic European metropolis. Somewhere in this thought process, I peered up from whatever newspaper or magazine I was rereading for the twenty-eighth time, more out of habit than any particular sense of hope at this point. I caught a glimpse of a head of bright-red hair walking across the hall. It was the Old Man!

"*Oscar!*" I yelled out a little too excitedly, as half the train station turned in my direction. He reached me and I hugged him like an over-excited mother whose child has just returned safely from war overseas. "Holy shit, you're alive! Where have you been? Were you arrested? We called everywhere and couldn't find you! Are you injured? You look pretty good, what happened?" I looked him up and down and he indeed seemed intact.

He took what I assume was a strategic pause to answer. "Yes, I'm fine. Before I say anything and you get the urge to flip out, please remember that when you left me at Ungdomshuset to go spend a night in a hotel with Lena, I didn't give you any trouble for it." I wasn't at all seeing how this was relevant right now, but it was indeed true. Following Gothenburg, we took a few days off and traveled to Copenhagen with Lena before continuing south to Barcelona. While our Copenhagen home at Ungdomshuset (the Youth House) was great, Lena and I decided that we needed at least one night of privacy before temporarily saying goodbye to each other, and so we invested in a hotel room. Let's just say the Old Man wasn't invited to join us.

"And even though it wasn't your fault, please also remember that while you spent two nights in Swedish suburbia never-never land with Lena, I was still at Schillerska being bowled down five flights of stairs and used as the Swedish anti-terror squad's new foreign Jewish plaything." I was starting to understand where he was going with this, and I tried to respond as calmly as possible. We did after all still have like a month of traveling through Europe together ahead of us, so it would have been unwise for me to try to murder him in the middle of a Catalan train station.

I took a deep breath and responded. "Oscar, I've spent the last three days sitting in this train station like an idiot. When I wasn't bored half to death, I was talking to the legal aid hotline or the kind CNT friends who tried to help, and together we were going through hospitalization lists, arrest lists, even names at the morgue to try to find you. If this story doesn't somehow involve you having been arrested and joyously released, or a miracle on the level of you having been seriously injured and magically now healed, or even better died and resurrected three days later because you are in fact the Jewish messiah, there is a good chance that I might kill you myself right here and now." I don't know how much of that I actually said out loud, probably not much of it. Maybe I just went with, "Uh-huh, so what happened?"

"So when the cops showed up, we just started running … and running … and running. I lost you, like, immediately. And I was running with crutches! So I wasn't very fast, but I guess I also wasn't *thaaat* slow, since they didn't catch me. But I kept getting baton blows from behind. *Bam! Bam!* Like five times right on the back."

I interrupted to say, "Yeah, that seems about right. It seemed like they were way more interested in beating the shit out of anarchists than making arrests. Anyway, yeah, and then?"

He continued, "I don't know, the adrenaline gave me wings, I guess, and I managed to lose them after turning a corner. I didn't really know what the hell to do, I'd lost you, there wasn't anybody I knew, and so I just made a split-second decision and the best idea I had was to throw myself under a parked car and hide there."

I did my best not to laugh, but his storytelling skills were on point as usual, and it again seemed like every time I went on some kind of rampage, the Old Man was the one who paid the price.

"I must have hid under that car for like thirty minutes, no idea. But a pretty long time to be lying on your stomach in the street. At least this time I still had clothes on and there were no dogs barking in my ear. Anyway, so I think the coast is finally clear, and I crawl out from under the car, and I see like five more people emerge from under some other cars a few meters away."

I imagined what the civilian passersby must have thought seeing a bunch of scraggly kids randomly crawling out from under cars in broad daylight in the middle of Barcelona and couldn't help laughing. "I started talking to them and it turns out they were a group of anarchists from Madrid, and we started chatting. About racism, political theory, Latin America, whatever. And they shared their weed with me, and then we just sat on some park bench getting stoned."

I gave him my best Tucker Carlson look. You know, the one he thinks conveys concentration but to most of us looks more like *I don't understand what in the hell it is that you are saying.* First of all, why on earth are these people taking illegal drugs to a demonstration? Second, why are you accepting drugs from strangers? Third, in what universe is sitting in the park for hours chatting and getting stoned the correct course of action after getting separated due to police attack, instead of, oh, I don't know, maybe heading to our prearranged meeting point? But thinking this was the climax of the story, the arc of the "please don't flip out" plotline, a stupid mistake that would lead to an arrest or something justifying the three-day disappearance, I again opted for silence. It was all pretty stupid, but sometimes a good anecdote is born from less-than-stellar decision-making, and knowing the Old Man, "getting stoned and talking politics in a Barcelona park with strangers I met while crawling out from under a car" was one he would cherish. If it had ended up costing a few days in prison, well then, he had probably already learned his lesson and didn't need lecturing from me. "So they picked you up at the park? How did you get out? How come you didn't show up on any of the arrest lists?" Nothing could have prepared me for what came next.

"Huh? What? No, no. Remember where I said to please not flip out? They invited me to spend the night at the beach with them, and I really wanted to keep getting stoned, so I said yes and decided to look for you the next morning at the station. And this just somehow turned into a three-day-long orgy of being at the beach, going swimming, lying in the sun, sleeping in a tent, and just being stoned out of our minds all day and all night." He topped it off with, "I was really enjoying myself and really needed some peace and quiet after all the stress." Years later Oscar revealed to me that his motivation for his beach vacation was not just his desire for weed and relaxation, but also that he had a crush on one of the people he'd met in the Madrid group and couldn't bring himself to say goodbye.

Honestly, I don't recall killing the Old Man that day, and since we embarked on numerous adventures together later on, it seems unlikely that I did. I don't even remember any kind of argument or fight following this. This bothers me now not so much on principle but because it seems like simple bad storytelling, the least believable part of a pretty solid chain of wild stories, a good movie ruined with a poor and unbelievable ending. When I said as much to the Old Man twenty years later, his response, true to form, was simply, "I guess I'm just difficult to get mad at." By itself maybe not a satisfactory explanation, but combined with my relief that he had miraculously reappeared at a point when I was reaching the conclusion that he was most likely dead in a ditch somewhere, and the general level of "crazy experiences normalized" in our lives, I guess explanation enough.

And so we returned to our squat, which photographic evidence now proves looked like a hovel out of a 1930s rural Spanish village somehow dropped into the middle of modern-day Barcelona but to us felt like an unimaginably luxurious resort, even conveniently located not too far from the beach. Once I was done demanding that we stay at least another two days, since I too felt I deserved to lie on the beach like a lizard in the sun, to which Oscar not surprisingly agreed, I blurted out, "I told you that stupid second demonstration was a terrible idea."

Oscar took a small pause before replying, "I know it's probably not a good time strategically for me to start a big argument here, but, um, *I* told *you* that the second demonstration was a terrible idea, which you basically ignored with silence, and then you said we should probably start heading there."

Hmm, maybe I had thought it but didn't actually say it out loud. "So, what you're saying is we both thought it was a terrible idea, but went anyway?"

Escape to 1936: Sunday, June 24, Sometime in the Early Afternoon

In the kingdom of bad ideas, this one was pure-blooded royalty. Even Oscar and I, incorrigible crazies, weren't convinced as to the wisdom of this. Only a few hours after thoroughly taking apart one of Barcelona's main thoroughfares, the plan was for all the anarchist crazies in Barcelona to reconvene at a park for another demonstration, exclusively anarchist. Not a semi-clandestine, word-of-mouth kind of thing. An actual public demonstration, with a likewise public time and place, some park somewhere in a central part of the city, and with a clearly anarchist character. Not necessarily meaning combative, but still, you know, if I were the cops and I were looking for the guilty parties of the riot that had taken place *that very same day*, this would be where I might want to drop by and take a look. So, this being a poor and terrible idea, it goes without saying that the Old Man and I were there.

Not to disappoint you, but there is no epic and unexpectedly uplifting plot twist here. There were a few hundred of us, I don't think more than three to five hundred, still solidly in the "calmly milling around at the meeting point" phase of things, when our suspicions were rapidly, and violently, confirmed. In the middle of a warm and sunny Barcelona afternoon, it was suddenly raining police officers. As in dozens of police vans filled with riot cops from the Policía Nacional speeding toward us from all sides. As they like to do in the Spanish State, they drove past or next to us, and then swarms of overexcited cops came flying out of their vehicles, shooting *bolas de goma* and swinging batons wildly. Not the way one would imagine a law enforcement professional might, but swinging with both hands the way a baseball player does when going for that memorable home run.

No heroic resistance was possible, and nothing positive or memorable comes to mind here. Well, memorable maybe, but definitely not positive. We scattered like terrified prey from a pack of wolves, sprinting in all directions. And this fiasco is worth mentioning, if nothing else because this too is a part of the reality of choosing to engage in mass militance. Sometimes, you are simply routed by the enemy. It may be due to poor political or tactical decision-making, or it may be because of the state's (or fascists') larger numbers or better preparedness. In this case both poor political as well as tactical decision-making were to blame, with no massive show of force or brilliant political chess maneuvers on the side of the state or cops necessary. The anarchist nuts had simply decided to reconvene after a successful mass action (tactical stupidity) and do so in a manner that was isolated from any other political currents or demonstrators that could either stand in solidarity or, pardon our honesty, serve as cover (political *and* tactical stupidity).

I immediately lost the Old Man, and I hadn't quite made it a block when several vans caught up to us. Cops flew out, and almost immediately a group of ten or fifteen of us were surrounded, pinned against a wall by a line of baton-swinging cops standing a few meters away. Again, as in Gothenburg, the question in my head was: Certain arrest or likely injury but possible escape? But unlike the situation in Gothenburg, this one didn't allow the luxury of calmly pondering the question while sitting in a classroom, with about the same urgency as one might display in a school debate on the pros and cons of the random history subject of the day. This was a split-second decision. Fling yourself right now at the cops and possibly suffer a broken arm but escape, or forever hold your peace. Well, maybe not forever, but definitely for a good few days while in jail. That said, had I been afforded the time to think about the specifics of this particular situation, of the prospect of imminent arrest and becoming a prisoner of the Spanish State, the following not insignificant factors would have played a role in my decision-making process.

While Spain is, at least on paper, a normalized Western European democracy much like all the others, its twentieth-century history leading up to the year 2001 was very different from that of the rest of the Western European countries. Most significantly, while most Western European states took the form of relatively liberal welfare-state democracies post–World War II, Spain was a dictatorship led by General Francisco Franco from the fascist victory over the combined forces of republicanism and anarchist social revolution in 1939, following a three-year-long civil war ignited by a military uprising against the democratically elected republican government.[6]

Sitting out World War II as an officially neutral country, Franco ruled Spain until his death in 1975, at which point the so-called democratic transition process began. To be concise: Franco himself stated a few years prior to his death that he was leaving *"todo atado y bien atado,"* which roughly translates to "everything is tied up safely and securely," by which he meant that Spain would suffer no radical changes post-Francoism. While Spain did hold its first democratic elections in 1977 and ratified a new constitution by popular referendum the following year (although a majority of people in some parts of the Basque Country abstained from voting), there was never a systematic upheaval of its state apparatus, and certainly none of its repressive forces, such as the de-Nazification process in postwar Germany.

On the contrary, as part of its ongoing conflict with an array of revolutionary armed organizations, both from the independentista left, like ETA, and from "traditional" Marxist-Leninist armed organizations, like GRAPO (Grupos de Resistencia Antifascista Primero de Octubre, or "First of October Antifascist Resistance Groups"), who were active from the 1960s and '70s well into the 2000s, as well as the broad ecosystem of radical groups that employed tactics of mass militance and confrontation with the state, the Spanish State continued to rely heavily on the brutality and heavy-handedness of both its Guardia Civil and Policía Nacional forces and its judiciary. Throughout the 1970s, '80s, and '90s (and I'm sure beyond as well), the Guardia Civil and Policía Nacional were well known for brutal repression at demonstrations as well as beatings and torture of detainees. If the arrested demonstrator was particularly unlucky, they would then be handed a multiyear sentence by a judge thanks to one of the many antiterrorist statutes that encompassed the potential actions of virtually any person and organization of the extraparliamentary left. The two most striking examples of "Spanish democracy": the paramilitary death squads of the GAL (Grupos Antiterroristas de Liberación, or "Antiterrorist Liberation Groups") of the 1980s, created to murder and disappear militants of the Basque revolutionary movement and financed by the highest levels of the "socialist" government of Felipe González, and the constant outlawing of Basque political parties, organizations, and media through the use of laws banning organizations deemed sympathetic to armed struggle or that failed to denounce political violence.

And so, while it all happened in an instant, I knew all this and the answer was crystal clear: While already a firm partisan of attempted escape, if I had refused the possibility of going to jail in Sweden, there was absolutely no way I would expose myself to being a prisoner of the Spanish cops and a hostage of its legal system without a vicious fight. Injury was already rarely a concern that occupied my mind, as the cocktail of political fanaticism and the perceived invincibility of youth had me convinced this was not a worthwhile concern, so the decision was obvious.

I flung myself at the cop line. One knee forward to protect the midsection, much like a soccer goalkeeper coming out to intercept a cross. Forearms up, offered as potential sacrifice to protect the neck and face. From then on I recall two still images, like snapshots from an action sequence. First, the cop in front of me, eyes wide, face full of the intensity and hatred typical of cops who genuinely despise their demonstrator opponents, both hands on the baton and teed up for the home run swing. I closed my eyes and braced for impact. The next image is of me on the other side, frozen in the briefest of pauses to inspect the damage. I had felt no pain, but knowing how well adrenaline can mask it, I checked my arms. I was already sprinting away, in my best white anarchist Ben Johnson impression, when I concluded that the cop had either hesitated, or missed, or aimed at somebody else. I'll never know exactly how or why, but I had again magically escaped unscathed.

A few moments later, it started becoming clear to me that something even more magical and unexpected than once again being free and intact had occurred in the instant in which I had blinked. Much like Dorothy clicking her heels in *The Wizard of Oz* to be transported home, I must have unconsciously muttered something like "Please get me out of here" as I closed my eyes, and the fates had seen fit to transport me to the place and time in history they knew I was most taken with.

I had run into the narrow streets of old Barcelona, where I quickly came upon some fellow masked friends who were manning a barricade. It is difficult to overemphasize how narrow the "narrow streets of old Barcelona" actually are. A car can barely pass through some of them, and in this case a couple of overturned dumpsters and ten or so people were more than enough for a solid "front line." The barricade we were defending was located right in front of a building that sported a large white circle-A sign, next to a red and black banner reading "CNT-AIT!" It seemed I had been transported to 1930s Barcelona and found myself living inside one of the iconic "anarchists defend CNT building from the advance of state forces" pictures we have all seen.

Now, (over)excited as I was about this setting and backdrop, there were unsurprisingly a few differences between the historic images this was evoking in my mind and the reality of the situation. Our barricade of dumpsters and trash bags was less sturdy and stylish than the ones made of bricks and sandbags from the history books. Back then, the defenders were armed with rifles, we with mere rocks. While they were actually defending the building, as far as I could tell our barricade just happened to be in front of the CNT office, but the building was very much shuttered. Finally, there was the detail that, you know, while the historical anarchists acted with the support and participation of broad sectors of the local population in the context of a historic and sweeping social revolutionary uprising, in our case the neighborhood population, consisting of a lot of African immigrant families, looked at us with what I could only interpret as mildly annoyed boredom from their balconies and doorsteps.

And yet, as contrived as the comparison might be, and as decidedly unspectacular and historically irrelevant as our situation was, I couldn't help but feel emotional about where I was and the incredible history of anarchist struggle that had taken place in this city. For years in Paris I had listened in rapt fascination as the veterans of this struggle, or their children, talked about what they had fought for, what they believed in, and what they had ultimately sacrificed in the pursuit of those beliefs. Likewise, I had devoured any book I could find on the Spanish Revolution in Spanish, French, or English and immersed myself in all its different aspects. Understanding myself, my actions, and the movement I was a part of as the direct historical heirs to this movement was central to my perception of anarchism. We are today's representatives of a centuries-old tradition of struggle, of which the Spanish Revolution was arguably (inarguably?) the pinnacle.

The military conflict was of course one aspect of this history, an unfortunate necessity. But beyond that, the Spanish Revolution was the culmination of decades of anarchist education, agitation, and organization. It was a mass experiment, involving millions of people, in social revolution and workers' self-management. An upheaval that took place in rural settings, with massive voluntary collectivization and in many cases even the abolishing of currency, but also in urban Barcelona. The workers' takeover of numerous modern industries, the effective and efficient union operation of diverse means of production (socialization rather than nationalization), and the peace, order, and relative stability of anarchist-run Barcelona are all testaments to the viability of anarchism as a societal model for large, industrialized, modern urban societies. If there was ever a practical example of the

Barricades in front of a CNT office in Barcelona.

tactical efficiency of building dual power, of organizations of workers' self-management and defense such as the CNT and its militias, of specifically anarchist organizations like the FAI, so that when the time of revolution finally comes—*le grand soir*, in the millenarian terminology of the turn-of-the-nineteenth-century anarchists—the working class could seamlessly do away with the bosses and repurpose all that it had built for the common good of society, this was it.

But the Spanish Revolution was not an upheaval only of economic relations and state power (or the lack thereof). It was a social revolution in the literal sense, bringing with it drastic and almost immediate changes in gender dynamics and social relations.[7] Women formed their own organizations, with Mujeres Libres, a specifically anarchist women's organization, rapidly reaching thirty thousand adherents and women creating their own militias and fighting on the front lines as equals. The revolutionary spirit was so widespread, contagious, and unmistakable that even a person such as my great-uncle-in-law, who came from a relatively religious middle-class Jewish family who harbored few sympathies for radical ideas, would talk to me sixty years later around the family table with admiration and enthusiasm about what he had witnessed during those days.

He was a child, living in Barcelona at the age of eleven years old, when the war and revolution erupted around him in 1936, too young to understand much about the political forces shaping the world around him. These were by no means easy or pleasant times in his young life: he and his family had recently fled Germany, his older brother contracted meningitis and went from healthy teenager to deceased within the span of a week, and then the uncertainty of war and the spread of fascism eventually pushed his family to depart for South America. Yet, and I paraphrase him as he is unfortunately no longer with us to tell me once again in his own words, which lined up uncannily well with what I would later read in George Orwell's *Homage to Catalonia*: "I remember taking the tram in the city, and suddenly we didn't need to pay anymore. On it, from one day to the next, people were treating each other completely different. There was no more use of the formal *usted* or *señor* to refer to people. What I most remember is that people were eating on the tram, sometimes bread or even chocolate, and would freely offer to share with complete strangers around them."

I have little doubt that had the anarchists been victorious in the Spanish Civil War and the Spanish Revolution, it would have dramat- ically altered the course of the twentieth century, and potentially modern history as we know it. At the very least, anarchism would have remained a mass movement rather than receding from the forefront of the struggle against capitalism, as it did for decades, leaving the space of communism and anticapitalism dominated by the authoritarian tenden- cies of Marxism. But beyond that, the practical example of a successful anarchist society would have inspired millions across the world and lit a spark of social revolution that may have spread like wildfire.

The anarchists of that time almost changed the world; the dozen or so of us held our little barricade until a few cop vans showed up, at which point we presented a principled yet brief and symbolic resistance and then disappeared into the neighborhood. In the grand scheme of things, we neither affected nor changed much of anything. The question one might be asking is: Where is the connection between some kids on a barricade throwing stones at cops and the actual day-to-day organizing work of revolutionary unions and anarchist organizations that brought us as close as we have ever been in the modern world to the realiza- tion of our ideas on a mass scale? This supposed dichotomy that is so often presented to us, between the organizer and the "summit hopper," between the workplace or community struggle and rioting, or between the so-called established and formal structures and organizations of anarchism and the more fluid and amorphous groupings that are more often than not choosing to engage the state with possibly more anger than strategy? As is so often the case, the end takes us neatly back to the beginning, and the answer to a movement question is in the streets and in our praxis.

Our first glimpse of the city of Barcelona as we had emerged from the subway had been of the windows of the stores of the upscale Passeig de Gràcia crashing down. Banks, a Burger King, the iconic Tienda Inglesa, and all kinds of luxury shops. We had arrived at the Sants train station, the city's central station for long-distance trains, not thirty minutes earlier, thrown our bags in a locker, agreed on a spot to regroup should we lose each other during the day, hopped on the subway, and emerged directly to this new and inspiring sight.

We were at the large demonstration that had been called to protest the summit of the World Bank. A summit, mind you, that was not taking place, having been preemptively cancelled due to concerns about Gothenburg-like clashes. But the demonstration was held nonetheless, and we headed there as well because they had cancelled the summit but had neglected to cancel capitalism.

Property destruction, it goes without saying, was hardly a new sight to our eyes. And while we usually give it a solid two thumbs up, there were only a couple dozen people engaging in it within a demonstration of comfortably ten thousand people, but that was not a particularly new or inspiring sight either. Not being the types to wait around for an invitation, though, we quickly threw on jackets, gloves, and masks and began to lend a helping hand.

As the black-clad folks smashed bank windows or graffitied "Against Capitalist Society, Against the Forces of Order, and of Course Against Spain," we noticed that one of the blocs in the march would consistently erupt in cheers and applause.[8] It was not other participants in a black bloc cheering themselves on, but rather a group of several hundred people, an eclectic mix of young and old, men and women, with some looking subcultural but most like anybody's friend, mom, dad, or neighbor. It was the CNT and the anarcho-syndicalist bloc of the demonstration. They were participating in a different manner, marching calmly but firmly in a small sea of flags and banners, but clearly signaling their approval and solidarity with chants of, "*¡Eso no es violencia, eso es resistencia!*" which translates to "That's not violence, that's resistance!"

So while saying that we had found the answer to the question raised above is an exaggeration (here and everywhere, I will attempt to shy away from claiming to have the answer to this—or much of anything, for that matter), it was without a doubt a further practical example, from the CNT, a movement and an organization with one of the most solid histories in the world, of what we had been vehemently stating.

"We are complementary, not contradictory. We are often one and the same. The black-clad people you see at demonstrations are more often than not the same people putting in the day-to-day hard work of sustaining the anarchist movement," was more or less how Oscar or Jorge, ever more patient than I, often used to respond to the either-or framing of questions regarding the supposed dichotomy between local organizing and more spectacular bursts of conflict. In our own cases and in those of the friends and comrades around us, we knew this to be true. We volunteered at the local radical bookstore, attended coalition meetings, organized book fairs, put on concerts, contributed to speaking tours, and (in our eyes, most importantly) were responsible for the timely appearance of North America's only monthly anarchist publication. Considering how much of our existence was spent pulling all-night propaganda heists at Kinko's, licking envelopes, or standing in line at the post office, we did not take kindly to criticism implying that we somehow were in it for the thrills and had been neglecting the more mundane aspects of anarchist organizing.

The significant difference between us in the US movement and what we saw in Sweden, where I'd met with a long-lost CNT comrade from France in the middle of a black bloc riot, or in Spain, with its anarcho-syndicalist bloc, was that in the US we and the relatively small group around us did our best to wear all the hats, or at least as many as possible, in order to speak to a broader and more diverse group of people. These were actual examples of what we aspired to and were trying to efficiently work toward but did not to a meaningful extent possess in the US: a multifaceted, multigenerational movement, where some do all while all do some. But we are conscious that in the end we are collectively working toward a common goal, each making best possible use of the different tools in the very much varied anarchist toolkit.

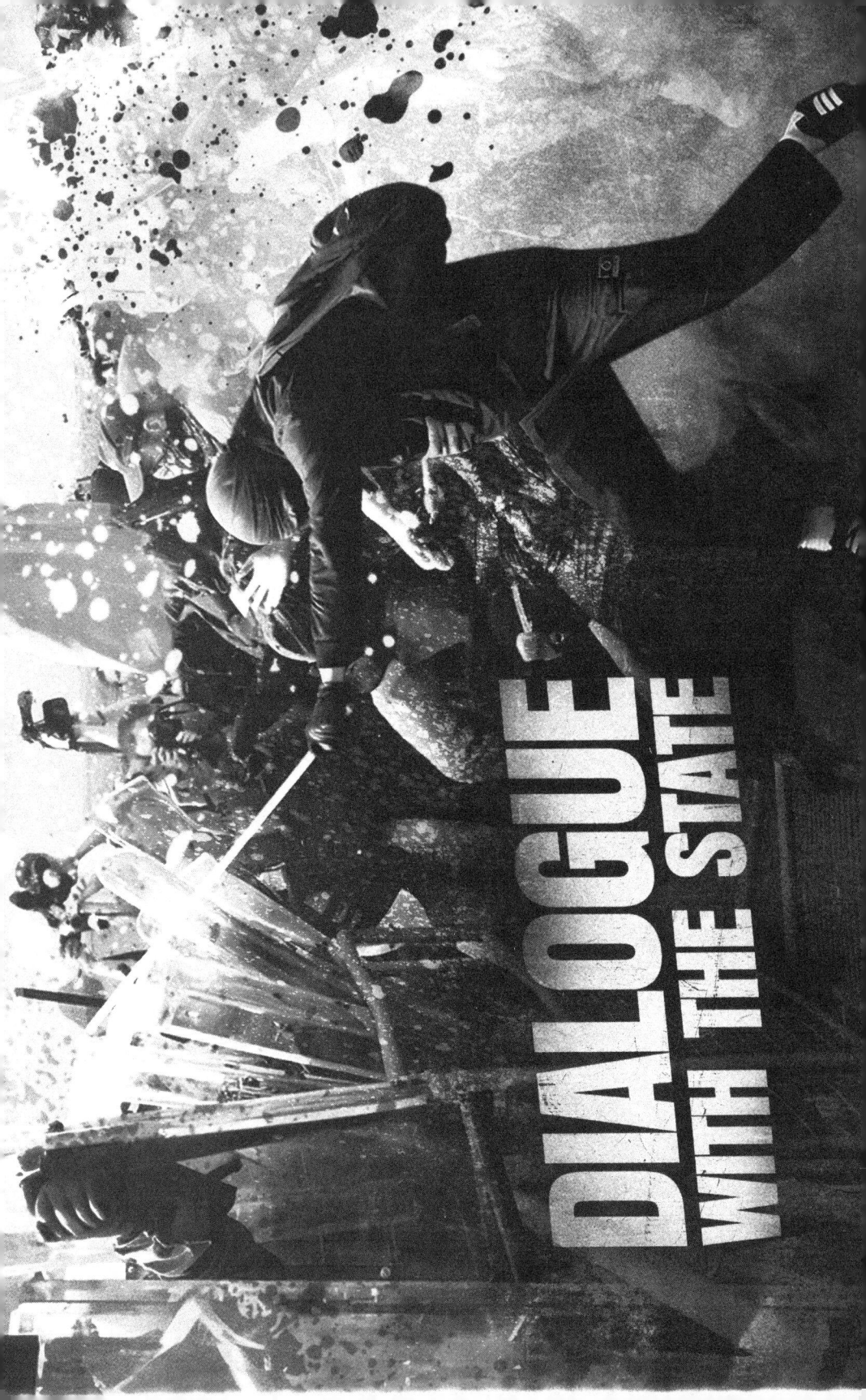
DIALOGUE WITH THE STATE

12
ON TOUR WITH THE HIPPIES: ESCAPE FROM SALZBURG

Petisovci, Slovenia, July 3, 2001

This was quite the unexpected turn of events. We were somewhere on a farm, somewhere in rural Slovenia. Across from me a small group of people was making puppets and clown costumes. The Old Man was off somewhere drinking wine and probably trying to debate some poor, unsuspecting victim about council communism or free jazz, while a random new friend was attempting to teach me how to juggle. I can't pretend to know what the post-revolution anarchist utopia will look like. But thanks to our half-week stay on a random farm somewhere in ex-Yugoslavia, I'm pretty sure I know what the "peaceful short-term anarchist retirement village as interlude between epic battles" looks and feels like. And this was it.

People from different backgrounds and cultures, debates and discussions to be had at will, and the leisure and freedom to do as we please, when we please. All of this set to the backdrop of warm and sunny summer days and impressive starry skies at night that us city dwellers often forget exist, located on a campground surrounded by beautiful trees and lush green fields.

Once again, it had started with Oscar frantically waking me from my peaceful rest on a convergence center floor, this time in the Austrian city of Salzburg, the day before. "Wake up! Wake up!" I knew enough by now to quickly shift from groggy to awake and aware. Also, in this case the confrontation had been the day and night before that, July 1, so unlike in Gothenburg it made sense to expect repression-related problems and inconveniences. "Friend John was in the city buying some food and passed by a newspaper kiosk. There's a picture of you on the cover! We need to leave the city, right now!"

"What, unmasked?!"

"No, no. Masked, but it's still not great. Friend John thinks he has a way to get us out of here without going by the train station. He's talking to some people right now. He's going to meet us here in a few minutes. He has a copy of the paper too."

Friend John, as we ceremoniously referred to him, was about our age, hailed from the Bay Area, was very familiar with our prestigious publication, and shared politics similar to ours. So, despite him having made the mistake of revealing to us that his dad was a hardcore hippie who went by the name of Tree, which in our immature minds was wildly hilarious and reason enough to tease him constantly, we quickly became friends. He was also one of the few international radicals who had traveled to Salzburg for the July 1 mobilization against this meeting of the World Economic Forum, which gave us even more of a reason to adopt him into our small anarchist traveling circus. This particular mobilization, possibly due to the relative weakness of the Austrian radical scene, or because of its chronological proximity to the Genoa mobilization, was by far the smallest of the Summer of Resistance tour stops. Oddly enough, there was even a total absence of the German antifa scene, and the demonstrations at their peak never had more than a thousand people.

If it's action you were looking for, this wasn't really the place to find it. It had all been relatively uneventful from that perspective. On the day of the mobilization, we had reached the police barricade, at which point we could go no farther in the direction of the summit. This was the cue for a few dozen masked autonomes and another few dozen of the Turkish crowd chanting, "Marx! Engels! Lenin! Stalin! Mao! VIVA! VIVA! VIVA!" to engage in a relatively uninspired exchange of blows and kicks with the Salzburg police, to the delight of a small horde of journalists. This was followed a short while later by another confrontation with the cops, in which the impromptu anarcho-Stalinist alliance seemed to find success in fighting the cops back, only to realize the cops had retreated strategically in order to lure us down a side street, at

WORLD ECONOMIC FORUM ATTACKED IN SALZBURG DESPITE PRE-EMPTIVE REPRESSION

As expected, Austria's far right government made use of almost its entire arsenal of repression in order to prevent disturbances at the World Economic Forum meeting in Salzburg from June 30 to July 3.

Schengen was cancelled, strict controls were placed on trains and at borders, over four thousand policemen (and women) were deployed, and all demonstrations were banned in the city except for the square in front of the train station.

All this for less than one thousand demonstrators (as this was soon after Barcelona and right before Genoa).

Despite the very uneven odds, about one thousand people managed to break out of the heavily guarded square and hold an illegal march in the direction of the congress center. Upon arrival at the security barriers, several attempts to enter were made (despite the pacifist attempts to stop them), as the photo to the right shows. The march made it to within 150 meters before being surrounded and trapped by police for over six hours. Twelve arrests were made.

FOURTH CONGRESS OF NEFAC

The fourth NorthEastern Federation of Anarcho-Communists (NEFAC) conference was held in Boston on the weekend of August 9 to 11.

Most notable, the Federation continues to grow at a steady pace, incorporating four new supporter collectives as well as several new individual members and supporters.

The four new supporter collectives are RASH Montreal, Black Hammer Anarchist Collective (NYC), Freyheyt (Toronto), and Barricada (Boston).

One of the most significant decisions of the conference was that the federation would like to see the anarchist movement begin to move away from "summit hopping" and towards community oriented initiatives with a militant backing, thus working to create a true dual power.

The federation also voted to involve itself in the organizing for the upcoming mobilization against the World Bank and IMF in Washington DC in order to present a viable alternative to purely symbolic action, in the form of real direct action.

Furthermore, NEFAC is publishing a call (included in the DC section of this magazine) as well as a four page tabloid to be distributed during the days of action.

The federation also made some structural changes, such as adding a "Friends of NEFAC" initiative for those who are supportive of NEFAC and desire to keep up with the activities of the federation.

An additional part of the conference included a women's congress as well as a people of color congress.

It is inspiring to see the continued growth of organized revolutionary anarchism in the Northeast, both in terms of numbers of people and theoretical development. We can only hope that the example of NEFAC will serve as a point of reference for the creation of similar structures across North America.

BARRICADA #8. SUMMER/SEP. 2001

Barricada report on the July 2001 anti-WEF mobilization in Salzburg.

which point we were promptly kettled by another line of cops behind us. And that's where we remained for hours, making the best possible use of our time chitchatting with our new Turkish friends. They seemed friendly enough, and they were certainly endearingly combative. We asked politely as to their political affiliations, although the chants had kind of given away the surprise, and they were indeed exiled militants of some Marxist-Leninist organization with all the letters of the alphabet in its acronym. We responded politely when they inquired the same of us, to replies of, "Oh, anarchists. In Turkey our organization maybe kills people like you. Ha ha ha, no, no … we are just joking, you are too irrelevant." It was all very reassuring. After hours of "negotiations," the police allowed us to leave in lines of ten, an impressive pile of discarded black clothing and flagpoles behind us as we departed the scene in the most innocent-looking lines of ten people we could muster.

"Dude, you're lucky I'm friendlier than you guys are and I already got us a ride out of here," were Friend John's first words when he finally returned with the newspaper, which he promptly threw in my direction. I looked at the picture plastered across the front page. From a security perspective it probably wasn't great, but it didn't seem that tragic either. It was a skillfully taken action shot from the brief confrontation at the security perimeter, which captured the precise moment in which a demonstrator's wooden pole, a demonstrator who may or may not have been me, in the midst of a rather artistic and dynamic pose, makes contact with a police officer's helmeted head.

"I mean, it's not great, and it's a fair argument for getting out of here sooner rather than later since there aren't exactly a million possible suspects, but I'm, er, I mean, the person is decently masked up. This doesn't seem to be the end of the world." To be perfectly honest, stupid, and superficial here, immediate safety concerns aside, I was already picturing proudly displaying this picture to my grandchildren someday, you know, if I *were* that person! The image even went on to be part of CNN's "breaking news" intro clip for a few years, which I always found entertaining, and in a particularly heartwarming moment, I spotted it as part of a larger antifascist mural in Germany a few years later.

Friend John, ever the patient one, went on to explain the entirety of the plot to me. "So, I only bought one newspaper, but exactly this picture is on the cover of *all* the local papers and *most* of the national ones." Well, that was sounding a little less great. I mean, I only really needed the one for memorabilia purposes, no need for the overexposure. "One of them runs it with the headline 'Vandals Spread Terror in the Middle of Salzburg.'"[1] Not the best representation, but nothing new for the mainstream press, I suppose. "Remember the hours-long kettle yesterday?" It hadn't been the most memorable day of our lives, but yes, I still recalled yesterday. "Apparently, the reason for that kettle was that a police officer was struck on the head and injured, and the objective of the kettle and the small group release was mainly to identify the person responsible. Are the dots connecting for you now?" And suddenly, I wasn't finding the situation quite as amusing anymore. "As you know, this city is pretty small. There aren't a ton of possible suspects here, there is only one train station out of Salzburg, and apparently the cops are going around it right now with pictures of activists, trying to make arrests." At that moment, I was officially no longer in the mood for ironic comments, even in my head. "Which brings us right back to how lucky you are that I socialize more than you guys, because I got us a ride out of here by car. It isn't exactly discreet, but it also isn't where the cops might be looking for black-clad black bloc monsters. It's in one of the Publix Theatre Caravan vans, it's leaving in thirty minutes, and they have room for all three of us."

If the colorful array of flip-flops, dresses, and dreadlocks we found ourselves sharing a van ride eastward with didn't give away that we were in a group that, while ideologically close to us, was culturally more than a little different from us, the first pit stop made the contrasts abundantly clear. We stopped at a picture-perfect idyllic lake, a postcard-like representation of how one might imagine the Alps in summertime, complete with green fields and snow-capped mountains in the background. And before we knew it, everybody was swimming naked in the lake except the Old Man, Friend John, and me. The three prude outcasts.

This is of course a reflection, and maybe a criticism, of us and our young and self-conscious selves, and nothing more. Anarchism should not be the domain of any one particular subculture, obviously. This particular crew we found ourselves riding with just happened to be different from the bubble we were used to finding ourselves in. Truth is, we would have gotten in that van even if they had been taking us to Romania to serve as migrant slave labor picking asparagus in the blazing summer heat, but it just so happened that we hitched a ride with a radical street theater troupe from Vienna, based out of none

The backyard and soccer field at the No Border camp in Petisovci, Slovenia.

other than the EKH, a former Communist Party of Austria headquarters turned legalized autonomous center, and this landed us at a Slovenian No Border camp.

Since then, I've been able to reconstruct where we were: the small Slovenian town of Petisovci, located one kilometer away from the Croatian border and two kilometers from the Hungarian border, making it a fitting location for a No Border camp. What I recall as a beautiful farmland paradise, I've since seen disparaged as a "decrepit socialist era campground."[2] For a moment I feared my recollections might be nothing more than a nostalgia-induced, rose-tinted-glasses hallucination ... until I remembered that I have the pictures to confirm my memories. What is etched in my mind are picnic tables for communal moments of talking and drinking, lying in the grass enjoying the shade under the trees, and the huge grassy field on which we played the world's worst games of soccer—maybe twenty people or so a side, with nothing whatsoever to differentiate who was on which team, in the evening darkness, and with a good half of the players more than a little tipsy from the wine. Essentially, forty happy little children chasing wildly after a ball in the darkness.

Post-revolution anarchist utopia? A scene from the No Border camp in rural Slovenia.

For days the maybe hundred or so of us enjoyed the freedom of alternating between lounging around like useless anarchist lizards in the sun and contributing productively to the infrastructure and daily life of the camp. We spent a lot of the day debating and theorizing, and a fair amount of our evening as well. The only difference was that thanks to the red wine, in the evenings we did so less coherently and with more agitated finger wagging and enthusiastic fist shaking. We were never wanting for good food, or even wine for that matter. We took happily as we needed, and gave just as happily as we could.

This parenthesis of self-care and calm in the midst of a summer of revolt was a beautiful little world. And a world that might just look like this, instead of the world of authorities, borders, work, violence, and exclusion that we currently inhabit, is definitely one worth fighting vigorously for. With that in mind, we departed for Genoa.

FROM RIOT
TO INSURRECTION

13
THE BATTLE OF GENOA
July 2001

Introduction: The Genoa Commune

At this point, as far as I can tell, aside from the detail that my limited grasp of Italian would be odd for a lifelong resident, all signs indicate that we have always lived in the city of Genoa. In the vertigo of our itinerant "summer of rage" lifestyle, and convinced as we are that the revolution is imminent, two weeks in one place might as well be a lifetime. During the course of our lifetime in Genoa, our favorite supermarket has shut its doors, and our ever-expanding little family now has an eviction on its record. Apparently, since the anarchists began frequenting the press center down the street there has been an unacceptable spike in shop-lifting at the local branch of the chain supermarket, and, although I can't imagine there might be any correlation, they've closed the place down. Meanwhile, the world the Ya Basta! network and the Genoa Social Forum envision is broad and inclusive, but not to the point of accepting that anarchists live and organize among them. And so once upon a time, a few days after our arrival in the city (a lifetime ago!), the family was forced to relocate from Carlini Stadium to the somewhat more austere living arrangements at the Albaro school. And so, as I sit in the sweltering Italian summer heat, pondering if I should trade revo-lutionary zeal for an office job with air conditioning and curious how it is possible to be both so bored and so anxious simultaneously, I am starting to become convinced that this has always been our existence, and might be forever.

★

Why had we been the first foreign anarchists to discover Genoa in the run-up to the G8 summit, arriving almost two full weeks before its scheduled date? Well, while to the reader of today, to whom the antiglobalization movement of the early 2000s might not be much more than a blip on the radar of history, this might seem like a delusional notion, those of us caught up in its whirlwind progress and explosive growth truly believed this was the vehicle that would lead us to generalized international social upheaval, systemic change, and anticapitalist revolution. Like I said above, some of us anarchists of the time—maybe the younger ones, the more passionate ones, the true believers, the innocent ... among which I and a lot of like-minded others found ourselves—believed it to be not only possible but potentially imminent. Oscar, discussing this view twenty years after the fact, puts it bluntly: "It was pretty insane. Insane and vanguardist. Your view was that beyond the vanguard of, what, maybe five or ten thousand anarchist militants who actively took part in the clashes of the antiglobalization movement, there was this sea of discontent, just lying dormant and latent among broad sectors of society at large. And that a few thousand radicals could release a wave of rage and discontent that could no longer be contained, culminating in some form of revolutionary upheaval ... if only they managed to light the fuse at just the right place, just the right time, in just the right context." The right place. The right time. The right context. We had become convinced that the G8 summit in Genoa was precisely that place, that time, and that context.

The right place, as the geography of the city made it, in the words of CNN, "a security nightmare. It is a port, with access from the sea, and has a backdrop of hills. Its central streets are narrow and winding, making hit-and-run violence of the type seen recently at the EU summit at Gothenburg ... difficult to contain."[1]

Beyond its physical characteristics, there was the political makeup of Genoa. Within Italy's already strong traditions of both orthodox left-wing movements and autonomous structures of the radical left, Genoa was the "Red City." A city whose population had always been staunchly working class, antifascist, and pro-union. It was a city in which, if we played our cards right and were disciplined with our militance, we would, as in Quebec City, be viewed as allies by the residents, while the state, with its army of containers, fences, tanks, and twenty thousand police officers, would be seen as the occupying force. But unlike in Quebec, this was a population with cultural and political traditions that we saw as apt to induce them to move massively from tacit approval and support to active participation. And despite the thousands of heavily armed cops of all stripes amassed by the Italian state to oppose us, even the geography of the city would be to our advantage.

The right time. Directly on the heels of the clashes in Gothenburg, this would be the next episode in what was becoming a constant cycle of mobilizations and clashes. Movements thrive on momentum, and the momentum of decades of left-wing tradition in Italy and years of growth of the antiglobalization movement was expected to carry three hundred thousand people into the city of Genoa to oppose the G8, many of them with the explicit intent of breaching the "red zone" security perimeter.

As for context, in Genoa we saw the potential for a significant shift. A transition from symbolic and performative confrontations to revolutionary violence. Hundreds or even thousands of us revolutionary anarchists would swim in a sea of tens of thousands of radicals of other stripes, merging with hundreds of thousands of demonstrators and turning Genoa into an ungovernable city. While many satisfied themselves with the idea of delivering yet another unmistakable message of rejection and rupture on the world stage, of remaining within the realm of symbolic battle, within this context the maximalists among us were quietly picturing something more.

That we would overrun Genoa and establish the Genoa Commune. That we would generate a situation in which we could, by expelling the cops and with the support and active participation of the local population, manage to wrest away control from the state of a large territory in a First World urban metropolis for a period of hours, possibly days. With everything that entails: physical protection of the space, self-management of the liberated areas, redistribution of goods, neighborhood assemblies, and so forth.

That which some defined as vanguardism was what we interpreted as simply our desire to live the example of our ideas. To prove in action, not just argument, that the different world many desired, because of the discontent that stems from people's practical understanding that how they live is not a fatality but rather a calculated imposition, is not just desirable but attainable. That this world is not the best of all possible worlds, and that if we fight together we can bring about a better one. Not tomorrow, but today. The Genoa Commune would mark the start of the next phase in destabilizing the post–Cold War end of history.

This was the delusion, or the spirit of the moment—depending on how kindly we want to look back on it. So when the Italian government announced that in order to prevent unwanted elements from enter-ing the country to take part in the protests against the G8 it would be suspending the free movement clause of the European Union's Schengen Agreement ten days prior to the summit and reinstating border controls, we promptly took appropriate action. While confident that this probably didn't mean limiting the freedom of movement of fine, upstanding young anarchists such as ourselves, we chose to minimize risk and not find out. In practice, this meant that on July 9, ten days before the summit was to begin, our small crew of the Barricada and friends circle, the Australians, and Friend Noah, just one of the many tribes of the (in)famous anar-chist traveling circus, were already sporting our finest "college-aged tourists discover European beaches" attire and enjoying a magnificent sunny summer day on the beaches of the quaint Italian seaside town of Ventimiglia, the French-Italian border already safely behind us.

We Are the Birds of the Coming Storm: Albaro Campground, July 19, Nighttime

There's a soothing calm to the night before battle. The knowledge that the time for mobilizing, preparing, plotting, scheming, organizing, debating, and worrying is over. It's a feeling similar to what an athlete might experience before a big game. Of knowing that, for better or for worse, in a few hours (or in this case a few days) it will all be over. You might be victorious or you might be defeated. You will possibly be injured, or in our case killed or imprisoned—but you will be on the other side of the event for which you prepared with such dedication and intensity and which simultaneously caused you so much anxiety and excitement. All you can do is hope that you have prepared yourself and your proverbial teammates as best as possible, and that you will give the best you have to give when the moment of truth comes.

And we have done nothing if not give it our best, having just finished four days of endless, infernal, stressful, and anxiety-filled—yet in the

THE BATTLE OF GENOA

end comradely—anarchist general assemblies at Pinelli. Assemblies of hundreds, which doubled in size with new people night after night.

From a practical, tactical, and decision-making standpoint, these assemblies were more often than not dysfunctional and impractical. The black flag gathers under it a wide variety of practices, ideas, currents, and tendencies. Each of these has its own distinct views on just about every practical and ideological matter conceivable. Imagine a room with up to several hundred people, including autonomes from France, Italian and Spanish anarcho-syndicalists, insurrectionary anarchists from Greece, "autonome antifa" types from Germany, French anarcho-syndicalists from the CNT, German squatter anarchists, and anarchists from ex–Eastern bloc countries. Often we even had "warring" anarchist factions from the same country, some with a history of physical violence with each other, sitting at the same meeting. French CNT members would run into members of the *other* CNT and they would scowl menacingly at each other.[2] Greek insurrectionary anarchists would run into other, more virulently insurrectionary anarchists (I have no idea how to more accurately describe the tensions between these groups) and each would accuse the other of being "social cops" and "worse than fascists," and other such pleasantries. Eastern European anarchists would bristle at "leftist" anarchists from Western Europe using the term "communism." And so on and so forth.

It was, unsurprisingly, next to impossible to come to any kind of agreement on much of anything between such disparate groups, even though, contrary to the picture I have painted, there was "a lot of goodwill at the meeting," according to an eyewitness account from a Workers Solidary Movement member, who goes on to say, "Although things got heated occasionally (it was a long evening) for the most part things went smoothly—people waited their turn to speak, waited for translation, and generally respected the rest of the meeting."[3] But despite our most comradely intentions, serious disagreements remained. What was our objective or objectives with this action or mobilization? How would we relate to or interact with other movement actors such as reformist organizations, parties, or unions? What position should we take toward the mainstream media?

Not only was it next to impossible to reach any sort of consensus or decision on most matters, it was usually not even possible to come to an agreement as to *how* decisions would be taken and implemented, since opinions on accepted practice for this ranged from "delegates and majority vote will be fine" to "consensus or nothing" to "any kind of decision I have to adhere to is an unacceptable attack on my freedom and autonomy and as an anarchist I refuse to accept it."

But somehow, we managed to make it work and came to a generally accepted decision to march toward the red zone with the COBAS (Confederazione dei Comitati di Base) rank-and-file trade unionists, who had welcomed us marching with them, provided we refrained from property damage until we reached the inner city. The assemblies were also, despite the challenges and frustrations, unique opportunities for anarchists from different currents and traditions as well as different countries to forge bonds. In our case, my time in both Paris and Athens, as well as Barricada's ties to some Athenian anarchists, helped swell a few isolated affinity groups into a larger, very militant cluster—a cluster that finds itself together on this night at the campground most anarchists have migrated to and are using as home base.

The setting of this particular night demonstrates what many of us feel: that for us, at least at this moment, nothing exists outside of the momentous confrontation that is about to take place. The night is pitch-black. In the darkness, under the cover of pouring rain, one can make out the shadows of dozens of black-clad figures laboring intensely. We hear the sounds of metal and wood, hammers and knives, being used with silent determination.

An account in *Barricada* continues the description:

> Despite the pouring rain, the camp was in full swing preparing for the next day. People tearing up benches, breaking apart poles, fashioning long flag poles, pulling metal bars out of the ground, attaching flags to wooden beams, making molotov cocktails, and collecting everything that could be of use the next day and storing it for the night. It was clear that the coming days would be intense.[4]

Oscar, Lena, and I take a seat around a fire a few of the Parisian comrades have started in a makeshift fireplace, protected from the rain by an awning. We are soon joined by Marianthi and Nikos, two Athenian anarchists from a collective that corresponds with Barricada and with whom we've become closer during the course of the last few days. I make the appropriate introductions between the Parisians and the Athenians, both sides friends of mine but who do not yet know each other themselves. Having lived in both France and Greece, I am familiar with, and identify strongly with, both of these currents of anarchism and their particular regional peculiarities. They are both comfortably within the family of revolutionary anarchism and more or less friendly to each other, but their political cultures, organizational methods, and political priorities as far as their day-to-day organizing is concerned are very different.

On hearing that the Parisians are from the CNT, Nikos blurts out, "So why are you here?" He means it in a comradely and friendly way, but he is clearly curious.

Julien replies with a convincing case for the importance of anarchist workplace organizing, for an anarchism implanted firmly in the struggles and daily needs of workers and communities. "That's the priority of our agitation, and of my work as an anarchist. It's our bread and butter in the CNT, and what I believe will one day lead us to establish the conditions for a general strike. But of course, I also believe that the anarchist movement needs to be able to communicate through symbolic messages as well. To raise its voice on an international level, to show its internationalist and combative character, and its strength to pierce the veneer of capitalist stability. My priority is not summits, and some in the CNT see them as a distraction, but many of us feel these mobilizations and moments of mass resistance complement our work." Nikos and Marianthi nod approvingly and seem satisfied with the answer. In any case, they refrain from the critique of unionism, revolutionary or otherwise, which they might have presented at another moment.

They seem to find that their motivations are similar enough to Julien's, and this comradely late-night fireside chat is already illustrative of one of the stated reasons they are there: "Because it is a chance to meet with our comrades who will come from all around the world, a chance ... to promote continual conditions of communication and coordination of our struggle ... in order to create together moments of social counter attack."[5] It's not exactly how they said it that night, but their opinion, and that of many Athenian anarchists, is preserved in the text they published in *Barricada* titled "Genoa Will Not Be Porto Alegre."

"We're here to turn this summit into moments of ungovernability and insurrection. So that we send a message of rupture not just with the state, or the cops, or capitalism, but also to all the NGO scum, the

Stalinists, the reformists, the authoritarian pacifists, the nationalists. All of those who want to use this movement and this moment of rebellion as a vehicle to become managers of capitalism or to present us with a supposed better version of it." Marianthi's disdain for all of these is so strong that it looks like she is about to spit into the fire with disgust as she utters their names. She closes with dramatic flair. "We are here because we need to be wherever revolt happens, and at the same time we will work to make revolt happen wherever we are, like we do in Athens."

Lena, Swedish and succinct, says something to the effect of, "I'm an antifascist first and foremost. Capitalism is the breeding ground of fascism, so I fight to eliminate one if I want to exterminate the other. If the leaders of capitalism are having a party, I will be there to disturb it." Clear, concise, and to the point. "I've just never been to anything like this before except Gothenburg. That was much smaller, and it was still intense. So I'm curious what will happen tomorrow and what to expect."

She has wandered into the question on everybody's minds: What do you think will happen tomorrow? Everybody was pretty much in agreement as to the minimum expectation, as expressed by Nikos: "At a minimum, create chaos and disrupt the veneer of capitalist peace and invincibility. Show them that we are always more and more, and that eventually no army will be able to protect them or their society." The intermediate expectation wasn't too controversial either. "Maybe we can overrun the red zone, give them the scare of their lives, and delay or even cancel the summit."

It's when Nikos gets to the "maximalist" expectation for the coming days that two very distinct camps form within our little fireside group: "We will generate so many points of conflict, clashes will become so widespread, that the cops will not be able to hold the city. The people here are sympathetic to us, and a dynamic of widespread revolt can develop. We won't just smash and burn the symbols of capitalism—we'll open the shops and supermarkets, redistribute goods in an organized fashion. The heart of the city will be able to experience a temporary liberation from capitalism and have free access to whatever they need while tens of thousands of fighters keep out the forces of the state. For a few hours, or days even, we'll establish the Commune of Genoa."

If it were socially acceptable and not likely to break the comradely vibe, the Parisians might be laughing out loud at this part. Lena I can't really judge. The Old Man, meanwhile, glances at me, biting his lip and clearly doing his best to avoid rolling his eyes dismissively, and I know what he is thinking: *Great, now this crazy has found a whole nest of similar crazies.* He isn't wrong. I don't say it much, because even among the anarchists this is generally viewed as a wildly optimistic, not to mention potentially dangerous, perspective. But here is a whole anarchist scene, a combative and experienced one at that, who is boldly stating that such a scenario is at least possible.

I can tell that the Old Man is worried about us overestimating both our support and our material strength. He is probably also rightfully outraged about how crude our revolutionary strategy seems to be at times, because he has often said as much. "Who needs revolutionary thinkers and analysis when we have you geniuses," is one his favorite joking-but-not-quite lines reserved for Cadger and me when he catches us advocating for, essentially, "whatever, just push until it falls." If he were to say something right now, I'm sure it would start with, "Oh great, now it's 'push until it falls, at least in a small place and for a few hours.' Another great leap forward in revolutionary strategy and theory."

Taking advantage of the meditative lull in the conversation, Lena declares, "It's late and I'm going to sleep. You should all probably do the same." Her initial shyness has dissipated enough that she is now giving this group of comrades she has only just met mildly disapproving looks, implying, *Have you any idea how late it is?* But everyone takes her cue without argument. We say our goodnights with powerful hugs and intense looks. The unspoken message is abundantly clear: *I'll be at your side tomorrow. I'll be with you tomorrow. I'll protect you if you fall, care for you if you are injured. We'll advance as one and retreat as one. Together, we'll make history.* None of this is said out loud, but at the same time it couldn't be more loudly stated. This unlikely and eclectic group of people from the farthest corners of the world—Parisian anarcho-syndicalists, Athenian insurrectionists, a Swedish antifascist, a Chilean ultra-leftist, and one Argentine anarchist crazy—at least for the moment, have become a family. And we haven't even entered battle together yet.

Soon, the entire camp is asleep. As we quietly push open the door to the dark gym, we are greeted by the peaceful sight of hundreds of people spread out over every inch of the floor, sleeping placidly. Hundreds and hundreds of anarchists, who in a few short hours will fight some of the most intense battles with the police that Italy and Europe have seen in years, resting quietly. We enter the gym and quickly fall fast asleep, nestled comfortably in each other's arms and surrounded by a few hundred of our closest friends.

The Golden Horde: July 20, Approximately 11:00 a.m.

We've just finished the short descent from the campground to street level, down the narrowest of stairways cut windingly into a typical Genovese cliff, wide enough for only three people abreast. Our little international cluster of fifty or so people leads the way and is the first to reach the street. There's fifteen or twenty Athenian anarchists, ten or so of the Parisian CNT and Brigada Flores Magon crew, a few German and Swedish autonome antifas, some Eastern European comrades from Abolishing the Borders from Below, and of course the Barricada and friends crew, composed of Oscar, Lena, Friend Noah, me, and a few others. Oscar quips, "It looks like a scene out of *Braveheart*."

Looking around at the masked and often helmeted yet nonetheless perfectly familiar faces around me, I realize that I would feel safer and ride more confidently into battle with these fifty than with any group of five hundred random unknowns dressed in black. In many cases from personal experience, in others because their reputations precede them, but I know that everybody around us represents some of the most committed, experienced, and combative exponents of modern-day anarchism from around Europe and North America. Swedish antifascists from the Antifascist Action network who were not only unfazed by the events of Gothenburg and the subsequent repression but galvanized by them and out for revenge. Parisian CNT members with a general strike behind them. The ex–Red Warriors and Brigada Flores Magon crew, with well over a decade of fascist-hunting successes. Athenian comrades—many of them veterans of the November 17, 1995, Polytechnic occupation (the night I personally discovered modern anarchism), the riots that greeted President Clinton's visit to Athens in 1999, and the anti-IMF clashes of 2000 in Prague—who had been forging a path of uncompromising and militant war with the state for years. It is a veritable who's who of revolutionary anarchism. And that is just in the cluster of fifty or so of ours. It's safe to say that if there has been a militant struggle in Europe in the last decade—from antifascism to immigrant solidarity, from labor struggles to squatting—anarchist veterans of that struggle are in the roaring mob of hundreds descending this stairway.

As I turn to look at the stairway behind us, I see an image that is a poem. An exercise in mass militant poetry. Artists may put their poetry on a piece of paper or on a canvas, but the poetry of revolution- ary struggle is exclusively three-dimensional. It lives, breathes, and moves before your eyes. Fleeting by nature, it can rarely be adequately captured after the fact. We experience art and poetry that can only be appreciated by its protagonists and, perhaps, those lucky enough to experience the moment as witnesses.

The perfect blue of the late-morning summer sky is a backdrop to the dramatic cliff into which the narrow, winding staircase is etched. Today, the staircase is packed from top to bottom with black-clad combatants radiating passion, conviction, and emotion in their move- ments and their voices. There is artwork in the contrasts within the scene, and the mass of people provide the poetry as the first roars of "No nation! No border! Fight law and order!" echo through the city of Genoa.

We might not be the Golden Horde of Nanni Balestrini's 1970s Italy, when an entire generation of rebel workers defied state, parties, and bureaucratic unions to produce beautiful scenes of thousands spilling out of Italian factories to take on the cops and the society they defend, while hundreds, maybe thousands more went a step further and took up arms against modern capital.[6] But for today, we might be the next best thing: the Golden Horde of international anarchism. Thousands upon thousands lending not just our time and our minds, as every single comrade in this crowd surely does in their hometown, but also our bodies to the pursuit of articulating a wholesale rejection of the entirety of the existing order. We have come, if not from all corners of the world, at least from all corners of Europe and North America to take on the capitalist powers, the leaders of this world, and their private army of almost twenty thousand police officers. It's been barely ten years since the supposed "end of history" and the definitive victory of capitalism, and yet here we are already—ready to take it on headfirst and convinced that if we just push hard enough, we can bring it crumbling down. Whether this is a strategically sound course of action, and to what extent we are delusional, is and will be in the future the subject of much and heated debate. But in this moment, it matters next to nothing. What matters is expressed in the first sounds of breaking glass and the

Molotovs flying through the air to greet the first cops on the horizon: that the time for talking is over. We have declared that we would wage war against capital, the state, and all forms of domination—our war, the social war—and that time has come. It's time to "make total destroy."

A View from a Hill

From our perch high in the peaceful hills of Genoa, we're looking out at a dream. Our eyes scan the cityscape, taking in the sights and sounds of what is happening all around us. Thick columns of smoke in different shades of white, gray, and black billow across the city. We can't make it out from where we are, but they are coming from burning barricades, the flames of looted and burned banks, and the fires of an armored carabinieri transporter that has been overrun and set ablaze. The sounds of clashes ring in our ears. In one direction, we see groups of people running back and forth, in and out of our line of sight, as we hear tear gas canisters explode around them, quickly followed by expanding plumes of smoke. From another direction, we hear roaring chants. We can't quite make out what they say, but chances are it's the popular rallying cry of *"Genova libera,"* Italian for "Free Genoa." From seemingly all directions comes the din of sirens wailing, the sounds of ambulances and cop transports crisscrossing the city in a cacophony of shrill noises. Every once in a while we hear the distinctive *pop-pop* of gunfire, and we again wonder if the bullets are lead or rubber. It's a solemn reminder of how we got here, of the ferocity of the battles that led to warning shots being fired in our immediate vicinity twice, and then the use of tanks to disperse us.

We're a group of no more than twenty comrades, made up of Oscar, Lena, Friend Noah, some Athenian comrades, and a couple of unknowns who have been "pushed into the outskirts of the city" following the latest in a series of intense clashes since we left the campground.[7] The past five hours have been eventful. We clashed with the cops almost immediately after descending from the campground, with several hundred of us being cut off from the larger bloc, eventually forced to retreat into the convergence center by the sea, where we barricaded ourselves and expected the day to end in a pathetic fiasco, with us being mass-arrested only an hour or two into the clashes. Instead, we found an escape route by way of a winding walkway along the waterfront. Once regrouped, we unfortunately clashed with some of the COBAS

Clashes on July 20, 2001, in downtown Genoa.

members, who, unhappy with the premature property destruction of the black bloc, were mainly intent on getting their bloc safely back to their camp without drawing more cops toward them.

It was a sad and concerning moment. Those who we saw as militant comrades just a few short hours ago, who had held open the gates to the GSF center for us as we retreated, had become just Stalinists to be combated. Again, those who stood literally back to back with us, keeping an eye on the nearby cops while batons swung one way and the other between the COBAS lines and us, were the Athenian comrades. The standoff lasted almost twenty minutes, with sporadic bouts of fight-ing that sadly yielded some minor injuries, along with some internal COBAS conflicts between those intent on holding the line against us and those wanting to let us pass.

Eventually, they "stepped back and allowed the bloc to pass. At this point, most of the black bloc people present decided to change and disperse in order to reach other areas of the city where the possibilities for action were greater."[8]

I can't remember how exactly, or where or when, but soon after our waterfront escape the Athenians and our crew managed to again find a decently large and combative bloc of people as we reentered the city. We found ourselves far from the red zone, but at least headed in its general direction, now numbering "more than 2,000, including at least 400 in the black bloc."[9] We were pulling dumpsters and whatever we could find into the street behind us to cover our rear, but all in all the march was relatively uneventful. Suddenly two carabinieri vehicles appeared on a side street to our left, driving at full speed before stopping about thirty meters from the bloc and shooting tear gas in our direction. As an anonymous comrade from France put it, "I don't know what they were doing there, but it wasn't safe."[10]

Not safe for the cops. We all realized it more or less simultaneously. "Between the two trucks there's maybe thirty cops maximum and us ... we are hundreds."[11] Some sixty of us charged toward their vehicles, and stones and bottles rained down on them. The cops made no attempt to exit their vehicles, though one in each truck shot tear gas canisters through an opening in the roof; they rapidly desisted when several stones impacted their helmets.

We reached the vehicles, quickly surrounding them. Metal bars, batons, and crowbars smashed against their windows. They cracked, spiderwebs of impact marks streaking across them ... but they held.

> The trucks don't move. The one on the left is finally able to retreat thirty meters, but not the one on the right. Their special windows are all beaten in, but holding. People had the idea to check if the front doors of the vehicles are locked. Bad luck for the cops ... they weren't. The doors opened!!! The cop on the passenger side managed to quickly shut his one, but not the driver—who after being pulled halfway out of the vehicle was desperately pulled back in by the other cop, but not before taking several blows to the head. The situation looked dire for the cops.[12]

There was visible fear in the cop's eyes as he was almost pulled from the vehicle. I had time to notice that he was relatively young, probably not much older than me. We had nothing against him as a human being, but in that moment the issue was the role he served, both on this day as well as on every other day of his career as a police officer. Accustomed to giving orders, to being the bully, to giving commands and receiving obedience—he was suddenly faced with a group of people who had no respect for this authority, no fear of his uniform, nothing but disdain for the green, white, and red flag on his vehicle.

It was at that point that we heard the detonations. Unlike what you might be familiar with from movies, the sound of gunfire is distinctively anticlimatic. The *pop-pop* of bullets pierces the moment precisely because it's an eerily understated sound that stands out among the constant roar of explosions and ammunitions that are the more common soundtrack to mass militance. It was a blur from there. As we sprinted away from the vehicle, I looked around to see if my comrades were with me, spotting only Oscar and Lena. I looked for anybody on the ground, anybody fallen. "The shots came from the second truck. I saw the driver outside, taking cover behind his open door."[13] My last image of the scene is of the cop standing by the door of his truck, gun in hand, in trademark "cop who has just shot warning shots into the air to dissuade an advancing mob" pose.

This was the first in a series of intense confrontations, and it was quickly followed by a protracted battle in the form of a "massive confrontation with hundreds of carabinieri under and in front of a tunnel which led to the general area of the red zone."[14] The clash was more intense than anything I've ever experienced. Enormous, seem-ingly rotating units of cops. Many hundreds, possibly thousands, of us. Nothing in Gothenburg, Quebec, or Washington comes near to the intensity of these battles. The cops were generous with the tear gas, which I could swear was more noxious than what they used in Quebec City. The carabinieri were also making use of some kind of projectiles that we couldn't quite place. And, most significantly, they were (like us) light and mobile. They charged quickly and often, and as they came close we could see that this was a highly politicized country and the police forces seemed to personally despise us.

The feeling was mutual, and we repeatedly replied to the carabi-nieri charges with counterattacks of our own. The crowd, pleasantly diverse and multilingual, was resilient and determined. We turned the sky dark with stones, and again, eventually cornered and frightened cops resorted to gunfire, although this time we didn't see where it came from, as an armored carabinieri vehicle was overrun and set ablaze.

In our last act before arriving at our scenic suburban perch above the city, we were not shot at but rammed by tanks driving full speed across our barricades and into the mass of people confronting them. My last thought before literally running for the hills was, "What the fuck? They're not going to ram those things into us, are they?" The assumption was that they would rev the engines a bit and maybe advance, with cops slowly following behind, eventually pushing the barricade apart. But in another sign that we'd reached a new level of escalation on both sides of the barricades, they did no such thing. The tank in front instead flew at full speed across the bridge, into and through the barricades. None of the five or six hundred of us there, "two hundred black bloccers and several hundred others" made up of activists of different stripes and locals, were inclined to pull a Tiananmen Square reenactment. The barricades broke, the tank exploded through them, and it continued forward at full speed. It made no attempt to slow down or avoid the people in its path. The street was narrow, the sidewalk almost nonexistent, and the risk of death by tank trampling very much real. We sprinted and scattered in all directions.

It was the end of what had been an hour-long battle on this bridge near via Tolemaide. Via Tolemaide was where the White Overalls bloc was trying to reach the red zone, and we heard that their contingent was huge, numbering potentially over ten thousand people. But cops blocked our way and the next battle erupted. There were charges and countercharges constantly swaying back and forth across the bridge. "Eventually, through the use of abundant amounts of tear gas, the police cleared the bridge," but they positioned themselves at the other end and did not advance.[15]

> Everyone then set about building barricades along the bottom of the bridge and out along the street, using the small dumpsters, materials from a gas station, some newspaper cases, and metal fences nearby. Once the barricades were built, people began collecting stones and other materials to defend against the tear gas canisters and the large canister bullets.[16]

We were like ants, laser-focused on building the colony. Everybody was pitching in, everybody was fortifying the barricades or gathering ammunition. But it was not just foreign anarchists and black bloc folks. I'm not sure where they came from, how they joined us, or when the dynamic developed, but we were outnumbered by Italians, many of whom were clearly locals, as they indicated to us where materials were to be found and which streets to be aware of possible police appearances from. It was an interesting indication of what the dynamic might have been in the city, and this, coupled with how close we were to reaching the larger mass of demonstrators, had us quickly forgetting that we numbered only a few hundred. We were determined to make a stand at this location.

And under normal conditions it might have been a valiant stand. But as soon as the tanks rolled in, it was over. Whatever illusions we had of being able to hold this position and being able to ward off or eventually push back the cops in a protracted face-to-face battle scattered to the four winds as we tried desperately to dodge the incoming tank. As I sprinted away and out of the city, out of the corner of my eye, I caught flames rising from inside a nearby bank.

★

For the next hour, as we've made our way through the "steep, small, and winding hills," we have been torching luxury cars as we retreated and building barricades behind us.[17] As we ascend into the hills, we don't know if cops are on our tail, although we assume that the most likely answer is that they aren't. As the hundreds of us scattered, only our small group chose to flee toward the hills. But if cops do happen to appear behind us, we're such a small group that our only defense is to keep them at a distance thanks to the flames, the barricades, and the illusion of our group being larger in number. So less to make a statement than for our own safety, we've been extra aggressive in our retreat, and this has meant that numerous vehicles have been repurposed for barricades or set aflame. Our militance is as real as can be, but we are consciously trying to create the illusion of numbers. Communicating preemptively that if you come near us, we won't be going down without a fight.

Our geographic isolation is the result of my assessment on this day in Genoa, as well as on many adventures with the law over the years, that if you have already "done things," if cops have gained the upper hand or dispersed your group, if you can't extirpate yourself from the streets to a safe place or in an anonymous vehicle, and if you don't know where your enemies are located around the area, then it's always wisest to go on long, random, meandering hikes around the outskirts of the city until things die down, safer options arise, or you simply reenter the city hours later and ridiculously far from the original area of conflict. It's a strategy that over the years has taken me on beautiful solo sightseeing walks or yielded stimulating peaceful conversations with my comrades on the outskirts of Thessaloniki, in the suburbs of

An overturned car ablaze in downtown Genoa on July 20.

Strasbourg, through the posh islands of Stockholm, and everywhere in between. So today, when the tanks came rolling in and it looked like all hope was lost, we noticed the small, winding road leading away from the city and into the hills—and we aimed straight for the hills, and a small group of comrades did the same.

We're well over an hour into our retreat into the hills of Genoa when we decide that we are safe from potential carabinieri at our rear and reach the perch providing us the panoramic bird's-eye view of the city, where we rest.

The scenes unfolding below us are too far away for us to join. For once, we are content as spectators. I'm driven constantly by a some-times exhausting feeling of obligation to push things forward. My comrades—and it's probably a big part of why we are comrades—are not much different. The "what if nobody throws the first stone?" anarcho-anxiety, leading us to make sure that if nobody else throws it, we will. And for all we knew, our proverbial as well as very literal stone throwing in our series of clashes with the carabinieri might have been, aside from Ya Basta!'s ritualized civil disobedience, the only conflict taking place in all of Genoa.

But as we stand on our perch high in the hills, it becomes abundantly clear that we were simply one front in a city full of clashes. That the bloc that split from us after that fateful first encounter with the carabinieri, and who knows how many other thousands of comrades who spilled across the city, have created an entire cityscape of confrontation. For once I have the peace of knowing that, while my comrades and I have contributed more than our fair share, we are living a moment of generalized revolt that extends far beyond our actions.

★

The panoramic painting unfolding in front of us is a living illustration of revolt and negation being transformed into mass collective action. The embers of negation—the unmediated act of open battle with the state, capital, and its army—have scattered across Genoa and sparked a prairie fire. The city is on fire, it is a dream, and it fills me with a sense of both peace and joy difficult to explain. But I can already feel the disdain and hear the pearl-clutching gasps of the reformists and pacifists around us if they could hear that the sight of a city on fire, of clashes and violence, fills my comrades and I with a sense of peace and fulfillment. I can see their righteous indignation at confirming that anarchists are indeed nihilists simply interested in destruction. That those of us present in Genoa on this day "held the view that anarchy is based on chaos and destruction rather than a well thought-out political ideology defined by compassion and self-governance," as some supposed comrades later claimed.[18]

While I resent having to write this, there's maybe no better time for a quick and reasoned tour of the issue of violence than during our peaceful hillside interlude, as we sit and watch the scenes unfold before us, reveling in the violence of our camp. Even acknowledging the topic feels almost like a concession and reminds me of a thousand too many conversations I've found myself reluctantly trapped in when in nonpolitical social settings. And I'll engage the subject much as I do in polite society, when—in a loud bar, during dinner, or at a party—somebody inevitably remarks, "Did you know that Tomas is an anarchist?" as a topic of exotically interesting conversation. While most will find it quaint and mildly interesting, at least one person in the group, almost without fail, will gasp or point out self-righteously that "anarchists and the anarchist movement are actually very violent, and I'm against violence."

Massive clashes between police and demonstrators in the vicinity of the red zone.

It's at that point that I more often than not lose the little patience I carry with me to begin with for situations when others take the liberty of making a political zoo animal out of me in loud and poorly suited social settings without my consent. I take the bait, and with the world's most thinly veiled contempt, I reply that if they really want to discuss the issue of violence, it would be my pleasure—because I, too, abhor it.

From wholly nonpolitical people, the objections usually take the form of "but you throw stones and set fires, anarchists have placed bombs, killed people, it's all so violent." And even from those who politically think or feel themselves somewhat closer to us, there are similar if more nuanced questions or objections. "There's violence throughout your political life, and throughout your anarchism." "It's not normal for most people, it's not their experience. At least not in this form, and it scares and distances people from your objectives." "You need to at least explain how you, and your comrades, developed this relationship to violence in order to be relatable."

On the surface they seem like logical questions. While we might sometimes forget this detail in "our circles"—and even if we know that the overwhelming bulk of our time and efforts as anarchists is spent writing, discussing, agitating, and generally participating in mundane and seemingly endless meetings—most people do not spend decades

The huge Ya Basta! bloc heads toward the red zone.

of their lives throwing fire, wearing helmets, building barricades, or being regularly in the general vicinity of bombs, explosions, gunshots, prison sentences, injury, and death. In short, civilians are not generally exposed to this kind of violence, and most certainly don't perpetrate it themselves.

Or at least they don't perceive it this way. And there lies both the crux of this question—the question of violence—and my annoyance and dismay at having to constantly address it, either among apolitical civil society or when faced with the infuriating indignation of politically inclined people who are in fact defending structural violence. For it is not violence per se that society—and, for that matter, even leftist or activist or anarchist or radical or whatever you may want to call it circles— takes issue with. The issue is with the often spectacular nature of "our violence," with who chooses to make use of it, and in what context.

Our violence, spectacular as it is when taking the form of the flying Molotov, the flaming barricade, the baton striking the police- man's helmet or fascist's back as he flees from our fury, is intermittent. It punctuates a moment or a situation, articulating it symbolically or challenging it practically—just as it challenges the state's monopoly on violence. This violence surprises or shocks some, because it is not the violence we are used to. It's a striking contrast to the monstrous, systemic, and continuing violence of capitalism and class society that is often less direct and less immediate, and to which most have become numb.

We have become as a society wildly unaccustomed to liberatory violence, but we are numb to the violence of the bully, the violence of everyday life, the dull daily horror necessary for the gears of modern nation-states and capitalist society to maintain the grinding of their normality. We could fill countless pages with the specific, needless barbarisms of modern capitalism. Human beings worked to death; thousands dead every year in the world's largest economy from preventable illness due to lack of access to health care; homeless people freezing to death outside the entrances of empty homes and hotels; refugees drowning by the thousands at the gates of Fortress Europe or dying of dehydration at the US's southern border; not to mention the violence of alienation, of forcing humans to devote the majority of their lives to repetitive and mind-numbing labor, forced to rent their bodies simply to exist in society—when human progress could allow us to all live plentiful lives with significantly less work. And all this is simply a drop in the bucket of the panoply of systemic violence that is basic to capitalist and nationalist normality, without even making mention of the gruesome bloodbaths in their inherently cyclical outbursts of crisis, wars, and genocides. The state is a machine of constant, brutal, murderous violence at which no one bats an eye.

And so, as in Genoa, as one comrade put it, when it is "a stone against a helicopter, a stick against an armored car," we are supposed to take seriously those who claim that it is us who revel in violence? "There is no comparison—they are the real butchers, they are the ones whose hands are covered in blood from not only the silent holocaust but from the massacres in Chechnya, the Gulf War, Latin America and many other places." Our "violence is less than a fraction of a drop of water in the entire oceans of the world when compared to theirs and ... they live in a state of constant denial."[19]

There are those who will psychologize us, claim that our violence is a political scaffolding constructed to justify our violent natures or personality traits to ourselves. Yet, in my case, I have a lifetime of empirical evidence that proves the contrary: I am a "stops to greet dogs" kind of guy, the perpetual friendly "has I tolllld you how much I lof you?" drunk, the peace and love and laughter and munchies stoner, never struck a child or partner and shudder at the thought, get very queasy around blood, don't participate in combat sports—and in fact plan to outlaw them when I'm finally elected president of the world. I can't even really enjoy TV shows when there's too much death or suffering, much less the news. I have essentially never been in a fight outside of those with political reasons, and even then, because my violence is ideological rather than personal, my one phobia is knives—which frighten me when in the hands of my opponents and which I refuse to wield or use myself. If this is a violent personality justifying itself through political struggle ... weird!

If I as an anarchist have exerted violence, it has been in the realm of the specific and immediate violence to stop a deportation. Violence to prevent fascists from successfully living out their exterminationist fantasies. Violence to help somebody avoid eviction, to defend a squat or social center. Violence in solidarity with workers defending their dignity. Violence to prevent immediate harm and human suffering—and in general to defeat the system that makes all this needless suffering possible. In short, violence to defend my autonomy against oppression, and violence with and on behalf of the oppressed against their oppressors. And because the violence of capitalism and nation-states is constant and systemic, we as anarchists do not need specific acts from the state in order to justify our attacks—our violence. We do not need to contextualize our violence as "they attacked us first" or moan "but the repression." We are not victims, nor are we misguided youngsters pushed to irrational acts by circumstance or impulse. We are not violently lashing out due to an inability to formulate a coherent political or revolutionary strategy.

On the contrary. My violence, our violence, is that of the combatant choosing to engage a criminally monstrously violent system. Because I am perfectly conscious of the historical fact that violence, not in isolation but as an element of broader social movements and societal upheavals—even in those that have been whitewashed decades after the fact, like Martin Luther King and the civil rights movement of the 1960s, Gandhi and the fight against British imperialism, or the Stonewall riots—has always been a motor of social change, of ending oppression, and of progress. Aversion to it, leaving it exclusively to our oppressors, only serves to defang movements of resistance and render our world ever more unlivable.

Which is precisely why the machinery of consent manufacturing, firmly in the hands of the defenders of the status quo, has done the job it has at building an intellectual argument positing all violence outside of the state as illegitimate, criminal, irrational, and terroristic. To do so, it has elevated capitalist reality to the condition of a quasi material religion. In order to justify human suffering in an era of unprecedented abundance, the sanctity of capital and the dehumanization of "others" have coalesced to develop a "common sense" in which commodities and borders are valued above human life. It's a process that began with the fall of the Eastern bloc and the globalization of capitalism and has frighteningly accelerated in the thirty or so years since, eroding the postwar consensus of the liberal capitalist welfare state. A consensus that posited, or at least so went the discourse if not the actions, that all life has value and is to be protected. While this was much less so in the US, where marginalized and oppressed communities continued to suffer double oppression due to the racial nature of US capitalism, in the case of Europe, for example, an effort was made to guarantee the basics—housing, health care, education—at least for those parts of its population with the privilege of citizenship.

The progressive "victory" of the logic of greed and capital, its advancement on the collective psyche, is eroding this consensus. Life is more and more seen as having less value if it is not productive. The obsession with youth, and the acceptance of those with less access to health care dying younger, are tacit expressions of the normalization of this crude equation: If you produce less value, not for society but for the capitalists to whom you rent your body and labor, then your life is less significant. The collective reaction to the hundreds of thousands of deaths caused by the COVID pandemic is a stunning confirmation and acceleration of this process: The old, the sick, the marginalized ... their deaths are not so tragic. I'm shocked when I think about it, until I remind myself that tens of thousands are allowed to die from prevent-able illness every year in the richest and most materially advanced society in the history of the world, simply because they lack proper health insurance. And nobody bats an eye at this unspeakable violence and preventable human suffering.

In the immediate aftermath of the COVID pandemic's "acute phase," we saw how quickly the so-called retail heroes and essential workers, who during the height of the pandemic were forced to choose either exposing themselves and their loved ones to illness or suffering dire economic consequences—all in the interest of allowing for the continuation of capitalist normality and the further accumulation of capital—were cast aside and their lives downgraded to disposable as soon as the pool of labor was deep enough to replace them.

I'm concerned that as we slowly move from tacit to overt acceptance of death at the altar of the market and productivity, with Republicans openly expressing on TV that Grandma should do her patriotic duty and die for the economy, how long can it be until our very existence is presented matter-of-factly as an economic equation and the advance of capital destroys even the most basic humanist consensus? This, coupled with the growing fascist movement and its inherently geno-cidal ideas, is the cauldron brew from which the ever-increasing cycle of racist mass-shooting events and other atrocities is feeding itself.

Mixed together, it's a kind of grotesque, religious-like blend of nationalism and capitalism, gradually replacing humanism and now wielding the power of the state, industry, and the media. A totalitarian theocracy, an ideology of capital, whose god is commodity and whose first commandment is the accumulation of capital. Its principles and tenets, like in the darkest times of the church's rule in the Middle Ages, are not to be questioned. They are self-evident. The violence commit-ted to preserve its rule and order is judged to be normal, even natural; it is unquestionably accepted, barely acknowledged. Like in the Crusades, no amount of senseless human suffering, ecological destruction, or mass death is too great a sacrifice at its altar—and the only mortal sin, which will brand one a heathen and a terrorist, is effective resistance against it.

All of this while we live in the bounty of industrialized society, in which technology, human progress, and automation have given us the means and tools to live lives of fulfillment and leisure, free from the chains of work for survival. All of this suffering and death are avoidable, intentional—and there is no greater violence than inflicting needless, optional, voluntary pain and suffering on individuals, on society, and on the planet.

It is precisely because I abhor violence, and seek to end the system and material conditions that breed it, that I am proudly and uncom-promisingly violent in my opposition to it. In the words of Luisa Toledo—who lost all three of her sons in the battle against the violence of capital and dictatorship, two of them on the same day, but remained unbowed until her last breath—I strive to be "capable of being beautifully violent, to mask up and take to the streets and oppose everything which represents this horrific system of dominance."[20] History will judge us, and I am confident about how it will look back on our actions and our violence: as the only signs of humanity (of "civilization") and dignity among the barbarians and their apologists. I'm not interested in the judgment of this "desert," of today's morally bankrupt society. Nothing could matter less to me than its morals, its outrage, its breathless need to analyze the completely anecdotal violence of the oppressed, of violence committed in the pursuit of liberation.

I am only interested in joining with those who identify the violence perpetrated daily around us, who identify that being forced to choose between wage slavery or hunger by those who have seized the collective wealth of society for themselves is not freedom but a daily, constant, and grinding violence exerted on their very existence. I am interested in advancing the program to end violence, to attack its roots and causes: poverty, hunger, nationalism, religion, inequality, hierarchy. To replace the society of violence with the world of solidarity, mutual aid, freedom, and socialism.

And yet, obviously, fighting the cops and the state is by no means equivalent to actually building the liberated world of our dreams—a task that is significantly more painstaking, slow, and difficult. My dream is not of the chaos and violence, obviously, but I value them as the necessary prerequisite for what comes after. And in the clashes I see the negation of what I reject, the birthing pains of the world to follow. The cops we battle and the banks we dismantle are the physical manifestations of state and capital. These are the guardians and symbols of our daily oppressions. Capital, which benefits from the workplace where you sell your body for x hours per day, alienated from your desires in order to survive. The false freedom of choosing between wage slavery or poverty and destitution. The cop, whose gun and baton make possible the existence and preservation of this order. Who will harass you in the street and imprison you if you rebel.

They are the representatives of these ideas and their systems of dominance that penetrate every aspect of our daily lives. Just as the Propagandists of the Deed were once told that "you can't blow up a social relationship," we are today told essentially that we can only vote and hope this world away, if that. Minds colonized by capitalism try to convince us that this is the best of all possible worlds. So when from our perch on the hill we see that thousands have come together to reject this narrative, to put their bodies at the service of the struggle for total liberation, and that collectively—if only for a moment in time, in a small corner of the world—we are sending the old world and its guardians on the run, we see it as steps successfully taken on the long and difficult path to the realization of our dreams.

How could it fill us with anything other than the purest, most immense joy? On behalf of our movement, our anarchism, we collectively boldly proclaimed ourselves a movement of attack, not resistance, and told our enemies that we would be coming. To expect us. The view from the hill spoke, stating clearly that the message was no longer in the future tense, it was now firmly grounded in the present: We are here.

★

As we sit in the shade of the tree line on our perch above the city, observing the sights and sounds of the clashes below, I'm flanked by Lena on one side and Oscar on the other. Masks are off, and our normally chatty group is unusually silent. Taking in the enormity of it all. I turn toward the Old Man, who catches the look in my eyes and the self-complacent grin spreading across my face. "Don't say it." He laughs, and knows what's coming, because although it's obvious, I absolutely can't help myself.

"So, Old Man, who's the fucking crazy now, huh?" A needless "I told you so" moment among friends and comrades. "I don't know about you, but to me it seems like the maximalists and our delusions might have been right about this one." Lena hits me on the arm and chides me for being "shildish." It's all in good fun, among comrades who are happy to be in the wrong.

Oscar begins to admit, with one of the broadest smiles I've ever seen him wear, that "I never expected you to be right about this dynamic, about there being so much—" Oscar stops mid-sentence as we all catch a sudden burst of movement to the right side of our panoramic view. There's running and commotion among a few dozen carabinieri who had been lounging around in an open parking lot, where "six armored vehicles and two carabinieri Land Rover Defenders" are parked.[21] They are guarding the front entrance of the Marassi prison. As they lob a

Demonstrators charge at a police line in Genoa.

few tear gas canisters toward a corner of the square, we see dozens of masked people emerge, headed straight for the cops and the prison, throwing stones and objects as they advance. "The carabinieri vehicles, with the group still at a distance, fall back and ... at this point, with the square empty," dozens more black bloc participants come into view.[22]

The Marassi prison, emptied of prisoners prior to the summit, is under attack by a column that has broken off from the bloc that headed into the city when we split after the original clash. This bloc, "which eventually swelled to over three thousand people, marched for several hours through the city, destroying all the symbols of capitalism in its path."[23] Windows shatter, the signage on the front is demolished, and a Molotov cocktail sets the main entrance aflame. The slogan of "fire to the prisons" has become literal, unfolding in front of our eyes, and is again set to the backdrop of the state's guardians lost in a panicked retreat. In the last few hours, we have seen cops on the run, we have forced them to pull their guns on us in desperate last acts of defense, they have rolled their tanks at us, and still the city remains ungovernable.

It feels and sounds almost dishonest to claim it now, but I'd rather tell a dishonest-sounding truth than an honest-sounding lie. We were looking into history, right in front of our eyes, and we knew it. We could tell that something momentous, something incredible, was happening this day—and that we had the militant privilege of witnessing it. We lost our sense of caution. Whoops and cheers erupted as stones and fire hit the prison. The wave was breaking, although not in the direction we thought. We know now that it broke against us, and that this was the high point. But nothing and nobody could have convinced us in that moment that the exact opposite wasn't the case.

Energized and inspired like never before, we head back toward the city on fire.

"It Was a Bullet That Did This"—The Death of Carlo Giuliani: Piazza Alimonda, July 20, 5:27 p.m.

From the account of the anonymous comrade from France:

> That's why they had to send those thirty or forty cops to the small side street, to the left of the first lines of demonstrators. They must have thought that the front ranks would be afraid of a charge on the flank that would cut them off from the rest of

the demonstration ... and that they would move back a little bit, thus reducing the pressure on the police on via Tolemaide, or maybe they were trying to dissuade us from spreading out into the small streets on the left and thus extending the perimeter of the fighting. I don't know why they did it but, in any case, it wasn't a good idea because there were a lot of angry people arriving to support the front lines and occupy the space gained during the charge of the demonstrators, and the few dozen cops were very quickly charged by at least sixty or seventy people.

The cops retreated to a small perpendicular street as we continued to charge them. The more they retreated, the more we charged. We chased them down the small perpendicular street and came out into a small square with a church. The cops continued to retreat under the projectiles. Many of the demonstrators had iron bars or pickaxes. We outnumbered them and they were trying to avoid contact with us. The cops went to reform their line at the entrance to a street that led to the square. When they withdrew, they left two small carabinieri jeep vehicles twenty or thirty meters behind them. The situation was violent, fast, and confusing, so I'll be careful.

Both cars tried to back up, but for some reason at least the second one couldn't. The vehicle then found itself cut off from the rest of the cops and in contact with the protesters, who began throwing stones and hitting it with metal bars or poles. The rear window of the vehicle was broken, I didn't see how but it was gone. I was about ten meters away from the vehicle ... and with a bit of an elevated view because I was on the steps of the small church. That's when I heard the first detonation, quite loud, dry, and close. I instinctively ducked and thought it was a gunshot. I looked straight ahead at the police line at the entrance to the small street to see what was happening, if they were shooting or charging. They were about thirty meters away, and through the tear gas I couldn't see much.

I think there was another bang. I swung around, still hunched over, went down a couple of steps to the back ... and crouched down behind who knows what for cover. I stood up a little. Right in front of me, still about ten meters away in my opinion, was the

Für die Macht der Reichen 'gehen sie über Leichen!

Am 20.Juni 2001 wurde Carlo Giuliani in Genua von einem Polizisten bei den Protesten gegen den G8-Gipfel erschossen und anschließend von einem Polizeiwagen überfahren. Bei diesem Vorfall handelte es sich nur um die Spitze des Eisbergs: Polizeiübergriffe, Misshandlungen, psychischen und physischen Misshandlungen auf den Polizeistationen. Nach offiziellen Angaben sind 500 Demonstranten verhaftet und 200 verletzt worden. Viele Menschen werden noch vermisst.

Seattle * Göteborg * Genua :
Die Revolte ist gerechtfertigt!

"They'll walk over corpses to defend the power of the rich! Seattle—Gothenburg—Genoa: Revolt is legitimate!"

back of the carabinieri's jeep with its window smashed in. I could make out movement inside…. I think (but it's a bit confusing, I can't be categorical) that I saw, through the broken rear window, quite distinctly, two helmeted cops, bent over or crouching down, close together. I saw the "light spot" of a hand, chest height, along with, in the extension of this hand, a black and shiny mass.

I immediately realized that it could only be a handgun and that it was from this weapon that the detonations came. I assumed they had fired in the air to get away. The cops (because there seemed to be two of them) seemed agitated and were looking out the broken window, pivoting slightly, to see if any protesters were approaching. I couldn't see what was happening on the ground…. When I looked in front of me again, the carabinieri's car was gone. I got up and moved forward. There were very few people in front of me. I had the feeling that the noise was decreasing considerably for a few seconds, followed by some shouting.

I thought something was wrong, that something bad had happened. I saw a few people running and they stopped six or seven meters away from me on the left. I got closer. There were four or five people in a circle. I went around them and saw someone on the ground. A tear gas canister rolled by us. I shot it back at the cops who were not moving, still about thirty meters away. I turned around to look at the guy on the ground again. His feet were near mine. I remember his white T-shirt and his sticky black hood glistening with blood. I saw a puddle of blood widening from his head. I noticed he was oozing blood from his left eye socket. I realized it was a bullet that did this and that the shots had not been fired into the air. I took a few steps backward, holding my head....

The little group of six or seven cops had gotten even closer. They were maybe ten meters away. We backed off and the line of cops that was following the little lead group at a distance started to charge, so we got the hell out of there.

We didn't know what to do because we thought the guy on the ground was badly hit but not dead. We didn't check to see if his heart or pulse was still beating. If we had understood that he was already dead, obviously, we would never have left his body in the hands of the cops and we would have carried him to via Tolemaide where we would have caught an ambulance. (I don't dare to imagine the effect it would have had on the hundreds and hundreds of people who were there.)[24]

"Don't Clean Up the Blood": Armando Diaz School, July 21, Shortly Before Midnight

"Hey, are you coming? It's late and I'm tired!" Lena is standing by the doorway while I sit at the computer in one of the offices on the first floor of the Genoa Social Forum media center, a three-story building on a narrow side street. It's almost midnight on the night of July 21, and after two days of nonstop clashes, Lena logically wants to go to bed. Our home, at least for the night, is directly across from the media center. A place we and some others have relocated to just a few hours earlier, judging that the risk of a raid at Albaro, from where a large section of the black bloc had emerged in the previous days, was too high. So we've moved to a place we assume will be inhabited mainly by "less-confrontational elements" and which we've deemed to be significantly safer. A school located directly across the street from the media center: the Armando Diaz school.

In Loving Memory Of a Fallen Comrade

Carlo Giuliani is not a victim of police brutality. He is another dead man in the fields of social war. Carlo Giuliani is not a hero. He was revolutionary who - with dignity - decided to resist violently against what was oppressing him.

We remind all those who will try to build their political careers on t blood of our dead comrade, that he was one of those who you call "provocateur" and "hooligan." Carlo Giuliani does not fit in their funeral orations, or in their crocodile tears.

We do not feel pity for Carlo. He died for something we would die and for something that we have dedicated our lives. For freedom. Carlo will always live in the hearts of the revolutionaries. The struggle continues...

They murdered an anarchist

He lay on his back in the street. Eyes closed, arms at his side, legs, akimbo, blue jeans but shirtless. He looked almost peaceful, except for the massive pool of blood that trickled out of two bullet holes to his head.

This young anarchist, Carlo Guiliani, 23 years old, would never again protest, dance, sing, attend meetings, or embrace friends, brush his teeth, or cook breakfast, or love another anymore, murdered in cold blood by police on a sunny afternoon in Genoa, Italy.

Moments later, Carlo encircled the globe, entering homes thousands of kilometers away via the Internet, photographed from a dozen different angles. Once passionate, alive and angry. Seconds later, silenced and still, felled by two gun shots then run over by a police jeep escaping the murder scene.

Millions of us never knew you, Carlo, anarchist brother, but now your name is stenciled on the tongues of the speechless, your lifeless body now fixed in the minds of the incredulous, immortalized on the front page of newspapers. You, alone, within a circle of dozens of blue-helmeted riot cops, staring vacantly, and puzzled over your corpse.

Carlo, you died like a butchered dog in the street, so that a gang of wealthy, powerful criminals could shake hands, smile, slap each others' backs and drink fine Italian wine safely, knowing they had a 20,000 strong body guard, prepared to tear gas, beat and even murder protestors like you, like us, to allow them to conduct their sordid

We know they are not troubled by the death of one anarc or a handful of anarchists, they oversee the daily violence the State, of Capitalism obliterating whole families, comm ties, towns, regions, tribes, the needless, preventable de of millions worldwide.

One less 'troublemaker' won't stop them.

But Carlo, you tried, and they made you pay with your life

Your blood Carlo, was hosed away into sewers where it mingled with the blood of the homeless, with the blood of those forced to beg and starve everyday, with the blood broken boned, poisoned, beaten workers, men, women a children with the blood of others who died at the hands o police, soldiers and hired assassins, your blood infused all with a fierce rage. The rage of the forgotten, the voice the expendable victims of a money-crazed world gone m

And this blood red rage, rose from the sewers, and pour out of the mouths of screeching rats and spilled into the streets of Genoa, into palaces, boardrooms, reception ha limousines and stained them all red, a carpet of blood. It overflowed into rivers and oceans touched continents fa away and crept onto beaches at night staining them red. oozed its way onto signed agreements, memos and doc ments that seal our fate, but which we never see & stain them red, too.

To remind everyone of the rage of those like Carlo, who so others can profit. To remind them that this blood red has just begun

Back cover of the Summer/September 2001 issue of *Barricada*, in memory of Carlo Giuliani.

333

"Five more minutes and I'll be down," I reply. I'd like to say that I'm busy hastily writing dispatches for *Barricada* about the weekend's events. It's definitely what I *should* be doing. Writing about the widespread clashes on the 20th that turned Genoa into a citywide theater of open revolt and confrontation. About the death of Carlo Giuliani. About how we witnessed our movement splinter in front of our eyes, as those we thought of—despite our differences—as comrades embraced the wildest conspiracy theories about militant actions and declared us fascists and cops in disguise. About how on the day following the death of Carlo, well over a hundred thousand took to the streets—and while thousands of revolutionaries concentrated their rage against the cops and the symbols of capital, we at the same time had to fight off the hordes of authoritarian pacifists who declared us, for engaging in militant resistance, the culprits of repression. There was a lot to write home about.

But it's unlikely that I was doing my homework, considering the next issue of the magazine wouldn't come out until September. So it's more likely that I'm either obsessively checking the collective email or indulging in my out-of-control Indymedia newswire addiction (think Twitter before we had Twitter). Whatever the case may be, I'm not quite ready to log off. "Fine, I'll wait for you outside downstairs." I barely acknowledge her, while Oscar—who is lying in a corner of the room half awake—musters a half-hearted thumbs-up gesture. Lena exits the scene and heads downstairs, where Friend Noah, the Australians, and a few other comrades are still lounging around outside the building.

★

I've survived a shocking amount of extreme experiences relatively unscathed. I usually like to point out that while luck and fate do indeed always play their role—you can do everything right and still be arrested or injured, and you can likewise do everything wrong and still escape consequences—this one, what is about to happen, feels like the purest of dumb luck. An Inspector Gadget level of luck. Obsessiveness. Internet addiction. The dumbest of luck, a coin toss in our favor from the stars. Except for one enormous detail: We are here, hanging out in a restricted access space, instead of across the street. A media center that only credentialed journalists can enter. While we may not be journalists, we are indeed credentialed. You make your own luck.

Whatever it may be—those five minutes spared Lena, Oscar, and I (as well as several of our friends downstairs, who might have headed across the street with us) from experiencing what would possibly have been life-altering trauma in the form of days of beatings and tortures the likes of which most of us associate only with the darkest days of South American military dictatorships. A series of events so brutal and violent that Amnesty International would go on to declare them "the most serious human rights suspension in Europe, after World War 2."[25]

★

I don't know how long it's been since Lena headed downstairs. Thirty seconds? Maybe a minute? Two? Definitely somewhere in the span between nothing and not much. The earth begins to shake. A low, rumbling sound, growing louder and louder, rises from the street and through the open windows. Oscar bolts upright. I'm thinking it and he says it. "Earthquake?!" For the briefest of moments, I think to myself what a fittingly dramatic, if rather unfortunate, climax to the weekend it would be if it were to be capped off by a natural disaster.

As we race to the windows, we begin to hear the roaring of a jeep motor and uniformed men yelling, "Go! Go! Go!" We lean out the windows and immediately realize what is happening. The rumbling was the sound of hundreds of boots striking the pavement as they ran up the narrow street. Racing toward us from our right is a small army of cops, led by an armored van. We will later learn that these are mobile divisions of the Polizia di Stato from Genoa, Rome, and Milan, with support from a battalion of carabinieri. The gaggle of people lounging around outside the media center flees back inside. We're expecting to be raided, but the van turns to the right, toward the building directly across from us. They are aiming, at least at first, for the school.

The van struggles with the gates for a few moments. It's at this point that the mob of extremely agitated cops discovers Mark Covell standing in the street. He tries his best to explain to them in Italian that he is a journalist, but "within seconds, he was surrounded by riot-squad officers thrashing him with their sticks. For a while, he managed to stay on his feet but then a baton blow to the knee sent him crashing to the pavement." He is now "lying on his face in the dark, bruised and scared," but his ordeal is just beginning. "A police officer sauntered over to him and kicked him in the chest with such force that the entire lefthand side of his rib cage caved in, breaking half-a-dozen ribs whose splintered ends then shredded the membrane of his left lung." He hears police officers laughing, as "a group of officers occupied the time by strolling over to use Covell as a football. This bout of kicking broke his left hand and damaged his spine."[26]

The van succeeds in breaking open the gates, sending the 150 or so cops pouring into the school courtyard, racing toward the building's main door. Mark Covell's ordeal may be coming to an end, but for the ninety-three people inside the Diaz school, it is just beginning.[27] The building's doors swing open, and we watch with growing impotence and dread as the officers easily remove a hastily constructed barricade and enter the building. From here on, our vantage point is reduced to hearing the shrill screams of fear and pain coming from the open windows and getting the occasional glimpse of a baton-swinging officer as some scenes momentarily play out in front of the windows and in our view. But the testimonies that would later emerge from inside, where what Michelangelo Fournier (at the time assistant chief of Rome's mobile police squad) would later describe as looking like a "Mexican butcher shop" is unfolding, are harrowing.[28]

A 2008 article in *The Guardian* is illustrative in this regard, and also makes clear that those inside are not what one would call "the heart of the black bloc." As the police pour into the Diaz Pertini school, they can be heard yelling, "Black Bloc! We're going to kill you."[29] It's possible that, hyped up by their superiors or just misinformed—or quite simply not caring about the distinction—they truly believe that they are about to face the anarchists who "caused violent mayhem in parts of the city during demonstrations earlier in the day." But they are mistaken. So much so that this particular sleeping space, provided by the Genoa city council as a base for demonstrators, has "even posted guards to make sure that none of them [the anarchists] came in."[30]

One of the first to encounter the riot squad is thirty-five-year-old Belgian economist Michael Gieser. Gieser has just changed into his pajamas and is in line to use the bathroom when the raid starts. He describes how, believing in the power of dialogue, "he walked toward them saying, 'We need to talk.' He saw the padded jackets, the riot clubs, the helmets and the bandannas concealing the policemen's faces, changed his mind and ran up the stairs to escape."[31]

The account in *The Guardian* continues:

Others were slower. They were still in their sleeping bags. A group of 10 Spanish friends in the middle of the hall woke up to find themselves being battered with truncheons. They raised their hands in surrender. More officers piled in to beat their heads, cutting and bruising and breaking limbs, including the arm of a 65-year-old woman. At the side of the room, several young people were sitting at computers, sending emails home. One of them was Melanie Jonasch, a 28-year-old archaeology student from Berlin, who had volunteered to help out in the building and had not even been on a demonstration.

She still cannot remember what happened. But numerous other witnesses have described how officers set upon her, beating her head so hard with their sticks that she rapidly lost consciousness. When she fell to the ground, officers circled her, beating and kicking her limp body, banging her head against a near-by cupboard, leaving her finally in a pool of blood. Katherina Ottoway, who saw this happen, recalled: "She was trembling all over. Her eyes were open but upturned. I thought she was dying, that she could not survive this."[32]

According to *The Guardian*'s report, based on the work of public prosecutor Emilio Zucca, "none of those who stayed on the ground floor escaped injury." Zucca, with his own staff as well as the help of Covell, "collected hundreds of witness statements and analyzed 5,000 hours of video as well as thousands of photographs." According to Zucca's prosecution report, "In the space of a few minutes, all the occupants on the ground floor had been reduced to complete helplessness, the groans of the wounded mingling with the sound of calls for an ambulance."[33]

The Guardian continues:

In their fear, some victims lost control of their bowels. Then the officers of the law moved up the stairs. In the first-floor corridor they found a small group, including Gieser, still clutching his toothbrush: "Someone suggested lying down, to show there was no resistance. So I did. The police arrived and began beating us, one by one. I protected my head with my hands. I thought, 'I must survive.' People were shouting, 'Please stop.' I said the same thing ... It made me think of a pork butchery. We were being treated like animals, like pigs."

Officers broke down doors to the rooms leading off the corridors.... Gieser was out in the corridor: "The scene around me was covered in blood, everywhere. A policeman shouted 'Basta!' This word was like a window of hope. I understood it meant 'enough.' And yet they didn't stop. They continued with pleasure. In the end, they did stop, but it was like taking a toy away from a child, against their will."[34]

Police officers spread themselves across the building, beating and abusing essentially every single person they encounter: "Several victims describe a sort of system to the violence, with each officer beating each person he came across, then moving on to the next victim while his colleague moved up to continue beating the first. It seemed important that everybody must be hurt." In yet another testimony, a twenty-six-year-old care worker from London, Nicola Doherty, describes her partner, Richard Moth, lying across her to protect her: "I could just hear blow after blow on his body. The police were also leaning over Rich so they could hit the parts of my body which were exposed." In the course of the beating, she suffers a broken wrist while trying to protect her head with her arm.

The Guardian continues describing the intensity, ferocity, and sadism with which the carabinieri systematically comb the building: "In one corridor, they ordered a group of young men and women to kneel, the easier to batter them around the head and shoulders. This was where Daniel Albrecht, a 21-year-old cello student from Berlin, had his head beaten so badly that he needed surgery to stop bleeding in his brain." While using their batons as weapons against the defenseless demonstrators, they grip them at right angles, so as to strike hammer-like blows inflicting maximum damage.

Not content with the violence, the police show that humiliation is also the order of the day. Examples abound, such as "the officer who stood spread-legged in front of a kneeling and injured woman, grabbed his groin and thrust it into her face before turning to do the same to Daniel Albrecht kneeling beside her; the officer who paused amid the beatings and took a knife to cut off hair from his victims, including Nicola Doherty; the constant shouting of insults; the officer who asked a group if they were OK and who reacted to the one who said 'No' by handing out an extra beating."

Some are almost able to escape, such as Karl Boro, who makes it up to the roof only to reenter the building and receive a beating that leaves him with "heavy bruising to his arms and legs, a fractured skull, and bleeding in his chest cavity." Similar is the fate of Polish demonstrator Jaraslaw Engel, who is caught in the street by police drivers after exiting the school through the construction workers' scaffolding. The cops then "laid him on the ground and stood over him smoking while his blood ran out across the Tarmac."[35]

And finally there is Lena Zuhlke and her partner, Niels Martensen, two students from Germany who find a hiding place inside a cupboard on the top floor of the school. Eventually discovered, "Martensen was dragged out and beaten by a dozen officers standing in a semicircle around him" while "Zuhlke ran across the corridor and hid in the loo." Again, the chronicle in *The Guardian* is painfully eloquent:

> In the corridor, they set about her like dogs on a rabbit. She was beaten around the head then kicked from all sides on the floor, where she felt her rib cage collapsing. She was hauled up against the wall where one officer kneed her in the groin while others carried on lashing her with their batons. She slid down the wall and they hit her more on the ground: "They seemed to be enjoying themselves and, when I cried out in pain, it seemed to give them even more pleasure."
>
> Police officers found a fire extinguisher and squirted its foam into Martensen's wounds. His partner was dragged by her hair and tossed down the stairs head-first. Eventually, they dragged Zuhlke into the ground-floor hall, where they had gathered dozens of prisoners from all over the building in a mess of blood and excrement. They threw her on top of two other people. They were not moving, and Zuhlke drowsily asked them if they were alive. They did not reply, and she lay there on her back, unable to move her right arm, unable to stop her left arm and her legs twitching, blood seeping out of her head wounds. A group of police officers walked by, and each one lifted the bandanna which concealed his identity, leaned down and spat on her face."[36]

While we in the media center are still unaware of the unusual ferocity of what's happening across the street from us, it's clearly nothing good, and we're pretty certain that our building will be next.

We're sitting on the floor in the hallway, maybe forty or fifty of us, in a deathly silence. The decision has been made to all be in the hallway together, so as not to leave anybody alone and exposed to potential violence from the police, who have indeed entered the media building—fifty-nine of them, to be precise. And so we sit on both sides of the hallway with our backs against the walls, as masked police officers pace menacingly back and forth. The cops are like characters out of a second-rate police thriller. Beer bellies, hairy forearms, and if we could see their faces, I'd bet good money that at least a few of them would have mustaches. One paces quietly but menacingly, striking his baton against the wall at random intervals and in the vicinity of the heads of those who dare to make a sound. Another one alternates between yelling threats and insults at us.

They saunter along the hallway, looking us up and down one by one. I feel Lena give me the slightest of nudges with her shoulder. I turn to catch her trying to point with her eyes at my shoes. Immediately, it's clear what she's trying to call my attention to, and I can feel the cold sweat of worry starting to form on my neck and trickle down my back. My left shoe carries with it the telltale signs of street clashes— that unique mix of dirt and difficult-to-explain splatters of different colors of paint, mixed with splashes of the telltale grayish-white faded stains of whatever the hell it is we throw on ourselves to combat the effects of the tear gas. Am I being paranoid? Are they even looking for specific people to arrest here? I don't know, but this is the most concerned and scared I've been all weekend, all summer, maybe even all my militant life. Because I'm acutely aware that if things were to suddenly go south here, I have absolutely no agency in the situation. There is no degree of fanaticism, no smooth talking, no fast running, no combative instinct that could possibly save me. The space between me and the butchering across the street, not to mention the one still to come at the police station, is nothing more than the whims and attentiveness of the two masked cops pacing the hallway in front of us. Just as I'm doing my best to discreetly position my feet so as to hide one shoe with the other, a woman's voice echoes loudly from the entrance to the hallway.

The woman, elegantly dressed, storms into the hallway like she owns the place. Our initial thought is that she is some high-ranking cop. But she immediately heads toward the cop who seems to be in charge and begins berating him. "What the hell do you think you're doing? We have rights in Italy, you can't treat these people like this. You need to get out of here right now," was the general gist of it as it was later translated for us. Apparently, she was some parliamentarian who just happened to be giving an interview with mainstream media on one of the other floors. Her presence, and her words, are like showing a cross to vampires. As quickly as they appeared, they left. Although, as we would learn in later days, the reason might not have been the presence of the parliamentarian, but rather that they had accomplished the task they had entered the building to perform.

We make our way outside and take it all in:

Ambulances began to arrive and the massacre that occurred in front began to become evident. We watched the horror unfurl before us. About 50 or so riot police stood guard in front of the school gates, and vans, trucks, and re-enforcements waited at either end of the street.

One by one our comrades were brought out on stretchers, some conscious and others not, and several still inside the sleeping bags they were in when the police arrived.

The cop who appeared to be in charge made a show of pulling on a warm up jacket which had an Italian flag sash around it. Evidently, they were quite proud of the work they had done.[37]

Eventually, the cops leave and we walk over to the school, to document what happened as well as to collect the comrades' belongings. Immediately, the brutality of what has just happened comes into graphic focus: "Upon entering, the sight one was greeted with was of nothing but blood, flesh, teeth, and urine. Everywhere somebody had been sleeping one could see a corresponding pool of blood."[38]

Oscar, speaking twenty years later, still vividly recalls the scene: "There were pools of blood everywhere, puddles where people had pissed themselves, teeth scattered on the floor, blood stains on walls and furniture. That's the main thing: teeth, blood, and urine. I remember looking at you and thinking that I couldn't believe what we had managed to escape. But on the other hand, I remember thinking that we always somehow managed to walk away unscathed from really bad situations, and that it was thanks to your fanaticism. While some close comrades were in there, as usual it was again mainly the pacifists, the unorganized, the low-hanging fruit who the cops ended up getting. Those in constant motion—like you, probably answering an email or drafting a text—might face higher consequences in general if caught, but are rarely caught."

Back at the Diaz school, surrounded by the smell of urine and the sight of blood-stained walls, I'm taking it all in. Making it a conscious point to remember every detail of this experience, to let it harden me. Should my understanding of the vicious and violent nature of the state ever falter or my conviction ever wane. But I'm thinking not just of the barbarity of this raid. I'm taking note of everything we've lived over the past few days. Of our experiences with the reformists, the NGOs, the Stalinists, the pacifists, and even some who share with us the label of anarchist. Of who shares our convictions both in word as well as in deed, and who doesn't. Of who stood side by side with me, with us, when it was literally the sea to one side, the cliffs to the other, the cops to our front.

I remember a comrade's raised fist as he was being stretchered away from the Diaz school.

I'm drawing the lessons of Genoa. I interpret that these are all signs of an ever-growing and intensifying clash. Of a state fearful of us and lashing out ever more aggressively. The only retreat we understand is forward, and we have no intention of backing away from whatever might come next.

The Lessons of Genoa: Beyond the Antiglobalization Movement, from Riot to Insurrection

The scene is reminiscent of war movies, when children and refugees sporting faces weary with exhaustion and fear board trains transporting them out of the conflict zone. Hundreds of us have loaded ourselves onto several buses and traveled as a caravan from the media center to Genoa's main train station. Our objective: a train to nearby Milan, where the historic Leoncavallo social center is providing shelter (not to mention food) for activists as they make their way out of Genoa.

We're an eclectic mix on the buses, mainly composed of "refugees" from the media center, those fortunate enough to find ourselves inside it when the cops invaded the Diaz school across the street. The tense silence isn't just a factor of our collective exhaustion. Beginning with the generalization of the clashes, intensified with Carlo Giuliani's death, and reaching its boiling point with the raid on the Diaz school, there has been a veritable storm of rumors, conspiracies, and mutual accusations laying bare the tensions and contradictions between the very different political currents and traditions that make up the broader so-called antiglobalization movement.

We look at each other with silent distrust, and in some cases thinly veiled contempt. Our frayed nerves and the raw emotion of what many of us have lived through in the last forty-eight hours makes for some short fuses. The clashes are one thing, and at least for our spectrum nothing too out of the ordinary. But a comrade is dead, and most people on this bus have only barely escaped South American-level beatings and torture inside the Diaz school by virtue of pure strokes of luck. Instead we were forced to stand idly by as we heard soul-curdling screams of pain and terror coming from our comrades across the street.

★

When it came time to assign responsibility for these events, I like to think most of us anarchists took the strategically sound and politically mature route: The clashes are the expected consequence of an assertive and growing revolutionary movement encountering an occupying army of twenty thousand cops. Carlo's death is unfortunate and tragic, and we fully intend to avenge it, but it's not surprising considering the virulence of the clashes and how our fighters at times overwhelmed and overran the carabinieri. The Diaz school raid? The wounded ego of those same forces of repression, on the one hand hungering for vengeance and on the other under significant pressure from their leadership to show that they had struck a blow against "the black bloc" with a media-friendly display of arrested foreigners and confiscated weapons.

But among the reformists, the Ya Basta!/Tute Bianche spectrum, and the pacifists, and incredibly even picked up by some who we thought to be comrades, a completely different narrative had taken hold: a conspiracy-laden narrative not unlike that which took hold of so many well-intentioned liberals during the George Floyd uprising, in which white supremacists set fire to Minneapolis's Third Precinct and cops were placing convenient stacks of bricks on street corners. The post-Genoa narrative was so mired in conspiracy theory, so ignorant of the standard procedures and activities of undercover cops in social movements and mass mobilizations, so incapable of imagining regular people taking agency and control in choosing their forms of struggle, and so convinced that any exertion of violence outside the channels of the state can only be the work of manipulation and outside agitators that I still have trouble representing it objectively.

In this fairy tale narrative, which is presented as "not an opinion but a fact, underlined by testimonies and images," a "police black bloc" appeared at regular intervals in Genoa, destroying property and giving police pretext to attack otherwise peaceful demonstrators.[39] The existence of this mysterious police black bloc was taken to be undeniably confirmed thanks to pictures of groups of undercover cops dressed in black sometimes standing around and sometimes discreetly moving from demonstrators to behind police lines. According to a spokesperson from the People's Global Action Network, "There exists numerous evidence (photos, videos, testimonies) that a large part of the damages were perpetrated by these fake black blocs (composed of police or fascists)."[40] Similarly, representing another aspect of the conspiracy theory—that when not directly carried out by cops, property damage in Genoa was permitted by cops—two ATTAC spokespeople claimed with confidence that "any person present in Genoa saw how the forces of order allowed the black blocs to devastate the city."[41]

This conspiracy theory permeated even into anarchist and antifascist circles, as evidenced by the fact that all the above quotes were in fact published as matter-of-fact statements in a 2002 book published by the French anarchist and antifascist No Pasarán network (*Gênes: Multitudes en marche contre l'Empire*, or "Genoa: Multitudes in action against empire"). One of the most vocal and well-known advocates for it was none other than David Graeber, who wrote:

> The police had provided a "Black Bloc" of their own. Over and over, on Saturday came reports of a mysterious group of 30 to 40 "anarchists" whom nobody else had ever seen before; huge guys, for the most part, and extraordinarily violent—willing, even, to physically assault other (real) anarchists who tried to stop them from attacking small shops and setting fire to cars.
>
> By the end of the day, after countless sightings of these "Black Blockers" emerging from police stations, hobnobbing

with carabinieri or assisting with arrests, the only question left in anyone's mind was whether one was dealing with undercover cops or fascist vigilantes working with the police. (The tendency of carabinieri stations to sport portraits of Mussolini and fascist insignia inside suggested this might have been a somewhat blurry distinction.)

The phony bloc would suddenly appear, smashing windows and overturning dumpsters, right next to each column the cops wanted to attack; the police themselves would show up a few minutes afterward and proceed to lob massive amounts of high-intensity tear gas and pepper spray into the area just after the phony bloc left; this would be followed by baton charges meant to break bones and splatter blood.[42]

Graeber and others are in fact correct in some of their observations, just comically incorrect in the conclusions they draw from them. Were there undercover cops among the bloc, usually in groups? Absolutely, and we don't even need to see the images of those potential cops to assume so. In fact, you should always assume that to be the case, as a matter of basic operational practice at militant demonstrations and mass mobilizations. They are always there doing what they do. In a mobilization such as Genoa, that means things like "identifying the national origins of participants, identifying particular individuals, evaluating how many experienced and organized groups are moving amongst the mass of isolated and inexperienced people, studying riot strategies from close up, evaluating offensive material available (quality, quantity …), listening to conversations or otherwise gathering intelligence (objectives, routes, informal organization, etc.)."[43] As a very standard operating procedure, they generally do not intervene or attempt to make arrests on site, except sometimes once people are dispersing, for obvious reasons.

And yes, there absolutely were times when elements of the black bloc were able to calmly partake in property damage or otherwise move around relatively undisturbed. But the reason for this is exactly the same as the one the good demonstrators of Graeber's Genoa were tear-gassed or otherwise attacked soon after the appearance of people dressed in black—and it's not because of the success of a cynical and brilliantly executed plan to manipulate violent anarchists in order to beat innocent demonstrators. The actual explanation, as is often the case when debunking conspiracy theories, is much more simple: because the bloc, like most other groups during those days, had been dispersed into multiple groups acting autonomously and dynamically throughout the city. This overwhelmed the cops, who simply could not attack all elements in all places at all times, and also created a city pockmarked by a constantly shifting terrain of clashes and front lines. And so, such as was our case during the two days of clashes, sometimes we fought intense mass pitched battles with the cops, sometimes we were caught in panicked escapes by people retreating from battles we didn't even know had taken place, sometimes our retreats would land us smack in the middle of a mob of pacifists or the Tute Bianche, and sometimes we had the luxury of peacefully lounging around and resting while some- body took apart the nearest bank or built barricades for the inevitable arrival of the cops. On just about any given street you could turn a corner and suddenly find yourself in the middle of any of the above scenarios.

Graeber would double down on this perspective and conspiracy theory in a 2002 piece in *New Left Review* in which he states that the "scrambling of conventional categories" of confrontation, as the Ya Basta! spectrum interpreted the mediated spectacle of choreographed "clashes" that they had developed, was so challenging to the state and the forces of order that it "makes them desperate to bring things back to familiar territory (simple violence): even to the point, as in Genoa, of encouraging fascist hooligans to run riot as an excuse to use over- whelming force against everybody else."[44]

This is dangerous logic, because it implies that if we behave well enough, or act "creatively" enough, we can somehow achieve our political objectives without incurring the wrath of the state. It is the liberal logic of the bad demonstrators bringing misfortune upon the good, peaceful, and reasonable demonstrators—but shrouded in radical vocabulary. Not to mention that in the specific Italian context, it is even more acutely misguided and ahistorical. As one comrade succinctly put it, "Fascist culture in the police has remained unchallenged since the end of the Resistance," which is still permeated by a "brand of old-style fascism where everyone is a communist and communists deserve a good beating," regardless of circumstance.[45] As importantly, if not more, we would argue that the threat to the state, and what led it to "the use of overwhelming force against everybody," was definitely not the theatrics of a sector of the antiglobalization movement that had taken to self-policing its tactics in the face of an opponent who never intended to return it any such courtesy. A self-policing developed so as to make radical politics more palatable to the mainstream media and appeal to the morality of a society that views the state as all-powerful and rejects any challenges to its monopoly on violence. The threat to the state was an ever-growing international movement, becoming more and more assertive, knitting networks across the globe among different political cultures and backgrounds; converging struggles for freedom of movement, for workplace democracy, and against the prison-industrial complex; and developing a praxis of direct democracy and militant confrontation. That this convergence of struggles and the intensity of the clashes, as well as the widespread abandonment of the Ya Basta! spectacle in favor of organic and unmediated clashes with the state and its forces of order, reached a high point in Genoa—one neither the state nor the reformists could control—is what truly threatened them and spawned the absurd conspiracy theories.

The reality in Genoa was that tens of thousands of people from across the globe and from all walks of life came together and attacked the state and its defenders. Some, like the several-thousand-strong black bloc, came with that explicit intent, while others, thousands of disaffected people from the Ya Basta! bloc and thousands of locals, were simply radicalized or inspired into action as the days developed. This is what put Genoa, if only temporarily, out of the control of the state and generated its violent backlash. Where the inadvertent cheerleaders of the state as all-powerful and all-consuming saw a conspiracy that interfered with the controlled and mediated spectacle they had planned for, we saw organized resistance fuse with genuine and spontaneous rebellion. This is something Ya Basta! and the reformists from ATTAC (Association pour la Taxation des Transactions financières et pour l'Action Citoyenne, or "Association for the Taxation of Financial Transactions and for Citizen Action") and company had not come for. David Graeber and Ya Basta! essentially explicitly state as much when, referencing the death of Carlo Giuliani, Graeber writes that "as soon as they heard that someone had died, Ya Basta! pulled their people out. This was not the sort of battle they had come for."[46]

And here is where we agree. Obviously, we had not come with the intention of seeing a comrade be killed. But we had most definitely come with the purpose of creating as massive and intense of a confrontation with the state as possible—with no concern for media opinions or mediated clashes, which is not what Ya Basta! and the reformists had come for. Riding on the bus out of Genoa, looking at the faces around us, we began coming to a lot of conclusions that might seem self-evident today but were revelatory then. A lot of the conclusions we would soon outline in *Barricada* in a piece titled "The Lessons of Genoa." That a lot of these people might be well intentioned. That we might indeed have a lot of things in common. That the antiglobalization movement might be a convenient sea for us to swim in, both tactically and as far as radicalizing sympathetic people eager to change the world around them. But that we were not, and could not, call ourselves one movement. It wasn't just our tactics that were different (something that in and of itself would have of course been fine). Our objectives were different. They wanted a controlled and mediated spectacle and were shocked when neither the cops nor the anarchists nor other discontents followed the script. The NGOs and reformists—of which Ya Basta! was essentially the "radical vanguard"—wanted an act of mass street theater, with the participation of a controlled and docile mass, directed by them. As large as possible, but tame, so as to be used as a bargaining chip to earn a seat at the table, to manage capitalism, to tame it and render it more humane. Our objective, on the other hand, and in the words of a great early twenty-first-century Greek anarchist philosopher, was to "make total destroy." Or as *Barricada* put it:

> We as anarchists are not interested in watered down demonstrations and false declarations of war. We are not interested in, and believe there to be no such thing as, a common ground for dialogue with the rulers and exploiters of the Earth. Likewise, we have no interest in their political schemes and maneuvers. We are indeed "the ungovernable force," content with nothing less than total social revolution with the aim of a creating a new society based on the principles of workers self-management, mutual aid, decentralization, direct democracy, freedom, and socialism.[47]

To us, the periodic summits that marked the watershed moments of the antiglobalization movement were symbolic moments of governance, synonymous with symbolic moments of dominance. And as such we were determined to at the very least not allow them to pass incident-free,

Poster released in the aftermath of Genoa by antifa groups from Germany.

and in the case of Genoa move from a symbolic moment of governance to a practical moment of insurrection. We left Genoa determined to "shed the weight of trying to appease the rest of the 'anti-globalization movement'" and "begin focusing on creating a real revolutionary anti-capitalist movement from below" that satisfies itself with "nothing less than the total destruction of state and capital."[48] Summits from now on would be potential moments of insurrection and, as before, of symbolic messaging to the state. But also a place to assert ourselves as a movement in the face of the NGO-reformist complex of the antiglobalization movement. We would "constantly go where they go" in order to "ruin their parties, crash their debates, and turn their futile attempts to appeal to power into insurrectionary events where people are encouraged to think and act autonomously."[49] In what is essentially a definitive statement of divorce in the family, in "The Lessons of Genoa," *Barricada* called for a strategy toward the reformist wing of the antiglobalization movement of "constant harassment, sabotage, exposure, discrediment, propaganda, action, and counter action."[50]

But if our messaging and stance toward other actors of the antiglobalization "movement" were shifting ("movement" being a word we

349

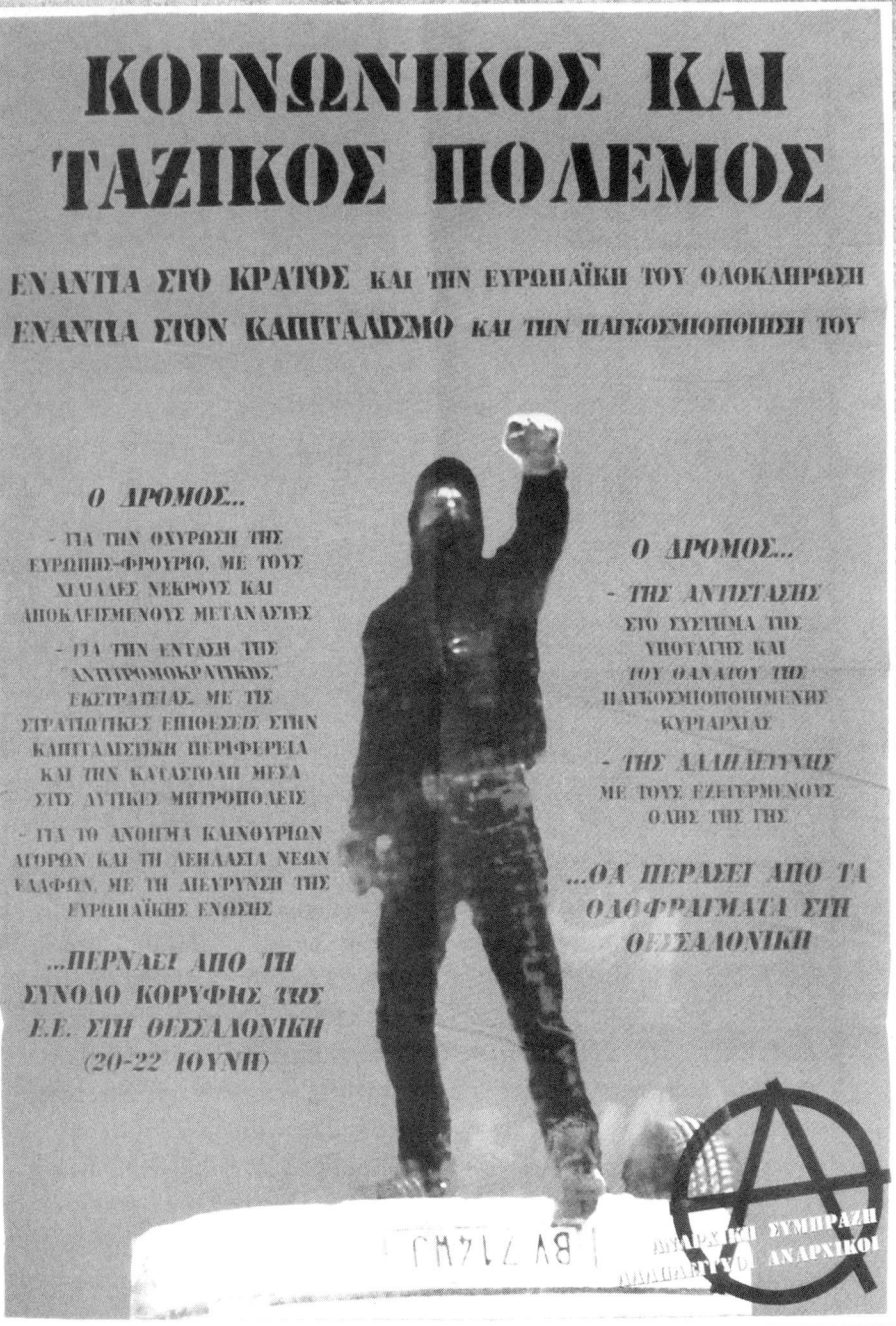

Julien Terzics, ex–Red Warrior, drummer of Brigada Flores Magon, and CNT member, stands defiantly in the face of the forces of repression. Poster by Athenian anarchists with image from Genoa and headline "Social and Class War."

began putting quotes around), the essence of our strategy and messaging toward the rest of society remained unchanged. If anything, we left Genoa even more firmly convinced of its validity. That capitalist globalization was not an inevitability, that there were indeed masses of people resisting, and doing so not just with words but with very concrete and tangible actions. It was also a message of disobedience and rebellion to those in power. No walls can stop us. No borders can contain us. No armies of cops can defeat us. And every time we successfully delivered that message, we grew as a movement. Not only did we attract new people to us, but our activists and militants grew bolder and more daring, making us not only more numerous but, just as importantly, more combative, more confident, and more effective.

While liberals and reformists, and even many who were at least on a theoretical and intellectual level revolutionaries, shied away from confrontations as they grew increasingly violent, we saw the increase in repression and confrontation as a partial victory in and of itself. Not at all because we believed, as many in the antiglobalization movement seemed to, that being victimized by the state was somehow morally positive and politically useful. Completely to the contrary, we actively made it a point to criticize that mentality and say that if the state was lashing out, it was precisely because it was under attack and because we had declared war on it. It was not a coincidence that *Barricada*'s post-Gothenburg analysis was loudly headlined "We Are Victors, Not Victims," nor was it a coincidence that many anarchists, both insurrectionary and otherwise, from Greece to Boston and many places in between, enthusiastically adopted the "Another War Is Possible" slogan adapted from the antiglobalization movement's "Another World Is Possible."

The way we saw it, the democratic state's power rests on consent. The greater the level of consent in society, the less the state is required to take off its peaceful mask and resort to the violence at its root to maintain itself. The greater that level of consent, the more cover the state will receive from society at large when faced with resistance, a society that will cheer the violence used by the state to suppress dissent. The more frequent, more effective, and more massive the confrontation, the greater the rupture in social consent. The greater that rupture is— the deeper the attack on the state's monopoly of violence—the more room rebels have to build dual power and to develop, establish, and strengthen structures of resistance and bases from which to launch our attacks and wage our war (be they networks, organizations, occupied spaces, or what have you).

Be Realistic, Demand the Impossible: Another War Is Possible

I sit slouched and tired on the train out of Genoa. As we begin our trip toward Milan, the hills of the city come theatrically into view. Physically I'm on the train, but figuratively I'm back on that hillside. The glow of the fire on the prison walls has burned the moment into my memory. On that hillside, under the trees, with those comrades, where I realized I want nothing else and nothing less than this. Not just in the pursuit of the anarchist idea, but in all of life, in everything I do and live. If it's not epic and awe-inspiring, life-changing and all-encompassing, and at the same time beautiful and enthralling while dangerous and terrifying—I don't want it. I will never know if I was born this way or if the collective experiences of our youth made me this way, but it has ended up being my nature in life, love, work, and sport. A double-edged sword giving me the power to constantly demand, and expect to achieve, incredible and impossible things—like years later recovering my broken body and making it stronger than ever despite a cacophony of experts telling me that there was no hope—while also a brutally fanatical and exhausting voice rarely allowing me to understand when a cause is lost, when the cops are too many, the fascists are too strong, or the love of the person you want to grow old with has been irretrievably extinguished. I blame and thank Genoa, Gothenburg, a hundred battles that came after, and a thousand nights conspiring to attack prisons and presidential palaces for the person I am. For planting so deep within my conscience the belief that anything and everything is always somehow possible.

How could I believe anything other than that if I crashed into the wall enough times, alone or ideally with my friends, if we threw ourselves at it with enough courage and conviction regardless of the steel, stone, or cement meant to stop us, that it would cede? We were barely in our twenties and had already toppled fences made to protect the world's most powerful with the ease of a summer breeze blowing away a feather. We were told it was impossible to live in or organize out of places that didn't belong to us, took them regardless, and stayed for years. We had crashed presidential parade routes, hunted fascists, and done it all while joyously living, laughing, and loving (yes, I've just quoted this deeply intellectual work of pop culture art).

We had no idea that soon we would be orphans of a movement. Some moving on, some scattered across the world, some injured, some imprisoned, others exiled. For all we knew, this was the world and would always be. As far as we could tell, now that our friends numbered in the thousands rather than the dozens or hundreds, we could allow ourselves a future in which we could live, organize, and rebel ever more boldly. That as the slogan went, another world *was* indeed possible, and we would wage our war—the social war—to ensure that possibility became reality.

If we could dream and achieve anything, no matter the enemies, no matter the armies of the state, no matter the tanks—why wouldn't the logical next step be to burn down the prisons, storm the palaces, and build where they once stood the society of our dreams?

ACKNOWLEDGMENTS

I've been fortunate enough to travel an incredibly long road, along which I've had the privilege of meeting countless people. Individuals who have touched my life, shared in my militancy, and helped shape my understanding not just of what anarchism means and what it means to be an anarchist, but also of the existential concepts of solidarity, mutual aid, friendship, and resilience. I will not list them all here, because I am unable to. Too many are names I never knew, as our movement, lifestyle, and security culture demanded of us, and others the passage of time has, embarrassingly, taken from me, but they are no less important. Most importantly, though, it is because this work—and my limited but earnest and honest attempts to re-create the spirit and tone of our times is, among other things, precisely that— is a thank-you in and of itself to all the friends and comrades with whom I shared the road, the general assembly, the barricade, and the conspirative moment.

There are some, however, whom I do need to specifically mention.

Gabriel Kuhn and all the participants of the CrimethInc. ex–Workers Collective in general—as well as one of them very specifically—come to mind, as without their prodding this book (or any of the other many books that have sprung from this project) would simply not exist. They believed in me, trusted me, were patient with me, and generally held my hand throughout the process (as did the kind people at PM Press).

Another thanks is owed to the many comrades, some who still believe in the anarchist ideal and others who do not, who accepted to be interviewed and gave me numerous hours of their time so that we could reminisce about that era, flesh out ideas, remember grievances, and unwrap memories that had merged and meshed together so that we could correctly represent the historical events in this book. This includes the Barricada friends, Jorge and Old Man Oscar; Victor, Mateo, Patre, and all the comrades from Brigada Flores Magon and crew; Felham from Antifascist Action Stockholm; Nicolas Phebus from NEFAC Quebec and another ex-NEFAC comrade who now lives in the Carolinas; Edgar Partisano from Catalunya; and several Athenian comrades whose testimonies mainly ended up in other forthcoming book projects.

Last, but certainly not least, the family I have chosen. My mother, who now that I am a parent myself I understand must have existed in a state of never-ending anxiety and worry, knowing as she did that if there was a stone in the air or a street on fire essentially *anywhere* in the world, there was a good chance her child was involved. My sister, who has been all things at all times to me—psychologist, counselor, cheerleader, and generally infallible support at my side. My children, whom I love endlessly, and who have bravely borne the consequences of actions not of their choosing. My partner, who might not share in my ideals or vision of the world but understands that these ideals are the parameters that shape my conscience and make me who I am, and who I am is a person she chooses to love and share her life with.

Nadie se salva solo.

NOTES

Foreword

1   Francis Fukuyama, *The End of History and the Last Man* (Free Press, 1992).
2   Patricia Cohen, "Why It Seems Everything We Knew About the Global Economy Is No Longer True," *New York Times*, June 18, 2023, https://www.nytimes.com/2023/06/18/business/economy/global-economy-us-china.html.

Introduction

1   "I am, somehow, less interested in the weight and convolutions of Einstein's brain than in the near certainty that people of equal talent have lived and died in cotton fields and sweatshops." Stephen Jay Gould, *The Panda's Thumb: More Reflections in Natural History* (W.W. Norton, 1980).
2   Karl Marx, *Critique of the Gotha Program* (PM Press, 2022).

Prologue

1   Peter Kropotkin, "'Anarchism,' from *The Encyclopaedia Britannica*, 1910," Anarchy Archives, accessed October 25, 2024, http://dwardmac.pitzer.edu/Anarchist_Archives/kropotkin/britanniaanarchy.html.
2   Chairman Gonzalo, leader of the Communist Party of Peru–Shining Path, was captured by a Peruvian antiterrorist squad in Lima, Peru, on September 12, 1992. At the time, the Maoist insurgency controlled large swaths of the Peruvian countryside and boasted over twenty thousand armed militants.

2   33 Rue des Vignoles

1   To be honest, it has for a while only been partially cobblestone lined, as most of the alley past the entrance has been cemented for a few decades now. But let's please not allow a detail like reality to get in the way of painting a pretty picture.
2   Officially, the CNT is a revolutionary union and "apolitical," therefore not

explicitly calling itself anarcho-syndicalist. Also, for the sake of objectivity: At that time, there were two CNTs in France. One, generally referred to as CNT-F, with its headquarters at 33 Rue des Vignoles in Paris, and the other the CNT-Bordeaux faction. The split took place in 1993, mainly, but not exclusively, around the question of participation in workplace union elections. The CNT-F, with its approximately five thousand adherents to the one or two hundred of the CNT-Bordeaux, was the significantly larger of the two. In the present day, there has been yet another split, the details of which I am less familiar with, which took place in 2012 and in which yet another CNT, under the name CNT–Workers' Solidarity, has emerged.

3 Le Conseil National de SIA, "Brève histoire de S.I.A.: Son origine, son oeuvre, ses buts," article published in the 1978 edition of the SIA's annual calendar, https://cras31.info/IMG/pdf/sur_sia_extrait_du_calendrier_1978.pdf; translation by the author.

4 CNT-AIT, "S.I.A.: Une autre conception de la solidarité," CNT-AIT Toulouse website, October 21, 2017, http://www.cntaittoulouse.lautre.net/spip.php?article887; translation by the author.

5 Nicolás Pan-Montojo and Guiomar del Ser, "Remembering the 4,427 Spaniards Who Died at the Mauthausen Concentration Camp," El País, August 9, 2019, https://english.elpais.com/elpais/2019/08/09/inenglish/1565343422_748912.html.

6 Sueña Radio, "CNT Españoles en el exilio," radio interview with Manuel Rodriguez, January 6, 2016, audio, 25:45, https://archive.org/details/AaaMontajeManuelCNTEnElExilio/AaaMontajeManuelCntEnElExilio5.mp3; translation by the author.

7 Sueña Radio, "CNT Españoles en el exilio."

8 Evelyn Mesquida, La Nueve: Los españoles que liberaron París (Ediciones B, 2016); translation by the author.

9 Mesquida, La Nueve.

10 Miguel Íñiguez, "Nota biográfica de Manuel Lozano," Todos los Nombres, accessed October 29, 2024, http://www.todoslosnombres.org/content/biografias/manuel-pinto-queiroz-ruiz; translation by the author.

11 Mesquida, La Nueve.

12 Mesquida, La Nueve.

13 Françoise Cariès, "Ces Espagnols ont libéré Paris," La Dépêche, August 23, 2004, https://www.ladepeche.fr/article/2004/08/23/256182-ces-espagnols-ont-libere-paris.html; translation by the author.

14 Mesquida, La Nueve, 241.

15 Mesquida, La Nueve, 119.

16 Laurent Giménez, "Agosto 1944: Los Españoles en la liberación de Paris; Testimonio de un anarquista español," Memoria Libertaria, August 27, 2018, from a pamphlet originally written in 1985, https://memorialibertaria.org/agosto-1944-los-espanoles-en-la-liberacion-de-paris-testimonio-de-un-anarquista-espanol/; translation by the author.

17 Giménez, "Agosto 1944."

18 Giménez, "Agosto 1944."

19 Sueña Radio, "CNT Españoles en el exilio."

20 Commission Journal, "CNT: Après la scission, quel futur?," Alternative Libertaire, January 6, 2013, https://unioncommunistelibertaire.org/CNT-Apres-la-scission-quel-futur-5164; translation by the author.

21 That band, Brigada Flores Magon, would a short time later become four skinhead guys and one Black woman, and rapidly go on to become an international reference for anarchist and antifascist punk rock and Oi! music. As you might have deciphered from my description of them, they were a "redskin" band, which has nothing to do with the anti-Indigenous slur but is rather short for "red skinheads," a term used to refer to left-wing skinheads. Their drummer, Julien Terzics, was one of the founding members of the legendary antifascist street gang the Red Warriors and can even be seen sitting in the passage of the 33 Rue des Vignoles in the relatively well-known documentary *Antifa: Chasseurs de skins*, which translates to "Antifa: Skinhead hunters." The name might sound confusing, considering I just mentioned that they too were skinheads, but they referred to themselves as "reds" and to the Nazis as "skins."

Brigada Flores Magon and the crew around them would later provide a great deal of the impulse behind the formation first of RASH (Red and Anarchist Skinheads) Paris and soon after an entire network of RASH groups across France. RASH Paris in turn produced the fanzine *Barricata* (the first few issues of which I'm proud to have collaborated on), which eventually grew into a well-respected and professionally produced magazine that ran for almost a decade.

To this day, the influence and contributions of Brigada Flores Magon, its ex- or current members, and its crew are very much outsized for what basically began as a gang of young, street-level leftists. Along with over two decades as a band playing in support of anarchist and antifascist causes while terrorizing Nazis and nationalists across Europe, Julien Terzics was the owner of the Parisian "antifa bar" Le Saint Sauveur, Yann Levy is a respected movement photographer, Fred Alpi has published a book and is an accomplished singer-songwriter, Victor "Le Chinois" runs the record label Discos Machete in Mexico, and Nicolas Norrito is the cofounder of the prolific anarchist publishing house Libertalia, which also runs a bookstore in the Paris suburb of Montreuil. The anarchist record label and clothing company Fire and Flames, which turned twenty years old in 2022, also grew out of the crew around BFM.

22 Interview with Victor, 2020.

23 Interview with Victor, 2020.

24 Editorial in *Pravda*, October 17, 1937.

3 "Europe, Jeunesse, Révolution"

1 One of these confrontations, between a small group of antifascists and Jeunesses Nationalistes Révolutionnaires (Revolutionary Nationalist Youth) members on June 5, 2013, even claimed the life of a young antifascist and CNT member, Clement Meric.

2 For the record, the CNT officially defines itself as "revolutionary syndicalist" rather than anarcho-syndicalist. In practice, it seems to be "a distinction without a difference."

3 With notable and tragic exceptions, such as the 1995 murder of seventeen-year-old Ibrahim Ali by a Front National postering crew in Marseille.

4 Tristan and Matéo, "Ce que c'était d'être un skinhead antiraciste dans la France des années 1990," *VICE France*, November 15, 2016, https://www.vice.com/fr/article/wdmaey/etre-un-skin-antiraciste-dans-la-france-des-annees-1990; translation by the author.

5 Incredibly, I have been able to find video of another one of the confrontations with the fascists, at the same spot as the one described above, that occurred a

few months later. The video is from November 1998. The location is exactly the same, as are the motives on both sides. In this case, the fascist group is a little less "diverse" than in the confrontation described above, and our dispersal is due to the intervention of the police. You can find it at the following link, or by searching on YouTube for "Manif Anti IVG Télé Bocal." If you speak French, the whole thing is worth watching; if you don't and are just there for the superficial action, then what you are looking for begins at roughly 2:40: https://www.youtube.com/watch?v=8dDS0T_flgQ.

6   I use "skinhead" in connection with Nazis very grudgingly. While there have of course been many who identify as skinheads who are Nazis or fascists, even the vast majority in the 1980s, original skinhead subculture was a blend of Jamaican and British working-class youth influences. Racist skinheads are therefore inherently a contradiction.

7   Marc-Aurèle Vecchione, dir., *Antifa: Chasseurs de skins*, documentary, Resistance Films, 2008, posted February 2, 2023, by Resistance Films, YouTube, 1 hour, 5 min., 13 sec., https://www.youtube.com/watch?v=soIUEkICiVU. The documentary is available with English subtitles and is highly recommended.

8   Vecchione, *Antifa*. "Lynching" in this context is French slang to describe a serious beating of many against one individual.

9   Again, "redskins" in this context has no connection to the slur for Indigenous peoples but is rather short for "red skinheads," which was the youth subculture the Red Warriors either identified with or gave birth to, as the name implies, of left-wing skinheads. By the late 1990s, France had a solid network of redskin bands as well as red and anarchist skinhead groups.

10   The JNR dissolved sometime in the mid-1990s, only to be revived in 2010 by Ayoub. In 2013, they were administratively dissolved (de facto banned) by the French state. The cause of their ban was originally "incitement to racial hatred," which a court later struck down while maintaining the ban, considering that the JNR constituted a "private militia."

11   The subway security camera footage of his death is readily available on the internet.

12   The quote he was referencing is actually from Kwame Ture: "If a white man wants to lynch me, that's his problem. If he's got the power to lynch me, that's my problem. Racism is not a question of attitude; it's a question of power."

13   "Du bon usage des morts," *REFLEXes*, May 12, 2006, https://reflexes.samizdat.net/du-bon-usage-des-morts; translation by the author.

14   "Du bon usage des morts."

15   "Du bon usage des morts."

16   "Du bon usage des morts."

4   The 21:03 to Marseille

1   Paris's Lycée Autogéré (Self-Managed High School) is an experimental public school founded in 1982 that "places students in a condition of autonomy, encouraging them to resolve challenges themselves, in a collective manner if they so choose." Academically the school rejects grades, while structurally its day-to-day operations are decided on collectively by teachers, students, and staff in a directly democratic fashion, principally through working groups and assemblies. Unsurprisingly, the school has steadily provided new and young blood into the anarchist and antiauthoritarian movement, and similarly unsurprisingly, it was a target of a fascist attack in 2018. The high school's website, in French, can be found here: https://www.l-a-p.org.

2   "Lutter auprès des sans-papiers: Histoire du CAE Paris," *Courant Alternatif*,
     February 1, 2006, http://oclibertaire.free.fr/spip.php?article115; translation
     by the author.

3   "Un bilan critique du Collectif Anti-Expulsions d'Ile-de-France," *Cette Semaine*,
     no. 85 (August–September 2002), https://cettesemaine.info/cs85/cs85cae.
     html; translation by the author.

4   Jacques, "Étrangers expulsés, étrangers assasssinés!," *Le Monde Libertaire*, May
     14–20, 1998, available at https://ml.ficedl.info/spip.php?article3761; transla-
     tion by the author.

5   Storming the Bastille Police Station

1   The "plural left" coalition was actually composed of the aforementioned three
     main parties, as well as a small group of significantly smaller center-left and
     left-wing parties. In the legislative elections of 1997 that saw them rise to power,
     the Socialist Party drew 23.5 percent of the vote, the Communist Party a very
     respectable 10 percent, and the Greens another 6.8 percent. In that same election,
     Jean-Marie Le Pen's far-right Front National party gained over 14 percent of the
     vote, a number we found back then already incredibly alarming. Little did we
     know what was still to come.

2   Agence France-Presse, "Expulsions gare du Nord," *Le Parisien*, June 13, 1998,
     https://www.leparisien.fr/paris-75/expulsions-gare-du-nord-13-06-1998-
     2000114210.php; translation by the author.

3   The Bonnot Gang was a group of (in)famous French illegalists and individualist
     anarchists who were active in the Paris area from approximately December 1911
     to March 1912. Their claim to fame, besides the daring and adventurous nature of
     their exploits, was that they were the first to use an automobile for the purposes
     of robbery or expropriation. French police mounted a massive operation to track
     down the members of the gang and also used the gang's activities as pretext for a
     much wider crackdown on the anarchist movement, something that led many of
     the more organized or moderate wings of French anarchism to explicitly distance
     themselves from the activities of the gang specifically, as well as from illegal-
     ism in general. Jules Bonnot, the most recognized of the gang and its supposed
     leader, was eventually surrounded in April 1912 in a garage on the outskirts of
     Paris, where he kept over five hundred police officers at bay for hours, before
     they laid a dynamite charge under the building and eventually fatally wounded
     him.

4   Agence France-Presse, "Expulsions gare du Nord."

5   Collectif Anti-Expulsions, "Arrêt immédiat de toutes les expulsions," *Le Monde
     Libertaire*, September 2, 2007, https://www.monde-libertaire.fr/?page=archi
     ves&numarchive=9998; translation by the author.

6   "Un bilan critique du Collectif Anti-Expulsions d'Ile-de-France," *Cette Semaine*,
     no. 85 (August–September 2002), https://cettesemaine.info/cs85/cs85cae.
     html; translation by the author.

7   Émile Henry was, even among anarchists, a controversial figure. Aside from
     the deep rift between organizational anarchists and the illegalist propaganda
     by the deed wing, Émile Henry vocally espoused the idea that since the entire
     bourgeoisie as a class are responsible for, and benefit from, the exploitation of
     workers and the oppressive class structure, there are literally no innocents among
     them. His second bombing, that of the Café Terminus, claimed one life and was
     explicitly justified by him with this line of reasoning: that it was a rich person's

café and therefore there were no innocents there. While most "propaganda by the deed" anarchists saw the different branches of the state and its representatives as legitimate targets (heads of state, judges, police, soldiers, important capitalists, etc.), the line of indiscriminate attacks against "the rich" probably marks a dark moment in anarchism, when it came most near to actual indiscriminate acts of terror. His closing statement at his trial is a revealing look into this questionable line of thinking, while at the same time a moving example of defiance in the face of imminent death. He was executed by guillotine on May 21, 1894, at the age of twenty-one.

8   From Émile Henry's closing statement. See "Le 8 novembre 1892 explosait le commissariat de la rue des Bons-Enfants," *Rebellyon*, November 8, 2023, https://rebellyon.info/Le-8-novembre-1892-explosait-le-19084; translation by the author.

6   This Hotel Is a Detention Center

1   Back then, the French state could only hold undocumented immigrants for a period of ten days, at the end of which, if they had not yet been deported, they had to be released again until their eventual date of deportation.

7   Every Airport and Train Station a Battlefield

1   Emmanuelle Cosse and Brigitte Tijou, "Siamo tutti clandestini," *Vacarme*, no. 8 (May 1999): 23–26, https://vacarme.org/article20.html; translation by the author.

2   Keir Milburn, "Italy's Disobedients—Return of the Tortoise: Italy's Antiempire Multitudes," in *Globalize Liberation: How to Uproot the System and Build a Better World*, ed. David Solnit (City Lights Books, 2004).

3   Milburn, "Return of the Tortoise."

4   Cosse and Tijou, "Siamo tutti clandestini."

5   Muriel Bernardin, "Le Collectif Anti-Expulsions," *L'Oeil Électrique*, no. 25 (September–October 2002), http://oeil.electrique.free.fr/article.php?numero=25&articleid=450; translation by the author.

6   Bernardin, "Le Collectif Anti-Expulsions."

7   The entire situation can be seen here: "Swedish Student Stops Deportation of Asylum Seeker on Plane," posted July 25, 2018, by Newsweek, YouTube, 4 min., 18 sec., https://www.youtube.com/watch?v=VnTgW0I8_ls.

8   Bernardin, "Le Collectif Anti-Expulsions."

9   Davis VanOpdorp, "Elin Ersson Fined for Anti-Deportation Protest," *DW*, February 18, 2019, https://www.dw.com/en/elin-ersson-sentenced-to-fine-for-anti-deportation-protest/a-47560924.

10   "Un bilan critique du Collectif Anti-Expulsions d'Ile-de-France," *Cette Semaine*, no. 85 (August–September 2002), https://cettesemaine.info/cs85/cs85cae.html; translation by the author.

11   A demonstration on June 19, 2001, that drew tens of thousands of participants and, in an unusually successful display of discipline on behalf of so many radicals, remained completely conflict or incident free, so as to create a space where "illegal" immigrants could participate without risk of arrest.

12   Sebastian Weiermann, "Angst vor dem Gipfel," *Jungle.World*, June 4, 2015, https://jungle.world/artikel/2015/23/angst-vor-dem-gipfel.

13   From the Argentine newspaper *Clarín*, December 1, 1999; translation by the author.

8 The Inauguration

1 Barricada Collective, "Account and Analysis of Inauguration Day RAAB," in *The Black Bloc Papers*, ed. David Van Deusen and Xavier Massot (Breaking Glass Press, 2010), 116–17.

9 "We Have Nothing, Destroy Everything! Everybody to Quebec City!"

1 Autonomous Organizing Collective of Anti-Authoritarians from the Midwest, Northeast, Montreal, and Quebec, "Revolutionary Anti-Capitalist Offensive, Spring 2001," originally published in *Barricada*, no. 5 (March 2001), reprinted in *The Black Bloc Papers*, ed. David Van Deusen and Xavier Massot (Breaking Glass Press, 2010), 132–33.

2 *Barricada*, no. 5 (March 2001).

3 Ingrid Peretz, "Accused Summit Plotters Inspired by Zola," *Globe and Mail*, April 22, 2001, https://www.theglobeandmail.com/report-on-business/accused-summit-plotters-inspired-by-zola/article1180556/.

4 "Quebec: Free the Germinal 5!," A-Infos, May 5, 2001, http://www.ainfos.ca/01/may/ainfos00138.html.

5 Peretz, "Accused Summit Plotters."

6 Gabriel Sainte-Marie, "Chronique d'une infiltration policière—Le groupe Germinal," *L'Aut'Journal*, July 2001, http://archives.lautjournal.info/autjourarchives.asp?article=261&noj=201; translation by the author.

7 Alexandre Popovic, "L'affaire Germinal: L'Art d'infiltrer un groupe militant," La C.R.A.P. website, accessed December 5, 2024, https://lacrap.org/sites/lacrap.org/files/laffaire_germinal.pdf; translation by the author. This is an excellent and informative document prepared by the "C.R.A.P.," which in French stands for Coalition contre la Répression et les Abus Policiers, or "Coalition Against Repression and Police Abuse." Highly recommended if you speak French.

8 Sainte-Marie, "Chronique d'une infiltration policière."

9 Popovic, "L'affaire Germinal."

10 Popovic, "L'affaire Germinal."

11 Popovic, "L'affaire Germinal."

12 On one occasion they even went as far as inventing a fake gift certificate for a paintball match, which had supposedly been a gift to the sister of one of the undercover agents who was unable to use it, as a pretext to meet other members of Germinal.

13 Sainte-Marie, "Chronique d'une infiltration policière."

14 "Quebec: Free the Germinal 5!"

15 Isabelle Mathieu, "Sommet des Amériques—Arrestation de six activistes," *Le Soleil*, April 19, 2001; translation by the author.

16 "Quebec: Free the Germinal 5!"

17 Patrick Lagacé, "6 activistes de Montréal arrêtés avec du 'matériel émeutier,'" *Le Journal de Montréal*, April 19, 2001; François Cardinal, "Premières arrestations au Sommet—La police détient six activistes présumés," *Le Devoir*, April 19, 2001; translations by the author.

18 MaRK, "Breaking the Barricades: Quebec's Carnival of Resistance Against Capitalism," *Northeastern Anarchist*, no. 2, available at https://mirror.anarhija.net/lib.anarhija.net/mirror/m/mb/mark-breaking-the-barricades-quebec-s-carnival-of-resistance-against-capitalism.pdf.

19 MaRK, "Breaking the Barricades."

20 In *Barricada* no. 7 (May 2001), an article titled "The Black Bloc Visits Quebec: The

Chronological Account of a Participant" describes the encounter: "Somebody decided that, since the policeman was alone, it would not be much of a problem to slash the tires of the squad car. Apparently, the policeman, infuriated, decided to jump out of the car and arrest the tire slasher. At this point several people reacted to perform an unarrest. According to the policeman's version of events, one person pushed him back with a baton and another struck him in the face with a metal bar, causing the officer to bleed profusely. At this point the officer managed to pull out his gun, and how a further escalation of the conflict was avoided nobody seems to know. This incident would become very important as throughout the weekend police attempted to arrest people and charge them with 'attempted murder' as a result of this incident."

21   Cindy Milstein, "Something Did Start in Quebec City: North America's Revolutionary Anti-Capitalist Movement," *Scoop*, June 1, 2001, https://www.scoop.co.nz/stories/WO0106/S00004/something-did-start-in-quebec-city.htm.

22   Milstein, "Something Did Start in Quebec City."

23   Milstein, "Something Did Start in Quebec City."

24   "Quebec City Eyewitness Analysis: Free Trade Area of the Americas (F.T.A.A.) Summit, April 19–22, 2001," *Inside Front*, no. 14, 106–11, https://cdn.crimethinc.com/assets/journals/inside-front-14/inside-front-14_screen_single_page_view.pdf.

25   Milstein, "Something Did Start in Quebec City."

26   Milstein, "Something Did Start in Quebec City."

27   MaRK, "Breaking the Barricades."

28   Nicolas Phebus, "Did We 'Radicalize This'? An Insider's Look at the Quebec Protests," *Northeastern Anarchist*, no. 2, available at https://theanarchistlibrary.org/library/nicolas-phebus-did-we-radicalize-this-an-insider-s-look-at-the-quebec-protests.

29   Phebus, "Did We 'Radicalize This'?"

30   MaRK, "Breaking the Barricades."

31   MaRK, "Breaking the Barricades."

32   Northeastern Federation of Anarcho-Communists, "Anarchists: You Only See Them When You Fear Them," text from NEFAC tabloid distributed during the FTAA summit, A-Infos, April 20, 2001, http://www.ainfos.ca/01/apr/ainfos00340.html.

33   This catapult would later that day be used as pretext for a police snatch squad to arrest Jaggi Singh and charge him with two counts of possession of a dangerous weapon. He was held in prison for seventeen days.

34   Paul Shukovsky, "FBI Raids Media Center: Stolen Security Plan for Quebec Meeting Was Put on Internet Here," *Seattle Post-Intelligencer*, April 23, 2001.

35   Shukovsky, "FBI Raids Media Center." The same article goes on to quote an anonymous federal criminal justice source who states that "the speed with which the sensitive stolen document appeared on the Internet speaks to the sophistication of the movement that is opposed to unrestricted global trade. The fact that you have something of this magnitude out there on the Web, it really shows these groups are strong, resourceful and resilient."

36   The documents in question are no longer anywhere to be found on the internet, so I've recollected and reconstructed what they said to the best of my abilities.

37   Popovic, "L'affaire Germinal."

38   MaRK, "Breaking the Barricades."

39 MaRK, "Breaking the Barricades."
40 MaRK, "Breaking the Barricades."
41 MaRK, "Breaking the Barricades."
42 "Blocs, Black and Otherwise," CrimethInc., November 20, 2003, https://crimethinc.com/2003/11/20/blocs-black-and-otherwise.
43 Phebus, "Did We 'Radicalize This'?"
44 Phebus, "Did We 'Radicalize This'?"
45 Interview with Nicolas Phebus, March 2021.
46 Interview with Phebus.
47 Interview with Phebus.
48 Interview with Phebus.
49 Interview with Phebus.
50 Phebus, "Did We 'Radicalize This'?"
51 Phebus, "Did We 'Radicalize This'?"
52 Interview with Phebus.
53 "The Black Bloc Visits Quebec: The Chronological Account of a Participant," *Barricada*, no. 7 (May 2001).
54 MaRK, "Breaking the Barricades."
55 MaRK, "Breaking the Barricades."
56 "Black Bloc Visits Quebec."
57 MaRK, "Breaking the Barricades."
58 MaRK, "Breaking the Barricades."
59 "Quebec City Eyewitness Analysis."
60 "Quebec City Eyewitness Analysis."
61 "Quebec City Eyewitness Analysis."
62 "Black Bloc Visits Quebec."
63 "The Black Bloc in Quebec: An Analysis," *Barricada*, no. 7 (May 2001).
64 "Black Bloc Visits Quebec."
65 "Black Bloc Visits Quebec."
66 "Black Bloc in Quebec."
67 "Quebec City Eyewitness Analysis."
68 Phebus, "Did We 'Radicalize This'?"
69 Phebus, "Did We 'Radicalize This'?"
70 "Quebec City Eyewitness Analysis."
71 Interview with Phebus.
72 "Black Bloc Visits Quebec."
73 "Black Bloc Visits Quebec."
74 "Quebec City Eyewitness Analysis."
75 "Black Bloc Visits Quebec."
76 "Quebec City Eyewitness Analysis."
77 "Quebec City Eyewitness Analysis."
78 Popovic, "L'affaire Germinal."
79 Popovic, "L'affaire Germinal."
80 Popovic, "L'affaire Germinal."
81 MaRK, "Breaking the Barricades."
82 Interview with Phebus.
83 Interview with Phebus.
84 Interview with Phebus.
85 Interview with Phebus.
86 "Quebec City Eyewitness Analysis."

10   Days of War, Nights of Love

1   *Sudaka* is a derogatory term usually used by Spaniards to refer to immigrants from South America, or South Americans in general. Like many such terms, it has been reappropriated, and we often use it among ourselves in a self-deprecating manner. It is one of those terms that we use among each other but would react strongly to if it was spoken by a Spaniard, particularly as it would usually come in the form of *sudaka de mierda*, which essentially translates to "fucking South Americans."

2   There has been some turbulence over the years, but as of 2020 the AFA network in Sweden was still standing.

3   The Antifaschistische Aktion/Bundesweite Organisation was formed in 1992 by some of the more well known, structured, and movement- and coalition-building-oriented autonome antifa groups in Germany, including Antifascist Action Berlin and the Autonome Antifa from Göttingen, better known as the [M]. It dissolved following a congress in April 2001, one of the first victims of the growing anti-imperialist versus anti-German rift in the autonome and antifa movement.

4   Ya Basta! communiqué, June 14, 2001.

5   "Göteborgskravallerna 2001," June 14–17, 2001, posted June 6, 2011, by Tomas Bergqvist, YouTube, 32 min., 56 sec., https://www.youtube.com/watch?v=vNLmn3Qe1z0. The sequence begins around 3:35.

6   I wasn't aware of this until I discovered the video years later, but it seems a few minutes after this another, more sizable group emerged from the school in the same fashion we did (we have no idea where they came from). Their escape is even more epic, as in what can only be described as a Scandinavian-demonstrator-versus-cop interpretation of *American Gladiators*, they fought their way past cops who were perched on top of the containers as they made their escape into the crowd.

7   Stephen Castle and Andrew Grice, "We Won't Give an Inch to Anarchist 'Circus,' Vows Blair," *Independent*, June 16, 2001, https://www.the-independent.com/news/world/europe/we-won-t-give-an-inch-to-anarchist-circus-vows-blair-9164554.html.

8   "Blair: Anarchists Will Not Stop Us," *BBC News*, June 16, 2001, http://news.bbc.co.uk/2/hi/uk_news/politics/1392004.stm.

9   I can't believe we have to say this, and yet out of experience here we are: This is not actionable intelligence, it's just something to be aware of in your surroundings. Please refrain from yelling "COP!" at random people because they look "out of place." That is wildly irresponsible and dangerous, and it can result in serious consequences for that person if you are making a mistake.

10   Tobias Hedkvist, "Regulating Resistance: The Ideological Control of the Protests in Gothenburg 2001" (Communication in English paper, Malmo University, 2006), 19, https://mau.diva-portal.org/smash/get/diva2:1483243/FULLTEXT01.pdf.

11   "Göteborgs Kravallerna 2001," posted May 17, 2008, by munkiEda1337, YouTube, 3 min., https://www.youtube.com/watch?v=k3bKpfP43SI. Rock-throwing police officers can be seen at approximately 2:25–2:35.

12   He was subsequently tried and convicted for "rioting" and sentenced to six months in prison.

13   "Wisemen," Wikipedia (Sweden), last modified July 17, 2024, 20:19, https://sv.wikipedia.org/wiki/Wisemen.

14   Interview with Felham, September 2020.

15   Hans Abrahamsson, "Debatt 13/8: Felaktiga hotbilder låg bakom polisens ager-
      ande," *Göteborgs-Posten*, August 13, 2006. English translation available here:
      https://web.archive.org/web/20100601195146/https://www.eurotrib.com/
      story/2007/3/19/152213/911.

16   Abrahamsson, "Debatt 13/8."

17   Abrahamsson, "Debatt 13/8."

18   Revolutionary Front was very much a "street activism"–oriented network of
      activists who broadly described their politics under the keywords of "Socialism,
      Anti-Fascism, Women's Struggle, Class Struggle, Internationalism." They were
      most renowned for their ambushes and home visits to Nazi militants, usually
      culminating in breaking down their doors with an axe. Many of these ambushes
      were filmed and then used for propaganda purposes under the banner of Revfront
      Media. These videos are still available on YouTube, as is an English-language
      interview with *VICE News* in 2014 ("The Rise of Sweden's Far-Left Militants,"
      https://www.youtube.com/watch?v=U1MYMVfyHi0). Highly recommended
      viewing.

19   From the early 2000s onward, far-right and neo-Nazi groups demonstrated in
      the Stockholm suburb of Salem to remember Daniel Wretström, an eighteen-
      year-old Nazi killed during a fight with other local youths, apparently initiated
      after he drunkenly hurled racist insults at a girl. For over a decade, Salem was
      the scene of a mobilization of often thousands of European Nazis—and coun-
      termobilizations from the AFA network led to significant clashes with police
      officers protecting the march. It's in the course of one of these mobilizations
      that Felham and I first met.

20   Interview with Felham.

11   The Cancelled Summit: Our Anger Is Always Justified

1   This may seem like a detail, but it is important in that *independentista* is a specific
      term to define themselves and their movement that partisans of independence
      from the Spanish State who come from a left-wing perspective choose to employ.
      There is no English translation for *independentista*, the closest equivalent being
      separatist. But *separatist* does have a Spanish-language equivalent, *separatista*,
      which the left-wing pro-independence movement rejects (along with *nationalist*,
      for obvious reasons), as it implies that they are separating from an actually exist-
      ing whole rather than seeking independence from the politically and militarily
      sustained construct of the Spanish State. *Separata*, short for *separatista*, is also
      commonly used as a derogatory term by Spanish nationalists to refer to Catalan
      separatists.

2   You might know it as "Spain." I can't bring myself to utter the word without air
      quotes.

3   A few years later, I had the (mis)fortune of being in a small Basque town on the
      night of the transfer of local power from the left independentista group Batasuna,
      which had been outlawed and prevented from participating in elections, to one
      of the Spanish nationalist parties. This was one of the typical fortresses of the
      independentista left, where the Spanish State was nothing more than a despised
      invader and the imprisoned and exiled youth of the town were seen as long-lost
      heroes. On the eve of the transfer of the levers of local government from Batasuna
      to the Spanish political forces, the Guardia Civil moved in to "pacify" the town,
      establishing a quasi military occupation of all streets and public spaces of the
      kind one associates with the peak times of the Troubles in Northern Ireland.

4   Pere Ríos, "La compleja red de la violencia antisistema," *El País*, October 20, 2001, https://elpais.com/diario/2001/10/21/espana/1003615213_850215.html; translation by the author.

5   In 2017 the Catalan Parliament approved the holding of a referendum on independence from the Spanish State, which was eventually held on October 1 of that year. The Spanish State did not recognize the legal validity of the referendum, arguing that the question of seceding from the Spanish State itself was illegal, as there was no legal framework to do so. In response, and to prevent the vote from taking place, it sent thousands of police officers to Catalunya to confiscate ballot boxes and on numerous occasions violently attack voters, in images that were widely seen internationally. Despite the efforts of the Spanish State to criminalize the referendum, there was a 43 percent participation rate, with 92 percent of participating voters choosing yes on independence.

6   Portugal and Greece are the other two notable exceptions to the rule. Portugal was ruled by a military dictatorship until the Carnation Revolution in 1974, while Greece was ruled by a series of military juntas from 1967 to 1974.

7   With the obvious and glaring limitations of the time, which included, for example, some anarchists espousing homophobic views.

8   The graffito comes from a quote from *Por amor a Cataluña* by Eduardo Goligorsky (Flor del Viento Ediciones, 2002)—some shitty book by some shitty pro-Spain author lamenting the possible destruction of the Spanish State by the leftist forces of disorder, or something like that.

12   On Tour with the Hippies: Escape from Salzburg

1   *Kronen Zeitung*, July 2, 2001. The translation of "Chaoten-Terror mitten in Salzburg" is paraphrased, as there isn't really an adequate English translation for *chaoten*.

2   Maple Razsa, *Bastards of Utopia: Living Radical Politics After Socialism* (Indiana University Press, 2015).

13   The Battle of Genoa

1   "All Aboard the Anarchy Express," *CNN*, July 11, 2001.

2   "Vignoles" versus Bordeaux. I was a member of one for several years, but not the other, so I am very much biased here.

3   "Eyewitness Account of the Genoa G8 Protest," Workers Solidarity Movement, July 20, 2001, archived at https://web.archive.org/web/20240222211550/http://www.wsm.ie/c/eyewitness-account-genoa-g8-protest.

4   "The Black Bloc in Genoa: An Affinity Group's Account," *Tute Nere*, reprinted in *Barricada*, no. 8 (Summer/September 2001): 7–10, available at https://archive.org/details/black-bloc-006/page/n3/mode/1up.

5   "Genoa Will Not Be Porto Alegre," *Barricada*, no. 8 (Summer/September 2001).

6   *The Golden Horde* is the title of Nanni Balestrini's definitive work on Italian revolutionary movements of the 1960s and 1970s. Balestrini himself was a cofounder of Potere Operaio and a supporter of the influential ultra-left group Autonomia Operaia. He was accused of membership in a guerrilla organization in 1979 and fled to France. A novelist, he is most well known for his 1971 novel about workers' struggles at the Fiat factory in Milan, *Vogliamo Tutto* (We want everything), which this author strongly recommends.

7   "Black Bloc in Genoa."

8   "Black Bloc in Genoa."

9   "Témoignage d'un anarchiste sur les événements du vendredi 20 juillet 2001 à
      Gênes," *Cette Semaine*, no. 83 (September–October 2001): 25–31; republished
      on A-Infos on August 6, 2001; archived at https://archive.wikiwix.com/cache
      /?url=http%3A%2F%2Fcettesemaine.free.fr%2Fcs83%2Fcs83temoibb.html;
      translation by the author.

10   "Témoignage d'un anarchiste."

11   "Témoignage d'un anarchiste."

12   "Témoignage d'un anarchiste."

13   "Témoignage d'un anarchiste."

14   "Black Bloc in Genoa."

15   "Black Bloc in Genoa."

16   "Black Bloc in Genoa."

17   "Black Bloc in Genoa."

18   Adam Porter, "It Was Like This Before," in *On Fire: The Battle of Genoa and the
      Anti-Capitalist Movement* (One Off Press, 2001), 75.

19   Jazz, "The Tracks of Our Tears," in *On Fire: The Battle of Genoa and the Anti-
      Capitalist Movement* (One Off Press, 2001), 88.

20   Luisa Toledo Sepúlveda, born in 1939, was a militant of the socialist Allendist
      tendency in Chile during the 1960s and 1970s. After the military coup of 1973,
      which ousted President Allende, she became active in several anti-dictatorship
      and pro–human rights initiatives. On March 29, 1985, her sons Eduardo (twenty
      years old) and Rafael (eighteen), both members of the clandestine Movimiento
      de Izquierda Revolucionaria (Movement of the Revolutionary Left), fell in a clash
      with police officers. The date of their death is remembered to this day as the
      Dia del Joven Combatiente (Day of the Young Combatant), with clashes and
      attacks against police across Chile. A third son, Pablo, was found dead in 1988
      following the explosion of a bomb he was carrying. After the death of her sons,
      Luisa continued to be active against both the military dictatorship and its partial
      democratic continuity. She attempted to light herself on fire in 1991 as a protest
      against the lack of investigation and clarity into the death of Eduardo and Rafael.
      During the Chilean uprising of 2019, at over eighty years old, she could be seen
      in Plaza Italia among the demonstrators, urging them to battle and lauding their
      commitment and bravery.

21   Transcript of witness testimony given by one of the police officers in a trial of
      twenty-five demonstrators for G8 actions, June 8, 2004. Originally posted on
      www.supportolegale.net; translation by the author.

22   "Secolo xix: Quei no gloabl li avrei manganellati," Comitato verità e giustizia
      per Genova (Committee for Truth and Justice for Genoa), June 2, 2004, http://
      www.veritagiustizia.it/old_rassegna_stampa/secolo_xix_quei_no_gloabl_li_
      avrei_manganellati.php.

23   "Black Bloc in Genoa."

24   "Témoignage d'un anarchiste."

25   "Al G8 la più grave violazione dei diritti umani," *Il Secolo XIX*, October 30, 2008,
      https://www.ilsecoloxix.it/genova/2008/10/30/news/al-g8-la-piu-grave-
      violazione-dei-diritti-umani-1.33367778; translation by the author. While I
      appreciate Amnesty International taking what happened at Diaz school seri-
      ously, I have to assume they mean "the most serious human rights suspension"
      in what is traditionally considered "Western" Europe, given the massacres and
      ethnic cleansing that took place in the 1990s during the wars in the former
      Yugoslavia.

26 Nick Davies, "The Bloody Battle of Genoa," *Guardian*, July 17, 2008, https://www.theguardian.com/world/2008/jul/17/italy.g8.

27 Mark Covell suffered eight broken ribs and went into a coma due to the beating he received that night. He would go on to launch a civil case for compensation against police officers involved in his beating, as well as taking the Italian government to the European Court of Human Rights. In 2012 he was finally awarded €350,000 in damages by the Italian state, on the condition that he drop his case before the ECHR.

28 "G8, Fournier: 'Sembrava una macelleria,'" *La Repubblica*, June 13, 2007, https://www.repubblica.it/2007/06/sezioni/cronaca/g8-genova/g8-genova/g8-genova.html; translation by the author.

29 Davies, "Bloody Battle of Genoa."

30 Davies, "Bloody Battle of Genoa."

31 Davies, "Bloody Battle of Genoa."

32 Davies, "Bloody Battle of Genoa."

33 Davies, "Bloody Battle of Genoa."

34 Davies, "Bloody Battle of Genoa."

35 Davies, "Bloody Battle of Genoa."

36 Davies, "Bloody Battle of Genoa."

37 "Black Bloc in Genoa."

38 "Black Bloc in Genoa."

39 Wu Ming, in *Gênes: Multitudes en marche contre l'Empire*, ed. samizdat.net (Éditions Reflex, 2002), 196.

40 Olivier, "Action mondiale des peuples," in *Gênes: Multitudes en marche contre l'Empire*, ed. samizdat.net (Éditions Reflex, 2002), 276.

41 Rafaele Laudani and Fiorino Iantorno, "Attac Italie," in *Gênes: Multitudes en marche contre l'Empire*, ed. samizdat.net (Éditions Reflex, 2002), 272–73.

42 David Graeber, "Among the Thugs: Genoa and the New Language of Protest," *In These Times*, September 3, 2001.

43 "Témoignage d'un anarchiste sur les événements du vendredi 20 juillet 2001 à Gênes," *Cette Semaine*, no. 83 (September–October 2001): 25–31; republished on A-Infos on August 6, 2001; archived at https://archive.wikiwix.com/cache/?url=http%3A%2F%2Fcettesemaine.free.fr%2Fcs83%2Fcs83temoibb.html; translation by the author.

44 David Graeber, "The New Anarchists," *New Left Review*, no. 13 (January–February 2002).

45 Becky, "An Italian Job," in *On Fire: The Battle of Genoa and the Anti-Capitalist Movement* (One Off Press, 2001), 69.

46 Graeber, "Among the Thugs."

47 "The Lessons of Genoa," *Barricada*, no. 8 (Summer/September 2001).

48 "Lessons of Genoa."

49 "Lessons of Genoa."

50 "Lessons of Genoa."

IMAGE CREDITS

Page 12: Anarchist pamphlet about November 17, 1995
Page 20: C. Martin / Instagram: @cedric_martin_photographe
Page 24: Tomas Rothaus
Page 29: Courtesy of Archivo Fundación Anselmo Lorenzo (CNT)
Page 38: Courtesy of Archivo Fundación Anselmo Lorenzo (CNT)
Page 40: C. Martin / Instagram: @cedric_martin_photographe
Page 44: C. Martin / Instagram: @cedric_martin_photographe
Page 47: C. Martin / Instagram: @cedric_martin_photographe
Page 50: Raphael Kessler
Page 54: C. Martin / Instagram: @cedric_martin_photographe
Page 56: C. Martin / Instagram: @cedric_martin_photographe
Page 59: Beatrice Walylo
Page 63: (top) Maxwell Aurelien James; (bottom left) © VINCI – Black Lines 2024 @blacklinesbl; (bottom right) Machete Records
Page 72: C. Martin / Instagram: @cedric_martin_photographe
Page 81: Bruno Amsellem
Page 104: Tomas Rothaus
Page 107: Tomas Rothaus
Page 111: Antifascistische Linke International
Page 112: Antifaschistische Aktion
Page 119: Tomas Rothaus
Page 122: C. Martin / Instagram: @cedric_martin_photographe
Page 126: C. Martin / Instagram: @cedric_martin_photographe
Page 127: C. Martin / Instagram: @cedric_martin_photographe
Page 128: Clarín
Page 155: *Barricada* no. 5, March 2001
Page 158: *Barricada* no. 5, March 2001

INDEX

Page numbers in *italic* refer to illustrations. "Passim" (literally "scattered") indicates intermittent discussion of a topic over a cluster of pages.

ABOUT THE CONTRIBUTORS

Tomas Rothaus is a lifelong anarchist and antifascist as well as an athlete and a father. He was born in Buenos Aires, Argentina, and his nomadic life led to him moving around, with stops in Athens, Boston, Buenos Aires, and Paris, followed by longer stints in Germany and more recently returning to Argentina. He has been involved with a broad range of organizations, including the CNT-Vignoles, Collectif Anti-Expulsions (Anti-Deportation Collective), Barricada Collective, Northeastern Federation of Anarcho-Communists, Antifaschistische Linke International, and Acción Antifascista Buenos Aires. Over the past twenty-plus years he has been an active participant in militant demonstrations and antifascist mobilizations ranging from the Bush inauguration and the FTAA summit in Quebec in 2001 to the 2007 G8 summit in Rostock, Germany, and the 2011 mobilization to stop the march of several thousand neo-Nazis in the city of Dresden.

CrimethInc. is a rebel alliance, a decentralized network pledged to anonymous collective action—a breakout from the prisons of our age. We strive to reinvent our lives and our world according to the principles of self-determination and mutual aid.

ABOUT PM PRESS

PM Press is an independent, radical publisher of critically necessary books for our tumultuous times. Our aim is to deliver bold political ideas and vital stories to all walks of life and arm the dreamers to demand the impossible. Founded in 2007 by a small group of people with decades of publishing, media, and organizing experience, we have sold millions of copies of our books, most often one at a time, face to face. We're old enough to know what we're doing and young enough to know what's at stake. Join us to create a better world.

PM Press
PO Box 23912
Oakland, CA 94623
www.pmpress.org

PM Press in Europe
europe@pmpress.org
www.pmpress.org.uk

FRIENDS OF PM PRESS

These are indisputably momentous times—the financial system is melting down globally and the Empire is stumbling. Now more than ever there is a vital need for radical ideas.

In the many years since its founding—and on a mere shoestring—PM Press has risen to the formidable challenge of publishing and distributing knowledge and entertainment for the struggles ahead. With hundreds of releases to date, we have published an impressive and stimulating array of literature, art, music, politics, and culture. Using every available medium, we've succeeded in connecting those hungry for ideas and information to those putting them into practice.

Friends of PM allows you to directly help impact, amplify, and revitalize the discourse and actions of radical writers, filmmakers, and artists. It provides us with a stable foundation from which we can build upon our early successes and provides a much-needed subsidy for the materials that can't necessarily pay their own way. You can help make that happen—and receive every new title automatically delivered to your door once a month—by joining as a Friend of PM Press. And, we'll throw in a free T-shirt when you sign up.

Here are your options:

- **$30 a month** Get all books and pamphlets plus a 50% discount on all webstore purchases

- **$40 a month** Get all PM Press releases (including CDs and DVDs) plus a 50% discount on all webstore purchases

- **$100 a month** Superstar—Everything plus PM merchandise, free downloads, and a 50% discount on all webstore purchases

For those who can't afford $30 or more a month, we have **Sustainer Rates** at $15, $10, and $5. Sustainers get a free PM Press T-shirt and a 50% discount on all purchases from our website.

Your Visa or Mastercard will be billed once a month, until you tell us to stop. Or until our efforts succeed in bringing the revolution around. Or the financial meltdown of Capital makes plastic redundant. Whichever comes first.

Argentina, A Tale of Two Utopias: Anarchism, Soccer, Neoliberalism

Tomas Rothaus with a Foreword by Gabriel Kuhn

ISBN: 979-8-88744-147-4
$22.95

A Tale of Two Utopias takes us through the outsized and unexpected remnants of the influence of anarchist ideas and practice on modern-day Argentina—from the names of popular pastries to the foundation of numerous soccer clubs—until we arrive at the explosive intersection of anarchism, football, and the crisis of neoliberalism.

This is a thrilling first-person account of the December 2001 uprising in Argentina that marked the end of the neoliberal experiment of the 1990s, narrated by an anarchist participant in the clashes that laid siege to the presidential palace and forced the president to resign and flee on a rooftop helicopter. *A Tale of Two Utopias* weaves together two simultaneous yet seemingly unrelated events of those "days which contain decades" of Buenos Aires in December 2001: the uprising and the first championship in 35 years of the popular football club Racing Club de Avellaneda.

Alternating between urgent narration and historical account, and accompanied by over 150 photos and illustrations, *A Tale of Two Utopias* has the reader walking the streets of a Buenos Aires on fire, while finding the time to take us on a lovingly traced tour of the rich history of Argentina's anarchist movement of the early twentieth century (then among the largest in the world)—and it is also a compelling account of the trauma inflicted by Argentina's numerous dictatorships.

"*A Tale of Two Utopias weaves complicated histories of anarchism, football, resistance, and everyday life in Buenos Aires into an artful narrative of youthful exuberance and political turmoil. As opposition boils up again today in Argentina, this riveting snapshot of popular outrage from below presents readers with a fascinating point of inflection to connect general strikes and dreams of revolution, past and present.*"
—Mark Bray, author of *Antifa: The Anti-Fascist Handbook*

We Go Where They Go: The Story of Anti-Racist Action

Shannon Clay, Lady, Kristin Schwartz, and Michael Staudenmaier with a Foreword by Gord Hill

ISBN: 978-1-62963-972-7 (paperback)
  978-1-62963-977-2 (hardcover)
$24.95/$59.95   320 pages

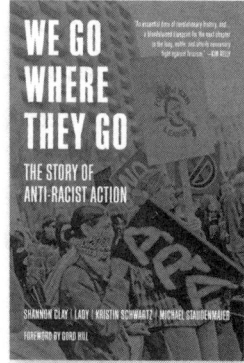

What does it mean to risk all for your beliefs? How do you fight an enemy in your midst? *We Go Where They Go* recounts the thrilling story of a massive forgotten youth movement that set the stage for today's antifascist organizing in North America. When skinheads and punks in the late 1980s found their communities invaded by white supremacists and neo-nazis, they fought back. Influenced by anarchism, feminism, Black liberation, and Indigenous sovereignty, they created Anti-Racist Action. At ARA's height in the 1990s, thousands of dedicated activists in hundreds of chapters joined the fights—political and sometimes physical—against nazis, the Ku Klux Klan, anti-abortion fundamentalists, and racist police. Before media pundits, cynical politicians, and your uncle discovered "antifa," Anti-Racist Action was bringing it to the streets.

Based on extensive interviews with dozens of ARA participants, *We Go Where They Go* tells ARA's story from within, giving voice to those who risked their safety in their own defense and in solidarity with others. In reproducing the posters, zines, propaganda, and photos of the movement itself, this essential work of radical history illustrates how cultural scenes can become powerful forces for change. Here at last is the story of an organic yet highly organized movement, exploring both its triumphs and failures, and offering valuable lessons for today's generation of activists and rabble-rousers. *We Go Where They Go* is a page-turning history of grassroots anti-racism. More than just inspiration, it's a roadmap.

"*I was a big supporter and it was an honor to work with the Anti-Racist Action movement. Their unapologetic and uncompromising opposition to racism and fascism in the streets, in the government, and in the mosh pit continues to be inspiring to this day.*"
—Tom Morello

"*Antifa became a household word with Trump attempting and failing to designate it a domestic terrorist group, but Antifa's roots date back to the late 1980s when little attention was being paid to violent fascist groups that were flourishing under Reaganism, and Anti-Racist Action (ARA) was singular and effective in its brilliant offensive. This book tells the story of ARA in breathtaking prose accompanied by stunning photographs and images.*"
—Roxanne Dunbar-Ortiz, author of *Loaded: A Disarming History of the Second Amendment*

It Did Happen Here: An Antifascist People's History

Edited by Moe Bowstern, Mic Crenshaw, Alec Dunn, Celina Flores, Julie Perini, and Erin Yanke

ISBN: 978-1-62963-351-0
$21.95   304 pages

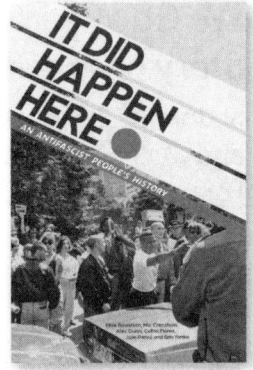

Portland, Oregon, 1988: the brutal murder of Ethiopian immigrant Mulugeta Seraw by racist skinheads shocked the city. In response disparate groups quickly came together to organize against white nationalist violence and right-wing organizing throughout the Rose City and the Pacific Northwest.

It Did Happen Here compiles interviews with dozens of people who worked together during the waning decades of the twentieth century to reveal an inspiring collaboration between groups of immigrants, civil rights activists, militant youth, and queer organizers. This oral history focuses on participants in three core groups: the Portland chapters of Anti-Racist Action and Skinheads Against Racial Prejudice, and the Coalition for Human Dignity.

Using a diversity of tactics—from out-and-out brawls on the streets and at punk shows, to behind-the-scenes intelligence gathering—brave antiracists unified on their home ground over and over, directly attacking right-wing fascists and exposing white nationalist organizations and neo-nazi skinheads. Embattled by police and unsupported by the city, these citizen activists eventually drove the boneheads out of the music scene and off the streets of Portland. This book shares their stories about what worked, what didn't, and ideas on how to continue the fight.

"*By the time I moved my queer little family to Portland at the turn of the millennium, the city had a reputation as a homo-friendly bastion of progressive politics, so we were somewhat taken aback when my daughter's racially diverse sports team was met with a burning cross at a suburban game. So much progress had been made yet, at times, it felt like the past hadn't gone anywhere. If only we'd had* It Did Happen Here. *This documentary project tells the forgotten history of Portland's roots as a haven for white supremacists and recounts the ways anti-racists formed coalitions across subcultures to protect the vulnerable and fight the good fight against nazi boneheads and the bigoted right. Through the voices of lived experience,* It Did Happen Here *illuminates community dynamics and lays out ideas and inspiration for long-term and nonpolice solutions to poverty and hatred.*"
—Ariel Gore, author of *We Were Witches*

The Hands That Crafted the Bomb: The Making of a Lifelong Antifascist

Josh Fernandez

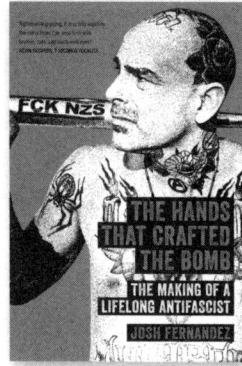

ISBN: 979-8-88744-023-1
$22.95   256 pages

Josh Fernandez is a community college professor in Northern California who finds himself under investigation for "soliciting students for potentially dangerous activities" after starting an antifascist club on campus.

As Fernandez spends the year defending his job, he reflects on a life lived in protest of the status quo, swept up in chaos and rage, from his childhood in Boston dealing with a mentally ill father and a new family to a move to Davis, California, where, in the basement shows of the early '90s, Nazi boneheads proliferated the music scene, looking for heads to crack. His crew's first attempts at an antifascist group fall short when a member dies in a knife fight.

A born antiauthoritarian, filled with an untamable rage, Fernandez rails against the system and aggressively chooses the path of most resistance. This leads to long spates of living in his car, strung out on drugs, and robbing the whiteboys coming home from the clubs at night. He eventually realizes that his rage needs an outlet and finds relief for his existential dread in the form of running. And fighting Nazis. Fernandez cobbles together a life for himself as a writing professor, a facilitator of a self-defense collective, a boots-on-the-ground participant in Antifa work, and a proud father of two children he unapologetically raises to question authority.

"Fernandez is scathing on the corporate-minded liberals who talk about equity and diversity, antiracism, and gay rights but can't deal with people actually defending themselves or challenging authority. What he offers instead isn't heroics or militant slogans or even measured analysis—it's the messy story of a 'fucked-up person' trying to 'channel rage into something less destructive,' a guy who tends to run face-first into danger but also has the good sense to run away screaming when confronted with a knife-wielding racist. Fernandez's account of violence, trauma, and loneliness is hard to read in places, but there's an underlying sweetness here, a hopefulness about flawed people helping each other out, a sense that if we can get past the lies, we can remake this world together."
—Matthew N. Lyons, author of *Insurgent Supremacists: The U.S. Far Right's Challenge to State and Empire*

Fire and Flames: A History of the German Autonomist Movement

Geronimo
with an Introduction by George
Katsiaficas and Afterword by Gabriel
Kuhn

ISBN: 978-1-60486-097-9
$19.95   256 pages

Fire and Flames was the first comprehensive study of the German autonomous movement ever published. Released in 1990, it reached its fifth edition by 1997, with the legendary German *Konkret* journal concluding that "the movement had produced its own classic." The author, writing under the pseudonym of Geronimo, has been an autonomous activist since the movement burst onto the scene in 1980–81. In this book, he traces its origins in the Italian *Autonomia* project and the German social movements of the 1970s, before describing the battles for squats, "free spaces," and alternative forms of living that defined the first decade of the autonomous movement. Tactics of the "Autonome" were militant, including the construction of barricades or throwing molotov cocktails at the police. Because of their outfit (heavy black clothing, ski masks, helmets), the Autonome were dubbed the "Black Bloc" by the German media, and their tactics have been successfully adopted and employed at anti-capitalist protests worldwide.

Fire and Flames is no detached academic study, but a passionate, hands-on, and engaging account of the beginnings of one of Europe's most intriguing protest movements of the last thirty years. An introduction by George Katsiaficas, author of *The Subversion of Politics*, and an afterword by Gabriel Kuhn, a long-time autonomous activist and author, add historical context and an update on the current state of the Autonomen.

"The target audience is not the academic middle-class with passive sympathies for rioting, nor the all-knowing critical critics, but the activists of a young generation."
— *Edition I.D. Archiv*

"Some years ago, an experienced autonomous activist from Berlin sat down, talked to friends and comrades about the development of the scene, and, with Fire and Flames, *wrote the best book about the movement that we have."*
— *Düsseldorfer Stadtzeitung für Politik und Kultur*

Who's Afraid of the Black Blocs?
Anarchy in Action around the World

Francis Dupuis-Déri
Translated by Lazer Lederhendler

ISBN: 978-1-60486-949-1
$19.95   224 pages

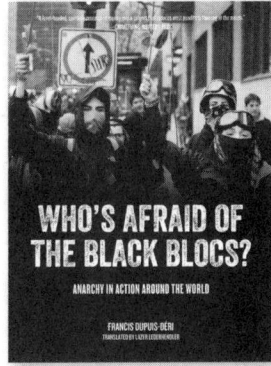

Faces masked, dressed in black, and forcefully attacking the symbols of capitalism, Black Blocs have been transformed into an anti-globalization media spectacle. But the popular image of the window-smashing thug hides a complex reality. Francis Dupuis-Déri outlines the origin of this international phenomenon, its dynamics, and its goals, arguing that the use of violence always takes place in an ethical and strategic context.

Translated into English for the first time and completely revised and updated to include the most recent Black Bloc actions at protests in Greece, Germany, Canada, and England, and the Bloc's role in the Occupy movement and the Quebec student strike, *Who's Afraid of the Black Blocs?* lays out a comprehensive view of the Black Bloc tactic and locates it within the anarchist tradition of direct action.

"*A level-headed, carefully researched inquiry into a subject that reduces most pundits to foaming at the mouth.*"
—CrimethInc. Writers' Bloc

"*Francis Dupuis-Déri's discussion of Black Blocs is intimately well-informed, truly international in scope, and up-to-the-minute. He treats the complex issues surrounding the tactic with an admirable balance of sympathy and sobriety. This book is the ideal antidote to the misinformation spread by the establishment, its defenders, and its false critics.*"
—Uri Gordon, author of *Anarchy Alive!*

"*Wearing black to mask their identities, the Black Bloc fights injustice globally. Although little is known about these modern Zorros, this book critically reveals their origins and prospects. I heartily recommend it.*"
—George Katsiaficas, author of *The Subversion of Politics*

"*The richness, imaginativeness, and sheer learning of Francis Dupuis-Déri's work is stimulating and impressive. The whole book turns on a fascinating blend of the rigorously analytical and the generously imaginative. It was high time that it should be translated into English, as this well-established anarchist classic will both delight and inform.*"
—Andrej Grubačić, Professor of Anthropology and Social Change, California Institute of Integral Studies, and coauthor of *Wobblies & Zapatistas*

Three Way Fight: Revolutionary Politics and Antifascism

Edited by Xtn Alexander and Matthew N. Lyons with a Foreword by Janeen Porter and an Afterword by Michael Staudenmaier

ISBN: 979-8-88744-041-5
$24.95   416 pages

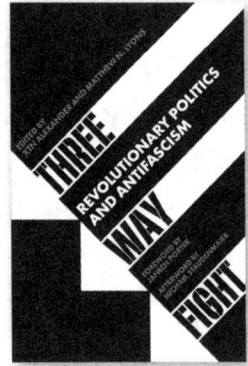

What's the relationship between combating the far right and working for systemic change? What does it mean when fascists intensify racial oppression and patriarchy but also call for the downfall of economic elites or even take up arms against the state?

Three way fight politics confront these urgent questions squarely, arguing that the far right grows out of an oppressive capitalist order but is also in conflict with it in real ways, and that radicals need to combat both. The three way fight approach says we need sharper analysis of far-right movements so we can fight them more effectively, and we also need to track ongoing developments within the ruling class, including liberal or centrist efforts to co-opt antifascism as a tool of state repression and system legitimation.

This book offers an introduction to three way fight politics, with more than thirty essays, position statements, and interviews from the Three Way Fight website and elsewhere, spanning from the antifascist struggles of the 1980s and 1990s to the political upheavals of the twenty-first century. Over fifteen authors explore a range of topics, such as fascist politics' relationship with patriarchy and settler colonialism, Tom Metzger's "Third Position" (anticapitalist) fascism, conflict within the business community over the 2016 presidential election, and the Trump administration's shifting relationship with the organized far right. Many of the writings address issues of political strategy, such as tensions between radicals and liberals within the reproductive rights movement and the George Floyd rebellion, video gaming as an arena of political struggle, and the importance (and challenges) of approaching antifascist organizing in ways that are militant, community based, and nonsectarian.

"Three Way Fight *not only represents the most pressing and insightful analysis on the far right available, but it is also written from within the movements to fight back. Offering some of the most explosive documents from the recent antifascist movement, these authors chart a new course for understanding the far right. A great read for both newcomers and longtime antifascists,* Three Way Fight *is simultaneously a documentary history of twenty-first-century antifascism and a theoretical evolution in the way we understand the future of the far right.*"
—Shane Burley, author of *Why We Fight: Essays on Fascism, Resistance, and Surviving the Apocalypse*

Wobblies and Zapatistas:
Conversations on Anarchism, Marxism and Radical History

Staughton Lynd and Andrej Grubačić

ISBN: 978-1-60486-041-2
$20.00   300 pages

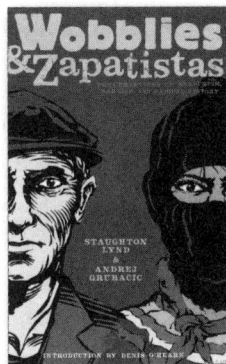

Wobblies and Zapatistas offers the reader an encounter between two generations and two traditions. Andrej Grubačić is an anarchist from the Balkans. Staughton Lynd is a lifelong pacifist, influenced by Marxism. They meet in dialogue in an effort to bring together the anarchist and Marxist traditions, to discuss the writing of history by those who make it, and to remind us of the idea that "my country is the world." Encompassing a Left libertarian perspective and an emphatically activist standpoint, these conversations are meant to be read in the clubs and affinity groups of the new Movement.

The authors accompany us on a journey through modern revolutions, direct actions, anti-globalist counter summits, Freedom Schools, Zapatista cooperatives, Haymarket and Petrograd, Hanoi and Belgrade, "intentional" communities, wildcat strikes, early Protestant communities, Native American democratic practices, the Workers' Solidarity Club of Youngstown, occupied factories, self-organized councils and soviets, the lives of forgotten revolutionaries, Quaker meetings, antiwar movements, and prison rebellions. Neglected and forgotten moments of interracial self-activity are brought to light. The book invites the attention of readers who believe that a better world, on the other side of capitalism and state bureaucracy, may indeed be possible.

"There's no doubt that we've lost much of our history. It's also very clear that those in power in this country like it that way. Here's a book that shows us why. It demonstrates not only that another world is possible, but that it already exists, has existed, and shows an endless potential to burst through the artificial walls and divisions that currently imprison us. An exquisite contribution to the literature of human freedom, and coming not a moment too soon."
—David Graeber, author of *Fragments of an Anarchist Anthropology* and *Direct Action: An Ethnography*

"I have been in regular contact with Andrej Grubačić for many years, and have been most impressed by his searching intelligence, broad knowledge, lucid judgment, and penetrating commentary on contemporary affairs and their historical roots. He is an original thinker and dedicated activist, who brings deep understanding and outstanding personal qualities to everything he does."
—Noam Chomsky

Zapatista Stories for Dreaming Another World

Subcomandante Marcos
Edited and translated by Colectivo
Relámpago/Lightning Collective with a
Foreword by JoAnn Wypijewski

ISBN: 978-1-62963-970-3
$16.95   160 pages

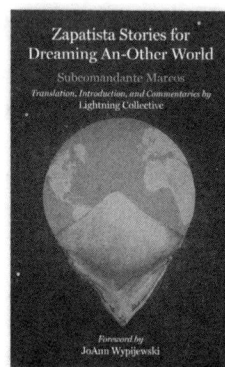

In this gorgeous collection of allegorical stories,
Subcomandante Marcos, idiosyncratic spokesperson of the Zapatistas, has
provided "an accidental archive" of a revolutionary group's struggle against
neoliberalism. For thirty years, the Zapatistas have influenced and inspired
movements worldwide, showing that another world is possible. They have
infused left politics with a distinct imaginary—and an imaginative, literary,
or poetic dimension—organizing horizontally, outside and against the state,
and with a profound respect for difference as a source of political insight, not
division. With commentaries that illuminate their historical, political, and literary
contexts and an introduction by the translators, this timeless, elegiac volume is
perfect for lovers of literature and lovers of revolution.

"From the beating heart of Mesoamerica the old gods speak to Old Antonio, a
glasses-wearing, pipe-smoking beetle who studies neoliberalism, and both tell
their tales to Subcomandante Marcos who passes them on to us: the stories of
the Zapatistas' revolutionary struggles from below and to the left. The Colectivo
Relámpago (Lightning Collective), based in Amherst, Massachusetts, translates and
comments with bolts of illumination zigzagging across cultures and nations, bringing
bursts of laughter and sudden charges of hot-wired political energy. It seems like
child's play, yet it's almost divine!"
—Peter Linebaugh, author of Red Round Globe Hot Burning

"This is a beautiful, inspired project. In a joyful Zapatista gesture readers will
welcome, this volume invites us to play, to walk on different, and even contrary
paths through smooth and crystalline translations that bring these 'other stories'
to life. The translators' commentaries preserve a delicate balance of expertise
and autonomy as they illuminate the historical, political, and cultural forces that
provoked the stories' creation. Among these forces are Zapatista women, whom
the translators rightly dignify in their meticulous and provocative introduction. This
volume is a gift to so many of us as we (attempt to) bring the Zapatista imagination
to our students and organizing communities."
—Michelle Joffroy, associate professor of Spanish and Latin American & Latino
Studies, Smith College and co-director of Domestic Workers Make History

The Angry Brigade: A History of Britain's First Urban Guerilla Group

Gordon Carr
with prefaces by John Barker
and Stuart Christie

ISBN: 978-1-60486-049-8
$24.95   280 pages

"You can't reform profit capitalism and inhumanity.
Just kick it till it breaks." —Angry Brigade, communiqué

Between 1970 and 1972, the Angry Brigade used guns and bombs in a series of symbolic attacks against property. A series of communiqués accompanied the actions, explaining the choice of targets and the Angry Brigade philosophy: autonomous organization and attacks on property alongside other forms of militant working class action. Targets included the embassies of repressive regimes, police stations and army barracks, boutiques and factories, government departments and the homes of Cabinet ministers, the Attorney General and the Commissioner of the Metropolitan Police. These attacks on the homes of senior political figures increased the pressure for results and brought an avalanche of police raids. From the start the police were faced with the difficulty of getting to grips with a section of society they found totally alien. And were they facing an organization—or an idea?

This book covers the roots of the Angry Brigade in the revolutionary ferment of the 1960s, and follows their campaign and the police investigation to its culmination in the "Stoke Newington 8" conspiracy trial at the Old Bailey—the longest criminal trial in British legal history. Written after extensive research—among both the libertarian opposition and the police—it remains the essential study of Britain's first urban guerilla group. This expanded edition contains a comprehensive chronology of the "Angry Decade," extra illustrations and a police view of the Angry Brigade. Introductions by Stuart Christie and John Barker (two of the "Stoke Newington 8" defendants) discuss the Angry Brigade in the political and social context of its times—and its longer-term significance.

"Even after all this time, Carr's book remains the best introduction to the culture and movement that gave birth to the Angry Brigade. Until all the participants' documents and voices are gathered in one place, this will remain the gripping, readable and reliable account of those days. It is essential reading and PM Press are to be congratulated for making it available to us."
—Barry Pateman, associate editor, The Emma Goldman Papers, University of California at Berkeley

Creating a Movement with Teeth: A Documentary History of the George Jackson Brigade

Edited by Daniel Burton-Rose
with a preface by Ward Churchill

ISBN: 978-1-60486-223-2
$24.95   320 pages

Bursting into existence in the Pacific Northwest in 1975, the George Jackson Brigade claimed 14 pipe bombings against corporate and state targets, as many bank robberies, and the daring rescue of a jailed member. Combining veterans of the prisoners', women's, gay, and black liberation movements, this organization was also ideologically diverse, consisting of both communists and anarchists. Concomitant with the Brigade's extensive armed work were prolific public communications. In more than a dozen communiqués and a substantial political statement, they sought to explain their intentions to the public while defying the law enforcement agencies that pursued them.

Collected in one volume for the first time, *Creating a Movement with Teeth* makes available this body of propaganda and mediations on praxis. In addition, the collection assembles corporate media profiles of the organization's members and alternative press articles in which partisans thrash out the heated debates sparked in the progressive community by the eruption of an armed group in their midst. *Creating a Movement with Teeth* illuminates a forgotten chapter of the radical social movements of the 1970s in which diverse interests combined forces in a potent rejection of business as usual in the United States.

"Creating a Movement with Teeth *is an important contribution to the growing body of literature on armed struggle in the 1970s. It gets us closer to knowing not only how pervasive militant challenges to the system were, but also the issues and contexts that shaped such strategies. Through documents by and about the George Jackson Brigade, as well as the introduction by Daniel Burton-Rose, this book sheds light on events that have until now been far too obscured."*
—Dan Berger, author of *Outlaws of America: The Weather Underground and the Politics of Solidarity*; editor of *The Hidden 1970s: Histories of Radicalism*.

"*The popular image of the 70s urban guerrilla, even on the left, is that of the student radical or New Left youth activist kicking it up a couple of notches. Daniel Burton-Rose's documentary history of the George Jackson Brigade is an important corrective in this regard. The Brigade, rooted in prison work, white and black, straights, bisexuals and dykes, was as rich a mixture of the elements making up the left as one could perhaps hope for. We all have much to learn form the Brigade's rich and unique history.*"
—André Moncourt, coeditor of *The Red Army Faction: A Documentary History*.

Abolishing Fossil Fuels: Lessons from Movements That Won

Kevin A. Young

ISBN: 979-8-88744-033-0
$22.95   264 pages

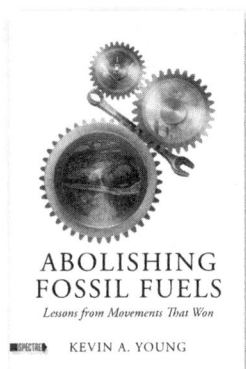

Climate destruction is a problem of political power.

We have the resources for a green transition, but how can we neutralize the influence of Exxon and Shell? *Abolishing Fossil Fuels* argues that the climate movement has started to turn the tide against fossil fuels, just too gradually. The movement's partial victories show us how the industry can be further undermined and eventually abolished. Activists have been most successful when they've targeted the industry's enablers: the banks, insurers, and big investors that finance its operations, the companies and universities that purchase fossil fuels, and the regulators and judges who make life-and-death rulings about pipelines, power plants, and drilling sites. This approach has jeopardized investor confidence in fossil fuels, leading the industry to lash out in increasingly desperate ways. The fossil fuel industry's financial and legal enablers are also its Achilles heel.

The most powerful movements in US history succeeded in similar ways. The book also includes an in-depth analysis of four classic victories: the abolition of slavery, battles for workers' rights in the 1930s, Black freedom struggles of the 1950s and 1960s, and the fight for clean air. Those movements inflicted costs on economic elites through strikes, boycotts, and other mass disruption. They forced some sectors of the ruling class to confront others, which paved the way for victory. Electing and pressuring politicians was rarely the movements' primary focus. Rather, gains in the electoral and legislative realms were usually the byproducts of great upsurges in the fields, factories, and streets.

Those historic movements show that it's very possible to defeat capitalist sectors that may seem invulnerable. They also show us how it can be done. They offer lessons for building a multiracial, working-class climate movement that can win a global green transition that's both rapid and equitable.

"Of the many present crises facing the future of humanity, climate change and its threat of mass extinction appears to be the most daunting. Kevin Young argues compellingly, however, that electoral strategies to fight climate change are a dead end. Rather, his study of past successful movements suggests that radical upsurges, the building of disruptive mass movements, including demonstrations, civil disobedience, and large strikes, are more compelling alternatives for stemming the tide, while ultimately only the end of capitalism will save us. A tour de force!"
—Michael Goldfield, author of *The Southern Key: Class, Race, and Radicalism in the 1930s and 1940s*

But: Life Isn't Like That, Is It?

Boff Whalley

ISBN: 979-8-88744-089-7 (paperback)
      979-8-88744-091-0 (hardcover)
$19.95/$29.95   288 pages

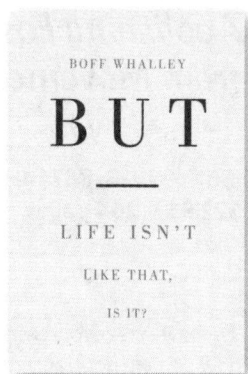

Life's stories are always prone to disruption and digression, thwarting the neat storybook narrative we love so much.

Almost all of our stories follow the same basic pattern: beginning, middle, end: exposition, action, and climax. It's a neat and tidy way of telling a story. But life's not like that, is it? It doesn't obey the rules. Life's stories—like the stories told here in *But*, personal and impersonal, historical and contemporary—are punctuated by disruption, derailment, and digression.

Stories where the good guys lose. Stories where the bad girls win. Stories that just stop in the middle. Stories that fizzle out or simply never get going. Stories that don't make sense. Stories that start where they should end and end where they start. Stories that go round in a cyclical loop, forever. Unfinished stories. Unstarted stories. Stories that stutter and mumble, that cough and splutter.

That's what we have here in this book: real stories, that do all of the above. That's why this book is called *But*. Because the but is there to disrupt the easy normality of the way we tell our stories. This book is a collection of stories about real lives, real people, and real life. Stuttering, wayward, disjointed, funny, ridiculous, and unplanned.

Praise for Boff's other works

"Free-thinking and mercurial, [he] is by turns rebellious, exuberant, fierce, kind, funny and invigorating."
—Jay Griffiths, author of *Wild*

"A stirringly evocative, riveting, hilarious, nostalgic, important book."
—Damian Hall, author of *We Can't Run Away from This*

"A strange, exhilarating blast of a book, throbbing with energy and sweaty authenticity."
—Richard Askwith, author of *Feet in the Clouds*

"A most enjoyable look at fell running with a punk soundtrack and attitude. It all makes for a great read, and I'm happy that Killing Joke may have been along for the ride."
—Big Paul Ferguson, Killing Joke

Sober Living for the Revolution: Hardcore Punk, Straight Edge and Radical Politics

Edited by Gabriel Kuhn

ISBN: 978-1-60486-051-1
$22.95   304 pages

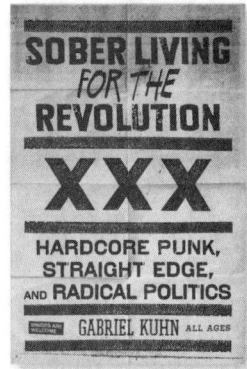

Straight edge has persisted as a drug-free, hardcore punk subculture for 25 years. Its political legacy, however, remains ambiguous—often associated with self-righteous macho posturing and conservative puritanism. While certain elements of straight edge culture feed into such perception, the movement's political history is far more complex. Since straight edge's origins in Washington, DC, in the early 1980s, it has been linked to radical thought and action by countless individuals, bands, and entire scenes worldwide. *Sober Living for the Revolution* traces this history.

It includes contributions—in the form of in-depth interviews, essays, and manifestos—by numerous artists and activists connected to straight edge, from Ian MacKaye (Minor Threat/Fugazi) and Mark Andersen (*Dance of Days/* Positive Force DC) to Dennis Lyxzén (Refused/The (International) Noise Conspiracy) and Andy Hurley (Racetraitor/Fall Out Boy), from bands such as ManLiftingBanner and Point of No Return to feminist and queer initiatives, from radical collectives like CrimethInc. and Alpine Anarchist Productions to the Emancypunx project and many others dedicated as much to sober living as to the fight for a better world.

"Perhaps the greatest reason I am still committed to sXe is an unfailing belief that sXe is more than music, that it can be a force of change. I believe in the power of sXe as a bridge to social change, as an opportunity to create a more just and sustainable world."
—Ross Haenfler, Professor of Sociology at the University of Mississippi, author of *Straight Edge: Clean-Living Youth, Hardcore Punk, and Social Change*

"An 'ecstatic sobriety' which combats the dreariness of one and the bleariness of the other—false pleasure and false discretion alike—is analogous to the anarchism that confronts both the false freedom offered by capitalism and the false community offered by communism."
—CrimethInc. Ex-Workers' Collective

Soccer vs. the State: Tackling Football and Radical Politics

Gabriel Kuhn
with a Foreword by Boff Whalley

ISBN: 978-1-62963-572-9
$20.00   352 pages

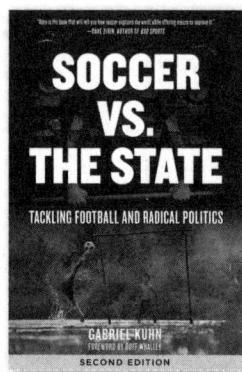

Soccer has turned into a multi-billion-dollar industry. Professionalism and commercialization dominate its global image. Yet the game retains a rebellious side, maybe more so than any other sport co-opted by moneymakers and corrupt politicians. From its roots in working-class England to political protests by players and fans, and a current radical soccer underground, the notion of football as the "people's game" has been kept alive by numerous individuals, teams, and communities.

This book not only traces this history but also reflects on common criticisms— that soccer ferments nationalism, serves right-wing powers, and fosters competitiveness—exploring alternative perspectives and practical examples of egalitarian DIY soccer. *Soccer vs. the State* serves both as an orientation for the politically conscious football supporter and as an inspiration for those who try to pursue the love of the game away from televisions and big stadiums, bringing it to back alleys and muddy pastures.

This second edition has been expanded to cover events of recent years, including the involvement of soccer fans in the Middle Eastern uprisings of 2011–2013, the FIFA scandal of 2015, and the 2017 strike by the Danish women's team.

"Gabriel Kuhn's Soccer vs. the State *is a wondrous reminder of all the times and ways and places where football has slipped its chains and offers what it always promised: new solidarities and identities, a site of resistance, a celebration of spontaneity and play."*
—David Goldblatt, author of *The Ball Is Round* and *The Game of Our Lives*

"There is no sport that reflects the place where sports and politics collide quite like soccer. Athlete-activist Gabriel Kuhn has captured that by going to a place where other sports writers fear to tread. Here is the book that will tell you how soccer explains the world while offering means to improve it."
—Dave Zirin, author of *Game Over* and *Brazil's Dance with the Devil*

"Gabriel Kuhn has written the programme notes for the most important match of all, The People's Game vs. Modern Football."
—Mark Perryman, cofounder of Philosophy Football